VAGABONDING IN AMERICA

A GUIDEBOOK ABOUT ENERGY

text and photos by ED BURYN

poems, drawings and appendixes by STEPHANIE MINES

RANDOM HOUSE · BOOKWORKS

First printing, April 1973   25,000 copies in paperback
                                1,500 copies in cloth

Book design and cover design by Ed Buryn
Cover art by Michael McMillan
Typeset by Vera Allen Composition Service, Hayward, California
        (Thank you Vera, Dorothy and Irene)
Printed and bound under the supervision of Peggy de Ugarte, Random House

Articles about aspects of vagabonding (thank you, friends):
        Train Travel As It Is, by Deetje Boler (Chapter 4)
        The Bus As It Is, by Thomas Kramer (Chapter 4)
        Motorcycling As It Is, by Norm Albers (Chapter 10)
        Bicycling As It Is, by Gini Howe (Chapter 11)
        Hitchhiking As It Is, by Mac Groben (Chapter 12)
        Minnesota is 300 Miles (Song), by Alice Rogoff (Chapter 12)
        Fruit Harvesting As It Is, by Joe Gaspers (Chapter 14)

This book is co-published by   Random House Inc.
                                 201 East 50th Street
                                 New York, N.Y. 10022

                          and   The Bookworks
                                 1409 Fifth Street
                                 Berkeley, California 94710

Distributed in the United States by Random House and simultaneously published in Canada by Random House of Canada Limited, Toronto.

Library Of Congress Cataloging In Publication Data

Buryn, Ed
        Vagabonding in America

        1.   United States Description-Travel 1960-5-Guide book.
I.   TITLE.
E158.B97   1973   917.3'04'92   72-12220
ISBN 0-394-48272-7
ISBN 0-394-707973-x (pbk)

Manufactured in the United States of America

This book is dedicated to

MY PARENTS

Kazimierz and Josephine Buryn

and to

MY CHILDREN

Jan and Sierra Buryn

for linking me into the chain of life.

TABLE OF CONTENTS

Chapters

Appendixes

The United States of America was settled by "vagabonds"
— movers and adventurers.
Vagabonding is in our blood, and its energy is in our
people and our land.
It's in you, too.

This book is about how you can release that energy
to live better.
It's also a portrait of America — what it is and
how to experience it.

Welcome To

VAGABONDING IN AMERICA

"The Creator made the world — come and see it . . . !"
—Pima Indian Prayer

The First Day

We began on a hot day.
Into the Sacramento Valley, into
the flat, dense bowl of heat.
We opened everything
and let the hot air in.
And then there was green, deep green,
and height.
                    Mountains!
Where we camped was pine needles,
cold mountain water,
hard Sierra granite.

    In the darkness
    everything was alive.
    A tree fallen into the cold onrush
              of water,
      each branch a priest
       dancing to the water music.

This was the place
and this was the first day.
A blessing upon us
who have ventured forth into Your world,
if there are blessings left
then please
a blessing upon we
who are children going forth
onto the Land.

About This Book

1

Definitions

THE BEGINNING OF THE BOOK This book happened because two people asked me to write it. One said he'd publish it; the other said he'd read it. A complete communications network.

It happened like this. Not too long ago I wrote a book called *Vagabonding In Europe And North Africa*. It isn't just about places— it's about getting back to the basics of the travel experience and making it joyful and inexpensive. The book is selling OK, and I've heard from hundreds of readers who used it and liked it. A completely good trip.

As a result, my publisher and friend Don Gerrard asked me if I'd be interested in writing a book about America. Frankly, I wasn't too hot for the idea because I knew that vagabonding in America would be a harder gig than Europe. The old-time values of America — freedom, dignity, brotherhood — are great, but the present-day style of America — materialism, unrestrained development, bigotry — makes it a hard place to stomach, especially for the vagabond. I was afraid of America. It wasn't just a question of my hide (tho that too) but of my consciousness. I'm an American — my mind is made up. I didn't want to be confused with new information.

Then I got a letter from Rick Rova, a reader of mine in North Dakota, who suggested I write a book about America, because he wanted to read a book like that. He'd read my book, been to Europe, and agreed with what I said, but now he wanted to know how to keep the good trip going here, how to come back with all the excitment Europe generates, how to stay turned on in America. Can one vagabond in America in a way that's fun, but also makes you a better person? God knows we need a guidebook to America that tells what it's really like, that tells how to see it in a meaningful way.

I thought more about it and said, "Well fair enough, it's worth a try." So I went to America to see what I could find — but I decided beforehand that I would tell the truth about it. I would call things the way I saw them, not the way somebody out to sell books or tourist services wanted me to. This is not a Chamber of Commerce trip, with praise only. Neither is it muckraking. It's about America, just the way it is, both up and down — sometimes an uptight downer, sometimes a downright uplift.

"... nothing prepared me for crashing when I came back from Europe to the States. In Europe I learned to deal with things as they came up — I had to, because things were all so far-out and new to me. But back in the States I kinda slipped into the old rut again and lost that excitement ... I'm not sure I can explain it better than that. I hope you know what I mean.

I guess I'm saying that the vagabonding experience doesn't have to end and begin in Europe. You know that I'm sure, but no book or friend in Europe layed on my head how *not* to lose it. Why not an extension then on how to keep together what you learn — live — feel in Europe and how to start putting it together in the States? Make sense or not?"

—Rick Rova
Letter, 27 Feb. 1972

TRAVELOSOPHY Seeing America is no pipsqueak adventure. It's the real thing, Coca-Cola and all. But there are better and worser ways of doing it, and Americans have been notoriously insistent on the worser ways for a hundred years or so. In fact, Americans are bamboozled about travel. They love it but don't understand it. They do it but get nothing from it. It's like fucking — if you do it without thought or feeling, it's just masturbation. Wasted juice.

I want you to think about travel. In this book I will lay a lot of personal philosophy on you. Don't be mad. A book about travel without a philosophy of travel is like a stew without vegetables — watery and unhealthy. After you dig these philosophical vegetables of mine, you may find that the stew is outrageously delicious and good for you.

Travel is not just moving over the earth from one place to another in some kind of conveyance. It's not about where you're going or how you're getting there. It's not about getting away from it all, at all. In fact, more the opposite ... a way of getting to it all. Travel is a metaphor for life. By that I mean travel is a dramatization of life, a way of experiencing it more intensely and self-consciously. Traveling is not so much an action as an enlightened state of consciousness, opening you to fresh experience, to fresh looks at the world and yourself in it.

People leading their daily lives, meshed in their routine patterns, get stale and energy-starved. We need stimulation and new perspectives; in short, we have a basic drive to get stoned; that is, energized, intoxicated with life. It's what keeps the human race sane, and we do it with booze, dope, poisons, weirdness, or whatever it takes to get us off. My premise is that traveling in America can get you stoned in a way that's healthy, fun and cheap. That's my travelosophy.

To get started without confusion, the rest of this chapter "defines my terms", the terms being the words of the title: VAGABONDING in AMERICA, a GUIDEBOOK about ENERGY.

VAGABONDING: A DEFINITION "Vagabond" continues to be a misunderstood word. Apparently the image that comes to mind for most people is a male hitchhiker, young and penniless. If that's what you think a vagabond is, please slip your mind into neutral for awhile and listen to this.

Vagabonding is an outlook on travel. The real definition of a vagabond is someone not entangled in travel arrangements. Vagabonds can travel by airplane or car-camper, be any age or sex, can be affluent or broke. It's a general style of traveling, yet it's as individual as you or me. Vagabonding means traveling light because "things" rob you of first-hand experience and weight down your spirit and your back. It means booking the details of your trip with an agent called Chance, and paying for your travels with pocket-money instead of bank loans.

It may sound strange but becoming a vagabond is a religious action. Ordinary tourists try to control their fate to protect their tender delusions from the shocks of reality. By pre-planning every aspect of their trip — whether vacation trip or life trip, they think they can circumvent the will of God or Fate. Vagabonds know better, and let things take their natural course.

The word "vagabond" is old-fashioned and vaguely disreputable, and I like it for both those reasons. It sets itself apart from today's slick modernity and sanctimonious respectability. As I see it, a vagabond is a liberated traveler. Contrariwise, a tourist is a pseudo-traveler, a sucker in economic servitude to travel agents, governments, businessmen, industry. Tourists are pawns with accessible bank accounts. Unfortunately, the tourist is also a human locust — a pest in small numbers, but potentially a swarming scourge that sweeps everything before it. Tourists bring their easy money, and upset the economy of the places they visit; they flaunt the customs, insult the natives. They leave behind a bad taste and a glut of money that threatens public morality and private integrity.

3

"It doesn't occur to most people that professional tramps make many more friends than people who stay put. You see, you get to know someone only for a short while and you show only your best side to each other. Then you part and these people remain your friends for ever."

"Rarely does it happen that a person giving me a lift doesn't want to take me home and introduce me to their family. People are so intrigued by my way of life and fascinated by the stories I have to tell. Because every vagabond is a storyteller — that's how we live."

"On the road, people confide their inmost thoughts. Preliminaries are dispensed with because you're coming from nowhere, going nowhere and you'll probably never see them again."

"People are wonderful, you know. Every person is better than he or she thinks. This is the high sacred secret of the road — the vagabond is staking his life that this is true."

—Kathleen Phelan
Article entitled *I Am A Vagabond*

Tourism destroys what it touches. The values that created the original tourist interest are inevitably eroded or simply grossed-out of existence by the profit-grubbers. Florida, for example, is a tourist catastrophe.

It's not only the influx of people that does it. The most destructive factor is that tourists spend their money as a way of avoiding personal involvement. They'll pay a hundred a day to a sleazy hotel that permanently destroys a beach before they'd dream of hiking to it and sleeping overnite on the sand. The tourist wastes his money and destroys his surroundings; the tourist accommodater sells his integrity and steals from his homeland.

But a vagabond — male or female — is different. As a vagabond, you're a person who's interested in spending as little money as possible. You don't want to disrupt anyone's economy, especially your own. You want to keep a low profile, living as the locals live, on their standards. You're interested in finding out the customs — observing them, practicing them, learning from them. You're especially interested in meeting people for the richness of involvement and sharing. You offer and expect friendship. You avoid fancy service, and know that honesty never costs very much.

When you travel as a vagabond you don't have to feel guilty that you're trying to live cheaply or willing to miss the neon nonsense. On the contrary, you'll be doing the places you visit a favor. Show yourself to them as a human being, not a jet-set zombie. Bring enough money to live, but not to upset life the way it is. When you travel, don't be labeled a tourist. Point out the difference. Tell them you're a traveler. Tell them you're a vagabond.

Each of us is a strand of life. If you let your strand intermingle randomly with other strands, you will never lack for interest or beauty. Let your trip be changed by who you meet and what happens; accept that you have the power to touch the lives of other people and change events. This is the vagabond mystique — the ability to be in close touch with other lives and other energies, which define and refine your own life and energy.

AMERICA: A DEFINITION I bogged down in trying to define America until I realized that I didn't need to define it for everyone, only for myself. The America in this book is a place I personally know about. I was born and raised in the northeast (New Jersey), grew up in the south (Florida), and have been living now a long time in the west (California). I just came back from over 15,000 miles of touring America — first alone (as a hitchhiker) and then with my lady Stephanie and our infant daughter Sierra (as car-campers). This is in addition to more than a dozen trans-American trips I've made by car, train, bus, and thumb — (I don't count airplane trips).

For me, America is a place so incredible that the mind can't hold it all. No man's experience can encompass even a fraction of its diversity, its fascination, its ugliness, and its exaltation. I love it in deep and complex ways. First, for its natural richness of land, climate,

beauty — all that it came with originally; and then for its ideals, its dream of justice and hope that people brought to it. But I also hate its lack of reverence for the land, its hypocrisy, its spiritual decay, its accumulating karmic burden. America is the most blessed and most cursed of nations. It's a paradox and a mystery.

Early-day America was a fantasy out of a Tolkein novel, an actual Middle Earth. From its sparsely populated eastern seaboard to the west lay a virgin land, unknown and unmatched. Settlers were hemmed in by mountains and near-inpenetrable forests for a thousand miles. Beyond that were the Great Plains and beyond that the Great Mountains and beyond that the Great Ocean. It stretched vast, pure and unknown, filled with strange wonders, peopled by mysterious civilizations. A new world full of treasures and hope.

Today, the frontiers have vanished, the unknown territory has disappeared. The Indians who lived harmoniously with nature, taking nothing from the land that they didn't give back, have been decimated. The exploitation started when the first white trappers encroached on the land, stripping it of its animal life to supply the fashion needs of the east and of Europe. After the trappers came settlers, expropriating land, chopping down forests. Then came the Army to mop up, to contain the remaining Indians on reservations. Industrialization was the next invader, radically changing the farms and cities in a quickening cycle of despoilation. Today the only enclaves of original America are the national parks and forests, yet the destructive process continues. Tourists pour in, and "developers" press in to suck out the last juices.

Meanwhile the American consciousness, a mantle once so bright in spirit, so colored with dignity and humanity, has become a threadbare cloak. Some claim we are totally selfish, powerful, hypocritical, dangerous to all that has beauty and soul. Others point to pollution, crime, despoilation as the hallmarks of the old America come to its last extremity. Fear and loathing are the watchwords.

Is this true? Hey, is this TRUE!? The answer is yours to make for yourself. I think there's truth in it, but there are other, happier truths abroad in the land, too. Vagabonds in America, I was told, are outlawed. It's dangerous to vagabond in America, they said. Freedom is out of favor; money is king. Well, I found that to be untrue. America is a vagabond's paradise . . . complex and difficult in its challenges, magnificent in its rewards.

It's up to you. Now is the time to go forth and define your country for yourself because it needs that definition more than ever. Go and see where this old America is at, and where the new America is going. Never mind what you read in the newspapers or books. It doesn't mean anything until you go and see for yourself.

My own trips have shown me much to be unhappy about, but my primary feeling is optimism, especially over the new America taking shape under the pressure of today's problems. The new America is about rejuvenescence, returning to the original humanist ideals. It's about a country deciding to change the patterns that no longer fit today's realities. It's about how dissolving patterns are releasing energy that is remaking America and creating a new world Renaissance.

The process is just beginning. The most evident signs are seen in young people, long-hairs, communards, vagabonds — but America's consciousness is changing at every level. Americans are turning from materialism to humanism ... from quantity of goods to quality of life. In the process, the nation is electric with energy, its people exciting, its creative outpouring incredible. Witness it for yourself, but in a way that makes you part of it. See America from the heart of its energy furnace, from contact with its people. See it as a modern-day vagabond.

GUIDEBOOKS: A DEFINITION I've been writing guidebooks of one kind or another for many years, and I'm coming to feel that there isn't much you can get out of them. There's only one way you can learn what's real and that's from your own experience. The most valuable knowledge comes from living and doing, not from reading. Nevertheless, I've always been an avid reader, and I get turned on by reading. I think the most important function of a guidebook is to stimulate you — tell you about why you should do something and get you into the spirit of doing it.

Practically all travel books tend to tell you about a hotel in Chicago that's the 16th greatest place in the world, or that car-camping in America is a sure way to get your rocks off, or that eight pairs of underwear are necessary when traveling east of the Mississippi. The truth, of course, is that traveling in America is not about those things. It's about what happens to your head while you're going through the motions. It's about the changes you go thru and the things you learn as a result. It's about the energy that comes rushing in on you when you're away from home, surrounded by strangers. And what you do with that.

Travel is about your inner self, and how you exchange energy between that inner self and the world. Guidebooks should suggest how to do that efficiently, productively, and creatively. And since that's what education should be, travel is also education, trying to define the world in a way that makes sense to you. Most schools and guidebooks make the same mistake. They try to put the world in some kind of can for you and say "Here, eat this mush; this is the way it is". In the way that schools can ruin your education and prevent you from learning anything, so guidebooks can spoil your trip and prevent you from getting high.

I remember once poring over two guidebooks with recommended tours so that I could see everything within a certain area. I'd spent a lot of time reading the books, investigating what there was to see, looking at maps, trying to figure out schedules. Afterwards, driving down the highway toward one of those areas I noticed I was chewing my nails, feeling an anguish in the pit of my stomach, and it came to me to stop and say, "What is this? What's happening to me?" And I realized it was those guidebooks at work.

They were "good" guidebooks — factual, complete, authoritative — but what's wrong with them, what's wrong with all guidebooks of their kind, is that they worsen an existing frustration. Let's face it; travel is frustrating because you can only sample the world as you pass thru it. All of us have an urge to go into more detail, we want to live more completely, we want to see more, we want to be everybody, to live every life. But you're only one person, I'm only one person, we can only go thru the world superficially, getting just a taste, feeling that we're not seeing as we could see, not experiencing everything there is to experience.

A guidebook which tells you all there is to see and do in a certain area can only reinforce this frustration. The writer has probably gone over that region a dozen times trying to pick up everything. We go thru in an hour or day or whatever, but with a consciousness that wants to see the five best things or the two best things, or see all ten things, and in a hurry. What happens is that we put ourselves on schedule. Tonight sleep here. Tomorrow be there. Next afternoon see this, drive over to that, then make it to such-and-such campground. So we get on the road and push ourselves because we don't want to miss anything. Even if we do see everything, we feel like hell afterwards because seeing everything isn't what travel is about.

It's the guidebook syndrome. Watch out for it. Never mind what the books say. See what you feel like seeing, and put quality into whatever it is. Take as much time as you need to do that. If the guidebook starts to get you uptight with other advice, for catfish sakes throw it away.

A few words about this guidebook before you throw it away: Guidebooks are notorious for being dull. To make this one more interesting, I've elected myself the main character — a kind of vagabond guinea pig sent out to test America for you. My trip won't be yours, but use it as a lens to focus on yourself and your own trip.

I've also added many choice photographs, poetry, and other insights to keep it moving, but in the end this is just a book. It's an abstraction of experience and thus less interesting than the real experience it's talking about. Read and enjoy it, but remember the purpose is to give you an understanding of vagabonding so you'll want to do it yourself. Do it. Then you'll have the real thing, which is always better than the book.

ENERGY: A DEFINITION I've discovered that the concept of energy is a useful way to think about life and especially traveling. By energy I mean vitalizing force, a primal juice that runs thru us. The source is the cosmos and the flow is life. Life is a mystery and so is energy, but both are real.

Structures or patterns of any kind are receptacles or storage areas for this energy. Anything that has form or shape is binding up a certain amount of energy because it takes energy to hold it in that shape. This includes everything from atoms (which release a lot of energy if they're broken up — note Hiroshima) all the way up to galaxies (which release even more energy if they come apart — note the end of the universe). People are energy structures too, of a lower order, but still a big deal if you happen to be one.

The way people live — all their myriad habits, routines, characteristics, traits — these are structures too. Civilization itself is a complex human group structure, and the social energy it contains is tremendous because so much individual investment of energy is sunk into it over thousands of years. Human history can be thought of as the story of man's attempts to build structures that capture cosmic energy in the most efficient and productive ways for everyone. Today's society is incredibly complex and interwoven, a veritable maze of energy storage. A powerhouse indeed.

Any single individual from birth to death undergoes a similar history of building life structures that hold enough energy to make him or her successful in whatever ways are important. These structures we call life patterns — psychic, social, sexual, cultural, etc. Patterns are energy-savers, and that is why we build and re-build them. They are frames of reference into which we can place our experiences. A pattern is protection against the unknown, against danger, against the void and its mysteries. Patterns are also called home. Without our patterns, we can't survive. Every single situation in life would be a total challenge, would require total marshalling of our strength and resources. Patterns buffer us from the recurring threats of life. We invest energy in a pattern, and it frees our attention (and surplus energies) for more pressing, non-recurring situations.

A pattern is like a dike that holds back the tide. The danger of twice-a-day floods can now be forgotten; only the irregular high tides are matters of concern. All our patterns function in this way to make available some free (uncommitted) energy. This free energy is then available to cope with life's special problems and challenges, those that can't be handled by our habit formations. But if these free energies have no challenges to face, new and useless patterns will be invented to use them up.

Today in 20th Century America, the pinnacle of world civilization, our fortress of patterns and structures both individual and societal, has completely protected us from the everyday threats of life. In fact, we have become hung-up in our patterns. We have so completely controlled our environment that little of our free energy is available anymore. It's all invested in routines, in doing the same things over and over because the challenges have disappeared. We've won all the big battles with our patterns. We've become decadent, as seen in energy terms.

The point of all this is to find what makes living and traveling fun. Personally, I'm sure that the fun comes from our surplus energies, in their play and exercise. Modern people frequently lack challenge because their energies are totally immersed in patterns. Their lives are dull because they're starved for free energy. Their lives crave challenge, crave to be used — but there are no challenges, and their uses are organized and repetitive.

What is clear is that people need to exercise all their capacities to live well. They have to work their muscles, their reflexes, keep alert and aware of themselves and their world. The biological reason is to keep them alive at full readiness to respond to sudden dangers. An important way that mankind does this is to get high on a regular basis. By getting high I mean tapping off some of the energy invested in those patterns, and letting it jiggle us, shake us up. This causes us to scramble to stay on top, to get some exercise.

There are many ways to get high, but I think every one of them involves disruption of patterns — a minor disruption for a minor high, and a pattern breakdown or dissolution for a total stoner. For example, a few ounces of alcohol somewhat disrupts your visual and motor patterns, your habitual inhibitions, and results in the high known as drunkeness. All races of mankind through history have indulged in it, and I would guess that it has survival value because it alters consciousness. An LSD trip is a much heavier disruption of patterns, and releases great blockbusting blobs of psychic energy that make it a very high experience.

America
taking me to you,
dragging my airy body
across your cities and plains.
America,
take me to you,
into your barren wasteland
plant the seed of my heart.
America, mother country,
homeland of my sadness
my burning eyes see you
          hungry,
America, the mother land.

Off The Tape
VAGABONDING AT HOME

Of course, you can also vagabond without leaving town. Your local beach, woods, meadowland, even neighborhood park is as good a place to make contact with the world and yourself as any fabled faraway spot. In my own locale, in San Francisco, some of the best and most rewarding travels I've ever made occured at Ocean Beach, which lies beyond 46th Avenue. Stoned trips I've made there, thoughts and visions I've had, new people and friends encountered, good experiences had — all these while vagabonding within easy walk, drive, bus, or hitch from my door.

Getting more mundane, the same is true of my front door. When I decided to tear up some sidewalk around my house to plant trees and shrubs, I learned more about my neighborhood and personally met more of my neighbors than I had since I moved in, years before. For example, that was how I met Tubbs, a retired neighbor and vagabond across the street. Tubbs invited me into his house and life, both amazing, both based on his Tahitian experiences as a seaman. Everywhere, anywhere is the location of life and adventure — if you open yourself to it. People are amazing everywhere, even next door, even across the continent. The story of a neighbor's life, if you could only know it, might just blow your mind, or change the course of your own life.

Pattern disruption is what travel is about too, and the reason we learn from it is it gets us high. But unlike drugs, it takes longer, lasts longer, is purely natural, and socially approved. When you leave home for new places, experience new adventures, and meet new people, your habitual patterns are altered and psychic energy is released. Uncertainty, even fear, become part of your life, but this new energy kicking around makes you able to cope, and to get excited about it too.

Travel is also a way of testing your patterns. Life is always changing, and patterns established to deal with life situations have to change accordingly. Unfortunately, they frequently don't. They get rigid, and because we're living in the middle of those patterns we're not aware that this change is taking place. Thus patterns can become outmoded, tying up energy we could use more productively. The problem is how to find the best ways of directing our energy, the best ways of leading life. We need to test our patterns to see if they're still working for us. What's needed is some kind of deliberate interruption that creates a new consciousness useful for evaluating the old.

The vagabond method of travel, in which you introduce new patterns, is one such way of pattern testing. You put yourself into the environment, and observe what happens — you rate what works. One proof that vagabonding works is coming home afterwards. You feel like a kind of superman, back from another realm into something bland and soft. That's because your energy, the ability of your mind to work, the sharpness of your senses, your awareness is higher than that of the people around you. The energy you freed by traveling makes you more alive in every way. But after being home for awhile, it all levels out, tho never to where you were before. You resume the patterns, reinvesting the energy . . . but the patterns are somewhat different now.

Understanding energy means being able to change your patterns in step with a changing reality. Traveling is one way of testing how you're doing, and having fun in the process. This is my formula for keeping your juices flowing, for staying high on energy all your life.

Off The Tape
HOMECOMING

I was born not far off the New Jersey turnpike, which is one of the world's most famous scenes of industrial desolation. Smog, smoke, noise, traffic, wire, steel, oil, gas, fumes, filth. New York is somewhere around here but you can't see it. It's been rendered invisible by air pollution. I saw only two green things anywhere nearby — some scroungy patches of grass between the freeways and a billboard advertising Kool cigarettes.

Driving down the turnpike I get the feeling that the main concern around here, is the apprehension of hitchhikers. Signs every few miles say "No picking up hitchhikers. No stopping except for repairs. No discharging or picking up of passengers." Even the Howard Johnson's restaurants on the turnpike print warnings on their placemats about how dangerous it is to pick up hitchhikers. Looking around me, choking on the smoke, eyes smarting, sick to my stomach from the slop they're feeding me, and sick at heart with the devastation and pollution all around me, what they're worried about is hitchhikers. Totally insane. Hitchhikers should get medals around here.

These environs are the braised loins from which I sprang, so to speak. Somewhere amidst all these towers — transmission towers, water towers, tv towers, telephone towers, smoke stacks, bridge towers, light poles, telephone poles, the whole place

is a forest of phallic things sticking up in the air. I turned off into Union City to find the house where I was born. Unfortunately, I knew the street but not the address. I guess I was hoping I'd recognize it from a long-ago picture I'd seen. Maybe it was fortunate that I didn't have the address, because I found the street completely filled with small shops, tenements, pizza parlors, drug stores, pool halls, laundries, parking lots — the whole gamut of ugly, struggling small businesses running for miles down the street. It was the local merchants' contest to see who could have the ugliest store. As usual, there were thousands of entries.

I was born in the back apartment of one of these shops, where my mother and father opened their first bakery. This is where they started on the long path that led from the barrens of industrial New Jersey to their present situation in the barrens of rural Florida. This is where I started too. How dreary. But at least I don't have any grand illusions about where I came from. The first-born son of an immigrant Polack. Born in the back of the shop on Shlock Row. Actually, I'm proud of that because it makes me All-American. There are few grand places to be born in America, unless you were born outdoors maybe. This makes me like everybody else in a certain way. In another way it makes me unique. So that's me, dreary but proud.

11

Why See America?

Is This Trip Necessary?

SELF-DISCOVERY FOR FUN
SELF-DISCOVERY FOR PROFIT
AMERICANS ARE PEOPLE
PRACTICAL REASONS
AMERICA THE BEAUTIFUL?
THE BEER CAN AS NATIONAL SYMBOL
HOMOGENIZING IS NOT GRADE A
THE AMERICAN MASS CONSCIOUSNESS

SIGHTS AND SOUNDS OF POLLUTION
SPEAKING OF AUTOMOBILES
IT'S A SMALL WORLD
WATCHING TELEVISION
OTHER OLD CONSCIOUSNESS
A NEW CONSCIOUSNESS
THE FUTURE LIES AHEAD
THOUGHTS ABOUT LIFE AND DEATH

SELF-DISCOVERY FOR FUN Yourself is all you've really got, and if you don't get a grip on him, her, or it, you haven't got anything. In ancient Greece the Oracle of Delphi (who was, of course, a woman) put it this way: "Know thyself." Now we have the answer, let's get to the question, which is: How do you find out who you are? The exact process is different for everybody, and it takes the best of us all our lives, working as hard as we can. However, we can start from what is evident: Go back to where you came from to begin to find out who you are.

Going to America means visiting your old home towns, finding where you grew up and were energized. It means rediscovering the past and integrating it into the present, not just your own past but our collective past. It's about finding patterns we didn't know existed, and deciding to either use or lose them. The cities and towns of America are artifacts of the American consciousness, and speak of who you are and how you got that way. Go and listen to them. And on your way, see and feel the American land — the spaces in between — the stage on which we Americans play our parts, and seek.

Journey to your parents and family, and in the process free yourself to know who you are. So many Americans mortally fear their parents, afraid of what their parents know about them, I guess. The problem is that everybody knows too little, not too much. Parents and children are just plain folks who need each other. Put family in your trip, so you can take heart from them.

Going to America means meeting people with whom you have something in common: your old friends and their people, your fellow citizens, your fellow Americans. They can tell you who you are if you listen. Part of the trip involves finding out who they are, and telling them. Visit the parents of your friends to learn about them, about their children, and about yourself.

Then there's going to America to understand the broader forces that shaped you as a citizen. Your country is a gigantic energy field whose effect on you is total and profound. It created you — economically, socially, politically, historically. Traveling thru it is a way of defining the structure so you understand it and how it works in relation to you. America can be a dike against the tide if you perceive how

Exercises

1) Draw a picture of yourself. Never mind that you can't draw, just put your pencil on the paper and follow how you feel about yourself with a line. What do you recognize in it when you're done? Now try it again, only with your eyes closed. What are the differences?

2) Write poems for these pictures or how you feel about them. Never mind that you're not a poet, just close your eyes and see what word or words come. They'll suggest others as you go. When you're done, think about the poem and what it means.

3) Make up a chart of your family and relatives, showing their ages, occupations, religion, consciousness, etc. How do you fit in? Find yourself in this chart; relate yourself to it.

4) Make up a similar chart with your close friends. Relate yourself to it in the same way.

5) Compare the two charts, and note where they're alike or different. Consider why.

6) Plan to visit family grave-plots on your trip. Look at family snapshot albums. Ask your relatives questions about what kind of kid you were, and have them tell anecdotes about you then.

7) Ask one or more close friends or relatives to describe how they see you. Don't respond at all to what they say; just listen quietly and think about it.

8) The next time you're afraid or embarrassed to do something while traveling — like going into a raunchy restaurant or avoiding conversation with a stranger, consider why you're feeling that way. Just once, for the sake of experiment only, overcome your fear, and see what happens. What do you feel about that.

9) On your trip around America, plan to have photographs of yourself taken (or take them yourself) in different places, but all the same way — same distance, angle, cropping. After your trip, collect and compare these pictures. See how different you appear in each. Think about why, think about where you were when the pictures were taken.

10) Take pictures of other people. (Go ahead, waste your film on strangers.) Just take pictures of other people doing things you find interesting. Afterwards, look at the pictures and see what they tell you. (And while you're taking them you'll be wondering why you're taking them — don't worry, that's why it's a good exercise.)

much of its reality is your own reality. Personally learning and feeling that you belong to each other is to free energy in yourself. Ignorance of America and its relationship to you can easily be a threat that drains energy away, handicapping you in far-reaching ways. Know thyself also means to know thy place. This trip is about energy.

America itself is in the midst of a self-discovery of immense proportions. It's all part of a new consciousness which I'll speak about in more detail later. The signs of this phenomenon are on every hand. One prominent example of the trend is the whole new industry in American artifacts and antiques, to which businessmen and auctioneers are flocking as prices for anything made before 1960 shoot upwards. There's a united interest in the United States, ranging the gamut from Athabasca to Zuni, from Acadia to Zion, from Adams to Zenger. It spans local, regional, and national issues; history, environment, cultures, personalities; everything and anything related to giving Americans a better sense of themselves.

SELF–DISCOVERY FOR PROFIT Then there's the Travel Industry — the TI — about which I'll say more later, and its efforts to help you discover America, or whatever reasonable facsimile of it turns out to be most profitable. Everyone with a buck to spend for advertising is getting behind the slogan "Discover America." All the oil companies are pumping money into propaganda, maps, data, tour guides, and travel directories. 1972 was Tourism Year of the Americas, with pictorial postcards and posters put out by the government. New travel magazines, new guidebooks, new publications by the dozen popping up all over. Almost every state in America is printing platitudinous tourist brochures and offering extravagant tourist services, dusting off their tourist sites, teaching their Indians to smile. We just had the national centennial of the National Parks (1872 – 1972). Besides the bi-centennial itself (1776 – 1976), new commemorative dates will no doubt be discovered.

Exploitation is, of course, an old story in America. Any kind of genuine peoples' movement is immediately spread-eagled and gang-banged by big business. "See America" is a bonanza for travel agents, the motel-hotel interests, the chain restaurants, the amusement parks, the publishers, the gasoline companies, and in fact just about everybody. Including you and me. And that's something to be aware of. Crass exploitation is the American style — it's gross but it pays the bills.

The problem is keeping straight in your head what it's all about. It's about Americans focusing on themselves as Americans, developing interest in their history and culture, getting insights into what it means to them as individuals. It's not about making money for the travel industry. It's not about creating 37 new jobs making plastic Uncle Sam dolls. It's about a spiritual and moralistic search, not an economic windfall. It's about a new concept of America, by Americans, for themselves. Discover yourself, but not by putting your head up your ass.

AMERICANS ARE PEOPLE

Today there's widespread cynicism about the American people — their make-a-buck mentality, their what-the-fuck morality, and all that _____ _____ (fill in the blanks). The American people collectively possess some traits not worth mentioning, and also have allowed themselves to be led on some strange trips. Yet here's the good news: Americans as individuals are great. The plain truth is that Americans are the most fascinating people in the world — with their background, they have to be.

America started off with a natural endowment of wealth — minerals, forests, rivers, soils, climate — unequalled in history. This wealth released its people, us, from the wheel of poverty so we became creative and productive, free, diverse and talented beyond any society to date. We've been made unique by a history which demanded our utmost in labor and dedication, inventiveness and courage. We've been made proud by a system of government that stimulated our hopes and dreams, that promised and delivered the most freedom any group of citizens have ever enjoyed. We've been informed by the most technological society the world has ever seen, by an incredible system of education, by a communications network that is the pinnacle of our industrial skill, by our transportation networks, by our mobility.

Today the entire world is affected in every way by Americans. We spurred an artistic and scientific Neo-Rennaisance, a cultural and technological revolution, an exploding political and spiritual consciousness. In all these things America is the world leader, and America itself is the primary arena for this massive and monstrous free-for-all of energy output. If you think this happened accidentally, if you think this happened because Americans are dummies, then you better think again. America and Americans are far out.

Looking back on my own three month tour of America just completed, it's easy to see that the most rewarding part of the trip involved encounters with Americans in all

America, the mother land,
scatter the seed of my aching
          heart
across the plains of Pennsylvania.
America, the motherland,
giving birth to deformed cities
that crumble and fall
and grovel at the dried tits
of the aging America motherland.
America, the motherland,
silent, white, hard working
standing flabby and old
outside rivers and hills
drinking the booze
you've stored for centuries
inside shady hollows.
America, the motherland,
sleeping in the humid summer
          night,
stroking smooth endless
          roads of death,
spurting oil and other
black juices,
gluttonous and generous
America
motherland,
stop this witchcraft,
look up to God
and arise.

walks of life. (Chapter 8 is all about Americans and how to meet them.) It'll suffice now to say that for all its beauty, wealth, attractions, climate, trips of all kinds, the people in America are still its best experience. No one gets more fully immersed in this experience than the vagabond.

PRACTICAL REASONS   OK. I've talked about beauty and philosophy, now let's get down to practicality and convenience. What are hard-headed reasons for seeing America instead of, say, going to Europe or abroad?

One of the best reasons is that you're already here. America is right under your feet, so it won't cost you much to get here. Traveling within America can be done *very* cheaply because you already know all about how to do it. If you own a car or motorcycle, you can travel for just gasoline costs and camp out. Even taking a bus or train from point to point is cheap when compared to overseas transportation. You can hitchhike, bicycle, or walk for next to nothing.

In the same way, you can live cheaply in America while you're traveling. You can shop in supermarkets. When you go to restaurants you know which ones are cheapest. You know how to cut corners in lots of ways because Americans all know that — we've been doing it right here for a long time. When it comes to lodging for the night, you can sleep in your car, camp out, or stay with friends and relatives. You know where and how to look for low cost rooms, and there's no language barrier. Much harder to do abroad.

So despite this high cost of living in America, you can probably travel more cheaply here than you can anywhere else, especially counting the cost of getting there. If you get in a jam or run out of money, better here than abroad. You're much closer to help to start with, whether it be a local soup kitchen or a telephone to call home or friends. For true-blue vagabonds without homes, it's easier to find work in America, from odd-jobbing and doing chores to part-time work or a full-time gig. Getting broke or in trouble abroad usually means no work, no help, not being able to speak the language — much grimmer. None of that applies here.

There are no language barriers, no paper-work barriers (passport, visas), no borders to cross. English-speaking doctors are available to cure the sick traveler, and even clinics to cure the indigent sick traveler.

Finally, you don't even have to give up the exoticism of culture shock. If you keep your eyes and ears sharp, your itinerary open, and your nerve up, you can find any number of situations in America that might blow your cool or turn your stomach. It might not be as exciting as Morocco, India, or Peru — but we have some foreign thrills in the form of our black ghettos, Indian reservations, Appalachian mines, city slums, environmental rapes, profiteering rip-offs, and esthetic disasters. Don't overlook this side of America or pretend it isn't there: it's what the travel agents don't mention because it's too real.

you are dying
LIVE LIVE LIVE LIVE LIVE LIVE

"FANTASYLAND"
San Francisco Chronicle

"In its first year, Disney World chalked up 11 million people, passing most National Parks and a whole bunch of European countries. Put 10,000 people on new payrolls. Boosted Orlando's 5000 hotel rooms to 36,000.

The best of original Disneyland has been duplicated: Nostalgic Tom Sawyer's Island. Pirates of the Caribbean. A sternwheeler steamboat is on the way.

Golf and boating. A Polynesian village. Old time steam railway. Marching bands. All the magic touch that goes with Disney productions — childhood fantasy you can live in. Like Disneyland, more adults than children.

Rates are competitively low: $29 a day in the Contemporary and Polynesian Hotels. That's for a couple, and you can add three children under 18 for free. (So hurry up and have three children or you're losing money.)"

AMERICA THE BEAUTIFUL? I frequently get the feeling that the world was created as a place to work out unbelievable ironies and cosmic jokes, a stage for serendipity before God's unimaginable eye. (I think that this is part of the Hindu explanation of God, too.)

Anyway, here we have America, the jewel in Natures crown, the pride of the planet, indescribably rich in unique wonders and natural beauty. And who should live here but Americans, a people polluting and destroying the radiance of the environment on a scale seen only in nightmares and Japanese movies. Indeed, it would seem that only the genius of God could pit against each other two such formidable opponents: On the left, clothed in purple mountain majesties — America the Angel, so vast in size and every inch so great that it seems incapable of being touched. But on the right, aha, we have Ourselves, this collection of devils rounded up from all over the world, so fiendishly ingenious and egotistically greedy that we've learned to disembowel the earth, darken the sky, sludge the rivers, even unstructure the atom. Our strength is multiplied with machines, computers, communications, pesticides, defoliants,

and even Mr. Clean. Who will win? What are the odds? What channel is it on?

The beauty of America is best typified by the American West where the open spaces haven't filled in yet, and doubtless never will. Everywhere some kind of infinity is suggested. Shadows of clouds lie upon the rugged landscape like islands in a vast sea. The expanse of the sky mirrors the expanse of earth below; both are lost in space. Dirt roads ride up side canyons and alluvial fans in straight lines for miles until they disappear from sight. The pavement is a ruled line pointing to the distant ranges of mountains. Telephone poles march away to infinity. Occasionally you see a rag-tag ruin still spanning time, a few sticks of wood above the sage, sometimes a crumbling wall or fireplace. The American west is cosmic because it so clearly reveals space, time and infinity.

Europe is in large measure about how man has harmonized with nature. By contrast, what is beautiful in America is the brute strength of its natural state, the infinities that are built into it. So much that people have done in America has been ugly and destructive, but the land still overpowers it, the land is so brutally strong that it transcends whatever man can do in the end, no matter what channel he's on.

In virtually every part of America some sort of natural beauty still dominates. No need to describe it, region by region, state by state, county by county. We've all been propagandized since we were little kids about how beautiful America is. Amazingly, the propaganda is true, and we knew it all along. In any part of America, as soon as you leave the city and go to the country, especially as you go to the less populated regions, the scene becomes something ranging between pleasant and inspirational.

What excites me is not just someplace like the West, say, whose scenery is unique in the world, but the total diversity of scenery throughout America. Alpine slopes, desert land, and flat plains. Coastal regions of every description, with bays, islands, and peninsulas. Farmlands and rural expanses, gentle and harsh. Arctic tundra and tropical jungles. Parklands, forest lands, green paradises of God. Water-works like lakes and rivers, streams and creeks, marshes and swamps, hot springs and geysers, fountains and waterfalls. Earth architecture of gorges and canyons, natural bridges and buttes, volcanos and caverns. And mountains, flowing free on so many horizons. Landforms and seascapes endless in scope and loveliness.

The spectacle of America has been conserved in our national parks, monuments, and forests. But don't go patting yourself on the back too much. It's true we did invent the national park idea, a great breakthrough in world consciousness. But even now, about 100 years after the first national park was dedicated, the percentage total of land set aside in our wilderness system isn't too impressive — 11 million out of 2300 million acres, or about ½ of 1% of our land area. That averages out to 20 people per acre, or about twice the density of the average large American city! In other words, if all Americans went to their wilderness areas at once, they'd be twice as crowded as they are now in the big cities. Ah wilderness. Ah me.

Off The Tape
DRIVING THRU CHICAGO

Entering Chicago on what looks like a 14-lane freeway: In the center strip, instead of a grass green divider lane is a two-track express-train system. There are more access roads off to the left; to the right are some other railroads. The freeways here are divided into expresses and locals!

Like all the giant American metropolises, no matter how many lanes of freeways there are, no matter how many new expressways and thruways they construct, there aren't enough of them. I'm sitting in the middle of a traffic jam right now — 7 lanes of traffic in my direction's all stopped or barely moving. Around me is a noisy, unnatural wilderness of metal, concrete, and brick. Nearby a billboard proclaims ALL FOR FUN.

. . . Now the highway has narrowed down to a more comfortable eight lanes, and traffic in the other direction as well as this one is stopped. That's more like it. We finally inch up to the source of the congestion, a fair-to-middling accident, with a couple of tow trucks around. We get by it, clear sailing again, 10 lanes now, all clear. For about two miles, that is, and then we come to a standstill again. A convenient electric billboard informs us that it's just after 3 o'clock, it's 88 degrees — just where you like to be on a nice warm afternoon. Later we come to the source of this congestion, yes it's another accident. This time the tow trucks haven't arrived yet. A woman is sitting in her car in the middle of the 10 lanes unable to get out, as isolated as if she were in a cabin in an Alaskan snow storm. She doesn't dare get out.

Hopefully, the special grace of the American land will inspire you, not only to look at it, but to love it; perhaps to work in the future to resist its further destruction. My own theory is that the paradox of American beauty and pollution is explained by our history. As Americans we believe in fighting and hating what holds us back. In the past it was Nature itself. The vastness was the enemy frustrating the dreams of the pioneers and presenting so great a challenge to the early American spirit. That battle is now won.

Yet the American spirit is so basically the same that it's still looking for challenge, still looking for an arena in which to test itself. That's one of the reasons why I think the future is hopeful. We're gradually turning our enmity away from nature and onto our materialism. The enemy is our own ugliness, our own undeveloped consciousness. We are the enemy.

The main problems now lie in our cities. American cities are uninhabitable by ordinary people and difficult for the rest of us. Born into a rich and beautiful environment, they flowered in the 19th century, but at the same time became centers of industry and money. In this century, they've become sick, and are rotting. Characteristically, American cities and towns are artificial environments, eyesores in relation to their natural surroundings. If one does harmonize with its environment then you know there's something unAmerican about it.

For example, San Francisco, where I live, is usually called the best American city because it is still beautiful. Preening next to the ocean and the bay, blessed with hills and parks and climate, it offers all the urban cosmopolitan and economic advantages — the pulse-beat of life, the tolerance and freedom to be yourself — yet it's not so large that it's completely lost its small-town atmosphere, its friendly sense of familiarity. But San Francisco is distinctly unAmerican in the traditional sense. SF is where beatniks, hippies, topless bars, and rock festivals originated. In elections of recent years, it is the only American city to vote for McGovern, por-

Off The Tape
MUD LAKE, IDAHO

A conversation between some of the restaurant patrons concerning what their kids could do in that town: one local man said that he and another neighbor were willing to donate land for a swimming pool. One lady said, "Yeah, I'd be willing to give a donation to build a pool. I've got one kid near growin up and I know she's gonna cost me money sooner or later." Another one said "Yeah, we oughta do something for the kids here. There's the church and the bar, and nothin in between. What they need is a hamburger stand and a dance hall." As we drive off, we see that the nearest thing to town is some kind of US Atomic Energy testing grounds. Mud Lake — all-American town.

nography, legalization of marijuana, ending the Vietnamese War, voiding the death penalty, and tearing down its freeways. Why? Because it's "the city that knows how."

Yet its being Americanized all the same. Not long ago I went downtown and strolled along a few blocks of Sixth Street, and here are some things I saw at random within ten minutes of each other: Streets torn up for subway, sewer, and high-rise construction; — attendent traffic jams, horns, fumes; trash burning in the gutters, doorways piled with wine bottles and litter, urine stains everywhere on the sidewalks; people hassling on the street — cursing, fighting, gambling, begging, dealing, pimping; a line of people selling blood; lines of empty storefronts, porny movie houses, hock shops, storefront missions, etc. Populating the streets was a diverse collection of drunks, cripples, prostitutes, hoboes, hoodlums, dope pushers, and poor people of every race, sex, age. These people and this place didn't just happen, they were made.

People are made to be what they are and this one area in San Francisco is only a taste of what's going on in big cities everywhere. Crime, corruption, pollution, paranoia, desperation. Ah city life, ah me. There is an answer, and it lies in changes of consciousness and national priorities. But in the meanwhile . . .

THE BEER CAN AS NATIONAL SYMBOL The American eagle is about to be extinct, so it's time to substitute something more representative of the American situation. This business of beer cans in America is as outrageous as anything else. There is hardly anywhere you can't find a beer can. In some parts of America, particularly the most isolated parts, like Monument Valley in the Four Corners country, the road is solidly lined on both sides with soft drink and beer cans. There are beer cans on the graves in the cemeteries of America. There are beer cans in the outhouses of the Sierra Nevada. There are beer cans even on the floor of your own car.

Pollution by beer cans is the symbol of the national problem of pollution, symbol of the American beer-can consciousness. Did you ever wonder why it should be beer rather than baked beans? Beer is alcohol. It gets you high, and Americans love to get high on energy busts. They like to move around, and they like throwing things — it uses their hands. They don't like using their heads, so they have low regard for their environment, for infringement on others, for human priorities. So, for at least right now, the beer can is our banner. It combines our need to get stoned, our technological skill in packaging and distribution, our disregard for subtler values. It's lucky when you live in America, where you can be anything, Budweiser.

HOMOGENIZING IS NOT GRADE A The process of making America more homogenous, of making more and more things look the same from automobiles to cities to life styles to clothing to food is essentially economically based. It's more efficient to streamline everything. It saves money, that is, releases money to be spend on even more things. Blah, Blah, Blah. What happens, unfortunately, is that distinctiveness gets wiped out, too. The rela-

tively few things that keep their character become enshrined and then themselves packaged and distributed. For example, the old sections of America are being canned for tourist consumption and thus become another commodity also. Very little is left to be itself anymore; it's preserved for eventual consumption and profit. Americans seem to be suckers for this. They eat processed food, buy the standardized cars, live in tract houses in planned suburbs, and are themselves, their lives, and all the things around them steadily cheapened by conformity.

You might think that from out of this homogenous society will come homogenous people. Not at all. In fact, this homogeneity inevitably produces the seeds of discord that flower into individuality. People need to express themselves, and conformist pressures only makes them strive harder to be different. A well-known photo-poster of a few years back showed a group of far-out-looking rock musicians standing in the street before a row of identical tract houses. The poster seemingly depicted the surreal contrast between these outrageous psychedelic freaks and the bland conformism represented by their background. But the poster was really just a portrait of the kids who grew up in those houses — those "freaks" are the natural result of that kind of homogeneity.

And so it is everywhere today. The commune-movement, the drug experimenters, the health-food craze, the pacifists, the conservationists, the hippies, the hitchhikers, the long-hairs, the free schools, the drop-outs, the entire "greening of America" revolution is the natural result, the reaction to the "Progress" mentality of the 1950's. That mentality of standardization for the sake of efficiency has suddenly become itself outmoded and old-fashioned. The affluent society, the people in power, the older generation have brought themselves to the point of decline. From this time on, they'll steadily lose their grip. The tide now begins to turn, slowly at first, but a new order is coming. You can be part of it.

THE AMERICAN MASS CONSCIOUSNESS Coming into Philadelphia thru a black neighborhood we see a large billboard advertising cigarettes. A black couple is smoking. They're very close to each other, and in large letters overhead it says "Naturally refreshing." In smaller letters at the bottom it says "No jive." Here's an ordinary example of the lying and corruption of the advertising industry and, by extension, the America that supports it.

First of all, it's selling only by sloganeering. Advertising in its early days tried at least to market the product on the basis of its merits. Almost all the big advertisers sell their products now only by slogans. In this particular case, the main slogan "Naturally refreshing" isn't true. To inhale cigarettes is neither natural nor refreshing. Even if you were to think of tobacco as a natural product, its treatment with menthol makes it unnatural. The addition of menthol does not refresh the lungs, that is, rejuvenate them when we smoke it in. Sloganeering usually simply avoids truth, but here is a case where it also lies. This particular example is underscored because it says "No jive" at the bottom. That's as if to say "this is the truth." But it isn't true, so to say it is just increases the magnitude of dishonesty.

"No jive" is also a racist statement, di-
rected at blacks. And showing blacks in the ad is also racist, especially since you only see this ad in a black neighborhood. Some people would say the advertising of cigarettes itself is a crime against the national health, but that doesn't bother me too much. People should have a right to their own poisons.

Nevertheless, that billboard sells an unhealthy product with an empty, lying slogan in a racist way. Naturally that billboard could be defended, no doubt with the argument that "it creates jobs." It sure is an all-American billboard.

SIGHTS AND SOUNDS OF POLLUTION Coming over the George Washington Bridge which leaps out from the Hudson River Palisades into the city of New York, the upper and lower reaches of the city can't be seen at all due to the smog and the smoke. The feeling of passing thru NYC on Interstate 95 is like being in the center of an automotive sewer. A cacaphony of noise. A kaleidoscope of dingy sights. Trains roaring alongside the freeways. Overpasses and underpasses — the sewer is multi-level. The roar of traffic — engines, diesels, horns, tires, brakes. Everything is drab — brown, gray, brick, slate. Even the moving cars are covered with layers of soot. The pavement, the walls, the buildings, are stained with exhaust smoke, with industrial soot, with the grease from the giant fart of the giant machine. At the edge of the pavement, patches of grass struggle to live, buried under a debris of junk: Mufflers, signs, tires, hubcaps, pieces of tar, stones, bricks, miscellaneous debris from the tide of mechanization that sweeps by. At one point on the center strip between lanes right after we come out of a dark tunnel, two sunflower plants turn their faces bravely upward from a field of beer bottles, cardboard, and tire tread fragments. New York in July can be beheld only with sore eyes.

And, of course, new road construction. Everywhere hiways being widened, new bridges built, new overpasses, more lanes please, give us more lanes. While we go thru bumper to bumper traffic they're building more lanes.

We've got 12 lanes, give us 15; more lanes so we can build more cars so we can have more traffic so we can have more lanes, please. That's the thing about materialism. Once you get started there's no end to it. No amount of things can ever be enough, and so the rape proceeds, the rape of nature, the rape of humanity. But the rape is seeking completion and it seems like it's going to get it sometime relatively soon. The orgasm of this particular 200-year rape is nearing. No doubt it's going to be quite a climax.

SPEAKING OF AUTOMOBILES, let's go to Detroit. The unholy source, the symbol of the American technological trip. Detroit seems to be reaping its ultimate reward for that reputation and my, does it fit. Much of the central city is a rotting carcass, a ghetto with buildings boarded up, all for sale or gutted. Fear rules the streets, the whole area has the appearance of being scored nightly by desperadoes. We visited a friend in a northern suburb. As we come into town, signs by the road say "Home of the 1970 Hockey Champs. No Hitchhiking. No Parking on Any City Streets between 3 AM and 7 AM." School bussing is obviously an issue because we see cars with bumper stickers saying "Judge Roth — Child Molester" and "Pith on Roth" and "Bus Kids? Truck Roth."

At my friend's house, a group of neighbors are on the lawn talking, and we overhear part of their conversation about blacks in Detroit. One man says, "I'll tell you what, the ones that love 'em are the sons of bitches that don't hang around 'em." The substance of the discussion was that you can't do anything for black people, that they tear up whatever you give them. The white consciousness always sees itself as the owner of all property, as the generous donor of goods to the blacks, and can't understand why blacks don't appreciate all they're getting, can't understand that the blacks don't want the gift, they want the power. In Detroit, the Mordor of American materialism, they don't yet understand that you can neither get nor give enough "things." The blacks are rioting while the rich get richer at Grosse Point. Society is collapsing but they're setting new production records for automobiles.

My friend's sister tells us how even a slight deviation on her part from the material ethic causes static from her nieghbors. For example, they make fun of or envy the fact that she travels a lot. They're suspicious about where she gets the money to do that even tho travel is a sacrifice for her. She travels to Europe and Hawaii by carefully saving money from a working woman's salary. Yet she is criticized be-

IT'S A SMALL WORLD As we near Disney World, Florida, we note that the surrounding area is a frantic construction complex — building today for tomorrow's tourists. Huge motels going up, hotels, gas stations, trailer grounds. Siphoning off from this, a four-lane divided hiway into Disney World itself thru a forested buffer zone. Early in the morning there are solid lines of traffic, a parade of out-of-state license plates, no cars coming out. Surreal. Pine woods on both sides. Blue sky, puffy clouds. Driving to meet our American fantasy. Welcome to the Magic Kingdom. The parking lot is an ocean of asphalt, with schools of cars systematically pulling in for feeding.

First impressions of Disney World all have to do with the amount of money involved, the amount of organization, the number of employees, especially the number of personnel directing crowds. Above all, a kind of mild amazement at the logistical feat. The nature of the attractions, the quaintness, the cuteness are secondary. This is a strictly American creation because it requires laboratories-full of technology, bank-vaults of money, and finally, a special consciousness to conceptualize the exhibits themselves. Main Street, Frontierland, Tomorrowland, and certainly Fantasyland, are all made-in-America-only. Pure Mickey Mouse.

It's a weekday in summer, the off-season in Florida. Yet Disney World overflows with people. For some of the rides there are long lines; for the rest of them there are short lines. One fellow I talked to said he'd been here six times. He's waited for some rides for two hours, and there are still some he hasn't gone on.

My most memorable ride was "It's A Small World" (the most expensive — an E ticket). We got into a boat in a dark waterway that disappeared into the bowels of this huge building. We swept forward in the current, full of anticipation. Entering a large room, I soon saw what the ride was going to be about, and my reaction was to feel insulted. The entire ride had but a single motif — thousands of two-foot dolls dressed in costumes of different lands,

cause she doesn't spend her money as her neighbors do, on cars and furnishings. As a working woman living alone, she doesn't have enough time to keep the grass mowed, which causes her neighbors to complain because it makes the neighborhood look bad. The good people of suburban Detroit are worried about the appearance of their neighborhoods while they're going spiritually bankrupt. They're destitute of quality in their lives, and they fear for their property, for their neighborhood. Why don't they fear for their souls? It's comic and tragic.

Leaving Detroit there's a huge sign that says "Ford World Headquarters" with one of those electronic billboards that gives news of the world, except in this case it gives sales figures, advertising slogans, and propaganda. Who cares?

animated and dancing to the tune of "It's A Small World." Room after room displayed these dummies in an orgy of overlapping music and color, lots of noise, things whirling and water swirling. As the insane music ran on and on, as each room revealed more and more dolls and sets, I realized it was completely bizarre and meaningless, and I dug it. Here was the ultimate tourist trip: You spend money and go nowhere. Nothing happens to you. It has no value as experience. You just rock gently and watch a million dollars worth of dolls do mechanical tricks in the name of the brotherhood of man. Ah man, ah me. An American Classic!

My sister, who lives in Florida and has visited Disney World several times, also sees it as a materialist hoax but said: "Let me give you a stock market tip. Invest in Disney World stock. It's going up. It's going to be a winner." Ah winners, ah me.

WATCHING TELEVISION Television in America is a complex matter, simultaneously a molder of opinion, medium of information, symbol of consciousness, entertainment center, home classroom, and social crutch — among others. I noticed that the way people relate to it shows the level of their consciousness. Most middle-class, middle-aged Americans use it as a social crutch. With the set on, all conversation becomes superficial, often to everyone's relief. No one has to speak, but if they do, no one has to listen — an ideal situation for handling company, or eating dinner with the family. Used this way, TV becomes an impediment to communication, an easy way out of social responsibility.

A related purpose of TV is to assuage the lonliness that Americans feel because they can't communicate with each other. TV projects the lonely man into a crowd, makes him feel less alone. Of course, the crowd is artificial, it's made of ghosts. Failing to seek other company is an easy way out of social interchange.

Meanwhile, for children TV is a home classroom. Kids raised on it learn fast, and what they learn is surprising. They learn about the commercialism of the medium, the dishonesty of advertising, the superficiality of the programming. What children learn from TV is an amazing testimonial to the wonderful design of human beings. They develop a higher level of consciousness than their parents because they see thru the artifice and concentrate on what values there are in it, such as language skills, information about the world, and social attitudes relating to TV itself.

OTHER OLD CONSCIOUSNESS In Nevada I overheard ranchers discussing the merits of various objects used to beat their kids into obedience. I heard them bragging about the brutality shown prostitutes in the early days of the West. In Idaho I heard them talking about preventing national forest lands from being designated as wilderness areas so they could use them for their own recreation and profit. On the road, I read about how the astronauts get rich from exclusive stories in magazines, how they set up trust funds for their kids by selling stamps from the moon. I observed how coldly many middle-class American families treat their children, as if they were possessions like their second car and their house in the country. I saw a parade of brutality, superficiality, coldness, pollution, greed, zombism, puritanism, alienation, racism, selfishness. I saw the old consciousness of America, and I think it's passing.

A NEW CONSCIOUSNESS America in its frontier and growth days was a hard land, lacking many of the most basic material rewards. But even without a pot to piss in, Americans had plenty of inner strength born of faith in God, in government, and in self. It was a place for materialist ambitions, since there was so little and the land promised so much.

Today the situation is at least partly reversed. The land has made good its promise, has been softened and made fecund. Now our outer strength, our store of goods and factories, is the wonder of the world — but we've begun to doubt our God, our government, ourselves. The ideas and ethics that brought us to this materialist peak are now exhausting our spirit and our resources. They are patterns from a simpler and grosser age, no longer appropriate to a world with more people and fewer resources.

What happened is that America went from one extreme to the opposite. We achieved great material prosperity, but became spiritually poor along the way. We gained more time off from labor and we live longer, but the quality of our lives is reduced to blandness and sameness. The time we spend on the job is less but also devoid of personal rewards or pleasure. Our technology has advanced, but is used more for exploitation and destruction than helping and building. Communication and transportation are far more rapid, but their content and style are vapid and dull. Racial equality is much closer, but those liberated lose their identity. Our understanding of life is increased many fold, but our capability to deal with it seems less, and our respect for it is no greater. Are we really better off?

This is the question that haunts todays' young people. They look around and see poverty of spirit, mediocrity, loss of identity, dehumanization, pollution, blandness, destruction. Is it any wonder they're turning away from the old-style American dream? Clearly they're "dropping out" from disgust. The politicians, the scientists, the economists — all the professional Americans — in the end came up with no human solutions at all. They only gave us words, and formulas, and money. It's not enough.

Clearly a new balance must be struck. The classic American goals need to be modified to account for the hidden costs we're just learning about. Americans are realizing that happiness comes from things like love and personal pride, not from new cars, campaign speeches, or scientific advances. Knowledge about life that you personally gain from living is always better than somebody else's advice, whether it comes

United States can become a world leader in a new way. We sold the world a materialist idea and now we can say "Stop the presses. We have seen your future and it stinks."

What America should do now is sell the world on a new kind of consciousness. So far, we've not taken that opportunity. The vested power structure in America, the government, the corporations, the military, the religious fronts, are all fighting for the status quo, still waving the flag and promising new cars. Too bad, because that's all over. For all their power, they aren't strong enough to hold the tide. In any case, the resources of the globe won't support much more exploitation, and any consciousness or power based on those resources must necessarily fade away.

What is the new American consciousness and how do you get it? In its basic form, it's very simple. It starts with the realization that happiness is about being alive, it's about being in love with life. This assumes that if we keep our material needs simple, there will never be a lack of a roof over our head or food to eat. Happiness is a spiritual commodity. It doesn't come from money. Next, the joy of being alive is a feeling gotten by using yourself, by exercising what talents you have, by using your mind and body. Making full use of yourself consists of finding worthwhile challenges to stimulate you into action. Education also comes from action. Finding more about everything, more about yourself, more in yourself, more about others, more in others, more about the world in which we all live together. Always learning, always moving toward sources of information and sources of energy. You can begin all of this by creating free energy in yourself, by starting to think about the patterns of life you have now, and how you can change them for more productive patterns.

The best way is to try something new, no matter what it is. It will make you question. Start with America. Start with yourself in your own country and go from there. But in traveling your country, be open to it. Experiment with new ways to see it, ways that you like, no matter what your travel agent says. Your most important responsibility at every level is

from your friend, boss, union man, congressman, or mother. If you arrange enough freedom and free energy for yourself, you'll always be able to think for yourself. You'll be less dependent on ruts and patterns, have control of your energy, and be able to release it at will.

Energy flow, whether for individuals or nations, cleanses consciousness, makes possible more energy release by adjustment of patterns. And this is where America is today — fiercely shook up by the forces of change, but charged with free energy it's using to evolve into a more mature nation.

Meanwhile, American-style materialism is still spreading in the world — to the Orient, to Japan, to Europe, South America, Africa. It will take them awhile to find out that materialism by itself is inadequate. That's why the to yourself. If you fairly serve yourself first, you will automatically serve your family, your country, your God. Discover yourself and you'll find the world. This book suggests ways to think about it and to do it.

THE FUTURE LIES AHEAD In fact, you can expect the future to be filled with lies. Where do you stand in this business of consciousness? Most likely somewhere in between the old and the new. No one is so developed in their consciousness that they can truly say, "I've run the course. I've done all I could." On the other hand, no one is so far gone that they can say, "There's no help for me — I can't change." To recognize that there's room for change is all the handle you need to begin. No matter what your patterns are now, you can release new energy from them.

Fear is usually what holds us back from doing what is right or desirable. We have so much invested in our old way of life that we hesitate. We're afraid to take any step toward a new way of life. But that's cheating yourself. The greatness of America and Americans lies in their freedom to pursue happiness, the right that's guaranteed them. The greatness is in the pursuit. The happiness in in the changing, not in the achievement. The happiness comes from experiencing what there is to be experienced without deciding beforehand what that should be.

To travel America now is to see options for other ways of living and thinking. It's about people everywhere facing the challenges of life by themselves for a change, and finding that the experience is a heady one, an exciting one. Americans are rediscovering the values of getting involved, and of thinking independently. Young people are in the vanguard, starting communes and farms, becoming craftsmen and independent workers. But the mass of America is changing as well, and can never be the same anymore.

The true richness of America lies in its myriad life alternatives. To travel America is to see every life-style that you can conceive of, everything from the ultra-spiritualist to the ultra-materialist, with every kind of gradation

and combination in between. What it represents is an awesome potential for quality of life. More than ever before, the potential of America. It's fantastic. There's a total renaissance in action, and America is at the center of it all. Its people sparkle with talent and ideas, with materials to put those ideas to work. They're charged with energy, they're remaking themselves, their country, and the world we live in, the most exciting time in history. I think today's enlightened Americans are the first truly international people in the world. Perhaps it could only happen in America, this ability to produce a new breed of people who achieved success, then went on to work for humanity and happiness.

Off The Tape
VIRGINIA CITY

In the graveyards of Virginia City, Nevada: Dead trees rising out of many of the graves. Decorative iron fences. Weeds grow rife all over. The wind howls thru you. I'm standing by a grave, way back in the hills. It's surface is completely cemented over, but cracked and buckled, with weeds growing next to some plastic flowers. In the background is the base of the mountain which I guess Mark Twain wrote about — Mt. Davidson. All that's left of the city is a series of tourist traps — decrepit monuments to what must have been a glorious past. In between the town and Boot Hill is a canyon, but it's piled up with mine tailings — more monuments. Then finally, the Boot Hill itself, magnificently unattended.

The tombstones are cracking under their weight, falling into the earth. Several of the stones are broken off. I'm standing in a portion of the cemetary where the earth itself has thrust forth its own monuments. Ancient, ragged stone comes up thru the earth very rich in color, dark hues. At the bases of the various monuments, both nature's and man's, are beer cans. Everywhere there's sage brush, some tumbleweed. As desolate a graveyard as I've seen.

A man just came by, a middle-aged man, and said to me "You have to see it to believe it, don't you?" He said his grandfather used to come here often; used to tell him about it, but he never believed it till he saw it. We talk some more amidst the stones, in the wind. He's a funeral singer, sung at a lot of graveyards but says he's never seen anything like this. "A lot of forgotten men here." He proceeded to speak feelingly and articulately about these men, about how they came from other parts of the world, seeking fortune and life . . . now they lie here in mouldering abandoned graves . . . lost even in memory. All the while he talked, his wife — a plain stout woman — said nothing. Finally I turned at her. Seeing I expected her to say something, she looked at me and said flatly, "Yeah, ain't it pitiful?"

THOUGHTS ABOUT LIFE AND DEATH We are all under sentence of death. To realize that is to be freed so that we can value our time here and make use of it all the more. Let me tell you the story of how I discovered I had cancer and what that meant to me.

It started on my most recent vagabonding tour. I was hitchhiking down the California coast, enjoying one of the more outrageous times of my life. I arrived in Laguna Beach one day, stashed my pack and decided to get some sun by the ocean. There were lots of people and I smiled at different groups. A woman with some children returned my smile, and as I walked past I saw next to her the Baba Ram Dass book *Be Here Now*. I said to myself, that's a good idea, so I stopped, said "Hello" and met a person who changed my life.

When I took off my shirt to get some sun, the first thing she said was, "You have a nasty looking mole there." She did volunteer work in the local free clinic, and that mole didn't look good to her. It's strange how these things work, for when she said that I got the flash: Cancer! I'd been aware that mole was discoloring and growing, but it never reached my consciousness until that moment, and then I suddenly saw all the malefactory possibilities. I had a sensation of my body fighting to contain the cells in that mole but felt I had to act quickly. I decided to return the next day to San Francisco and have it looked at by Wes Sokolosky, my own doctor in Pt. Reyes.

I flew back on a Thursday, telephoned Wes on Friday morning, went in the same afternoon. He removed it while I lay on my stomach on the operating table in his office. I watched a stream of blood flow to the floor from my shoulder. It slowly grew into a brilliant puddle, and I stared at it thinking, I hope this isn't too late. Later Wes assured me that mole cancer is rare, I was in good shape, and only 38. So I felt momentarily reassured.

Two weeks later on the road again, after recuperating and then renewing the hitchhiking adventure, I telephoned Stephanie from Wyoming knowing she would have the lab report. It was no surprise to me when she said it had been found malignant. I knew I'd been too late. The next morning I called Wes and he told me it was a spreading kind, not skin cancer. End of the trip.

On the plane home from Denver, I experienced a complete case of cancerophobia — unreasonable fear of cancer. I visualized my mole cancer, my melanoma already spread. I'd sprained my back a couple of months before and now I supposed the pain I still felt there was really the cancer already spread to my spine. This was prompted by a story I'd heard, ironically just the day before from a girl with whom I'd hitchhiked, about her boss whose back pains turned out to be spinal cancer. He died within two months. So, flying back in the plane I supposed I was going to die soon and tried to explore how that felt and how I felt about it. I was fascinated by the views of the Utah and Nevada desert passing below me, of the mountains and the land forms, and I watched them with abnormal intensity.

I had the feeling this was the last time I might see the earth from above. I thought how incredibly beautiful the workings of nature were, how every valley, every river, every ripple of water made its own shape as it went down the slopes, how it shaped the land, how ordained it was, how planned and how beautiful it was in that plan. I tried to accept the feeling that everything in life had a plan. If I had to die soon it was part of a plan and I had not to fight it. I had to give my spirit to the greater spirit in the sky, gracefully, without complaint.

But the thought kept crowding in that I was too young to die. My whole creative life was just opening up, I had just had my first successes in writing and photography. I was just now coming to spirituality, to a mature view of life. How ironic at this time to leave it all. It wasn't fair. I looked around me at the people smoking cigarettes and thought: Here they are violating the laws of cancer — yet they're alive and I'm dying. It was a battle between the negative thoughts and feeling sorry for myself, and the positive thoughts, the spiritual thoughts, wanting to yield myself without struggle to a greater fate.

Off The Tape
SANITY

We just passed part of a convoy of army trucks bound somewhere full of soldiers, carrying artillary pieces. As we passed them, they were all shouting "Take me home. I'm as sane as you are. Take me with you, I'm as sane as you are."

Yet, I still had hope, and promised myself that if I worked it out, if I could live, I vowed to remember how I felt then, and to live my life better and purer because of it. I had a rush of hope in which I saw that if I could get over this hurdle I would be stronger for it. It was an intensely dramatic moment in my life, and was itself full of life. Once again I realized that my life in its own way is a dramatic sample that characterizes all life.

Arriving home I saw soon enough that the knowledge of cancer had freed me from fear in a strange way. If I didn't have much time to live, I couldn't afford petty fears any longer. As life passes by, it is fear that keeps us from knowing it in its wholeness. That very weekend I made a number of important break-thrus. I took an acid trip I'd been afraid to take because of a bum one last year, I expressed and acted out my love for Stephanie with a clarify I'd been afraid of before. Healthy breakdown of patterns, new rushes of energy. Thus the nearness of death clarifies the opportunities for life, the foolishness of being afraid to live. I'm still learning about how to unravel all the layers of fear that keep me from complete honesty, from diluting the quality of life, but everything confirms the basic premise.

Meanwhile, the doctor trip wound up at UC Medical Center and their melanoma clinic. I had another operation on my back, and later, another on my right armpit. For the next few years, I'll be going back to the clinic for periodic checks to see if the cancer is actually gone. At the time of this writing (December, 1972), there is some doubt about it, but only time can tell. I've got my fingers crossed. In the meanwhile, I'm putting all I can into each day. My life is very full. Glory be. I intend to keep doing that always, whether I have a year to live, or fifty.

Whatever happens, I know the experience has made me a better person, more loving and giving, more human. It's a heavy life experience to look death in the eye and watch it draw near. Yet we're all in that situation, we're all under sentence of death. We need to realize it in some gut way so that we'll stop being afraid to live. One of these days your own death will be at hand. If you could see it coming, how would that make you feel? Could it be that you'd feel you hadn't used your time properly? If so, why not start to take stock now, and get that energy flowing? Get free of fear; get free. Take a look at yourself, take a look at the place where you live. This trip is necessary.

LETTER TO OUR FRIENDS
22 June 1972

Dear Eugene and Janet and, of course, Ona Blossom. Hello, hello. We are here in Bonifay, Florida, sitting around with Kazimierz and Josephine and Ed's sister Jane, after a dinner which included home-grown potatoes, corn, cucumbers, home-baked bread, fresh-caught fish, all grown and prepared by Josephine who has been up since 6 am, building with Kazimierz this house, and who is now washing the dishes absolutely forbidding me to help her. Sierra is playing on the floor, singing her songs of ectasy despite a slight fever which she has, I guess, from the changes in temperature she has been forced to undergo.

It has been a beautiful trip so far, a very real trip, with high points and low points. We have met some beautiful brothers on the road, seekers for the way, including one remarkable person who has been studying herbs, and who gave us some of his bread (herbs and seeds and flour — unleavened because he says leavened bread continues to ferment in your body). His eyes were so clear you knew that he was high and clear and it was a blessing to have him in the car.

Later we came to the red earth gates of Zion, Utah — a holy land where we hiked paths of deep red earth to an emerald pool at the back of a canyon where we swam and then dried our bodies in the sun. From Utah it was up, up, up to New Mexico where I met a great woman poet named Meridel LeSueur who has written a beautiful story about pregnancy. Meridel is now 74 years old, her face is lined with mystery and knowledge; she is a queen, an unknown queen.

New Mexico is elevating, that's all I can say, elevating. You float there, float in the clear blue sky, float in the white clean air. The Indians have sanctified the land. At the feet of the holy mountains of Taos, my family took a hot mineral bath, the three of us bathing in an island of warm water at the edge of the Rio Grande. And then we got stoned and hiked up the steep hill to see the smiling faces of some beautiful people. Ed and I are talking about living there and I feel right about it even tho I'm afraid to leave what I know in SF. But I love New Mexico, love what it has to teach me about the Indians, love what it reveals to me about myself.

The last few days have been more of an earthly struggle. The South — its very hot humid — hiking is a major expenditure of energy. And I don't feel very comfortable here — feel excluded, feel like an enemy. But then we came to Ed's parent's house, got

a true Polish welcome in the Middle of a Florida field and my baby has grandparents now, has been tossed and cooed and admired and I've been counselled ("don't you think she's hungry for food?" "so how long are you going to nurse her?" and the good old dependable Buryn, "let her cry"). Just like they said it would be, a family, home to my family at last, again.

And yet it is a family. Everyone is in the living room now, Ed's brother Henry who lives down the road and his wife Annette and their 2 kids and everyone else and the television is on and Ed is making jokes and drinking scotch and something.

I don't know where it's going from here, but I haven't known where it was going since the day we left. Ed is in charge of this odyssey. I make the soup and tend to the child and write in my black books (I'm carrying four of them with me, each for different classifications of information and I'm as attached to them as I am to Sierra). And I think this trip is becoming an important event in our lives, a true meeting with our country and so a good book will come of it.

Well there's nothing wrong with this home grown Bonifay stuff — comes on easy but does the thing. Ed's parents are talking about Ignatz and Josef and Poland and villages and peach trees and they're laughing about death (who's got the worst cancer?) Too heavy for me.

You are both in my thoughts and heart —

Stephanie

Off The Tape
CHACO CANYON RUINS

Built and occupied hundreds of years before Columbus. Left by thousands of inhabitants when Europe was in the dark ages. 800 rooms in a lovely canyon lost in the vastness of the southwest. There was originally a stand of ponderosa and pinon pines in the canyon, and the Indians chopped down all the trees for roof beams inside the houses. When the trees were gone, the land wouldn't hold water any longer and they were faced with drought . . . the entire site had to be abandoned. It's the same thing we're faced with now on a world-wide basis, except of course that we have nowhere else to go.

Where Is It At?

How To Find America

3

IT AIN'T SO EASY Stop and consider this: You can't see the forest if you're one of the trees. In other words, if you've never known any environment other than America, a strict rule of human nature says you're more or less insensitive to it. In other words, you can't get excited about something familiar. Why do you think most Americans would rather vacation in Rome, Italy than in Rome, Georgia? Partly because we already know about Georgia and guess what Rome is like . . . not too exciting, right? Travel must stimulate you, or it isn't worth a damn. (Why leave home if you like being bored?)

By God's merciful design, America is too big to be boring. Not many Americans know it well, and no American has seen all of it. Few Americans know the panorama of its history or feel its power sculpting their consciousness. Few Americans even realize the incredible range of experiences awaiting the traveler who seeks it out.

No land offers more, yet perversely no land can bore or corrupt more, either. Its communication networks work to impose a sameness of language and thought from northern tundra to southern sands. Most of its cities are interchangeable madhouses, its people uniformly wary and self-concerned. Its architectural styles, its man-made structures squat everywhere devoid of grace or inspiration, seemingly built just to make jobs for workers, to conduct commerce or maybe electricity.

America is a gigantic paradox. Therein lies the mystery; therein lies the fascination. How can a "land so blessed" be so scourged with problems and disillusionment? How can a people so materialistic and middle-class be so elusive, so full of genuine humanity and new directions?

To find America means struggling to pierce the cliches and slogans that hide its reality. It means deliberately attempting to escape the easy cynicism on one side, and the easy self-righteousness on the other. The truth is that for all its famous open spaces and open-ness, America lies hidden and closed to most travelers, and most of all to its own people. With all its easy blessings and freedoms, America quietly snares its native prey and clips its dreamers' wings.

To truly discover America, you must see it with fresh vision. The essence of the vagabond way is to consciously or unconsciously explore new experiences. This is exactly how we discover ourselves, also. The vagabond mentality gives you the impetus to push out of those old grooves into new territory — geographical, experimental, emotional, whatever. This newness in turn challenges the traveler, and tunes his senses. Freshets of energy miraculously appear, stimulating fuller functioning and vitalizing. One day you suddenly realize you're discovering a different America inside the bounds of that tired old one you knew before.

HOW TO DISCOVER AMERICA For the moment, never mind what all those travel advertisements say. Look at how Columbus did it. Pick a new vessel, a new crew, a new route, a new destination. Have a long talk with Queen Isabella. Concentrate on the treasures to be won, and piss on the perils. Planning is where to begin. Plan the broad aspects but leave the lesser details free. Planning consists of choosing places to go, ways to get there, things to do, and people to see.

First, pick a direction and a destination. You may think you know America because you've gotten used to your little sample of it. But no part is really like any other — not in geography, climate, history, or character. What new territory and places can you explore? New York is hardly San Francisco, and Fairbanks is far from Miami in all ways. The Rockies contrast with the Ozarks; the rapids of the Grand Canyon are nothing like the passages in Puget Sound. Consider the Florida Keys and the Maine Woods; compare the rivers of the Suwannee and the Columbia. Travel the Interstate Hiways and the Appalachian Trail. Compare the history of the Little Big Horn with that of Appomatox. Compare Capes Kennedy and Cod; Mounts Rushmore and Whitney. Do some research to find out about these and other specific places enroute — parks, historic sites, cities, attractions. (How to get this information is coming up shortly.)

Next, put life into your itinerary by doing something active. Your past travel activities barely scrape the surface of what there is to do. No doubt you've traveled far by car, maybe you've been car-camping. But have you tried bicycle touring? Sometimes simply seeing America minus a windshield reveals an all-new place. Ever roped your way up a mountain? That'll juice your glands and accelerate self-discovery. Tried any float-boating? Backpacking? Parachuting? Ever shop for antiques? Gone bird-watching? Ever visited a commune? Bathed in a desert hot-spring? Skied across a mountain range? Sketched a seascape? Cruised on a river steamer?

No place surpasses America as a recreational cornucopia. If you can't do it here, it's probably not happening anywhere. Feeling jaded with yourself and America? Try hitchhiking across it for a real adventure. Or how about just a taste of it by giving a ride to a hitchhiker? What about traveling to collect herbs, fossils, shells, or rocks ... zoos, battlefields, lighthouses, or graveyards? Want to be really far out? Go to a nudist beach for the first time, or to a palmistry reader. See a slum or a ghetto. Rent a bicycle. Introduce yourself to a hippy. Smoke a joint. Maybe find yourself an offshore island to comb the beaches and write love poems. Try it ... you'll like it. (How to get information is still coming up shortly.)

Last, and perhaps most important, plan to visit and meet actual human beings along your route. Think you've met all the American personality types? No one has yet, but it's a trip if you try. Psychological fun for the entire family. Don't forget about visiting friends, relatives, even business and casual acquaintances around the USA. Chapter 8 is all about how to meet and make the most of Americans.

One thing about your plan or itinerary. After inventing it, don't seal it in plastic and enshrine it as a holy document on your dashboard. Remember it's a fiction — a convenient one, of course — but that's all. Deviate from it every time something looks more interesting. Every place you see, everything you do, everyone you meet may suggest alternative ideas or activities. The plan doesn't matter — the doing does. The plan serves to get you doing, not to be the doing.

TRIPS TO TAKE At the back of the book you'll find a list of American "trips" — things to see and do — all researched to provide you with information. Compiled by Stephanie, its purpose is to give you new ideas, then point to what you need to follow through. Appendix 1 — Trips — includes book lists, book reviews, addresses, and miscellaneous information and comments. We've listed trips of basically four different types: *Outdoor* (wilderness experience, adventures), *People, Historical,* and *Cultural.* Use them as a starting place for ideas and plans. Brouse the back of the book before making plans.

THE TRAVEL INDUSTRY This is the collective title for a whole series of obstacles to seeing America in a meaningful way. I call it the "TI." The persons who love to be served by it I call TI-types, or TIts for short.

The TI corresponds in its own modest way to the military-industrial complex affecting us at the governmental level. The TI comprises the hotel, motel and restaurant chains, the resort and "amusement" complexes, the interlocking airlines and travel agencies. It is a huge business using computer-controlled reservations and pricing, offering profit-prompted tours and packages, setting phony standards of taste and popularity, employing advertising budget outlays that equal the gross national product of dozens of foreign countries.

The TI was born to suck TIts for profit. In other words, the TI sells travel services, not travel experiences. In fact, the TI shields you from experiences because they reduce profits. Moving your body from place to place makes money, but moving your heart or mind doesn't. The profits lie in the conveyances that motate people, the lodgings that rotate them, and the restaurants that potate them. What happened is that an industry founded to provide travel conveniences and services has gradually convinced itself that conveniences and services are synonymous with travel. It's a lie.

The primary damage is not to the American wallet. Americans who use the TI have too much money anyway, and the TI only takes what some other service industry will take

sooner or later. (Elementary economics teaches that dollars must be kept rotating for the good of the system.) The damage *is* heavy, however, on the American mass consciousness. TIts get the full treatment of luxury fare. They are always made comfortable. Refined and rich foods keep their bellies constantly full. Their eyes are pleased by the recurring sight of colorful and shiny objects of decor. They know they must be having a good time because all those other people just like them are there, too — and they look like they know they must be having a good time. Everyone is quietly aware of the potency of their dollars. What else could create total interlocking environments so artificial and yet so vast? Only dollars.

It's all a hoax perpetrated for the sake of those dollars. The computer-packaged tourist goes home bored but fatter, frustrated in experience but pleased at the power of his money. It doesn't take much of this artificiality to jade the erstwhile traveler. You can't get excited over something unreal, and that's

where our mass consciousness is today. Americans are locked into a coast-to-coast network of tinselled travel services that hide the reality behind advertising campaigns promoting luxury.

WHO USES THE TI? The TI and its services are everywhere. They are expensive and destructive. If you travel America totally free of the TI, you will cut the costs of your trip enormously and enjoy yourself correspondingly more. You will also clarify your consciousness and learn a great deal about yourself and your country.

The TI in fact serves only a relatively small class of higher-income and lower-consciousness Americans. Many need its services for business purposes and are not travelers at all, merely executives in the process of being executed a little at a time by their corporations. Others have seen too much TV and too many magazines, and spend their own money foolishly buying luxurious services they can neither afford nor enjoy.

Finally there is the large mass of Americans who are on the edge, so to speak. With varying degrees of sacrifice, they could afford to travel a la TI but they are reluctant. On the one hand, the glittering blandishments look good, but on the other hand they innately sense it's all bullshit. It's this latter group who are most capable of being liberated by a vagabond approach to travel.

To them, to you, I say: Travel the way you want to, not the way somebody wanting your bucks wants you to. Figure out your own ways to travel cheaply, without needlessly expensive services and equipment. Follow the lead of young people. How do they get by on next to nothing, and have such great times too? Surely you can see that if vagabonds travel cheaply and live richly, there must be a correlation between the two. There is. And I'll tell you more about it in future chapters.

For now, just don't rush into your travel agency and throw your money on the counter yelling "Book me a great trip." It won't work. In fact, there's no way the agent can do it. He probably doesn't even understand what you mean. It isn't good business.

PLACES TO GO This book does not list or describe "places," because places mean different things to different people at different times. For example, I liked Mystic Seaport, Connecticut, and recommended it highly to some friends about to visit New England for the first time. I told them about Mystic's authentic atmosphere, its original buildings brought from thruout New England, the active displays by genuine old-timers, etc. Well, they went there, and hated it. Before I could ask why, they described another place that had really turned them on—Old Sturbridge Village, in Massachusetts. What did they like about it? Well, they were charmed by its authentic atmosphere, its original buildings brought from thruout New England, its active displays by genuine old-timers, etc. So I said, "Hmmm . . . what goes on here?" The story was that they arrived at Mystic worn out from driving, irritable from hunger, found the Seaport full of tourists, and split in disgust. Obviously, no matter what they have to offer, places are just places. What makes them special (or not) is the complex combination of *you* and the *place* and the *moment*. (Sounds like a song.)

My friends had flown to New York, rented a car and wandered about New England more or less aimlessly for two weeks. They stayed in country inns instead of motels, shopped for antiques and water colors, and had great times with their kids making gravestone rubbings in old cemetaries. All of it was new to them, little of it was planned, and they loved it.

They were vagabonds — rented car, watercolors, kids, and all — and they were unlocking the complex combination of place, people, and time by flowing with what was happening instead of trying to control it. When they followed the plan despite indications that the time and mood were wrong, the place couldn't do it alone. The plan was a bust.

That in a nutshell is the story of so many tourists. They track down place after place according to plan and schedule. They try to capture the bird of experience in a cage of programmed travel. But the beauty of experience is its elusiveness, and to cage it is to kill it. The vagabond follows the bird on the wing instead, letting it lead the way. It always does.

Exercises

EXERCISES IN PLANNING

1) Contact at least six state tourist offices, telling them you want information about inexpensive and unusual vacation activities available in their state.

2) Write at least two wilderness societies asking for information about their outdoor outings.

3) Ask as many friends or acquaintances as possible about the best trips they ever had in America, and what made it so. (Be wary of those who extol luxury as the criterion of a good time; they're TIts.)

4) On several occasions, pick up hitchhikers with packs, and ask them about their experiences: Where they came from, what's the nicest part of their trip, are there any experiences or places they'd recommend?

5) Visit a travel agent and ask about excursion plans to other parts of America. If your vacation is short, ask about airline plans; if it's longer, ask about bus tours and Amtrac. Remember you want transportation, but don't close your mind to unusual package plans for special activities like skiing, skin diving, dude ranching, etc.

6) Write to distant friends and relatives, telling them your vacation is coming up and could you visit for a day or a week? Ask them if they'd like to visit you, too.

7) Write a short essay about what your dream vacation in America would be if you had the time, money, and/or freedom. When you get thru, examine the essence of your desires, and see if there are substitute or practical ways it can be at least partially achieved or approached.

8) Ask your spouse, parents, children what fresh ideas for vacations they have. (Don't be outraged when they tell you.) Write down each suggestion with advantages and disadvantages. Consider separate vacations. Consider leaving the kids home with relatives or neighbors. Never mind an idea that's crazy or impossible on the face of it. Are there ways to get round the difficulties? Can the idea be modified into practibility?

9) Everybody's got interests and hobbies, and somebody else has organized them into clubs and societies, Find out from your local branches where some distant ones are, and write them to ask about visiting privileges and amenities. Most organizations are only too happy to greet distant members and co-freaks of whatever persuasion.

10) Use your imagination. Consider your vacation a chance to be far-out. Ask your friends to brain-storm a vacation for you. Maybe you should all go together. How about trading each other's kids? Trip planning is when you start upsetting patterns and uprooting ruts.

11) Do this at least: Think seriously about doing *anything* you've never done before. Now tune in on how you feel about that as you visualize yourself actually doing it. Don't you get a twinging-jerking of certain muscles, an exciting-upsetting anxiety in the gut? That's a tiny energy-shot, a tickler urging you to open onto the full energy-wave. Keep at it. You'd be surprised where you might turn up . . .

INFORMATION SOURCES Since places exist everywhere except in a few other places, you need to know about some of them at least. And you should know about things to do, and what they cost, and so forth. Fortunately, there are even places to tell you this; there are even thousands of them — called tourist offices. In fact, there are so many bureaus of 'tourism,' 'publicity,' 'development,' 'visitors,' 'conventions,' and 'chambers of commerce' that the money they spend promoting tourism could probably give everyone a free vacation every year. Anyway, they exist to answer your postcards and letters with pounds of free maps, pamphlets, booklets, guides, fact sheets, directories, and garbage bags. It's relatively easy to collect a hundred pounds or so of printed paper for about $5 in postage. If you need fewer pounds, less postage will do. The bulk of this "free" "literature" is not helpful — four-color propaganda and commercial nonsense. Nevertheless, enough kernels of useful information are included with the promotional chaff that you should send for as much of the corn as you can stomach or find space to store.

Send postcards asking specific questions, assuming you know any, or ask for a broadside volley about tourist places, activities and sights, camping facilities, state parks, historical sites, special events, etc. Tell them how you're traveling; hint that you'll be staying awhile instead of just passing thru. When the stuff arrives, use it to get ideas and make tentative plans. Look at the back of this book for complete lists of state and city tourist bureaus; various travel clubs and pertinent societies; addresses of all national parks, forests, monuments, and other recreation areas; and of oil companies with map and touring services. That'll get you started, and God knows where you'll stop.

Many state governments operate information centers along the major hiways and interstates that cross their domain. These usually offer personalized (live) information as well as maps and brochures; amenities like toilets, tables, and trash cans. When you see one of these, pull over . . . have a pile of paper, or perhaps a piss or a picnic.

GUIDEBOOKS Books about traveling in America were not too numerous a few years ago, but today practically everybody and his dog has a See-America book out. (For example, even me. I'm my own dog, however.) None of these guides are needed, actually, but they all have some value. America is so big that most Americans don't know much about it, especially away from their own city or state. Thus, a good guidebook may be able to prove to you that other places are different from yours, or the same.

For example, did you know that Philadelphia and Los Angeles both have identical Independence Halls (including identically cracked Liberty Bells)? The question is: Which is the real one? That's what a guidebook is for. If you're driving through Texas, a good guidebook will show you the best way out. If you want to talk to an Indian, your guidebook will tell you How. Whatever your problem, some guidebook somewhere has the answer. All you have to do is pick the right problem.

Most of all, guidebooks are about getting to the "good parts." Virtually all guidebooks to America try to list and rate its top tourist places — cities, sights, hotels, restaurants. I think that kind of book is "efficient," and sometimes I even use one myself. (For example, I used a campsite directory.) However, no one information source or guidebook is the best for all situations or all locales, and as a vagabond you simply won't need them much. Remember that most of the standard guidebooks are the field manuals of the Travel Industry, and they present the same slick travel consciousness. Use the information if you find a book that fits your travel style and helps give you a better trip. But don't let it mold you into Mr or Ms Mass Tourist, USA.

A list of guidebooks and comments about each is given in appendix 3 at the back of the book. In addition, we've listed and commented on another selection of books (*USA Bookshelf* — appendix 2) that will maximize your experience with America. Reading some of these books can give you the background to appreciate aspects and artifacts of America that non-readers would only throw beer cans at.

TOURIST SLOGANS, ANYONE?

Alabama Has It All

Amazing Arizona

Arkansas — Its a Natural

Southern California: Best of all Vacation Worlds

The Golden World of California; The Glorious Land; The Redwood Empire

Colorful Colorado

Colonial Connecticut

Delaware: The State That Started the Nation

Fabulous Florida — The Sunshine State

Georgia: State of Adventure

Guam: Where America's Day Begins

Hawaii: It's More Than A Pretty Place; The Aloha State

Idaho: For a Change of Pace

The New Illinois/We Accommodate; Land of Lincoln

Indiana: The Center of Things

Iowa: A Place to Grow

Kansas: The Great State; Land of Clean Air & Clear Heads

Rediscover Kentucky

The Great State of Maine: Let Me. Entertain You; You'll Love Me. . . etc.

Begin with Maryland — So Much of America Did

Massachusetts: Custodian of the Nation's Heritage

Michigan: The Almost Islands of the Great Lakes

Marvellous Minnesota — 10,000 Lakes

Mississippi: The Hospitality State; The Place To Be

Missouri: The Cave State

Montana: The Big Sky Country

Nebraskaland: The Good Life; Where the West Begins

Nevada: Bet On It

New Hampshire: The State of the Arts

New Jersey: The NEW Jersey; The Garden State

New York: Vacationlands; The Empire State

New Mexico: Where The Fun Never Sets; Land of Enchantment

North Carolina: The Goodliest Land; Variety Vacationland

North Dakota: Go North to Dakota; Roughrider Country

Ohio Is Happening

Oklahoma: Tomorrow Country; See Oklahoma First

Oregon: State of Excitement; 24-Carat Vacationland

Pennsylvania/Excitement!

Rhode Island: America's First Vacationland

South Carolina: A Lot of It Looks a Little Like a Foreign Country

South Dakota: Of All Places!; Frontier of Pleasure

Tennessee: It Just Comes Natural

Texas: Land of Contrast

Utah: Discovery Country!

Vermont: The Green Mountain State

Virginia: Choose your Virginia

The Wonderful World of Washington: The Evergreen State

Wild and Wonderful West Virginia

Wonderful Wisconsin: A Land Made For Family Vacations

BIG Wyoming!

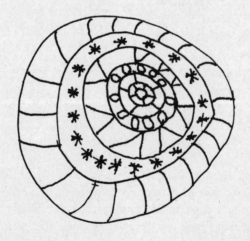

ROAD MAPS These are the common denominators of all American trips — the master reference works for all travelers. The best road maps are gasoline company maps, and they're free. However, one or two small points: First, if you buy your gas at the discount stations and u-pump-ems, they usually don't have many maps, or any maps. Next, you may need the map before you can locate one. For these reasons, a road atlas or a group of maps collected in advance is worth carrying. Amazingly, there isn't any really top-notch atlas in print. The best one, the Rand McNally Road Atlas ($2.95), which I used, still didn't have the required detail to get me happily thru all the places I went.

The problem isn't the map-maker; it's the size of the maps. Oil company maps are best because they're biggest (after unfolding) and can hold large quantities of detailed information. The best oil company maps are made by Rand-McNally and HM Gousha Co. Rand McNally makes maps for the National Automobile Club (NAC), for Mobil, Gulf, Standard, Phillips 66, Union 76, Boron, Husky, Triangle, Midwest, among others. HM Gousha makes maps for Texaco, Sunoco/Dx, Shell, Conoco, Chevron, Citgo, DS, Rose, among others. Almost as good are maps made by the Diversified Map Co and RR Donnelly & Sons (American,

Atlantic Richfield) and General Drafting Co (Esso, Humble). The poorest general road maps are the AAA maps, but only by comparison. Virtually all oil company maps show things like:

points of interest	national park map insets
campsites	paragraph descriptions
state parks	tolls
recreation areas	scenic roads
ski areas	tourist info addresses
monuments, memorials	police info
wayside parks	airports
information centers	counties
national features	yacht clubs
national forests	schools
mileages	ferries
distance charts	golf courses
cities index	townships
population	road types
city map insets	hiway numbers

3M Company also puts out a "Travelaide" series of interstate maps available at selected gas stations. They aren't too good, and advertise TI-type places to eat, sleep and amuse yourself.

What I would like is a major road atlas that compiles a whole set of oil company maps into one book about 20" x 30" in size, or a series of regional books. Since oil company maps are

Off The Tape
ECHO PARK

The proof of the joy of vagabonding is in the experience of being here at Echo Park in Dinosaur National Monument. We only came to the Monument by chance on our way to Yellowstone in Wyoming. I wanted to take a route I'd never been on before so I decided to cross northern Colorado and noticed that Dinosaur was on the way. After a long drive thru not particularly inspired desert country we came to Dinosaur and decided to detour up the 32 mile road that goes north off hiway 40. Thus we saw some of this canyon country, and from a place called Harpers Corner at the end of the road, we looked down 2500 feet to where the Green and Yampa Rivers join. We learned there was another 13-mile dirt detour that took you down there. Notwithstanding plans we'd made to be up in Wyoming the next day, it seemed more fun to explore the road down to Echo Park.

And so we discovered this incredibly beautiful piece of America. We spent the day swimming in the Yampa River amidst towering canyon walls, grassy tree-dotted meadows, and the constant whispering of the river. We sunned, we napped, we read, we played with Sierra, we luxuriated in paradise. Right now, I'm talking and walking the river alongside an ochre-colored sheer cliff that drops to the river's edge just at the point where the Yampa and Green Rivers join. The cliffs all around, the trees, the river, everything is now in shade except for one cliff-face standing alone, which burns an unforgettable gold in the intense southwest sunset.

Only the American West has this kind of scenery, among the most sublime country in all the world. Just a few years ago, this region was intended to be a dam site. Had that not been stopped by conservationists, this spot where I'm now standing would be under water. (Like Glen Canyon, gone under.) So much of America is already lost not only to the Army Corps of Engineers but to progress, to capitalism, to materialism. It's far better that a place like this should continue to exist than that a group of engineers and laborers and government technicians should continue to make that salaries. It's infinitely better that a place like this should continue to exist than that a reservoir be created to provide power for a billion more unneeded electric toothbrushes, to provide more water to create corporate farms to get more government subsidies for not growing crops, to provide more jobs so that more construction workers can buy more commodities.

Americans should be smart enough to realize that beautiful places are more valuable to us spiritually than bucks that can be extracted from them. Time to get it on. As Thomas Jefferson said, "I fear for my country when I reflect that God is just."

free, this type of atlas should be inexpensive, especially if subsidized and distributed by oil companies. How about it, Rand McNally?

Other road atlases are available free from a variety of sources — oil companies (Conoco, Shell, Amoco); from hotels and motels (Western Motels); from banks and private businesses . . . but none of them are worthwhile when actually on the road, where you need a maximum of detail to thread thru the urban interstate mazes, to explore back roads, to obtain useful information about the surrounding countryside.

Another source of excellent maps, often even better than oil companies, is state tourist offices. They all distribute free maps prepared by their own highway departments. They almost always provide more local information than gas company maps: for example, more city-map insets, more information about historical sites, parks, schools, as well as about laws and regulations. They also have more photographs, more propaganda pizzaz. Their only real drawback is that they come in odd sizes and in varying grades of paper (often too thick or stiff). If you write in advance for these, you'll have all the maps you need before starting out.

TIME TO DO IT An important part of trip planning is time — how much have you? Two weeks to see America won't do the job, but isn't hopeless. Three months — a summer — is about right for a major expedition. If you're a student, you've got the time. But what if you're a wage slave with two or three weeks, or what if you have the time but no money (unemployed or low income or low savings)?

Two Weeks Only? The worst situation is, naturally, the most common: The 50-weeks-on/2-weeks-off duty cycle of the wage earner or executive. Money in this case is not usually a crucial factor, and that's the best way to amplify your time allotment: Spend money to get somewhere quick, then hang around that one place and explore it. For example, westerners can fly to NY/New England, then rent a car or camper and go touring. For easterners, do the same in the reverse direction and tour

TOURISM AND ENERGY

Why do certain places become tourist attractions? What is there that connects a national park with a museum with a battlefield? What is it that moves people and imprints itself on their memory? I wondered about this, and first off I saw that time had something to do with it. A beautiful mountain, a famous painting, a historic building all "proved" themselves thru time in some way, but I realized that time is only a connection to a common ingredient from the past. What is it that is being transmitted thru time by these objects, by these places? Certainly that kind of transmission thru the fourth dimension requires a lot of energy, and . . . there was the answer: Energy itself. The attraction of all tourist places is that they were at some time places where energy was concentrated in some powerful way. The original energy is now gone, but it left behind certain artifacts — mountains, paintings, buildings — that people universally recognize as souvenirs or sign posts of energy release.

Tourists are notorious energy-freaks. They are always out dashing around for some kind of energy to get them high. What happens is they hear about or see a souvenir of energy — that is, a tourist attraction — and they think that maybe the energy will rub off. They want energy, so they go out after it.

When they get there, the catalytic power of the artifacts frequently works — it triggers a pattern disruption; a recognition, a restructuring, an input of new information. Meanwhile, all the other people there on their own energy trips are also releasing energy. The result of it all is a true energy high, at least for many of the tourists who come there. They're there to bathe in an energy pool. The energy is really their own, but the place releases it.

the San Francisco/Los Angeles circuit. Or expeditiously get yourself to a mountain region and back-pack for two weeks, or canoe-and-camp, or take a river float trip, or . . . you get the idea.

If money is a problem, first think again about why you're working at all (I mean, if you're going to be broke — why not at least have your time, rather than be broke and have no time too). Next, plan a new kind of vacation right in your own area. Every part of America, without exception, bears a better look by its natives, and promises adventure if only you open your eyes to it. But you may have to be more flexible or daring than before.

If stuffing the kids and lady in the car and touring your own state or tri-state region seems like a bore (or you already did that three years in a row), then do something new that turns you on. Look at the "Trips" appendix in the back. That's why we compiled it — for you to look at, and maybe act on it. Consider each trip seriously, one at a time. Something on that list should: 1) interest you, and 2) be financially feasible, and 3) suit your family, too.

Uncork some juice; unleash some energy. Even with only two weeks, some American vacation experience can still rattle your cage or shrink your spiritual hemorrhoid.

Leave of Absence. Another possibility for the two-week traveler is a leave of absence or

extended vacation. This particularly applies to employees who know they're needed by their organizations (mostly talented but timid executives). Perhaps you truly have the power to say "I'm taking my usual two weeks plus two more without pay, and if you don't like it, dump me." There are many, many people with this power who are afraid to test it. Corporations are amenable to blackmail because they're so accustomed to mediocrity as the performance norm that anyone really good can make them jump hoops. If you're someone like this, and your bosses won't play, you know of other places to go, of course. Don't be afraid to do it.

Your time off is probably your most valued commodity, anyway, so why not fight for it? I've known numerous talented engineers and executives who either work part-time or consult for great sums. They have lots of time for vacations. The real danger in doing this is that most of them finally quit altogether when they discover that they value the time off more than the money. A taste of freedom almost inevitably leads to a craving for it. Beware. It hooks you and it's wonderful. Most people can't understand this because they've never been free. They think it's impossible, whereas the truth is that freedom is right in front of you — you simply have to want it enough to take it. People fear the struggle for freedom but never credit the rewards.

No Money. Finally, what if you have plenty of time but inadequate funds? This is not too difficult a situation. Thousands of people — mostly young people who don't know any better — travel all over America with nothing at all. They hitchhike, they crash, they odd-job, they live in communes, they make it by drifting and hanging out. These activities can be negative or destructive, but it's all up to you. They can just as easily be positive and creative, and for most easy-going travelers, they are. Money is another American bogeyman that everyone bows down to and worships. Yet if you're willing to open yourself to a different kind of traveling, actually a kind of modern-day adventuring, then lack of money is not a great obstacle. More about this in chapter 5.

Midwest, I love you
most of all
tree shaded streets
kids on bikes
and jumprope
sounds of simple life
tinkling gently
in the summer afternoon
sun.

This is a great town for kids
But what happened to the adults?

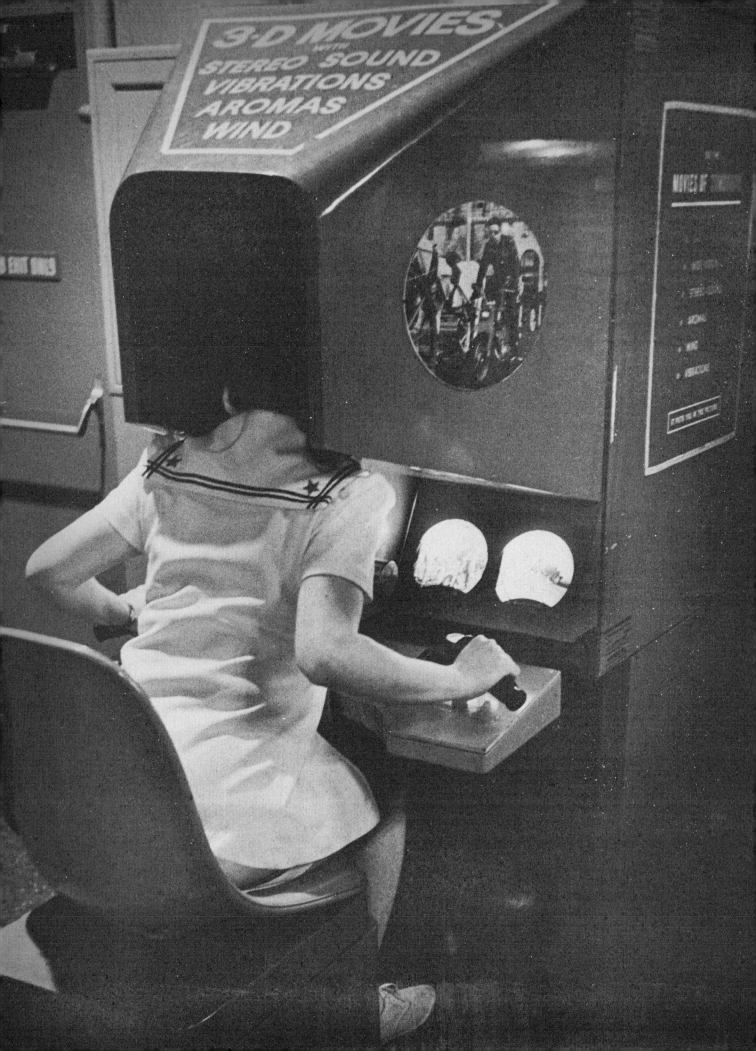

Making Your Move 4

A Transportation Survey

The Bus As It Is, by Thomas Kramer
Train Travel As It Is, by Deetje Boler

ATTITUDES This chapter is about how to go to America: a checklist of the ways to travel. However, your best and most exciting travel tool is your head. (It's that hairy knob on your shoulders.) Whichever way you travel, it's the contents of this neat knob — your ideas and attitudes — that determine the kind of trip you have. Most Americans don't really 'get off' seeing America. They "enjoy" humdrum trips that are something like visits to the barber or hairdresser — ritualistic and not unpleasant trimmings. But seeing America can be better than that — it can be like a sauna and massage.

This book frankly advocates new experience as the key to travel adventure. I intend to turn you away from conventional "touring" because whether or not you've done that already, it's boring. Spending a lot of money for ego and for security does not give you an exciting vacation, because it misses the point that protection is only incidentally related to fun. Being comfortably canned in chain hotels, being fed machine-masticated muck in franchise restaurants, being given second-hand experiences of life by artificial amusements is to submit to the worst, most banal, least interesting aspects of America. It's necessary to deliberately get away from what we habitually see and do in America because there's so much else to discover if we open our minds to it.

Vagabonding means not being afraid to do new things. This means traveling in a different way than you have before ... maybe car-camping instead of staying at Folly-Day Inns or Quantity Courts; maybe going by bus if you always take the car; maybe back-packing instead of flying, maybe bicycling instead of motorcycling. Think about how your trip could be different and better. Wouldn't it be great to *do* something for a change instead of having it *done* for or to you? How about taking a float trip down a wild river instead of watching some one else do it in a magazine or on TV? How about camping in New England, or touring ghost towns in Colorado, or collecting shells in Florida? Or a bicycling tour of Pennsylvania, a canoe trip thru Minnesota, or motorcycling the Northwest? How about combining several of these?

Your means of travel is not what your trip is about — but clearly the differences among the automobile, motorcycle, bicycle, thumb, backpack will dictate the style of your trip and have much to do with costs and planning and everything else. Think about how a different means of travel could turn you on — put your fantasy machine to work.

Next, vagabonding is about getting turned on by new places. How to see America as a new place is the question. It isn't easy, and you probably can't do it. But you can undoubtedly approach it more closely than you've done so far. First, reduce your dependence on the organized business establishments that exist for the sake of feeding and housing tourists. They will numb your senses and dull your appreciation. They are the dogshit on the daisies. Make an adventure out of finding neighborhood restaurants, funky motels, and forest campsites. Make fewer stops from the AAA guidebook and more from your own fancy. America is huge but homogenized. Most places look like a hundred others, especially if they're man-made. Seek out places that are different or unusual. When you get there, don't plan or make schedules. Approach America as an adventure instead of an advertisement. You can't feel alive and growing, you can't get excited, you can't learn anything if you plod thru the same trip(s) as all those other robotized tourists "discovering" America by the numbers.

Vagabonding is most of all about people — meeting them, being met, liking them, being liked, exchanging life and energy with them. Conventional tourism avoids contact with the natives. Instead, you meet the help and the service, the hosts and the hostesses. But where are the people who make you feel alive, whose story touches you or angers you, whose lives fill in the empty spaces of your own? Not happening. If you make up your mind to know people, you'll get help and friends everywhere. People are hungry to be known. Again, your attitude is the important thing.

Tourists tend to see themselves as cocoons of warmth traveling in a cold sea of strangers. They go slumming "out there" and then scoot for home and security again. Everyone feels that to some extent, but unfortunately most people feel nothing else. They get so tight that they take elaborate measures — at exorbitant cost — to make them feel secure on the road. This is where tours, agents, hotels, restaurants, guides, and conventional tourism come in. And this is where the fun of discovery goes out.

AMERICA BY CAR Every oil company (abbreviated EVOCO) is urging you to "Discover America by Car," and while their motives are purely selfish (EVOCO serves America), their recommendation is correct. America is best seen by car. By car I mean anything with at least four wheels and a motor (except certain models of tractors, earthmovers, and lawnmowers). An automobile gives you nearly complete freedom of movement at reasonably low cost in any weather or climate, it enables you to camp out in reasonable comfort, to bring friends or family (including children), to be unobtrusive and accepted everywhere, to cover the vast distances of America without great sacrifice. Almost all Americans already own a car and are completely familiar with its operation, needs, and maintenance. Most Americans, in fact, the huge majority, choose to see America by car. No need to sell it too hard.

Despite these many advantages, the car has one overwhelming disadvantage, one so familiar to us we can't even see it. That disadvantage is familiarity. We've almost all traveled by car since before we were born. There's no excitement in it. Driving around America can easily be, and usually is, the most monotonous and superficial trip of all. America is an automobile culture — the freeway society. While this makes motoring convenient, it doesn't make it much fun.

Motoring is a mass bowel movement via the Interstate Intestinal Hiway System. It means relating to an unending collection of gas stations, drive-ins, motels, and other bacterial growths along our arterial intestines. They're all a lot of crap, of course, and there's much more to America than this. Don't let it constipate your trip. Take positive steps to raise yourself out of the automotive ooze. That's why chapter 9 concentrates on trying to conquer the boredom and superficiality of automobile touring, as well as giving tips for its vagabond uses.

SPECIALIZED VEHICLES FOR RECREATION Included in this category are trailers, car-campers and pop-tops, piggyback campers, reconditioned school busses and postal vans, and of course the full-fledged "recreational vehicles." All have in common the fact that they can be lived in, which is good, but most of them also are so specialized that they can't be used for anything else, which is bad. They represent portable tract houses that waste both money and natural resources. Trailers and Winnebago-type recreational vehicles are the worst offenders, — as I will try to prove to doubting owners. Piggy-backcampers or pick-up trucks are almost as bad if the trucks are used for that purpose only, which is usually the case. The same applies to most pop-top camper vans, which are too encumbered with built-in appliances to ever see double duty once the tour is over.

51

Off The Tape
THE REC VEC FASHION SHOW

Announcer: "And this is Cindy. There are some gals who make $20 — $30 thousand dollars a year modeling in department stores, demonstrating mannequin modeling. Cindy is going to show us some mannequin modeling. It's very hard to tell which is a mannequin and which is real when a girl is very good. And if you didn't see Cindy walk out, I don't know if you would know if she was real or a mannequin. The dress is $23.00, completely washable. We twisted it around the hanger last night and it didn't wrinkle at all. Next we have Debbie in another long, sexy dress. Many of the dresses are backless with a long slit up the side. They're very comfortable. They show the legs, but just a little. The fabrics today are very light. You can hang about 12 of these in the back of your camper and not even know that there's that much of a wardrobe there. (applause) Next we have rather a sophisticated look in red, white and blue — Christine. This too is backless, not quite as sexy as the other dresses, but just as alluring. And today with the campers and all the different recreational vehicles that we have, some of you are going to think of having a wedding, and you'll drive the damper out to a hilltop and have a country wedding in light, washable clothes. And I'd like to show you what we think you might choose to wear. Our first model is Kim. This is in polka dots. The whole dress is $30.00, you could mix and match with many things in your wardrobe. Very feminine. Men like a woman to look like this. She's one of the guests at the wedding. Next we have — a little bridesmaid. Again, a washable dress, perfect for graduation or weddings, or just Sunday afternoons — a special dress. And next we have our bride. The peasant look, this is foile. It sells for $44 and is just lovely in your wardrobe."

The objections to all these factory-made campers are numerous and have to do with ecology, consciousness, and energy. First they're expensive and waste resources. They're sold by hucksters for the sake of profits only, with no love for the outdoors. These vehicles rip off the people that own them by cheating them of any type of wilderness camping experience — their home-on-wheels makes that impossible because no change of pattern is involved; no energy is released. Traveling is just like being at home watching travelogues on TV. The parks and natural lands of America that are wasted to make room for these vehicles, to make roads for them, to make blacktop "campsites" for them, the vile materialist consciousness that is perpetuated by them . . . these are all casualities of the Recreation Vehicle — a true abomination.

School busses (hippy busses), postal vans, and other converted-to-camping vehicles are considerably better because they make use of vehicles that would otherwise be junked. They're ecological. They're cheap to build and buy. They exercise your craft and skills if you make the conversion yourself. For most owners they not only serve as a general purpose vehicle but living quarters as well. Saves money, saves houses, saves minds. But they can be badly misused, too, of which more later.

If you already own a genuine Recreational Vehicle, and are angered or injured by my opinions, then hate me but listen to this. Your vehicle is a waste of materials and energy. It gives you comfort, convenience, and security — but not challenge, outdoor experience, knowledge, or wisdom. What you paid for it could have bought a suitable used vehicle and a better trip that could last much longer. Owning a "Rec Vec" (or "Recker") hurts *you* most because it deprives you of the chance to *do*. You're a traveling vegetable. The only good reason for owning one is if it's actually your home; if you're retired and want to vagabond "at home."

In chapter 7 about camping, I'll go into this subject further, not to insult or alienate anybody, but to show that there are better ways to go than in "Reckers". Being duped by the travel industry may not be your fault, but the time has come now to open your eyes.

MOTORCYCLING, USA Touring by motorcycle, while one of the great — maybe the greatest — way to vagabond, is not to be undertaken as lightly as car touring. With a car, you simply dump your stuff in the back, take on one or more extra people, pump in some gas, and you're off — probably for better than worse.

On a bike, it's hardly the same. First off, the kind of bike you ride is crucial. How safe will it be on a long road trip? How stable? How powerful? How comfortable? How noisy? If you already own a bike, is it suitable as a road bike? Should you sell it and buy another? The money outlay for a new bike is heavy, and buying a used one is risky.

When you get ready to go, how and how much you load it (saddlebags, pack, total weight, center of gravity, and more) are important. Then, what about the special clothes you need — leathers, helmet, boots, rainwear?

What about a windshield? What about theft protection and insurance? Both can be problems for bike owners.

Also, how experienced a rider are you, especially for the kind of trip you're planning? Have you done long distances and interstates before? How about back roads, dirt roads? How fast do you tire? Think about that one a lot — fatigue is nothing to casually ignore. Any long-distance bike rider will learn all about it the hard way. Fatigue can't be avoided, only forestalled.

What it comes down to is that motorcycle touring is more complicated than it might seem. Of course, the sensation and freedom of it, the sheer exhilaration of touring by bike is a fantastic payoff. With some thought and judgement behind it, you'll have the best trips there are. Chapter 10 is all about how to buy, ride, and vagabond by motorcycle.

HITCHHIKING FOR ALL IT'S WORTH Because it makes you depend upon other people, and because it makes you find yourself, hitchhiking is the best way to travel. It sensitizes you to experience. That's the theory. Hitchhiking in America, unfortunately, doesn't fully live up to the theory. The majority of Americans "never pick up hitchhikers" and a small but detectable minority of them love to hassle hitchhikers. Hostility is a constantly encountered reaction — from natives who'll hoot at you to cops who'll shake you down. Trouble-free tours are uncommon in long-distance hitching. What this means, really, is that hitching is not for everybody . . . it's not about to become the hottest thing in the field of mass transportation, but its popularity is nevertheless growing rapidly. In the end, it's up to you. Hitchhiking anywhere is full of uncertainty and discomfort, which is partly why it's also interesting and exciting. In America, especially, the vastness of the country and the hostility of the natives add new dimensions to the hitchhiking experience. Some people can hack it and love it; some people merely suffer thru it and hate it.

As a successful vagabonding adventure, it will only suit travelers who are young enough in spirit to try it; tough and resourceful enough to cope with its problems; and tolerant enough to forgive those people who make it difficult.

I personally think hitchhiking in America is a mind-expanding, magnificent experience, but that judgement accepts there may be great bummers too. It takes a special kind of traveler to do it. In addition, there are a lot of other factors involved in successful hitchhiking — attitudes, itinerary, equipment, techniques. Riding freight trains is another kind of hitching experience. I'll go into all of this in fascinating detail in chapter 12, a long chapter because the subject is dense.

BICYCLING AND WALKING If you'd like to experience America a little at a time (one of the better ways to digest anything), cycling and hiking are the most free, direct, and clean ways of all. They're cheap, they're healthy, they're creative outlets/inlets for energy and life. Like any other experience worth having, they make demands on you and test you in the process. It's right. Planning your tour intelligently is a paramount concern here, because America has too many vast areas that can literally swallow you up. You may get thru them alive but you'll wonder why you bothered to go in, or maybe to come out. Of course, there are happy fanatics (bless 'em) who occasionally circumcycle the country or cross-ambulate the desert for a lark (or for the recordbook), but that's a different trip.

For most people, walking to see America means hiking and back-packing in a preselected area. This is a classic American adventure, because nowhere else in the whole world can offer even a fraction of the outdoor locales, or variety of locales, that we have right here at home. Hiking in America is so accessible and gives back so many rewards for the effort that it's unthinkable to overlook or avoid. No matter how you travel, bring your hiking boots and a pack. Chapter 13 walks you all the way through this subject.

Bicycling the long distances is more feasible — that is, cycling tours of several weeks (or more) duration. But here, too, planning is vital, and equipment, clothes, and conditioning are no less so. The upsurge of cycling popularity in the face of all opposition is a spectacular proof of cultural change, but America is still a long way from being a cycling paradise. You'll have to choose regions that offer many things to see and enjoy in a relatively small area, and choose your roads carefully so you won't get mashed under somebody's steel-belted radials or other

great technological advance. You must have a good touring cycle with the right clothes and touring accessories, and finally you must have some cycling experience and physical conditioning. There are objective problems also, such as thieves, bad weather, and so forth.

Cycling enters you into an elite fraternity of stoned and free people, sound in body and mind, who can enjoy their travels and live their experiences in ways that the passing motorist can only dream about in his more lucid moments. Another travel combination, of course, is the motorist carrying his own bicycle. Now that's more like it. All this and more to be covered in chapter 11.

Off The Tape
BEACH WALKING

I'm on the beach at Big Sur, that's the sound of the waves withdrawing from a rocky beach after the first impulse of the wave rush comes up. Here it comes again. The beach here is all rock, the cliffs are all rock, the striations all behind me on the cliffs, boulders and pebbles of every size here on the beach. I wonder as I look at the waves, as I hear the sounds of the water pulling the stones back again and again, rounding them, always rounding them, making them smaller and smaller, I wonder how long it takes the ocean to work on a little piece of beach like this. How long does it take to make the cliffs retreat ten feet? The beach I'm standing on, fifteen feet wide, how many years of pounding of the ocean on this particular beach does that represent? Surely in a thousand years these rocks can't be worn down very much by the water. How about in 10 thousand, a hundred thousand? What about a million, or a hundred million years? I think the fascination with the ocean is because the ocean is timeless, the oceans have always been here and they always will be. I visit here on this little beach for a few minutes, but the ocean has been visiting here forever. I meet my master, a million times wiser, and I'm made humble.

CONVENTIONAL PASSENGER SERVICES
This includes airlines, rail lines (Amtrak), and passenger busses. All of these are the end of the line for vagabonds, not recommended except for certain circumstances. Travelers without cars, whether voluntarily or involuntarily, need these services. For people who can't afford cars, traveling by bus is especially suitable because it's cheap and reliable. For people with cars but lacking time or stamina, traveling by plane is the answer. Trains at this time are a sort of no man's land not good for anything except people who hate flying but want more comfort than the bus.

As usual, the costs vary inversely with the level of travel involvement. Air travel is expensive, efficient, fast and offers no involvement with traveling whatever. An airplane is a separate machine-made environment tightly insulated from the world. It's totally artificial but it gets you there fast. Train travel is similar in cost and concept but represents an earlier technology in that the traveler is not quite totally isolated. At least he can see the real world outside the windows and is allowed to breathe its air. Bus travel is the cheapest and least glamorous of public transportation services, and is the most real. Lets look at these in more detail:

AIRPLANES. These high-flying metal birds are symbolic of today's cultural characteristics: Speed, complexity, sterility, boredom, fear. Airplanes represent the extreme method of getting away from the concept of travel as experience. All the attractions and values are indoors and passive: Food, drinks, decor, dolls, movies, magazines, 'entertainment centers.' Meanwhile, travel — the idea of learning about other places and getting turned on enroute — has been redefined out of existence. Reality is perceived distortedly through a double-glassed peep-tunnel. Finally, the possible prospect of hijacking and the certain prospect of baggage search are the last surreal touches on this modern caricature of travel.

I travel by plane when I'm in a hurry, and always enjoy it for the novelty and the incredible beauty of the sky. But if I had to fly often, I wouldn't. The plasticity and boredom would be a total drag. Look at the people who

do fly frequently. If that's you, look at your-self. These people become increasingly inter-changeable, all wearing approved uniforms and approved personalities, yet secretly hungry for some kind of reality in their lives. The aging businessmen in bright shirts and checkered jackets look not just waxen and jaded but desperate. So do the stewardesses, despite their automatic smiles. Needy people unable to help themselves.

When you're in a hurry, travel by plane. That's the only reason to fly. Don't get hung on the much-advertised glamor. It's phony and without value. Try to meet people when flying. It's usually difficult to converse with a seat-partner because there's an unwritten code that frowns on it. Most airplane conversations are exercises in superficial communication, but breakthroughs do occur.

If you must travel by plane on your vaca-tion, especially to get somewhere fast so you can linger in leisure, at least try to save money doing it. Shop around to see if the airline(s) serving your destination or vicinity are offering any special fares. At this writing, the future for air fares is looking up. Various US airlines (for example, American and United) are announcing new charter fares that reduce rates around 50% or certain major routes, starting in summer 1973. Tickets must be bought 90 days in advance.

Excursion fares are the most common bargains, but there may be others. Some air-lines offer special stopovers destinations for little or no extra fare. For example, if you fly to Alaska from the South, you can get Hawaii thrown in at no charge on Delta Airlines, and a stopover in LA or San Francisco. Excursion fares usually mean completing your trip within 30 days, which works very well with short vacation trips. However, flying is usually re-stricted to weekdays and non-holiday periods.

Also check on family plans, night travel, or non-jet service for lower rates. Adult standby fares for passengers over 22 can save up to 50%, and are offered between certain cities by American, Continental, TWA, and United. (Youth Standby Fare for 12 to 21's is well-known and offered by most airlines after buy-ing the required airline ID card. However, it's being discontinued in 1973.)

Hawaii is a special case since you can't get there overland, at last report anyway. The lowest fares are offered in conjunction with package tours, and you might consider these if you'll be staying in hotels anyway. But since glitter and glamor is again the main commodity for sale, you can do better by going overland to a West Coast city, flying from there and booking your own less glamorous lodgings after you arrive. Excursion fares are offered from all but West Coast cities (which have all-year "thrift fares" instead).

For example, at this writing, weekday roundtrip excursion fare (30-day) from St. Louis is $343, but weekday thrift fare from San Francisco is $196. That means if you can get to SF from SL overland for less than $147 (the fare difference), you'll save money by going from SF. There is also a Youth Standby Fare with savings up to 25% over the standard economy fare. Once you're there, you can visit the other islands for just $9 each on what is called the Hawaii Common Fare. Ask about this at any airline office serving the islands, or ask the Hawaii Visitor's Bureau (address is in the back of the book) about it when you're writing for complete information on Hawaii.

Summing up, airplanes are good ways to get somewhere fast in sybaritic comfort. Fine for businessmen, and also for tourists without much time. But to those who rave about what a boon to travel the plane is, and all that, I say "Bullshit."

TRAINS. The good old days of train travel are over, of course, except in the movies, and in Europe (and the rest of the world). Trains in America are expensive anomalies, vestigial holdovers from a slower era before the technological proliferation of automobiles for private use and airplanes for commercial use just plain de-gutted them. The introduction of Amtrak, a noble attempt to save trains in the interest of National Defense, isn't working too well. (Amtrak's losses last year were estimated to be $125 million.)

For vagabond travelers, they're less than ideal. Routes are too few and runs not frequent enough, but most of all the costs are way out of line, frequently more than comparable airline routes. Amtrak needs to offer competitive prices if it hopes to survive. So far they've been trying to offer glamor and comfort, but they've no hope of competing with airlines on these scores. It's really too bad, because trains could be wonderful alternatives to the expense of planes and the discomfort of busses.

In the meanwhile, Amtrak at least offers an alternative. For travelers without cars, Amtrak is clearly the best way available if you have a little extra time and money. There's no doubt that it's a pleasant trip. I've heard many good reports from friends about the service, the food, and the friendliness of the passengers. And for car-owners who can't face the thought of another long car trip, Amtrak can be a first-rate vagabond adventure. Especially for first-time riders, children, and old-timers who haven't been on a train since WW II.

Personally, I love trains but my tens of thousands of miles of rail experiences were all either pre-Amtrak or in Europe, so I can't speak directly about what it's like now. (However, my friend Deetje has a report on it shortly.)

BUSSES. That leaves the continental busses — Greyhound and Trailways — and these are not bad. As elsewhere in the world, busses are the poor people's transport, and to travel by bus is to discover how the American lower classes and budget-minded other classes travel. It's a fascinating, sometimes disturbing, education. You'll meet the whole gamut of back--bone Americana — working men and women, minorities of all kinds, servicemen, drifters, young people . . . not always outwardly beautiful, but a storehouse of human, touching experiences.

Busses are pretty cheap and they go to most places (Greyhound has 100,000 miles of routes and is the only public transportation for thousands of communities). On the liability side, steady bus travel — unbroken except for short meal stops — is wearying, and sleeping on busses is not much fun. (On one of my many cross-continental bus trips, a sailor friend of mine and a female acquaintance he met on the bus made love for two nights on the back seat under a raincoat, proving some variations are possible.)

Generally you have no choice about where you eat, and the time alloted for meal stops necessitates ordering and eating with one eye on the clock. At some stops on the route, you'd be better off walking than eating, with the dual reward of getting needed exercise while avoiding silly food.

Busses are superb transportation over shorter distances, or used occasionally to take side-trips, as a relief from hitchhiking, and to bail out when you're stuck. Long-distance touring, especially on a bus pass, can work out happily if you get off the bus every few days. (I once traveled steadily by bus for seven days and nights on a roundabout tour and found myself remarkably unenthusiastic at the end.)

Off The Tape
FLYING HOME

Sometimes the beauty of flying is incredible. The sun has just gone down. We're flying high above a solid cloud bank. The sunset sky is to my left — a faint glow: Blue slowly turning to pale orange, pinkish, and below that solid gray, the cloud bank getting darker every minute, furrowed by little gullies. The dream withdraws into darkness, a manifestation of God briefly revealed. The world is so lovely. I love to see it, I love to travel thru its parts. I would like to live forever, but since I can't do that, I'll just see as much of it as I can while I'm able. How moving to see a town down thru the clouds, see the glimmer of humanity in the night. The settlements here are along the edge of the coastal fog bank. They look mysterious and enticing. How little is known of them flying above them so high, so fast.

The panorama of the Bay Area is as beautiful as I've ever seen it — a solid blanket of fog presses against a row of lights, a panoramic blaze of lights, patterns, and lines at random, holding back the river of fog. The brilliance extends for miles and miles to the north — a whole civilization lies below me, perhaps the best the world has ever seen.

Now we're out over the Bay; I can see the airport as a bright pool of light. San Francisco itself is hidden in fog to the north. Once again it seems so dream-like from the air, so rich in promise below — some kind of fantasyland, but there's no way to make contact with it up here. If you want to touch it, if you want to touch the people below, you've got to bring the airplane down, you've got to get out of the airplane, you have to go touch the people directly.

Coming in over the water, right alongside the Bayshore, coming down down, over the land, past the landing approach radars, I can see the strips on the runway below, see the lights on the runway. Touch-down. Engines cut back.

Off The Tape
HITCHHIKING OUT OF RENO

I just found out that the driver of this car, Steve, a young bearded guy who is a ski instructor at Lake Tahoe, is also a kayak freak. He's planning a kayak trip next year from the Pacific Ocean (Seattle, Washington) to the Atlantic Ocean by kayak — all on rivers and lakes. Except he's going to have to walk about 200 miles altogether, carrying the kayak on his back. It'll be four thousand miles of river and lake touring on the kayak, and he's going to take 4 or 5 months to do it. There are all kinds of adventures.

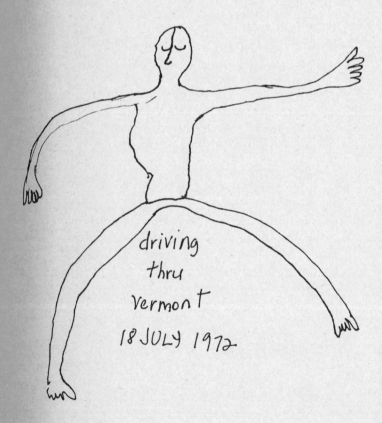

driving
thru
Vermont
18 JULY 1972

There are some long-distance bus passes available for bus-freak vagabonds on Greyhound Lines. One is the Ameripass — 60 days of unlimited bus travel for $150 (at this writing). That's quite a bargain if you're out to do a lot of traveling, and it also gets you discounts at hotels and sightseeing agencies across the country (and Canada). The Ameripass isn't offered during the summer, however, being an off-season inducement to travel.

Another pass is the USABUS pass — 21 days for $99, or up to three months for up to $198. However, this pass is essentially for foreign visitors and must be purchased out of the contiguous United States. It can be bought by Alaskans, Hawaiians, and overseas Americans, however.

The bus lines also offer sightseeing tour packages to most big cities and national parks, and I just read in the newspaper that Greyhound has teamed up with a charter flight company to offer combined air-bus tour packages. For more information about tour packages, don't ask me.

THERE'S MORE? The other travel means available are still many — for example, small boats (canoes, kayaks, inflatables, outboards, rafts) and animal stock (horses, mules, large dogs). But these are accessory trips only possible in combination or as part of other trips. Information about these can be found in the listings at the back of the book.

Other full-fledged, full-time adventures are cruising by yacht or powerboat, coastal piloting, island hopping, vagabond voyaging. However, if you don't already own a boat, or are not a long-time water rat, you're unlikely to go this route just yet. For now, it's beyond the scope of this book. A similar kind of adventure, aerial instead of acquatic, is touring by private plane. This does away with all the bummer aspects of commercial air lines and restores every bit of the adventure. However, its successful accomplishment demands an airplane. If you've got one, you've already thought about this kind of tour a lot, and have access to information sources. All you need now is a shove — or a good tail wind. Enough. The possibilities are overwhelming.

THE BUS AS IT IS
by Thomas Kramer

Try to leave home on your mother's birthday. After all, she launched you on your first excursion into this world. Thanks to my mother, I left with one of the best items one can have when travelling by bus: a pair of little cloth "booties" that airlines used to give you to put over your socks after you take your shoes off on the plane. If you keep your shoes on, your feet will swell up. Get on the bus, take off your shoes, put on your booties, and put your shoes on the rack over your seat. Even venture off the bus with them, except in really cold weather. If you have to sit next to someone, take the aisle seat so you can get to your shoes and other things without bothering your neighbor, unless its important to see something out the window. The window seat is also a good protection against possible discomfort due to the behavior of the person sitting across the aisle from you. A fat person will give you even better protection, as did a rather portly woman in New York who shielded me from the ranting of her neighbor who later slept twisting in his seat, falling on the floor, and later pissing thereon. But also love thy aisle-seat neighbor. Like the big black man out of Cleveland who saw me slicing into a large salami and said "I see you're going to DINE!" If you don't love him or are hard of hearing, you may find yourself hearing him say, as I did," I see you're going to DIE!" Be not afraid, your fellow bus rider will respect your status as a poor and equally weary traveller, very much in the same boat, or bus, as he is. He's not out to rob you, and any discomfort inflicted upon you will surely be inflicted back onto him because of the closely co-existent nature of bus seating and design. The thief can't escape nor can other crimes go undetected for long, so use the trip as a way of going out to people when they can't turn their backs on you. If the afore-mentioned fat woman had turned her back on me I surely would have landed in the piss-drenched aisle, having then to truly confront reality. For that is what the bus is . . . Reality with a capital R. It's the man in Cleveland who moved his family to safer ground after being robbed outside the Cleveland bus station. When I asked him where he had moved them to, he answered "the Bronx." It's the Indian alcoholics counselor who said, "I drink more than all those sons-of-bitches!" The big black lady who was on her way to Alaska after covering all the other states except Hawaii on the Greyhound Ameripass. When I found out she had two kids and a home back in Florida, I asked her what it was that she was taking a vacation from. She said, "the kids." I asked the old Swede next to me if that was water he was gulping out of a large bottle and he answered, "Ya, wid a liddle bit o' disinfectant in it."

Try to get off the bus every twelve hours if it's daytime and explore wherever you may be until the next bus comes to take you farther down the road. This gives you a good opportunity to dine on something a little more substantial than the food you packed (don't take peanut butter sandwiches) and, of course, to stay overnight and sleep. But if it's just for a couple of hours, use the time to walk after you've checked your bag in a locker at the station. This will give you the exercise you so badly need, especially if you packed peanut butter sandwiches. Or if you're too tired to walk, go to the nearest library, which should be fairly near to the bus station, as it most certainly is in Atlanta. Or go write a letter in the post office, which is right next to the New Orleans station. Remember to stake out the nearby restaurants before you choose one, or else you'll see the nicer one only after having mouthed some inferior fare. And be sure to check the bus schedule for variances in the amount of actual hours you'll be spending on either the express or the local bus. Check with more than one clerk since opinions will vary between the clerks in two different stations. It's a good idea to get your information straight or even your Ameripass coupon filled out for the next stop as soon as you get to a city, rather than having to rely on the phone or facing a huge crowd at the ticket window minutes before the bus is supposed to leave. When using the Ameripass in this fashion, you don't have to worry about changing your mind and destination; all you do is tear out your filled-in coupon and have them write you out another one. If you rely on the phone, some small town clerks will inform you of a bus which they won't designate as being either Greyhound or Trailways, only to have you discover when you get to the station that it's a Trailways and that your Greyhound Ameripass won't be valid on it. If you use the phone, ask them about this, since the two bus companies will often share the same station in a small town.

So ride easy on your bus trip, my friend, and remember to write home now and then to mom, she who so graciously gave you your bus-ridin' booties and bod.

TRAIN TRAVEL AS IT IS
by Deetje Boler

What shakes and rumbles and bruises your shoulders when you lose your balance? The Amtrac train from San Francisco to New York. What has constant 3-D color scenery streaming by as you sit and watch, or eat and watch, or talk and watch? The Amtrac train. What takes four days and three nights, with a four-hour stop-over in Chicago, to cross the continent? That's right.

My daughter and myself, with a month-old guinea pig, took the trip this summer, because I didn't feel up to driving that far, I don't like flying in airplanes, and we had once taken the Canadian train from Montreal to Vancouver and enjoyed it very much.

On the American train you have a choice between sleeping compartments of varying sizes (tiny-to-small rooms with doors and sinks and toilets and seats which convert into beds) or coach seats which lounge back (far more spaciously placed and comfortable looking than any bus seat); the Canadian train also has "berths," which are facing seats, open to the aisles in the day-time, and which a porter converts to curtained beds at night. By the way, the berths are set up lengthwise to the car in the Canadian train while the beds in the compartments on the Amtrac train are cross-wise. I found sleeping lengthwise far preferable — it had the super-comfortable lulling effect you might expect of a train's motion. Cross-wise you feel you might roll out of bed when the train changes speed, and Amtrac runs the trains so frantically fast that it jiggles and quakes rather disturbingly.

Actually, I found the Canadian train more comfortable for a variety of reasons. Not only were the cars generally in smoother running condition in addition to having the berth-cars, but the service was consistently better, especially in the dining car. The food, which was delicious, might have seemed even more so as it had been paid for in advance as part of the cost of the ticket, which was lower than for Amtrac — and on Amtrac you pay for the meals as you go. Furthermore, the scenery, especially going from the flat plains of Calgary into and through the Rockies, was more beautiful. We were heading west in

the Canadian train, which schedules Lake Louise in the daytime. I don't know what part of the country you go through in the day time when you're heading east on the Canadian train. But I do know that going east on the Amtrac train gives you a less spectacular view of the comparatively plain mountains around Reno (after upsetting views of stockpiles of what looked like guided missiles, as well as whole rolling hills of junked cars around the outskirts of Sacramento, then a dramatic lightening-flashed sunset on the Salt Desert, and the next day what seemed like endless rolling plains featuring snow fences guarding the railroad tracks, and butte after butte after butte. No trees, no animals, just rolling space. Dry grass and brown scrub brushes. You get that boring effect through the middle of Canada, too, but there it comes from rolling fields of grassy farmland.

After a day and a night of incessant movement, your perspective begins to shift. Time and space start streaming through you like an invisible curtain and eventually you can't tell one moment from another. Your senses drift. Everything is movement. Not only does your coffee-cup jiggle, but you jiggle. And outside, everything slides by with the same backward twist. Distant movement is slow, steady, slipping ahead of the near movement which wrenches from your eyes as soon as you grasp it and whips by out of focus. To rest your eyes you look far off — and there is that enormous country. On and on and on it slides. And you've only seen your one narrow, train-track slit of it. On both sides, more and more space.

With this awareness, you drop from Cheyenne to Denver and night falls awhile thereafter on what definitely has begun to feel more like the east — occasional gullies with water, tree-lined fields, crops, patches of houses, and sometimes a pretty little flat valley ushering a little river on its way, maybe even a weeping willow tree by the water. By morning you're, in effect, East, although it's called the midwest. In fact, I had no idea where I was; the only map provided had nothing on it but a red line indicating the train route on an outline of the United States which lacked even the States boundaries and the names of any cities other than those at which we stopped. (It would have been a greater service to provide the passengers with informative maps than to provide them with the heavily-made-up, smiling, uniformed, female "college student" who was, I suppose, intended to be your link with the outside world. No thanks.) Anyway, after the no-man's-land bread-basket of the non-rest midwest, a night's sleep produced Chicago coming up after breakfast. So, after two days of space, the urban blight started coming in the window — first the houses with the trees and an occasional backyard horse, then the lined-up houses, with fences, then closer houses with no fences, then duplexes, then apartments and businesses, then heavier businesses and slums, then solid slums, then downtown Chicago.

You have a four-hour stop-over here, and change trains. After finding a self-service baggage basket and putting our luggage in a locker, we took a city bus to the Chicago Art Institute. Very up-tight people there. Wouldn't let us bring in the little guinea pig in its little carry-cage (seemed to think it would swallow the El Grecos whole). Also wouldn't let us check it in the checkroom; in fact, a guard and a manager chased me down in the bookstore to loudly ask what I'd done with it — after I'd found an employee who agreed to keep it awhile behind the counter. Their nastiness kept us from enjoying the museum, as visions of them finding and confiscating the poor terrified creature kept crossing our minds. The fountain-side restaurant was over-crowded anyway, with a long line of hot people waiting to relax by the cooling water, so we walked back through the very large collection of many styles of painting and several rooms of small statuary, set up in heavily guarded square white rooms — rescued the guinea pig and went outside to sit on the grass in peace. I watched as elevators hoisted enormous metal bars to the top of an extremely tall unfinished building on the sky-line. I felt the grass and watched the birds hop and fly. We walked back to the train after eating hamburgers in a down-town white-collar lunch room, with the guinea pig under the table.

Our new train was a disappointment. Although it had a couple of carpet-walled cars on it, newly upholstered for looks, it also had broken platform doors between cars, unsummonable porters, a metal-screeching, run-down club car, no dome car, and what seemed to be deliberately slow service in the dining room. In addition, our porter took our bedroom for himself and switched us into one with the seats riding backward and no window across the aisle. This finally completely destroyed my sense of direction (since in Cheyenne they had put the engine on the back end of the train and thus pulled us what felt to be backwards all the way to Chicago). Consequently, I felt as if I were going West to New York, and I had no idea where North might be. In its favor, the air-conditioning worked better than that on the first train, we only had one day to spend, and coming into Pittsburgh at night is always impressive, with the fires in the foundries reflected in the river. That's late — one o'clock or so. Morning brings the more densely settled real East and, after breakfast, New York City. There we were coughed out on the morning hot Penn Station platform in the bowels of Manhattan, the center of the most swarming streets in this hemisphere. I went straight for a cab to take me to my first destination. Much as I love train travel, I was glad the trip was over, as I'd been left with the uneasy feeling that I'd been somehow disregarded by the entire railroad system, vaguely offended, probably tricked, and just plain taken all the way across the country. This had not been true of the Canadian trip, which enjoyed the benefits of passing through more attractive scenery, more comfortably, for less money. The disadvantage is getting up to Montreal and back down to San Francisco from Vancouver. Maybe the answer is to live in Canada in the first place, which, considering everything, does not seem to be a bad idea at all. I've been thinking about it long enough. Now that the U.S. election results are in, I feel outnumbered and perhaps surrounded by what may be a lot of either hostile, immoral, or stupid people.

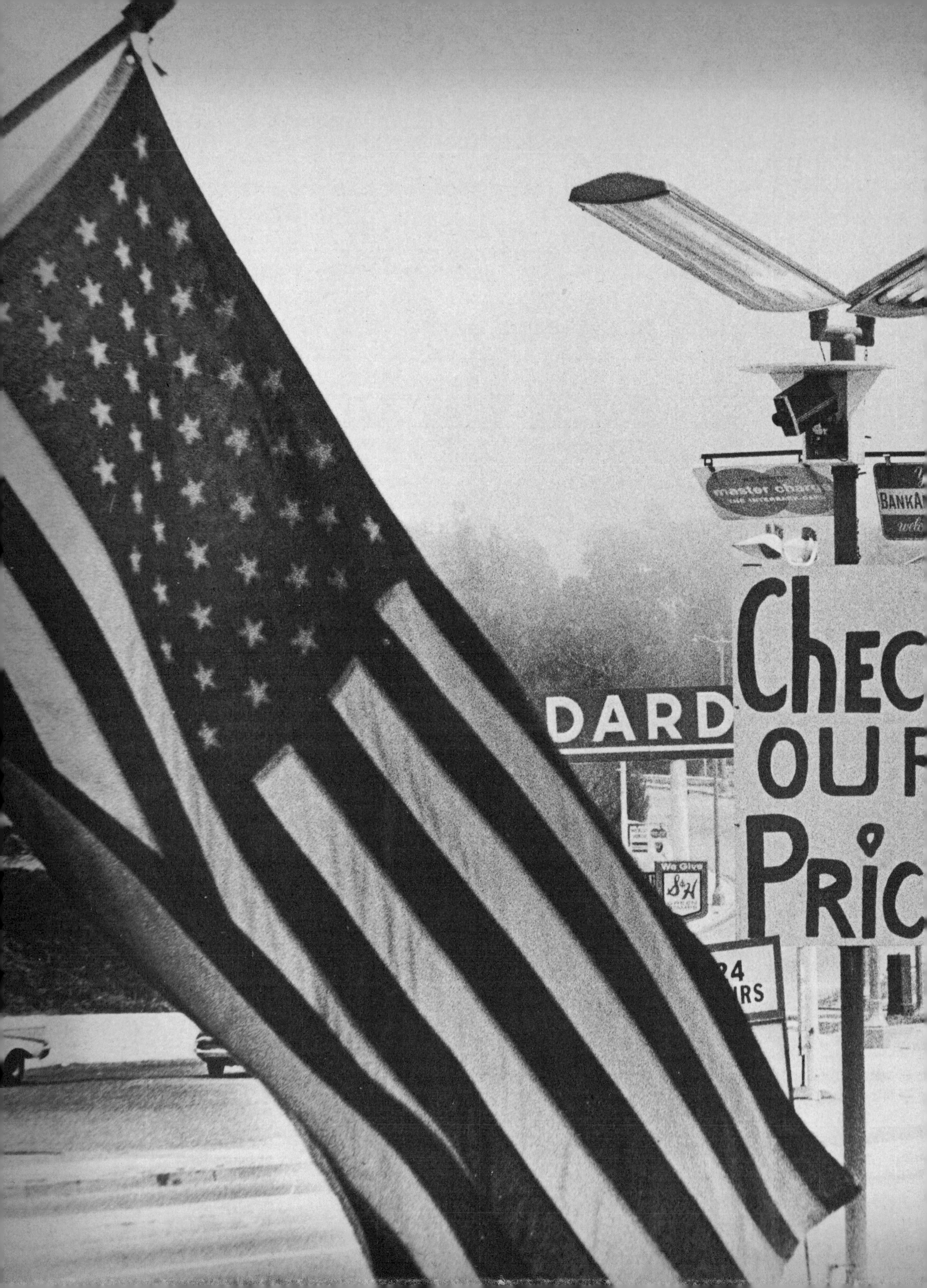
DARD
We Give
S&H
24
HRS
Chec
OU
Pric

Dollars And Sense

How To Use Money

5

MONEY AND ENERGY Money is an energy catalyst, and can even be thought of as energy. Of course, it's important. Like energy, tho, what matters is not how much you have, but how you use what you've got. How much of it is free for creative use, and how much is locked up in your life-bank? Needless to say, Americans have a lot of their money and their energy locked up in materialism. What is that all about, anyway? Actually our materialism is probably no worse than other cultures famous in history, especially the old aristocratic and monarchic societies of Europe. American materialism, however, is distinguished by its broad base and its use as an emotional release.

The wealth of America, widely distributed amongst all, created the broad base of materialism existing today — 200 million trained consumers straining at their paychecks to gobble up anything the factories can produce. But the "why" of it is the American work ethic — self-discipline and self-denial. Americans as a people are emotionally hung-up about how to gratify ourselves.

Gratification is another word for energy release, usually an energy exchange between parties or agencies of some sort. The energy itself is invested, as usual, in patterns of some

description. For example, love is a natural energizer that changes patterns and releases energy for exchange and mutual gratification. But Americans, as a Protestant-oriented, Pilgrim- evolved society, are conditioned to loving each other the same way they love God, abstractly and decorously. It's not a suitable outlet for gratifying the masses.

Similarly, gratification thru the world of direct experience is impossible for most Americans. Historically, they were tied to the land and their jobs, to their task of molding a democratic society under God — mostly a serious business with little opportunity for travel, the arts, cultivation of their "higher" selves. In fact, Americans for almost two hundred years experienced a national inferiority complex about how "uncivilized" they were, especially compared to Mother Europe.

As a result, there was just one way left for Americans to gratify themselves — thru work. And work they did; and work they still do. Americans made a reputation around the world that they still "enjoy" — they're working fools. Americans would rather work than fight, rather work than fuck, rather work than enjoy life. So their work has made them rich, and now what can they do with their money?

Here's a nice slogan as you enter West Virginia. The sign says "Welcome to wild, wonderful West Virginia." Except that you go down a little further on Interstate 64 and when it crosses the Kanahaw River, the town of Nitro shows up — an industrial complex going both up and down the river, smoke belching into the sky, one side from a huge mess of ugly buildings, and then up the river on the other side are some awesome skyscraper-size steam stacks, steaming into the sky. Wild and Wonderful indeed.

Nitro is only a warm-up for Charleston. It seems like a 1930's industrial town of the worst kind. Smoke stacks, ugly red brick buildings, box cars and tank cars, piles and piles of pipe running in all directions. Union Carbide, FMC, Dupont, chemical works of all kinds, industry, ordinance, trucks, trains, wires, towers, derricks, steel girders, pumps, pipes, nothing green, nothing live, all metallic and plastic. There's an island in the middle of the river here, sort of like the Ile de Cite on the Seine in Paris, but instead of being covered with cathedrals and graceful buildings, this one is a mass of storage tanks and smokestacks from shore to shore.

But the downtown section of Charleston itself looks pretty good. I guess that's where the money went. It even looks elegant, with Riverside Drive, big trees, stately homes, tall buildings. A historical marker that says Daniel Boone lived across the river for seven years. I wonder how he would feel about having opened up the West for this?

The haze and smog is so thick here in these hills that I would judge visibility to be about one mile. There are a whole string of unincorporated little towns all along the river, each with coal works and railroad siding. The whole river valley full of smoke. At one little town, a gigantic Union Carbide works of some kind spews smoke up into the air over acres of area. This whole run along the river is some kind of American horror show.

It strikes me that mining is a completely bad trip, whatever form it takes — whether it's oil, coal, precious metals. First of all, it rapes the earth of materials that can never be replaced by man. Minerals of all kinds should be used very carefully; they should be doled out. They are among the most precious things we have. Instead there is this rabid ripping away at the earth, pumping out its oil, stripping it away as fast as we can. Pell-mell, unrestrained consumption of our most precious resources.

Furthermore, mining creates untold human misery and greed. The men that work in the mines, the people that find labor thru mining industries, are notoriously poor and always have been, since the earliest days of history. They have constantly been exploited, while those who "own" the mines become fabulously wealthy. And they squander their wealth, never putting it back into the earth or into the labor that brought it out of the ground.

Then mining is ugly; mining destroys the land and the countryside. It kills the trees, it clogs the rivers, it poisons the air and the earth and the water. Lastly, mining feeds Technology which couldn't live without mineral resources. Technology feeds back and continues the whole process whereby more materials breed more destruction, more ugliness — so we need more minerals, more mining, more poverty, more exploitation.

In some ways it will surely be a blessing when mankind has finally stolen all the minerals there are. Perhaps that's when the millenium will be achieved. When man has to rely directly upon the organic kingdom for his needs and for his riches, he will be limited to a spiritual rather than a materialistic way of life. The original beauty of the Kanahaw River Valley makes all this so ironic. It reminds me of the Rhine River in Germany — wide, broad, steep forested slopes on both sides, roads along the banks. But here in America, instead of medieval castles and beautiful river towns, we have ugly poverty holes of Appalachia, we have the American modern-day equivalent of castles — they're called factories, industries.

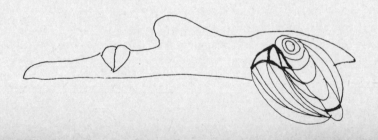

**&
THE
GREAT
SALE**

Well, money is a pattern too, but a terrifically potent and symbolic one. It's a medium of exchange for resources, labor, and products — all of which are themselves repositories of energy. That makes money a veritable symbol of energy itself, a powerhouse pattern invested with primeval force. It's easy to see that exchanging money, playing money games of any kind is a drug that can get you stoned, even freaked out. Far more people freak out on bad money trips than on bad LSD trips.

People will do anything for money — there's no end to its associations for both good and evil — and it's because of the energy it releases, the gratification it brings by its power to disrupt life patterns.

MONEY AND MATERIALISM For Mr Mass American, money is the most important energy in his life, certainly not the energy from love or living. He works his ass off at the factory or the office, but gets no joy from his work. Most of it is done by machines and routines anyway. He merely tends them, and delays his gratification until the paycheck arrives. Oh boy, MONEY! Energy! Power!

Now enter "things": now enter materialism. Here's a vast society filled with people making money on one hand, and factories making things on the other. Guess what? Exchange — Energy release — Gratification. And guess what else? It's a bum trip! It's a hangup of American society derived from outmoded ethics based on a religious view and a world view that have vanished into history.

Money is a symbol of wealth, and all wealth ultimately comes from the earth and its natural resources. To spend more money than is necessary, especially for things not needed, is unecological because it's not really money you're spending ... it's natural resources you're wasting. Every dollar represents some piece of our natural environment. We suppose that money rewards us for our labor, but we forget where the money came from originally. There's only so much left, and we can now see the darkness at the mouth of the tunnel we're headed for, unless we change our national consciousness about the uses of resources and money.

The situation today is that Americans *can* get their energy trips from original sources. In fact, it's imperative over the long haul for their survival as a society. It's time to get our psychic energy from experiences with people and with ourselves. We need to start becoming a society that gets high from experience instead of goods, from 'being' instead of buying. We need to cultivate energy exchange thru humanism, thru growth of potential in ourselves and in the quality of our participation in life. The means are at hand. Our machines can free us from the drudgery of survival; our technology has released adequate energy for everyone to pursue creative and humanly constructive lives.

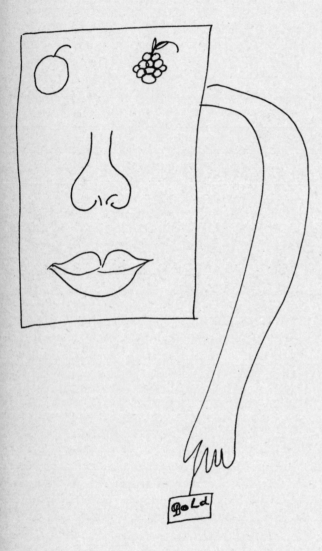

"Money has only one use — to give one independence from his enemies."

—Humphrey Bogart

MONEY AND FREEDOM.

People yearn for freedom. Time and again, one hears Americans complain that they want more freedom from their jobs, more time to travel, and so forth. These same people then turn around and show you their new car, or maybe even their new Recker. Somebody should point out that's where their freedom went, that's where their time goes.

Money is power, but only if you know how to spend it. Money can buy time, and time is freedom. How obvious, yet how universally ignored. For all their material wealth, or because of it, Americans are impoverished in personal freedom and individual consciousness. The energy their money represents, the power for self-liberation it possesses, is expended for ego-trips; for security; for keeping up with those assholes, the Joneses; for useless artifacts, literal junk of every description. Entering the average middle-class American home is like visiting a dungeon of the mind, where every object is a manacle subtly enslaving the smiling wretch who lives there, saying "See my new__ ? Isn't it great? I got it on sale for only $ __, a saving of $ __ ." The smile comes from gratification, but the situation is tragic, especially when multiplied a million-fold every day. There went someone's freedom. There went someone's consciousness. There went our natural resources. There went our greatness.

Freedom is, of course, just a feeling, and can be obtained in numerous inexpensive ways not related to money. However, most people don't know these ways, but, they do have money. It's what they're working for. Their big mistake is in spending it solely for the sake of fashion and comfort, or out of fear and ignorance. They receive this power — this money — then they foolishly piss it away on needless accessories and services.

The best use of money is to buy time. Time away from home, time away from the job, time in which to vagabond. There's the real power of your money — it buys you the space in which to explore your country and yourself at your leisure, as a full-time occupation.

It's surprising how cheap time can be. Keeping yourself alive in reasonable comfort doesn't cost much, actually. A little food, shelter, clothing, transportation can be worked out for a few hundred a month. As explained shortly, I made a three-month tour of America for five dollars per day, including transportation thru 40 states, and I lived well, even luxuriously at times. Time has a lot to do with enjoying life, and money enters into it only because money buys time. The most rewarding things in life are personal relationships and personal discoveries, and the more time you have the more likely you are to come into these rewards.

MONEY AND TRAVEL Its an old truism of travel that the less you spend, the more you can learn about the places you visit and the people who live there. It's easy to see, in energy terms, why that's so. The challenges of traveling require energy — a great deal of it. The flow of that energy is what makes travel fun. But money is an energy substitute. Spending more money means less energy is required; in other words, the challenges can be reduced with an energy substitute. The difference is in the quality of the experience: Energy is life, while energy substitutes are not. The problem is that the challenges can be eliminated entirely if enough money is spent.

Reduction of travel costs is an important goal, therefore, for lots of reasons. It means more energy and more fun. What costs money when you travel breaks down into four items: Transportation, Lodging, Food, and Other. Let's take these one at a time.

"THE SPECTER OF OIL SHORTAGES"
San Francisco Examiner

"The Department Of Interior proposes to lease 31,000 acres of oil shales in Colorado, Utah and Wyoming this winter to speed up large scale oil extraction processes. It is one of several steps being taken by the government to deal with the growing national oil shortage.

Major conservation groups, fearful of massive destruction of a starkly beautiful environment, are fighting the proposal. They are demanding that the government first try to reduce national oil consumption by adopting a comprehensive policy for the conservation of energy. Interior's reply is that the oil shortage is becoming so acute the country cannot wait on a long-range solution like a policy of reduced consumption.

The projected oil shortage over the period of the next 15 years is so great, and the consequences to the nation's economy and security so horrendous if a major shortage should actually develop, that the country simply cannot afford to delay moving on all fronts.

We are about to begin paying the price for what has been called our careless throwaway economy.

Given the total situation it seems to us that prudence dictates the most rapid development possible of all domestic energy resources, including the oil shales.

Inevitably the environment will suffer.

It is a price we must pay, the alternative being so much worse. The well-being of more than 200 million Americans, completely dependent upon an energy economy that cannot rapidly be altered, is paramount to all else."

69

TRANSPORTATION COSTS For many, this is the largest single expense, and in any case is intrinsic to traveling. The general rule in travel, as in everything else, is that freedom and cost are inversely proportional. The most expensive means of traveling give you the least freedom, the cheapest ways to travel give you the most freedom.

Public transportation — planes, trains, and busses — cost the most, and the costs are fixed . . . so much per mile, with no chance to save. Naturally, you also get the least freedom or flexibility — all schedules and stations are fixed. Planes and trains cost about five cents to seven cents per mile, basic minimum costs. Busses cost three cents to four cents a mile. Next comes private transportation, which lowers the cost and increases the freedom.

Basic automobile operating expenses are about three cents per mile but can be split amongst several travelers. Economically the chief disadvantage is the expense of buying the vehicle (car, truck, van, bus), but Americans either own one already or can buy one easily no matter what their financial status. Mobility and motorists are characteristic of America, which has more cars and roads than anything else except beer cans. (There are 3,000,000 miles of paved roads in the USA, and 125,000,000 vehicles. Americans drive those cars on those roads to the tune of 1-1/4 trillion miles annually.) The major impediment to complete freedom is that owning and driving a car constitute a major responsibility. You're always tied to your car both physically and spiritually. Finally, the fact that 100 million other people are traveling the same way may reduce the novelty of it all. So, if you're traveling by car to save money, be sure to read chapter 9 so you can get more fun out of it.

Motorcycles cost about one cent per mile or so to operate, less than a car with a single driver, but about the same as a car with several passengers. They're also expensive to buy, less convenient and comfortable, and more dangerous. Freedom mixed with responsibility.

Bicycling comes next. It costs nil per mile, but you still have to buy one and keep it going. It's cheap in cost and free in spirit. Its big disadvantages are limited range, limited comfort and convenience.

Hitchhiking also costs nothing per mile, and you own nothing at all with wheels on it. Altho you still depend on other people's wheels, at least you don't worry about paying for them or losing them. It's a wonderous release from responsibility.

Walking/hiking is finally the cheapest, freest way of all, bar none. No wheels to own, no wheels to need. Not too speedy though.

To travel cheaply, pick the cheapest means of transportation that meets your minimum requirements for adventure, mobility, comfort, and speed.

Next, take passengers to share transportation costs. If you can't bring passengers, at least bring companions to lower the overall costs. When traveling by car, buy the cheapest gas around and bring your own oil.

LODGING COSTS To reduce the costs of lodging, first dislodge yourself. The lodges of America, the roadside hotels and motels, are new-style highway bandits. They steal your money and rape your mind. Sure, they're luxurious but who needs it? You'll be asleep anyway. Costs of $10 to $25 per night are common, resulting from a travel concept dedicated to corporation values: phony efficiency and genuine spiritual corruption.

Fortunately, there are alternatives. I'll go into them in detail later, but here's a brief rundown: First is camping, whether you do it in private campgrounds, public campgrounds, or no campgrounds. No matter how you travel, camping is possible with just a minimum of equipment and cash. Chapter 7 is about this.

The next alternative is staying with friends and relatives. This is not mooching, because even tho free, it requires a big expenditure of social energy. Also, being a guest now obligates you to be a host later on, so it balances out. The greatest reward of being a guest is not saving money, but let's not overlook the lesser rewards either. Of which more later in chapter 8.

There are also lower-priced motels and hotels across America that skip the luxury to give you a more reasonable rate. How to find these and other lodgings is discussed in the next chapter. Finally, there are cheaper lodgings that you can't count on individually, but as a group exist in profusion — crash pads, missions, college campuses, casual quarters of whatever description. These won't be suitable for the average American family vacation, but can completely accommodate the young and adventurous vagabonds roaming America with little or no money at all.

FOOD COSTS The costs of eating are only one part of the American food dilemma . . . the other part is getting anything worth eating. A certain amount of cheeseburger/coke/french-fries is practically unavoidable . . . sometimes nothing else can be found. But to eat this stuff consistently, especially when it comes from chain-burger places, is to cheat yourself of nourishment and put your money in the wrong pockets. Good food in America — that is, fresh, high-quality food individually prepared by trained cooks — is either expensive or relatively hard to find, especially for the traveler passing through. But local cafes and restaurants *off* the interstates are good bets, and you can almost always find them with a minimum of personal inquiry. Preparing your own meals, especially if you're camping, will stave off both poverty and indigestion. Meal-making, particularly on an occasional basis, is fun, and you're sure of getting a good meal. Whether or not you're camping, the best and least expensive lunches come out of supermarkets enroute, and the roadside picnic sites are frequently beautiful and restful. More about food in the next chapter.

OTHER COSTS These shouldn't be overlooked, because so-called "incidental" costs can wipe you out. Almost all travelers underestimate these costs, which include admissions and other entertainment, souvenirs and gifts, reading matter and guidebooks, postcards and postage, laundry, phone calls, replacements for things lost or used up, and purchases of things you decide you need enroute which you overlooked originally. You can do without all of this, but it's a dreary trip that has no slack in it for an occasional monetary lark. However, the problem is usually overspending — needlessly — when buying souvenirs and entertainment. If possible, a maximum expenditure for "other" should be agreed upon beforehand, and a careful tabulation kept. This fund shouldn't include the emergency slush fund, which is another "other." The best way to cope with emergency money needs is to carry a general-purpose credit card or be sure someone back home can wire more money — yours or theirs — on short notice.

AMERICA ON $5 A DAY AND LESS Putting this all together into a concrete example, here's how the costs on my recent travels broke down. Situation: Car touring in a VW camper: myself, Stephanie and baby Sierra on the road for 71 days, covering 41 states and 13,500 miles. We set out to see America on a budget, but we weren't out to break any cost records either. The primary objective was to enjoy ourselves, exercising reasonable economies where possible. Per-day travel costs always leave out transportation costs, but that's silly because travel does involve transportation. I'll take those first. Our largest expense was gasoline ($270) at 16½ miles per gallon. Other automobile costs were turnpike tolls ($35), maintenance ($75), and parking ($8). Grand total for the car was $388, which figures to less than three cents per mile, or about $5.50 per day ($2.75 each not counting the baby as a person, or $1.85 each if we do). These figures are perfectly ordinary — neither low

nor high — but still show that cars go far for little. Only motorcycling or hitchhiking could cover as much distance for less money, and either would be far less comfortable, far more tiring, and impractical for a family. No wonder 90% of all Americans use their private car for vacation trips. (No wonder it's so great to go some other way, too . . .)

Getting on to the bonafide per-day results: Lodging (in our case non-lodging) amounted to less than 50 cents a night, or about 18 cents each. How was this miracle worked? Five nites sleeping in the car away from a campground, 21 nites sleeping in the car at campgrounds ($42 total), and 45 nights staying with people of various description.

Old Friends	14 nites
Relatives of friends	14 nites
Relatives	9
Friends of relatives	6
New friends	2
	45 nites total

Well over half the entire trip involved visiting people, who gave us lodging (and frequently food) at no cost. The money you save is not the reason for doing it, but nevertheless does make a big difference in costs. Meeting and staying with people is the most stimulating part of traveling America. It gives you the most genuine and rewarding trip possible. Naturally enough, it isn't easy. Half of the people we stayed with were new to us, and most of the rest not seen for years. That's a lot of social energy to tune into, and will power is required to do it.

Next were campgrounds — 21 nites for a total of $42, or $2 per nite ($1 each).

State Parks	8 nites
Nat'l rec areas	4
Nat'l parks	3
Nat'l forests	2
Nat'l monuments	2
Private campgrounds	2
	21 nites total

The most interesting thing about this is how we stayed at so few private campgrounds. This is worth noting because private camps average about double the cost ($3 — $6) of public camps. Casual camping — sleeping just off the road — for five nites was free and no problem.

Camping means being able to experience closehand the other side of America . . . the natural side, the land as it is, and sometimes, as it was. This is the well-known, the famous side of America, but it's being changed and threatened, just as all the rest. I would almost venture that seeing the USA without at least some camping experience is to miss the most classically American experience.

Food costs, in our case, came to $213 or exactly $3 per day — two adults and a baby. I didn't keep careful records — didn't separate food costs between restaurants and markets — but we frequently ate supper at a restaurant, never ate at a restaurant for lunch, and only occasionally had a restaurant breakfast. We ate most of our meals out of markets, prepared in the car, and these were certainly our best meals, on the average. (Even if your cooking isn't too great, you'll still eat better than at most restaurants.) After that came freebies from friends and other people putting us up. (The quality of these varied a lot, and naturally meant eating whatever was served, for better or worse. This especially affects travelers who are into vegetarianism, no preservatives, health foods, etc.) The rest came from restaurants, usually those chain chophouses, and we repeatedly got shitty food. A few one-only restaurants turned out fine, meaning good food at reasonable prices. Only one good chain restaurant. More about this later.

The final expense was "other." We found that $1.25 per day for each of us did it really well. This bought us some gambling, amusement tickets, guidebooks, postcards, gifts such as Indian necklaces, laundry, and assorted purchases like shoes and moccasins and brassieres and a baby's playpen, even. These expenses could be cut down or cut off entirely depending on your resolve and budget, or increased a lot, also depending. This is a personal matter. Do what you need to.

Anyway, for us it came together like this:

TOTAL PER-DAY EXPENSES

Lodging	$0.50
Food	3.00
Other	2.50
	6.00 per day
Total Auto Expenses (200 mi/day ave.)	5.50
Total Expenses for 2½ people	11.50 per day
or less than	5.00 per day each

Worked out another way, it comes to six cents per mile, or less than three cents per mile each. For comparison, the average American on vacation in 1971 in his private car spent almost 14 cents per mile in total expenses (according to my world almanac under Esoteric Trivia).

Just before starting the car trip, I went hitchhiking for two weeks alone, and my total expenses came to $1.50 per day, covering 1500 miles. On that trip I stayed mostly with people, but camped out in the woods (desert) a few nites too. So that's even cheaper.

OFF THE TAPE

Off The Tape
PORTRAIT OF THE ARTIST

Even in the bosom of his family, David must fight for his right to live as an artist. He gets little recognition tho his work is mature and important, and tho he teaches art at the university. He makes very few sales, so he gets no support. His relatives urge him to quit being an artist, to get a regular job because after all these years of struggle he still hasn't made it. At 36 he's spent his entire adult life as an artist and he's been almost continually poor the whole time. After five years of both starvation and notoriety in Copenhagen (where I first met him), he returned home to Detroit, primarily because it was his home and he could live in his sister's house for nothing. Now, as bad as it is here he's afraid to leave because he'll have to start all over again once more, just as he did when he went to Europe, just as when he came back from Europe. He'd like to leave for, say, California, but he'll have to start over again. It seems that David at one time worked for General Motors as a clay designer, as a clay sculptor making models in clay of new car designs. He could now be making $20,000 a year doing that. Also, it turns out that some of the people he worked with who stayed with it now have their own art interests on the side. They paint and they claim to be artists, they do a few paintings a year and in addition to having had their soul bought by General Motors, they still say they're creative artists. Nancy told the story of one such person who founded a gallery in Detroit which shows the work of so-called artists from General Motors who paint and sculpt in their sparetime. Their money has bought them the right to claim that they're artists. Meanwhile, someone like David not only gets no money for his work and no recognition, but he can't even get his work shown in a gallery like this because he doesn't work at General Motors.

CREDIT CARDS Don't scoff. Credit cards, the sure sign of middle-classness, are more useful to vagabonds than anyone else. They may brand you as being bourgeois, but look at it this way: You probably are. Vagabonds sometimes sport an air of irresponsibility — they need something to legitimize them. A credit card is a winner. Vagabonds sometimes need to get bailed out of a jam. A credit card is a winner. Moreover, simply owning one doesn't cost you anything. No matter how I travel, I've always brought at least one of the three major kinds of credit cards: Oil company card, bank card, and executive card.

Oil company cards (like Shell, Texaco, etc.) enable you to charge gas, oil, tires, service or repairs, and usually certain chain motel rooms and chain restaurant meals. Sometimes (like Conoco) you can cash personal checks by showing the card. Credit-wise, oil cards are the easiest to get. Even so, you should be over 21 and employed to be sure of getting a card.

Bank cards (like BankAmericard and Master Charge) are harder to get, but more flexible and useful. There's nothing within reason that you can't charge, including cash. It'll help when applying if you've already established credit and can prove reasonable stability. If you get turned down, try getting your own card on your parent's credit, or simply using your parents, or a friend's. But they'll have to be pretty good parents/friends for that, and so will you.

The hardest cards to get are the executive cards (American Express, Carte Blanche, or Diner's Club), and these are less useful to the vagabond traveler. They're for luxury lodging, dining, entertainment, and TI-type travel. They also don't have extended payment plans and they do charge annual dues.

Personally, I use credit cards only when I have to, but I American-expressly praise the Lord at that point. I've used them to prove I wasn't a total vagrant, to catch a plane home during emergency, for a shot of luxury when my spirits were shot, to get on a train when I was stranded, to buy a car so I could get out of Miami, and once even to buy a house. Handy little cards, those!

Check the following handy-dandy, all-in-one-charge-chart for more information.

CREDIT CARD INFORMATION

	Gas Cards	Bank Cards	Executive Cards
Nationwide	Some*	Yes	Yes
Cash Advances	No	Yes	Yes
Gasoline, tires, ect.	Yes	Yes	Yes
Motel/hotel charges	Yes	Yes	Yes
Restaurant charges	Yes	Yes	Yes
Repair service charges	Yes	Yes	Sometimes
Department store charges	No	Yes	Sometimes
Approval time	2-4 weeks	4-6 weeks	4-6 weeks
Under 21?	Students	Sometimes	Seldom
Use parents' card?	Yes	Yes	Yes
Credit requirement**	Easiest	Moderate	Strict
Membership fees?	No	No	Yes
Max. loss liability	$50	$50	$50
Credit plans	Revolving	Revolving	None
Credit ceilings (typical)	$500 or less	$1000 or less	$2000 or less
Interest on unpaid bal (typical)	18%	12%-18%	Overdue charge

*Texaco, Shell, Standard, American, and Continental only.
**Under 21, 21-26 (draft age), and women have it the hardest.

Addresses:

Oil Company Cards: Any major brand service station, or refer to oil company addresses in the back of the book.

Bank Cards: Bankamericard—Any B of A office, or Bankamericard Box 37114 San Francisco, CA 94137

Master Charge — Any affiliated bank office

Executive Cards: American Express Co. Box 1885 New York 10008

Carte Blanche Box 54116 LA 90054

Diner's Club 10 Columbus Circle New York 10019

TRAVELERS CHECKS AND SUCH Meaning, how should you carry money? Credit cards, of course, reduce your cash needs to start with. Beyond that, the answer seems to be some cash and the rest in traveler's checks. However, I'm personally not too fond of traveler's checks. They're occasionally difficult to cash, no matter what the ads say, and you're frequently required to show identification and get dirty looks for being a possible crook (or something — I don't even know what). On the last trip it pissed me off enough so that I finally cashed the last few hundred dollars worth all at once so I wouldn't have to keep messing with distrusting businessmen. In one large city (Washington, DC of all places) I almost couldn't get them cashed at a bank. (Insanely enough, the girl told me they sold 'em but didn't cash 'em.) The most recognized ones are American Express but you can sometimes get other brands for less than the stan-

dard commission (1% is standard), and some banks and businesses issue them free to their customers.

Traveler's checks can also be used illegally in several ways that I'll mention but don't endorse at all. One is to sell unsigned checks for something less than their face value (if you can find a buyer), then claim a loss and collect that too. The other way is to claim a loss and collect, but keep the original checks with no plans of ever cashing them. You use them only to prove solvency.

However, a brief personal statement about morality. Dishonesty is a bad trip, and it doesn't matter whether you're doing in American Express or your best friend. Telling the truth and being honest rewards you with self-respect and good karma; ripping off is another example of low-level consciousness, no matter how you justify it.

"Now listen to what Jesus said to his disciples. He said that any man that will come after me, he said Let him deny himself. Amen, and that's the thing that I want to get over to each and every individual person tonight and to everyone within the sound of my voice, that Jesus said that ANY MAN amen, speaking directly to his disciples and amen, directly to you and me today amen, he said if ANY MAN, amen, will follow me and come after me, he said LET HIM DENY HIMSELF. He said Take up his cross and follow me. Amen, now I want to ask you a question tonight, amen how many of us have denied ourselves, how many of us have denied our wants, amen, brother, I want this and I want that, amen. I think I need this but Jesus said Deny yourself. Praise God but you know tonight praise God that a lot of preachers get in the pulpit, amen and they get up to preach the word of God, amen and they're not even sent by Jesus, and they don't deny their own self, brother Dave, and they don't preach what God gave them to preach, amen they preach what they want to preach. Why? Because they looked over the crowd, amen they looked over the congregation and then they seized something to preach on and when you see them before your eyes, it's so easy to preach. Amen. My God! But Jesus said, IF ANY MAN WILL FOLLOW ME, IF ANY MAN WANTS TO GO WITH ME BROTHER JOHN, AMEN if any man wants to do what I will have him to do, amen, brother let him FIRST deny himself. Amen. If that self denial don't come, you're none of his. Amen, tonight, I don't care what you're doing, I don't care how many songs you've sung, don't care how many messages you've preached, I don't care what you've done for the Lord, amen brother, until you deny yourself, amen you're NOT his. He said if man will come after me, let him first deny hisself. Amen, brother Paul said praise God, in the word of God, amen he said I would die daily. Amen, brother, what was he dying to? Amen he was dying to the things of the world, amen he was dying to the things that that old fleshly man Paul would have wanted. He was dying, brother to the cares of his life. He was dying to the things, praise God that the flesh would want, he began to take up the things the spirit wanted. (Amen, come on brother, praise the Lord). Praise God. He said if any man is gonna follow me, let him deny himself, amen let's look at ourself tonight people, lets see how much denying we've done, amen let's be *honest* with ourselves, amen, let's see how much denying we've done. Amen. (You've got the message). Well I've done this, I've done that. You know I've done something else. Hallelujah. You know I went out today, and oh man, I just seen something that looks like something I just gotta have, oh Praise God I just gotta have it, I seen a new automobile or a piece of new furniture the women are saying, oh I just gotta have some furniture. Amen, Praise God. It ain't been many weeks ago, amen, just a couple of weeks ago when my wife just told me she just had to have a dinette set and a new rug, praise God. Amen and she didn't have to have it but, amen she just kept on till she got it. Amen brother, but let me tell you something tonight, amen, we need to be wanting the things of God, amen, we need to be denying ourself, amen and the things that self would want, amen. We need to be tiring ourself out, amen brother, that we have to work all the time that we don't have anytime for God tonight, amen. People say I just gotta do this. Just looks like I gotta have a new car. Looks like I just gotta have a new suit for preaching in. Hallelujah, most preachers can't even get in the pulpit and preach unless they got a nice suit on, a big neck tie. And brother let me tell you something tonight, Jesus said if you're gonna follow me, amen, he said Deny yourself. Amen, if I gotta have a suit to preach in, amen I'll just sit on my seat and listen to somebody else. Hallelujah. Well I'm glad tonite to know amen that God tole me praise God, amen and God tole me, I'll ordain you praise God, and God tole me Open your mouth and I'll fill it, amen brother and I've always learned to be that a way. And Jesus Christ praise God said I won't never leave you. I won't never forsake you. That's what he said. That's right. He said deny yourself, that's what he said. He looked over at me in other words just maybe like I would look over at Brother Dave amen he said now, Willard, if you'll deny yourself, amen take up your cross and follow me *I will make you fishers of men*. That's what he tole Peter one day, amen, he said Peter if you'll follow me he said I will make you fishers of men."

Food And Lodging 6

Merchandising Gone Mad

AMENITIES FOR SALE What value do you place upon eating and sleeping compared to the total value of your trip? For most tourists, eating and sleeping IS their trip. They leave home solely for the opportunity to eat and sleep more pretentiously than ever. Travel thus becomes a socially accepted cover for their real purpose, which is to indulge in glamorous amenities such as restaurant platters and hotel mattresses. This travel approach is widely extolled by everyone in the TI, and repeatedly promoted in their brochures and advertisements. As a result, I think everybody tends to confuse travel with its bodily comforts.

I would never argue that being able to eat and sleep well is important to the success of a trip, to your well-being, to the atmosphere of your travels. But there are two problems that arise. The first, the more obvious one, is the conflict between spending and experiencing, the more money you spend, the more you get away from the everyday reality and experiences of life — and as you lose those, the fewer benefits you get from the whole trip. You can pay plenty to eat and sleep, and still not get any satisfaction. That's what usually happens.

The second problem is more insidious, and is about confusing America with its Amenities. It's so easy to do. Suppose you only eat at Howard Johnson's Restaurants and travel only on the interstate hiways that connect them. Suppose you stay only at Holiday Inns. Now take a long tour of the United States this way (a lot of people do). OK, what would you think about America after you'd done that? Whatever it would be like, I think we'd all agree you'd be kidding yourself. It would be a horrendously misleading experience because your slice of America was all baloney.

The point is that as individual human beings grossly limited in time and space, we get only a thin slice of life anyway. So why not seek out as tasty a slice as possible? What you want is a slice of reality, not a slice of baloney. Now it just happens, as I've pointed out elsewhere in this book, and probably will again, that your ability to get a real taste of America depends not on how much money you're willing to spend, but on how much you're willing to save. It seems that America gives you an increasingly unreal look at itself the more money you spend. Conversely, the less you spend, the realer it gets. Ultimately this is because money is power, and can grossly distort reality. It almost always does — being around a lot of money is always unreal. It reminds me of something Anais Nin said in one of her diaries: "Poverty is the great reality. That is why the artist seeks it." And the vagabond too.

As a potential traveler, as a person of ordinary means, as an American who's interested in America, these things come together in the following way: It's important *not* to spend money because it wastes resources, dissipates your power (energy), amd makes it difficult to see America (distorts reality). If you really want value from your travels, it's important to economize. It's the only way to keep your vision clear. It's the only way to experience genuinely.

A THEORY OF SLEEPING Sleeping is a necessary human function that restores the body and spirits. Travelers in particular need this rest, and where possible, should get it daily. To fill this need, enter now the multibillion-dollar accommodations industry . . . the itinerant slumberer's ignoble servant.

Unfortunately, most of the industry is not content to rent you a warm bed in a dry room. They want to rent you a total concept of material comfort and mass-produced luxuries. What is more, they expect you to pay for it thru the nose. It's an old American sales technique: Find a need and fill it — with luxury extras for greater profits.

Marketing-wise, the industry's propaganda mills grind out the message that hotels are complete worlds of convenience and luxury. By implication, the real worlds of experience — so inconvenient and drab — become merely the unpleasant interludes between hotels. Again, it is this concept of travel services becoming the travel experience.

The truth is that travelers need accommodations that represent a sensible balance between services and costs. The exact balance is up to the traveler — anywhere from no services/low costs to total services/high costs. But Americans tend to go for the latter pri-

marily because they've been trained to demand it. However, it's true that most hotels offer nothing less, and Americans are collectively wealthy enough to pay for it.

My theory of sleeping is simple. Places to sleep should be comfortable enough to get your rest, and they should be free. All you need is a sheltered space big enough to lie down in, and after that no services or goods are required — you do the sleeping yourself. So why should it cost any money? The crux of the problem is finding that 'sheltered space.' If you're not prepared to camp, if you have no friends to stay with, if no one has offered you a place — its reasonable to rent a sleeping place for a night. But to pay $10 or $20 for it is outrageous. Occasionally a taste of luxury is a lark, but a steady diet of it makes you weird. Settle for less. Do yourself a favor, and downgrade the cost of your sleep. In the end, not being choosy and funky becomes a style that is always fresh, never boring. You don't get the chance to put on airs and worry about how you're measuring up in the Tourist Derby. You don't worry about how you're dressed or if the help approves of you, or about making reservations ahead on the computer, or whether your room will have a color TV set. You simply say "Fuck all that" and free yourself to have a good time on just a few dollars a day.

HOTELS AND MOTELS Not a bad idea. Travelers need places to sleep and clean up. Moreover, the advent of chain hotels and motels should have been an even better thing, because economies of scale and efficiency should have made chain hotel prices within reach of everyone. They should have become a total network of hostels which offered warm, dry beds and washing facilities at low cost. Instead, they became luxurious and expensive, frequently more so than the independent hotels and motels that they've largely replaced. As one report puts it, "Every 30 hours, somewhere in downtown America, an old hotel closes. Every 30 hours, somewhere in suburban America, a new motel opens."

But what hurts is not just the dollar cost,

but the cost in human values and individuality. The success of a chain like Holiday Inns is based on standardization. Every one looks the same and offers the same services — all 1500 of them, in every state and at least 26 other countries. Only the Army and the Navy have as many beds as Holiday Inns, and these organizations are just as standardized and old-fashioned. Every good-sized American city has at least one Holiday Inn, and as a perfect example of matching mentalities, Disneyworld in Florida is ringed by nine of them.

What are the reasons for this and similar triumphs of mass merchandising on the American travel scene? I think it's because Americans have a hunger for genuine experience, but are completely ignorant of how to get it. They rely on their money and materialism to do it for them, and so they wind up with spurious experience instead, with production-line luxury whose sterility paralyzes their souls and turns their brains to shit. It's bad consciousness.

This has come about not thru the innate stupidity of the American public. It's the result of decades of direct and indirect influence by a juggernaut materialistic ethic. Our industries, laboratories, unions, government have all closed ranks into a monolithic conspiracy to brainwash Americans into accepting anything that creates more dollars, jobs, or goods. We've believed it all, we've worked for it, we put our faith in materialism. Now it's starting to appear that we were sold a bill of goods, literally. Suddenly, America is way out of balance ... we've reached an extreme at which the cost in natural resources, in public morality, in quality of life measured in humanity and genuineness, is too great. We're at a cliff's edge beyond which lies national insanity and self-destruction.

"Double-think" is so common today we take it for granted. We wage war to make "peace." We slave to be "free." We dehumanize each other in the name of "humanity." We buy artificial products because they're advertised as "the real thing." We try to satisfy our hunger for experience by buying plastic substitutes. The genuine ways in which people can

live and be happy are hidden, shuffled aside, and ridiculed. Money has become a totem and a panacea. Everything reinforces the message that we can be happy if we spend money.

Until now. Today it's a new ball game. The holiday for Holiday Inns is about to be over. What this country needs for travel is a chain of low cost motels that offer clean and simple accommodations. Something better than dormitory style, but patterned on that idea. Nothing fancy — a place to sleep and get clean, to rest from the road. The cost should not be more than $5 a night and preferably about half that. Some kind of a folks hotel. The Volkswagon car was built on that idea . . . a basic car at a low price. Bigger, more powerful, shinier and fancier cars continue to sell, of course, but the future is going to start cramping their style soon. (Wait till gas prices go up a few hundred percent.) In the same way, luxury motels and that jazz are having a field day right now, but their future is limited. The way of the future lies in conservation of resources, not in further exploitation of them. There are indications that this is happening already. A new wave of budget-priced motels is coming into existence, contesting the mass chains. Some examples are Motel 6 (Calif), Scottish Elms (Tenn), Econo-Travel Motor Inns (Va), Thr-rift Inns (Va), and Days Inns (Ga) — all of which charge only six to eight dollars per nite for a single room. But more needs to be done, and will be. Can you picture it? "Vagabond Motels in all cities, all rooms two dollars including use of mixed showers and rumpus room. Nitely dances and community kitchen. Come one and all!"

There are inexpensive hotels in America, but most of them come under the category of "cheap" hotels, bringing to mind the image of sleazy wino-havens in the socially destroyed downtown areas of big cities. It's true, I think, that the least expensive hotels in America probably are to be found in the American slums, but there are a considerable number of others that don't fall into that category. All American towns have small owner-occupied motels and hotels offering rooms from five dollars up, usually in the outskirts and quieter

*   "Through clever and constant application of propaganda, people can be made to see paradise as hell, and also the other way around — to consider the most wretched sort of life as paradise."
—Adolph Hitler

CHAINS ON MY MIND

Holiday Inn	Marathon Motel
Sheraton	Red Carpet Inn
Hilton	Nutmeg Inn
Howard Johnson	Treadway Inn
Best Western	Walker Motel
Ramada Inn	Friendship Inn
Quality Court	Master Host
Travelodge	Albert Pick Hotel
Rodeway Inn	Colonial Inn
Superior Motel	Town & Country
Hyatt House	Marriott
King of the Road Inn	Stage Coach Inn
Admiral Benbow	

neighborhoods. Find them by local inquiry and diligent search.

In some parts of the country there are "guest homes" or inns, usually former residences that have been converted into hotels for travelers. These are usually less expensive than your standard hotel and far more interesting and comfortable. You get to know the proprietor on a human level and you get a completely different "feel" of America in these places. Student guidebooks, of which there are several (see appendix 3) sometime have pretty good listings of inexpensive hotels. Not all downtown hotel areas provide shabby accommodations either. Frequently older hotels provide inexpensive lodgings but will be clean and comfortable. They are often occupied by permanent residents who could add a lot to your travels if you're fortunate enough to meet them.

In the big cities, there are YMCA's and YWCA's. Incidentally, YMCA's frequently have rooms for families, and some of them even have rooms for women. Check the phone directory. There are youth hostels in America, tho not nearly so many as in Europe or as widespread. Most of them are in the east and New England, but there are some scattered thruout. If you're a member of American Youth Hostels or you join, you can get a complete directory of all American youth hostels. Write to: AYH, National Campus, Delaplane, Va 22025.

If you're a student or a young person in a university or college town, inquire about staying at a residence hall. There is almost always room for one more, and the cost is low — usually two or three dollars. Even if they don't have any room, you're likely to happen onto an offer to stay with someone or a warm place to crash. A new guidebook to US student accommodations has been compiled by the Council on International Educational Exchange (CIEE), listing youth hostels, YMCA's, YWCA's, college dorms, off-campus housing, etc. Refer to appendix 3 for more information about it.

CLEAN AGAIN AND ON THE ROAD

A Trip
is getting it on with people
putting yourself out there
being who you are
in someone else's space
unafraid
a thousand miles from home
two thousand miles from home
three thousand miles from home.

Off The Tape
DISCOVERY

We pulled up to a roadside table in Vermont to have our lunch. On a concrete table stood a root beer can with a little bouquet of flowers in it. Next to it underneath some rocks was a hand-written note that read: "God made flowers of all shapes and of all sizes and colors. He could have made just one, you know!"

If you come into a strange town and have no guidebook, not much money and a sense of panic, see if you can contact a Tourist Information Office or Better Business Bureau to recommend some hotel within your budget. Traveler's Aid Societies are perhaps the best clearing house source of information for cheaper accommodations. There are hundreds of them across the country, and most larger cities will have a Traveler's Aid office. The services they offer are extremely varied and broad in nature. They'll know of places to stay in every price range. If you're broke, they can help you with emergency housing and emergency food. They offer to assist stranded travelers, can contact home or help for you, can arrange counselling or referrals for travelers with emotional problems. In large cities, the Travelers Aid Society frequently has booths manned by volunteers at the bus station and the airport. Or check the telephone directory.

Another good bet is personal inquiry. Stop and ask someone if they know of an inexpensive place to stay. The key to doing this successfully is picking the right person to ask. If you're a student or young person, ask someone who looks like you. Frequently a good person to ask is a policeman. Often he'll be familiar with the worst places, and can steer you away from those at least. Cab drivers are another good source. If you make a determined effort to find lodgings by personal inquiry, one frequent result is an offer to stay at little or no cost in someone's home, in someone's extra room, someone's extra bed. If you really make contact with someone, they will be eager to help.

PEOPLE HOSPITALITY People are not necessarily so bad as they're made out to be. Americans are the friendliest people in the world but you need some kind of introduction to them. However, even the most informal introduction will often be adequate. Besides casual encounters, there is the person-to-person network of accommodations available thru friends and relatives across the country. This is a whole topic in itself, and I've devoted chapter 8 to it so I won't say any more now except don't overlook it.

CAMPING Sleeping outdoors is spacey. If you don't believe it, try lying on your back in a sleeping bag sometime, looking up at the stars. I bet you don't see the stars often and you've forgotten how amazing a sight it can be when the evening sky is clear and the moon is down. Modern man seldom sees the stars anymore, not the way his forebears did, not the clear way the Indians did. The starlit sky, any nite, anywhere is convincing proof of a cosmos beyond the paltry world we see around us now. What's amazing is that we're not even aware of it anymore. Our civilized routines have obscured the everyday miracles of life.

Camping puts creation back into focus, and in the process makes us see how many of our daily concerns waste our energy because they're unimportant in the larger picture of our lives. Camping restores you to nature, which is to say, back to yourself. Chapter 7 goes into this in more detail, with practical information on how to do it, how not to do it, what you need and what you don't need, how to find campgrounds, etc.

From the standpoint of finding a place to sleep, camping out is the number one solution for Americans seeking real experience at low cost. Public campgrounds (city, county, state and national) abound at costs from zero to three dollars per nite per vehicle. In addition, private campgrounds are springing up everywhere, with costs starting around three dollars per nite per vehicle. City campgrounds are appearing, too, offering an excellent alternative to motels and hotels at lower rates. (New Orleans will shortly have a 20-story campground with artificial turf and rooftop pool. As usual, American enterprise doesn't wait long to pervert a good idea.)

The chief problem with camping, in fact, is illustrated by the New Orleans idea. People agree to endure the comparative discomfort of camping for the dollar savings, but then start working to entirely eliminate that discomfort. As a result, campgrounds are turning into mobile slums — ghettoes of materialism in which the sense of the outdoors is perverted into gross travesty. Once again, folks, I say that the "discomfort" is necessary, and you

Off The Tape
CITY PARKING

The park I slept in last night was really pretty. It's right next to the Cache La Poudre River. Mountains off in the distance. Tall trees that the wind moved thru very hard last night, tall grass to make a comfortable bed. It's also a historic site. There's a plaque there marking the site of the stagecoach station when this was right on the Overland Trail. Just up the street from the park almost on the main street is the original oldest building in the area, a log cabin built in 1858. Almost every American town has a small local park like this that they don't advertise but which if you ask for is usually there. Travelers passing thru are allowed to stay there overnight.

shouldn't be in such a hurry to eliminate it by buying some new camping gadgets. That "discomfort" is reality. It'll keep you in touch with experience; it'll keep your head straight.

CRASHING This means going to sleep without fussing over *any* of the accepted amenities. There are various ways to crash and there are varieties of crash pads. For example, there are formal crash pads — places that exist for that purpose from night to night on a more or less permanent basis. The quickest access to these, I think, is to call the local "Switchboard" in whatever city you happen to be. The numbers change as the Switchboards go in and out of business according to the level of community support. But if you phone 'directory assistance', you'll get the current number if in fact there is one. For young people and hip travelers, Switchboards are useful traveler's aids. Then there are the Traveler's Aid Societies themselves, which in many large cities work closely with underground people to provide lodging and emergency travel services. Call the Traveler's Aid Society and see what they know about crash pads, about dormitory projects and the like. In general, any underground service can provide information about places to sleep. This includes free clinics, head shops, water

bed stores, health food stores, underground newspapers, and heads on the street. Same thing with the collegiate services: college bookstores, college campuses, student unions, dormitories, student newspaper offices, and students on the street are all sources of housing (and other) information.

The last place to get a good nite's sleep is to crash to earth, which means to just fall down where you are and make it a bed for the nite. However, you'll need at least a sleeping bag, and a tarp or tube tent would be handy for emergency shelter. Anyplace with a little privacy or protection will do — city parks, vacant lots, beaches. If you can get used to traffic noise, you can sleep by or beneath freeways, or in the adjacent shrubbery. Buildings under construction are great, especially on weekends because the workmen don't arrive in the morning. Other buildings include barns, sheds, empty farm-houses, garages, gas stations. Also abandoned cars.

You should carry insect repellant, groundcloth, and flashlite. Be prepared for occasional encounters with insects, mice, rats, cats, dogs, vagrants, citizens, and policemen. It's a good idea if your sleeping bag is drab in color, not one of those bright mountaineer's bags intended to be spotted miles away.

Exercises

LODGING EXERCISES

1) Find a room to rent for less than three dollars per person. Tell people you can't afford any more than that; see if they'll accommodate you anyway or if they have any recommendations. Pay attention to how people relate to you when you're out to rent a cheap room; some will scorn you; others will sympathize. Dig it.

2) Rent a room for at least $20 for the night. Enjoy the luxury of it all, but imagine how life would be if it were all like this. Try to meet other guests in the lobby or lounge, and find out where they're at.

3) Stay at an old-fashioned hotel in a small town (3,000 people or less). Strike up a conversation with the clerk or owner; ask what there is to do in town for an evening. Do it, whatever it is.

4) Stay at a somewhat rundown hotel in the downtown area of a big city. Try to figure out what that scene is all about, and who are the other guests sharing your life that night.

5) If you don't get satisfaction in a room or related service, try complaining to the manager or desk clerk. Particularly in a so-called better hotel, see what happens as a test.

6) If you got particular satisfaction or exceptional service, compliment the manager or owner. Tell him why.

7) When inquiring about a room, make a general rule of seeing the room first. In a bad hotel, it will get you a better room; in a better hotel, it'll put them thru a trip that should be interesting to watch. In a campground, drive thru first to look over the sites.

8) Call the Traveler's Aid Society for accommodations in a big city; take whatever they recommend within your budget allowance.

9) Stay at a guest-house or room in a private home. Local inquiry will usually turn something up. Compare it with hotels.

10) Some night when not feeling particularly tired, simply keep driving all night, or until you are tired. Then sleep in the car. Or alternate drivers so you can each get some sleep. Driving all night can be surprisingly painless when you've been in a steady routine. It can also change your perception of the trip.

POISON-FOOD
Reprinted from Good Times, San Francisco, Ca.

"Poison is as American as apple pie. Have some:

fruit juice. Fruits are bombarded with pesticides. The juices almost always contain DDT and the nerve-gas pesticide parathion (it killed the sheep).

milk. Cow's milk is still considered safe, because of the relatively low concentration of DDT in pasture grass. But women in England are being encouraged not to breast-feed their babies because the concentration of DDT in our diets has made mother's milk unsafe.

beer. To give it 'lightness and life' the chemical compound PVP is added. This ingredient is also used in hair sprays.

roast beef. A thick juicy slice comes from a cow born by artificial insemination, injected with sex hormones to increase fertility, fed synthetic hormones to induce rapid fattening, and shot with tranquilizers, antibiotics and insecticides. The sex hormones, an estrogen called stilbestrol, are suspected of affecting human sexual functioning. A real man's meal . . .

the cheeseburger. Hamburger meat is dyed. Worse, it may be treated with sodium sulphate in order to give it an appealing red color. This chemical is especially dangerous since it destroys both the black color and the rancid odor of bad meat. Cheese on top increases both the flavor and the poisonous content of one of our favorite dishes.

cheese. Cheese is processed by a multitude of chemicals. It is artificially thickened, preserved, flavored, and colored. One of the thickeners is also used to make cosmetics, another is used in printing inks. (Until recently cottage cheese preservative was also used to make contraceptives.)

peas and carrots. In order to retard spoilage, fresh vegetables are waxed with a parafin suspected of causing cancer.

bread. Wheat is stripped of all its nutrients; only the starch is retained because it holds synthetic vitamins and water so well. Emulsifiers keep bread soft but do not stop it from becoming stale. Bread is as plastic as its wrapper. It helps break strong bodies 8 ways . . .

candy. Top it all off with packaged candies, coated with shellac to produce an attractive glaze.

The most frightening additives are the carcinogens, which the Public Health service estimates include one out of every four substances injected into our food. Carcinogens are substances suspected of causing cancer. Carcinogenic substances are found in most food dyes and preservatives, and in stabilizers used in salad dressing, ice cream, chocolate milk, commercial whipped cream. Carcinogens include the estrogens injected into poultry and livestock, and pesticides. Radioactivity from fall-out or contamination from water or soil is also considered a carcinogen.

The major source of poison in our diets is DDT, the effects of which are cumulative. DDT may destroy our ability to reproduce by increasing the activities of enzymes which attach sex hormones.

It has been claimed that children may be more susceptible to carcinogens than adults. Today, cancer causes a greater number of child deaths than any other disease, and cancer deaths among children have increased 50% in the last decade.

The facts themselves are enough to induce nausea. Only one point need emphasis. Chemicals are injected into foods in order to produce more foods faster, in order to sell inferior products at a better price, in order to stretch the quantity of food at low cost to the producer. IN ORDER TO MAKE MORE MONEY. The farmer has been superseded by the food technologist who works for a food factory.

Chemical consumption is creating serious imbalances in our internal systems; it is producing ill health, and possibly death. Ironically, the chemicalization of the dinner table is affecting even the ruling class who wants the profits; they can't eat their money, and now they can't even eat their food."

A THEORY OF EATING. Eating, even more than sleeping, is subject to perversion and misunderstanding. It's one of the genuine pleasures of life and one of the special attractions of travel. The kinds of food people eat and the way they prepare it reflects their personalities, income, history, and geography. Sampling someone's diet or better yet, sharing it with them, is to learn a great deal about them. Of course, in America we're already familiar with our national fare, but you'll find regional specialties to excite your palate (if they're good), or pall your excitement (if they're not). Every part of America cooks in its own style, with its own preferred foodstuffs, based on local availability and local history.

The problem with eating in America is somewhat different than sleeping here. American lodging in general is adequate but too expensive, whereas the problem with food in America is that it may be cheap but it's usually inadequate. Bear in mind that when you're traveling, your food requirements generally decrease because your body does less work. Unfortunately, the boredom of modern travel frequently leads to overeating, and one of the most common ills suffered by travelers is constipation. But because the quality of food is so bad, the next most common problem is diarrhea. Finding a decent meal at a decent price is difficult to do consistently in America. You can either find good meals at expensive prices, or bad food at reasonable prices. Even for those people who can afford good food, the meals available are usually too rich or too large as a daily diet for travelers.

My theory of eating is simple: Travelers need to eat good food in relatively small quantities at reasonable prices. "Good food" means food that isn't spoiled by age, cooking or bad sanitation; hasn't been stripped of nutrition by factory processing; isn't polluted by chemical additives and insecticides; tastes good because of care and experience in preparation. "Small quantities" means eating according to your caloric and health needs, taking into account how much energy you're putting out. "Reasonable prices" is a relative term, depend-ing on the quality of the food and how much money you can afford. You're most likely to get it when you pay for food without an elaborate setting of decor, not atmosphere, and service.

Good food needs to be so carefully defined because there isn't much of it around. Unless you carefully select and prepare it yourself, you can't guarantee its goodness. A meal that tastes OK may be polluted or infected with bacteria, or it may simply lack any nourishment. Last year the US Senate was told by nutrition experts that the American diet is so "terrible" (at all economic levels, rich and poor) that it costs $30 billion a year in extra health care. Poor eating habits were blamed largely on the food and advertising industries, which were charged with "spending millions of dollars to develop and promote nutritionally worthless foods."

That refers to all food consumed, not just food available to travelers. Can you understand why it's even worse at restaurants that cater to travelers they'll never see again? Bye bye, baby ... take your indigestion down the road. "And remember folks, to keep from constipation, eat our food and try regurgitation."

Even where the intention is good, as in honest restaurants, private homes, and your own portable kitchen, you may be eating inadequately because shoppers are misled by packaging and processing to the point that they can't tell the food from the garbage. You may say, "Come on – we're all alive and healthy, you nut." But you better look again at rising disease and disability rates due to de-nutrified diets – at heart attacks, cancers, hypertension; at dental decay, at obesity, at digestive disturbances. You may not be as healthy as you think, you nut!

Tourists characteristically eat like pigs because food is the most exciting event of their day, even when it's awful. They munch their breaded poisoned frozen tasteless dogburger and say "Mmmm, that was worth driving 200 miles for, wasn't it?" Wrong again. Then they order another helping, plus dessert – anything

to stay away from the road for awhile. Even if the food wasn't very good, they'll say the decor was nice — the plastic flowers, the air-conditioning, the cute costumes, the color scheme, the scented toilet bowls.

The big question is: Can you get good food in America? If so, how and where? Let's look at the possibilities . . .

RESTAURANTS The best restaurant meal we got in America was at a cafeteria-style place in Arkansas — the Ozark Gardens Restaurant. For around two dollars each we had a delicious meal of fresh vegetables, choice of beef or chicken, dessert, and second helpings. It was a good meal because the food was fresh and tasty, self-served, inexpensive, and there was plenty of it. The restaurant was clean and pleasant, with good service, and the cashier was a nice lady who chatted about the locale (and how much it had worsened since the tourists came), asked where we were from, etc. It was a combination you'd think more places would attempt. Unfortunately, most haven't. (The only chain restaurant at which we thot the food good was Bill Knapp's, a midwest chain.)

The food problem in America, I think, is a combination of unconsciousness and greed. Maybe they're the same thing. There's no intrinsic reason for getting bad food in America — good food is available, easy to make, and it doesn't cost much. A good profit could be made by serving good food. But the American ethic calls for MORE profit, EXCESSIVE profit, and at some point along in there the food simply goes to hell. All the restaurants advertise good food for miles around and lots of money goes into that. More money goes into the building, the parking lot, the decor, the costumes of the girls, the music and lighting, the plexiglass tables, the expensive plastic flowers. And then when you sit down to the food you find that that's where they all agreed to cut expenses — by using "efficient" food and unconscious cooks.

Unfortunately, in today's restaurant business you make everything in batches by an easy formula that allows you to hire cheap help, then you put in preservatives, freeze the rest. You standardize everything for more profit. Cut it into equal size portions. Heat it a little on demand and serve it up. Most of it is muck. I mean, it's literally true that you can get a little patty of fried something-or-other at any restaurant and you can't tell what it is except that it's the protein entree — some kind of flesh, fish, fowl, or soy, but its identity has been processed away.

So what do you do? First of all, admit to yourself that you patronize these ridiculous restaurants primarily out of convenience (laziness) and from fear of the unknown. There are plenty of independent one-only restaurants around, but you don't know what to expect in them, and you're not sure how to find the good ones. Entering a strange restaurant in a strange town tends to frighten tourists, who would rather endure a mediocre meal at a familiar chain-restaurant than face up to finding and experiencing some local cafe. It's simply a matter of consciousness — knowing that other options are available and not being afraid of them. After that it's easy. As with any other fear, you simply move toward it . . . and it either retreats or disappears entirely.

MORE CHAINS ON MY MIND

Swiss Chalet	Hardee's
Stuckey's	Krispy Kreme
Howard Johnson	Long John Silver
Copper Kettle	H Salt Fish & Chips
Copper Penny	Hot Shoppes
Taco Bell	Howdy
Taco Tia	Bill Knapp's
Kentucky Fried Chicken	Sweden House
Burger Chef	Denny's
Big Boy	Sambo's
Burger Town	Carvel
Burger King	Dairy Queen
Borden Burger	Dairy Creme
McDonald's	Dairy Cream
Lum's	Dairy Dream
Royal Castle	Dairy Kreme
White Castle	Dairy King
Dutch Pantry	Dairy Bar
Horne's	Dairy Freeze
Ranch House	Dairy Princess
Morrison's	Dairy Sweet
Waffle House	Dairy Kool
Toddle House	Dairy Delite
Doggie Diner	Country Dairy
House of Pancakes	Kreme King
Pizza Hut	Fosters Freeze
Shakey's Pizza	Tastee Freeze
Red Coach Grill	

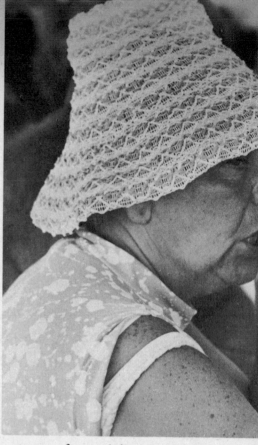

"FAST FOODS DRAINING U.S. RESOURCES"
Chicago Sun-Times

"America, a nation that delights in wheeling into a drive-in and gulping down an instantaneous meal, is squandering its natural resources and energy supplies on fast foods.

So concludes Bruce M. Hannon, an engineer at the University of Illinois, after studying the operations of a fast-food chain restaurant.

Hannon calculated that the McDonald's chain of 1750 restaurants used up the energy equivalent of 12.7 million tons of coal last year.

"That's enough energy to keep the cities of Pittsburgh, Boston, Washington and San Francisco supplied with electric power for the entire year," he said.

"It takes the sustained yield of 315 square miles of forest to keep McDonald's supplied with paper packaging for one year," he said.

McDonald's is the nation's fourth largest server of food. It trails only the Army, the Kentucky Fried Chicken chain and the Department of Agriculture's Food and Nutrition Service.

"My objective is not to pick on McDonald's. They're probably no worse than Burger Chef, Big Boy, Wimpy's, White Castle, Burger King, Dairy Queen and all the others. They are a symbol of our nationwide waste of material and energy resources.

I'm just trying to drive home the lesson that we cannot afford to keep on living as if there is no tomorrow."

As an experiment for awhile, try eating anywhere except at chain restaurants. First of all, the food won't be worse, most likely much better. The same holds true for the prices. But one of the best reasons is to get out from under the impersonal shroud that covers the American freeway driving experience. Local restaurants and cafes of Main Street America are full of life and warmth, personalities and characters. People talk to each other, exchange the latest gossip, even ask strangers where they're from and where they're going. It make take you 15 minutes extra to leave the freeway, drive into town and find a restaurant — but you're likely to observe more about that region over your meal than you could discover by eating for a week at the interstate chain-restaurants.

Looking back on a tour of America, some of the most interesting places of all were the funky restaurants, the family roadhouses, the ordinary cafes where America and its people can still be seen "in the rough" — farmers, truck drivers, local businessmen, ranchers, salesmen, housewifes, waitresses. By contrast, the bright sterility of the 'rest-stop' restaurant and its gleaming anonymity leads only to heartburn and heartache.

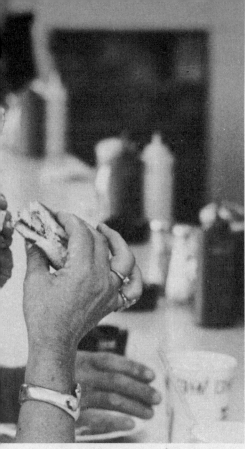

There is no infallible way to locate a good restaurant anywhere. You're on your own. Which is great, actually. Throw out the guidebook and make an adventure of it. When you get into town, drive around a bit, scout a couple of places. Maybe park the car and look them over on foot. Peer inside the window. Don't be shy; if someone stares at you, smile and wave. See if there is a menu or bill of fare posted on the outside (this European custom is slowly gaining favor with American restaurants). If in doubt, simply ask a passerby for the whereabouts of a place serving good food.

Once inside, don't worry about being a stranger. Hell, you're a customer and a person, just like everybody else there. They'll probably know you're a stranger anyway, so trying to look like one of the locals doesn't go far. On the other hand, don't make a big scene to declare your bravado and identity. You're just going to eat a meal in what is probably a pleasant place with good people in it, so stroll in nice and easy, sit down and relax yourself. Let the tension ease out of your body; relax those stomach muscles. Put the road out of your mind, turn your attention to your traveling companion(s) or to your surroundings, and enjoy one of the good experiences of life . . .

Off The Tape
RAILROADING YOUR STOMACH

In Albuquerque, we just ate at The Drumstick. I was attracted to the place because in big letters on the outside it says COME AS YOU ARE. Their specialty was chicken and I figured they couldn't foul up the fowl too badly. So we parked and went up to the door, where the first thing we saw was a sign saying Shoes Must Be Worn And Shirt Must Be Buttoned. So much for come-as-you-are.

I was prepared for perhaps a poor meal and glossy decor, but the reality exceeded my expectations. In the center of the restaurant were two large plastic geranium plants and two plastic trees. Surrounding them were the tables and chairs — a field of French-grill iron lawn chairs painted white. Around the periphery of the room were decorator carriage lamps and Japanese lanterns. Nevertheless, the main illumination came from fluorescent lamps nestled amidst the false beams on the ceiling. A Lionel train set circled over part of the room and was labelled the "Biggest Little Train in the World."

The chicken was breaded and fried into oblivion — dry and tasteless. Stephanie ate only a few bites and even I, the Polack slob, couldn't get all mine down. On the way out, the cashier sweetly asked how we liked it and Stephanie shook her up by saying it was "terrible." The girl was flustered — obviously no one had ever told the truth before. Why not?

MAKING YOUR OWN MEALS This is an obvious solution, at least part of the time. Even without a stove, you can make many of your own meals: cold cereals for breakfast, sandwiches for lunch, tuna salads for dinner. The materials are as close as your supermarket. The price is right and the effort is minimal. You don't get super meals from the supermarket, but they're frequently an improvement on what you can buy at your local greaseburger stand, and moreover, they're really easier than pie. Markets and stores are so plentiful across America that you need to buy only what you can eat at the next meal. Nor is there any shortage of places to eat. Roadside tables and parks, picnic areas and rest areas dot the American road system. Restaurant meals during the day, that is for breakfast or lunch, should be an occasional happenstance, to break the routine or sometimes to simplify a hectic day or a hectic schedule. You'll appreciate it most at the end of the day when you're tired. If you're making meals, supper's the hardest to prepare, takes the longest time, needs the most

equipment, and maybe this is the one you should consistently plan to buy ready made. It's also the one that gives you the best chance to sample the local specialty, to combine with the hotel stop, or to completely relax.

On the other hand, for those who are into cooking, chapter 7 on camping and chapter 13 on backpacking offer more information. Outdoor camp-cooking can be a great experience. Can you see yourself pulling into a campsite at some state park or other campground after a hard day of driving? Can you picture a beautiful spot, under some trees or by a creek, or at the base of some mountains, close to the grass and to the water, as you start the fire and get the first odors from the pot? Its fun and free, the cost is small, and good food is just one of the rewards.

SUPPER AT HOME How about a real home-cooked meal (as they say in the ads)? Sound better than a restaurant meal or a campsite meal? You bet, so why not show up for dinner at the homes of your friends and relatives, the homes of the people you visit, and the people who invite you into their homes? Anyone can arrange to stop across country and visit in private homes, and they should. These are usually the best meals of all because they're shared with people that you can relate to, people who feed you and share what they have with you as a gesture of their hospitality. To cook for a guest is an act of love and you'll got a few bad meals from an American host or hostess in their own home. Hospitality is an American tradition.

However, there are always social amenities to be observed, whose exact nature depends on the circumstances and your relationship to the people you're visiting. Sometimes it's OK to shout "What's for dinner?" when they open the door, but in other cases it'll cost you not only the meal but entrance to the house. Sometimes you'll know beforehand that you're coming for dinner, or that you're not. Frequently your visit will come on short notice, or no notice, and dinner may or may not be possible.

In general, you should call ahead to announce your visit by at least an hour and preferably more. If you don't know your host well, plan to pay a social call only, and count on nothing more. The offer of a meal or a bed must come graciously from the host without hints. It almost always does, but don't count on it — that's pushing your luck. Moreover, it makes you anxious about whether the invitation will be forthcoming. Relax . . . you'll get, you'll get!

Sometimes your host may be hungrier or in more need than you, so you should be the one to offer dinner — either by buying some food and cooking it, or by taking him out to a restaurant. Particularly in the case where you've received several meals or several days of hospitality, common courtest dictates that you offer to do dishes, cook meals, share food costs, or some similar gesture of gratitude in the form of work-sharing or cost-sharing.

OTHER FOOD TRIPS A couple of other food possibilities exist.

One is eating from roadside fruit and vegetable stands, which can supply at least the bulk of your between-meal snacks, and sometimes whole meals. The advantages are low prices for good merchandise, the opportunity to take a break from driving, and the down-to-earth character exuding from many of these stands and their operators.

This same produce can be gotten directly from the growing fields, too, if no one else is around. However, this is a snack possibility for hitchhikers and bicyclists, primarily. Motorists and motorcyclists who stop to pick fruit somehow seem far more like thieves. It's because they have a fast getaway vehicle, I suppose. If you're on foot, it seems natural to help yourself to a fruit tree occasionally.

Whether or not you're a student, eating at the cafeterias and student unions of colleges and universities is a good idea. There are usually some small cost savings, but the main benefit is again the *ambiance*. College campuses are always interesting, yet they're virtually *terra incognita* to most Americans past 25.

Exercises

FOOD EXERCISES

1) Figure or find different ways to eat supper for less than one dollar per person. Go to a supermarket and then cook for yourself, eat at a really cheap restaurant, buy some wine and eat at a friend's home . . . whatever.

2) Set out to eat supper for no less than $10 per person. Do this in some big city and dig the feeling of splurge!

3) Eat lunch in any small town (3,000 or less) not in an urban area. Think about how it's different from a city cafe, and speculate about the other customers. What kind of people do you think they are?

4) Eat lunch in a downtown lunch-counter or raunchy cafe in a big city. Bring the wife and kids — it's even better that way. How does this make you feel? Look at the other customers, and feel how it would be to live their lives.

5) If the food you get is terrible, and the waitress or cashier asks if you're enjoying it, take courage and say no. Tell her why. If the service is bad, take courage and don't leave a tip.

6) If the food you got was especially good, take the trouble to compliment the waitress, the cook, or the owner. Tell them why you liked it. If the service was especially good, thank the waitress personally and hand her the tip yourself.

7) When eating in restaurants, make a general rule about always asking the waiter or waitress what's good today, what do they recommend. It'll put you in human touch and improve your diet.

8) Go to a supermarket and buy the ingredients for a super picnic. Bread, cheese, lunchmeat, condiments, chips. salad, pickles, fruit, beer or wine, and whatever other delicacies you favor. Go out and find the prettiest, quietest spot you can. Enjoy.

9) Go into a restaurant and tell the waiter you want a meal for $_____ . Have him choose it and bring it . . . tell him anything he likes is fine; you want to be surprised.

10) Fast for a day or two. Think about all the trips that puts you thru. (Oh, it will!)

Off The Tape
TWO SCOOPS OF AMERICA

Here in Little America, America's new Travel Center. Open night and day. In Little America, Wyoming, 65 gas pumps. The driver of the car that picked me up stopped here for a break. I was going to get coffee, then looked at the menu and it said, 'dish of ice cream: 35 cents.' Well, I've had an upset stomach all day, probably from looking at the signs advertising Little America for hundreds of miles around. So I said to the waitress, 'Alright, I'll have some ice cream.' Later on when the bill came, the price of the ice cream was 45 cents. So I went and got the menu again and showed it to the waitress, that ice cream was only 35 cents. Well, she said, that's the price of one scoop, but unless otherwise specified we always give two scoops, and that's 45 cents. And I said OH and paid it. A little america, indeed.

Similarly, college students are probably easier to meet than any other group of Americans, and the quickest to help out if you need information or assistance.

If you're not a middle-class vagabond but more the lean and hungry type without money or friends in a strange town, look into what free meals are being offered. Most big cities have at least one soup kitchen in the downtown area, usually run by the Salvation Army or other religious mission service. Ask some of the local winoes where to get free meals, or call the local Switchboard or Traveler's Aid Society.

THE BEST MEAL STOP. Finally, there's the greatest meal stop of all: Fasting. That idea might strike you a little strange, but fasting actually helps travelers enjoy their trips more, and reduces food expenses. As I've pointed out, the tendency of travelers is to overstuff themselves with bad food. Fasting is a natural remedy that cleans out your body and straightens your head. Some of the character-

PROMISE KEPT
DREAM COME TRUE
ALWAYS OPEN - 17 MILES
LE AMERICA

istic side-effects of fasting are copious defecation and shedding of excess body mucus.

Other benefits are numerous and every one works for the traveler. First of all, fasting is a break from routine, and as you might expect from what I've already said about energy release, it gives you a noticeable energy boost. People who've never fasted think it tires you out, but the reverse happens. You feel alert and energized, yet calm. You perceive more; you experience more. And if the fast goes on beyond a day, you start to get quite stoned as well — very light and free.

I recommend an occasional one-day fast to all travelers as a kind of vagabond experience in exploring yourself. A short fast like that can't hurt you, and has every possibility of helping a lot — so why not try it? Get up one morning, simply skip breakfast and have juice instead. That's easy enough. Throughout the day, take juice or liquid breaks as you need. Put the energy that normally goes to meals into what's happening around you, and tune in on your own feelings. It's a good trip.

DAIRY DROOL

Soft ice cream stands are probably the most popular of the whole genre of American roadside restaurants. Look at how many different names they bear, proving the Yankee passion for ice cream (an American invention). And yea, verily, a thick frozen shake sucked up on a blazing afternoon drive thru American summer is one of the best things America has to offer. Mundane but great. If you order up a burger and fries with that shake, then you've got what makes most American mouths instantly fill with eager drool. None more so than mine, because I'm no more immune than you are. It's our American advertising heritage.

In Green River, Wyoming, on a parched and frustrating day, I flagged down a police car by honking and waving, then approached the patrolman and said, "This may sound silly, officer, but please tell me how to get to a Dairy Queen."

Camping And Car-Camping

The Outdoors Is In

7

CAMPING AND ENERGY Camping is a life-game in which we play at surviving in the forest primeval. It's make-believe for grown-ups, and it's fun to play if you don't bend the rules by making the game too easy. Things you take for granted at home, such as the electric light, become luxuries at the campsite — and you appreciate them anew when you're making do with equivalents such as a gas lantern or a candle. Many of your home comforts you'll do without entirely. Everything becomes a challenge again, and oddly enough, you find that it's fun to meet those challenges. Camping liberates you from your usual roles, too. For example, most men don't ever cook at home (it's against the roles) . . . but frequently do all the cooking at the campsite. It's more challenging than at home in your all-electric-kitchen, but mainly it's "manly" to cook outdoors — it allows you to change roles with

social approval.

What makes camping enjoyable is the new energy you release from new roles and new activities, in this case practicing survival skills like cooking, protecting yourself from rain, building fires, washing in icy waters, and all those "primitive" trips. The flow of energy released by those trips, primitive or not, is the great blessing of the outdoors. When you're playing at woodsman, problem-solving, and fire-starting, you're generating energy whose results you can see and feel directly — and you're alive in a way that feels good.

That's all there is to it. Energy flow feels good. Camping stimulates energy flow. Ergo, camping feels good. QED. Too much vehicle or too much equipment gets in the way of that energy release, and tho these gadgets blow up your ego and make the TI happy, they also tend to pinch off the energy.

The trick to it, just like everything else, is in finding the balance between, say, too much ease and too much challenge. The first is wasteful of materials and deadens the mind; the other makes you too afraid and uncomfortable. The first ties up all your energy in patterns; the other ties up all your energy in living without patterns. I suggest that it's everyone's task in life to develop the balance that works for them. In other words, some middle point that's up to you to discover will release the most free energy. So camping is like anything else. If you can get it together in that, it's a sign you can get it together elsewhere and vice-versa.

CAMPING AND THE TI Everyone understands that camping is a way to save money. Most campers started doing it because they couldn't afford anything else. But an amazing thing happened: They found it was more fun than any other vacation they'd had. They started to discover the relationship between value and cost again, namely, that the best ways to travel cost the least money. This is, of course, a basic tenet of vagabonding. Yet because of the efforts of the TI in particular, and the American merchandising system in general, this relationship between value and cost used to be one of the best-kept secrets of our time. Ah, Double-Think.

Vagabonds have always been disreputable in America, partly because they knew this secret and had to be kept down. Thus hoboes and hitchhikers represented an economic threat: they traveled free, flaunting the system. Anyone who traveled light and cheap was suspect. The backpacker/camper for decades was regarded as some kind of nut, not to be taken seriously. Bicyclists were even crazier, and more annoying because they messed up your car if you ran them over. Tramps and jobless drifters were the worst of all — raffish outcasts from the mainstream of society. Frequently they were even persecuted as criminals. These early-day vagabonds were the individualists of their time. While their contemporaries kept their proboscises perpetually to the car-

borundum, paying bills and dogging their duties, these vagabonds were out there on the road and out-of-doors, living better with little.

The secret has now leaked out. The importance of camping to America is that it is revealing the secret to the great middle-class mass of America. Camping is the way that anyone can avoid the outrageous travel costs heretofore foisted on the public. Air travel, first-class hotels, and expensive restaurants are the standard profit package in the Industry. For years, this package was used to promote economic snobbery. Camping was dismissed as something for people with no class ("slobs") or no money ("poor") or no style ("nuts"). These stigmas worked for years, until the people themselves created a camping tide that couldn't be resisted. The rise of the vagabond class never bothered the Industry; it's still considered the lunatic fringe. But the rise of camping is something else. It enables millions of people to enjoy the best times of their lives, and never once dream of seeing a travel agent. That means trouble to the TI.

Naturally the Industry is fighting back, and with considerable success. It turned instead to making money from campers, especially by selling them things they didn't need. The Industry started promoting camping and hiking when it re-defined campers as consumers who convert the wilderness into cash. They developed "recreational vehicles" that enable you to "camp" but cost even more than any airplane-hotel-restaurant package could. These vehicles not only ruin your ability to get genuine experience from the outdoors, but ruin the outdoors at the same time. The Industry developed a gleaming cornocopia of "camping equipment" for a mass market. Much of it is unnecessary or of questionable value, and most of it is cheaply made and poorly designed — profitable junk that falls apart or gets no use. The industry developed off-road vehicles (ORV's) such as snowmobiles, trail bikes, and dune buggies, which offer yet another mechanized thrill for the mechanical consumer. Naturally, the profits come directly from the natural environments that are decimated by the use

of these abortions. The Industry developed luxurious campgrounds at prices that hotels charged not too many years ago. The Industry developed tours in which you stay at "wilderness lodges" or trail camps after your daily dose of the outdoors; and pay dearly for your "camping" experiences.

In short, by co-optation and corruption, the Industry is trying to collect its dues regardless of the switch from conventional travel to camping. Ironically, the profits the Industry rakes off are not the real cost. The irony is dual: First, the money spent is actually a barrier that separates the buyer from the desired experience; second, the money spent goes into destroying the quality of the experience, and ultimately the very existence of the experience. As mentioned elsewhere, the amount of wilderness left is miniscule compared to the population now awakening to its values. Clearly, the only way to enjoy the wilderness without sacking it is by developing a higher mass consciousness. It seems that it should work, because curiously enough, the ways to get the most out of camping are the ways that least disturb the environment.

Off The Tape
SIERRA MEETS THE SIERRA

Last nite we slept at Indian Springs in Tahoe National Forest. In many ways, this is a typically American campground. The South Yuba River rushes by. Clean granite rocks. Nice stands of timber all around, surrounded by high peaks. And directly across from the campground is Interstate 80. There's constant freeway noise, especially of long distance trucks making their way to the west coast cities.

The campground is on the honor system. You fill out a card with your vehicle number, you pay two dollars and you put it in the box. It's a testimonial to the honesty of most Americans, when put on their honor. There are toilet facilities in the campground — for men and women there is a two-holer each, mint-scented, tho there's no shortage of dead flies around. Deep down in the shit-hole you can see beer cans amongst the other refuse. A purely American touch.

This is baby Sierra's first trip to the Sierra and I anointed her in the stream. She had let loose this incredible shit that was bubbling up over the edges of her diapers, so I stripped her and took her down to the Yuba River and dumped her in. She screamed some but it was fitting somehow that Sierra meet the Sierra this way. Earthy and watery at the same time.

101

CAMPING IS NATURAL Camping means living outdoors. By implication, it means discovering the values of Nature, all of which are (or were) outdoors. These values elude exact definition, but have to do with experiencing a natural environment from the inside (that is, from the outside). Not by observing, but participating. If you haven't hiked, swum, skied, climbed, been rained on, snowed in, exhausted by, or in some way personally involved with our forests, mountains, and canyon back country, no amount of photographs or text can render its incredible reality. Nature has no end of miracles on display for you, but you can only appreciate them by becoming part of them.

Come humbly and slowly. Watch and feel the vast energy shaping both mountains and mice, directing rivers and dewdrops alike, sprouting forests and flowers, creating canyons and clouds with equal patience. The stuff of eternity is under your feet; its workings are before your eyes; its energy blesses you with life. Beauty is not a spectacular arrangement of forms by an "artist" called God; it is simply the elegance and intricacy of every natural work, and the harmony and fitness of interaction between every natural work. We are all natural works. Becoming "unnatural" is what destroys our beauty, and causes us to destroy it around us.

Camping correctly means doing whatever brings you closer to Nature without destroying it or your appreciation of it. On the one hand, if you enter the wilderness unprepared, without adequate food or equipment you'll probably fail to appreciate it. (John Muir was an exception; he took almost nothing and was ecstatic.) The other extreme is to enter it with too much equipment, so that it isolates you from really coming into contact with the outdoors. This approach is wildly prevalent today, so let's have a look at what you actually need, starting with vehicles.

VEHICLES AND CAMPING I know you'll be sorry to hear this, but vehicles do *not* go camping. *You* go camping. It's necessary to make this distinction because many people think that camping means living in your car, whereas in fact, camping means living outdoors. Your car or other vehicle is just a means of getting to the camping place. It isn't the place. Thus, altho we all speak of car camping (and I do too), we should clearly understand the differences between living in your car and living outdoors. If you leave your car when you reach a campsite, put up a tent, cook outdoors, sleep in your tent, use your feet to travel when you move about, then all of that is certainly genuine camping. But when you travel by car, sleep in your car, cook in your car, that is emphatically not camping, but car-camping. The distinction is important because for the most part, camping is ecologically sound, whereas car-camping is not. Car-camping is economical and comfortable, but it is neither ecological nor an outdoor experience. Let's see what the criteria are for several kinds of camping vehicles.

ALL-PURPOSE VEHICLE In my estimation, the least specialized vehicle is the best because it serves the most purposes. A small, used van or pick-up is closest to being the ideal vehicle . . . it's a moveable space that can be used for any purpose. It can be bought cheaply, serviced easily, and driven either long or short distances economically. While traveling it can be lived in and when not being used for vacation travel or vagabonding use, it becomes a family car to haul groceries or the kids, or furniture, or tools, or whatever. Or it can be permanently lived in. It has side and rear doors for easy access, windows in the rear, and perhaps one window on the right side so that the driver can see into the truck's blind spot. More windows than that require curtains and cause heat loss in winter. For a better way to get light, build a skylight in the roof. The interior of the van should be left open insofar as possible, altho the sides should be paneled and insulated and a rug shaped onto the floor. With a portable stove and portable sink and sleeping bags to roll out at night, the vehicle becomes a sleeping unit. Move those objects aside and it can be used for anything else.

For more comfortable truck camping on a long trip, something like a postal van affords more space and hominess. *A book* called *Roll Your Own "* — see Appendix 1 under "Car Camping" — describes how to buy and equip these and other used vehicles for camping. One of its authors, Jody Pallidini, is a neighbor of mine and I've traveled in her van, "The Brown Rose of Tibet." Purposely drab on the outside, the inside is a blaze of color, with a skylite in the roof that keeps it brightly and warmly lit. Hand-done batiks, wall hangings, travel posters, Hindu posters, and portraits of Yoga masters cover the walls. There's some hanging lacework, a talisman of eagle feathers and bone, several sets of wind chimes in different colors, and examples of Hawaiian tapa cloth, Indian mirror cloth, and a patchwork bedspread. The bookshelf includes children's books and games — also Scrabble, Sorry, and Scam (the import game of dope dealing). For music, a tamborine and stereo tape deck. A charcoal/wood stove (pipe out the top) furnishes both heat and cooking. There's a couch on one side and a storage/pantry area on the other. At night, fitted boards and foam mattresses form a front-to-back, wall-to-wall bed. On the top is the spare tire, a rubber raft and oars. The truck's high road clearance and low-low gears mean it can go off the paved road, too. Clearly, it's a "recreational vehicle," but unlike the mass-produced ones, it's small, cheap, colorful, and has other uses.

CARS AND CAMPER VANS The ordinary passenger car is a specialized vehicle because it's intended only to transport people in comfort and style. Considering its limited services, it's a poor investment as a vehicle. No amount of chrome trim makes it suitable for camping, tho it helps if it's a model with reclining seats. If you load it with camping equipment such as tent, stove, sleeping bags, etc. — the car can be used for camping, but severe space problems are created. That's why a van is so useful — it's space hasn't already been permanently committed to seats and styling — it's still available for storage, for example.

If you insist on owning a passenger-type vehicle, then at least make it a station wagon. This goes a long way toward reclaiming usable space, yet retains the alleged dignity of the passenger vehicle. My first extended automobile tour of America — a six week 8,000-mile jaunt in 1956 — was via Ford station wagon, with a mattress in the back and a luggage carrier on top. My wife and I camped almost entirely by the roadside and in fields (got stuck a few times), and it was the first car that made me realize the utility of space. Afterwards, I bought my first van, and have owned one almost continuously ever since.

However, a commercial camping van, that is, one with built-in shelves and closets, built-in appliances and table, is already an over-specialized vehicle. The built-ins give you a measure of comfort that only serves to seduce you from the values of living outdoors, and usually cannot be removed easily if you want to use the space for something else later on. Since the innards are attached, you always haul them with you even when you're not using the car for camping (actually non-camping). Finally, these factory versions of camper vans are always expensive

The van-type camper is the most popular form of camping vehicle seen today, no doubt because they're a good compromise between the over-specialized in-one-way passenger car and over-specialized in-another-way Recreational Vehicle. But if you can make do without a super-duper model, you'll save money and enjoy yourself just as much. If you must have one, buying it second-hand can save you hundreds or thousands of dollars, and you'll get a better-equipped van which has been de-bugged and improved by the former owner. Or you can also buy a new or used stripped van and install your own camper kit. It doesn't require much skill, tools, or materials.

RECREATIONAL VEHICLES Going further toward non-camping are the super-specialized vehicles such as piggy-backs, trailers, and Winnebago-type land cruisers. They are useful only for car-camping — unlikely to be scooted about town or driven to work — and tend to be a waste of your money and our natural resources. The piggy-back camper can be an exception — at least when removable from the truck. However, few of its owners actually need or use a truck apart from camping. That is, they buy the complete package and never separate the camper unit from the truck.

One of the great success stories of recent years is the boom in Recreational Vehicles — Reckers — of which the Winnebago brand is the prototype and symbol. Winnebago Industries, Inc. of Iowa had 1971 sales of $133 million, and is building a second factory in Nevada which eventually will build 250 motor homes a week! The governor of Nevada welcomed Winnebago, saying it will "boost our economy while not polluting the environment." This is a fairly typical example of double-think, because while seemingly true, it's in fact a lie in the larger sense. The boost in the economy comes from using precious resources for trivial luxury products, ultimately a ripoff that destroys the larger economy, no matter what it does for Nevada right now. And while the factory may not pollute the Nevada environment, the products to be mass-produced there are expressly designed for destroying and polluting the wilderness of the whole country, as well as the quality of experience of the people that use them.

A park ranger in Grand Teton National Park told me that the founders of the Winnebago company are now all millionaires, and the money they've reaped comes directly out of the national parks and recreation areas of America — a direct rip-off. The ranger went on to say that people that own recreational vehicles ought to stay home. When they want to go to the Tetons they should relax in the privacy of their vehicles and pull down little Teton-painted windowshades, perhaps see a slide show on the walls. But if they want to see the Tetons, *really* see them, they should see them on the Teton's terms, which means leaving the Winnebago at home. The wilderness experience — the outdoor wonder of America — doesn't even begin to happen to you in your Recker. To bring a complete home on wheels into the woods is an insult to the spirit of camping and a vulgar show of ecological ignorance.

So, if you own one, sell it and start to kiss your ignorance goodbye. The money you'll have in hand will buy you a simpler, more versatile vehicle, and lots more time in which to enjoy it. You'll give up some comfort, certainly not to the point of suffering, and what you'll get back is far more than you gave up.

The only circumstance that justifies buying a Recker is for permanent or semi-permanent traveling on the road. Some retired couples choose to spend their last years vagabonding from place to place indefinitely. Other people take trips so lengthy that day-to-day comfort is important. Six months on the road, for example, makes you hungry for a little comfort. However, even in these cases, you're better off in one of the smaller models. Too much comfort leads to loss of experience, leads to isolation from what you came to see.

"ABORTIONS" This is my personal acronym for "American-Bought Off-Road Travel InventiON!" These uni-purpose wilderness vehicles, also called Off-Road Vehicles or ORV's, are the worst example of this specialized trend.

These ABORTIONS include trail bikes, snow-mobiles, dune buggies, all-terrain vehicles (ATV's), four-wheel-drive jeeps and trucks, and even power boats. All of them are characterized by the following: Internal combustion engine, fun to operate, don't need paved roads, little or no effort to use, and they tear up the natural environment. They now number about 5 million and their growth is explosive, much to the delight of the Industry and the terror of the conservationist. It's been estimated that an ABORTIONist causes 100 times more noise than the outdoorsman on foot and 200 times more physical damage to the landscape. Truly a curettage of Nature, a scraping away of its delicate life. Driving an ABORTION requires the least effort and the lowest consciousness of all. You pay your money, you go out to get your fun, and damn the wildlife, the ecology, the public, and the land.

The most widespread display of low consciousness on the American hiway is a Recker towing a power boat, with a trail bike strapped to the back, or some such variation. What's interesting is that the owner probably considers himself a cultural hero in his rig as it tears down the hiway on its way to tear up the woods. And he would get upset to be called by any of his true names. So powerful and successful are the propaganda mills of American industry that the menaces think themselves heroes.. Actually, this guy has the right idea: He wants to diversify his travel experiences with a variety of vehicles. His mistake is in buying expensive, motorized ones. He could just as well be driving a VW van with a small rowboat or rubber raft on top and a bicycle on the back. The idea is the same; the difference is the consciousness that underlies it.

There are other specialized vehicles, such as the motorcycle and the bicycle, of which only the bicycle can be said to be free of ecological taint. Yet both are at least much closer to the outdoors than any other kind of road vehicle. If you sleep out-of-doors while on a motorcycle or bicycle tour, then you can truly call yourself a camper because you live outdoors 24 hours per day — not just while stopped, but while moving as well. Riding a vehicle that exposes you to the air, to the scenery, to the sensation of movement is tremendously exciting, and is one of the primary rewards of these vehicles. It is claimed that ABORTION'S also reward their users with physical sensation and intimate contact with nature. The feeling is illusory in both cases inasmuch as the sensation comes from movement, not from being in true contact with nature. The motorcycle, at least, is on a road intended for that purpose so is relatively innocuous. Nevertheless, the bicycle is the only ecologically harmless vehicle.

"Once the whole is divided, the parts need names. There are already enough names."

—*Lao Tsu*
Tao Te Ching

NAMES TO BE NUMBED BY

Winnebago	Prowler
Covered Wagon	Mobile Traveler
Vagabond	Sycamore
Weekender	Silver Streak
Phoenix	Explorer
Bee Line	"Our Getaway Home"
Travel Queen	Land Master
Nomad	Road Runner
Northlander	Challenger
Skamper	Open Road
Stallion	Angelus
Holiday Rambler	Explorer
Ranger	Apollo
Safari	Four Star
Champion	Karibou
Swinger	Drifter
Royal Coachman	Sightseer
Nimrod	Siesta
Wanderer	et cetera
Hi-Lo	

Land Commander (You're following an Aristocrat)

Exercises

CAMPING EXERCISES

1) If you've got a car-camper in which you can sleep, then sleep outdoors for a change. See what a difference it makes in your feeling about the place. (It will.)

2) At a campground, ask around until you can get someone to come to dinner at your table, tent, or camper. (People might balk unless you tell them you made too much, and you need them to help you eat it.)

3) Ask neighboring campers to join you for coffee or tea after dinner at your tent. Put on a wood fire to spur conversation, which should be easy if you ask about them and their travels.

4) Start a driving day in mountainous, forested, or desert country and find a dirt road. Follow it for a few hours or a day; be prepared to camp by the roadside that nite. Bring ample food, water, supplies. Try to approach the beauty of the surrounding country however you can. Stop to survey the views or take pictures; take short or long hikes; stop to talk to other people along the way — tourists, rangers, Indians, hunters, fishermen, hikers.

5) Leave the highway at nite and find a place to park for the night without paying. Don't start looking till after dark and see where you wake up in the morning.

6) When you find a campsite you especially like, but have to leave in the morning to keep up with your itinerary, don't do it. Stay and settle for another day, or two, or a week. Try not moving for a whole day —relax by a mountain stream and fish, or read a book and sip coffee. Take a leisurely walk; meet some other folks, watch an animal.

7) Encourage your kids to meet other kids in the campground. If they're shy, introduce them to other kids yourself. Organize a popcorn fest after dinner for the kids all around.

EQUIPMENT FOR CAMPING The best way to learn about camping equipment is to write for free catalogs from mail-order suppliers, a whole gang of which are listed in the back of the book in Appendix 12 — Outdoor Equipment Suppliers. The stuff these guys will send you is exciting and educational. Most of the equipment is carefully described and illustrated, and comparing catalogs can give you an excellent idea of the range of equipment offered, and a good sense of their competitive features. If some of these suppliers are near you, visit their stores in person.

These suppliers offer the best outdoor equipment there is, and you shouldn't buy lesser quality. Buying discount-house sporting goods is false economy because the stuff is usually junk — poorly designed and/or badly constructed. In camping equipment, you usually get exactly the quality you pay for. If you buy only what you need, you can afford the best. Then it won't come apart when you're depending on it, and it'll last for years instead of months.

Talking or reading about how to select and use camping equipment is pretty dull. Actually, you don't need all that much, as I'll talk (briefly) about soon. There are many books available for novice campers about equipping yourself, and some are listed in the back of the book. However, you ought to be able to figure out what you need yourself. Consider carefully what your camping situations will be, and make a mental or actual checklist of the equipment you'll need to handle those situations.

For example, figure out how you're going to sleep. Will you be sleeping in the car on a mattress? Will you be sleeping outdoors on the ground? Sleeping in the car means you can do without a tent, sleeping bag, or air mattress. Sleeping outdoors means equipment. You'll need a sleeping bag for warmth, maybe an air mattress or sleeping pad to insulate you from the ground, and a ground cloth to keep your gear from moisture and abrasion. You also need something to shelter your sleeping rig in case of rain — a tent or tarp.

Going on to cooking gear is the same kind of reasonable process. Camping only in or near your car, you can use your regular kitchen pots, utensils, and accessories. But if you'll be hiking and cooking away from the car, you'll need a lightweight stove, pots, and food. Your range of menus will determine the extent and type of kitchen equipment you need to bring. People carrying their food with them on their backs should do some careful thinking about their menus and bring exactly what they need — no more, no less. Like, you don't need a spatula if you don't plan to make pancakes.

Most camp food can be prepared with a minimum of equipment. This is true even of car-camping where it's common practice to take everything from your kitchen and transfer it to your car. It's a mistake to make elaborate meals while camping. That's an indoor trip. Keep them simple but nourishing (and good). Otherwise you start longing for one more gadget, one more pot, an extra burner, an oven, egg-beater, waffle iron, and soon you'll be duplicating all the stuff you have at home because it comes in a slightly more lightweight camping version that you can cram into your car somewhere. Forget it.

Wherever possible, use something directly out of your kitchen at home. If you buy something you already have at home, it should only be because you're going to carry it on your back somewhere and it needs to be lighter, smaller, or more efficient. When you do buy camping equipment, buy absolutely the minimum amount. The more dependent upon equipment you become, the more likely you are to become a friend of the Industry and an enemy of the wilderness.

The same thing applies to clothing. Wear what you already have when it's impossible to do so. You should own a good pair of boots for the outdoors, but if you don't plan any extensive hiking, you don't need expensive hiking boots. Bring your old work boots to wear around the campsite. People who drive into camp in their tin-plated trailer or Day-Glo recreational vehicle, jump out wearing the latest in expensive down parkas, imported

GOLDEN EAGLE PASSPORTS

For $10 you can get the (1973) pass at all national parks and post offices. The pass admits a driver and passengers to any national park or forest for an unlimited number of times during the year. If you're over 62, it's called a Golden Age Passport, is free, and also gets you half-off on campground and other park fees.

Off The Tape
MARRIAGE

At a Maine campsite, we invited the neighboring couple to have tea with us after dinner. They were a young longhair couple from New Jersey, married just a few weeks. They were headed for Oregon and Washington to look for some land to start a farm. Once they got it, total self-reliance would be their goal; they were fed up with today's society. We asked why they got married when they had already been living together for some time. They said it avoided a lot of hassles, especially with her parents. She said it was amazing to see how getting married changed Jeff from a "no-good bum" into a "really wonderful person."

woolen slacks, mountaineering boots, then set up their elaborate kitchens and spend two weeks lying on their ass, guzzling beer and playing pinochle at night under the light of multiple gas lanterns, are caricatures, not campers.

The problems, as always, are ignorance and fear. People have always used money as a cover for ignorance but Americans, being rich, have built a reputation on it, especially in travel. Look at American tourists abroad; look at Rec Vec campers at home. Fear and ignorance interlock and reinforce each other: Ignorance makes you afraid, and fear makes you stupid. The truth is that you can't afford to be stupid when you don't have much money. That's one of the positive aspects of traveling cheaply. Vagabonds don't stay ignorant; they live and learn. Fear is also a natural companion to wealth. Money always makes you afraid, not only of losing your money but losing the energy that it stands for. Vagabonds don't have much money to lose and they're rich in energy, so they have less to be afraid of.

What it all means is that spending money on unnecessary equipment only builds a wall around you, keeping you from experiencing and gaining confidence in yourself.

SLEEPING BAGS Your sleeping bag should be your most expensive piece of equipment, and your most necessary one. You can make do with just about everything else when you're camping outdoors, but not without a good sleeping bag. You can go hungry for awhile or eat uncooked food, you can find natural shelters from the rain, and so forth, but if you miss your shuteye, it's only a matter of time until you crack up. A good sleeping bag is an investment in freedom. It frees you from your house, your possessions, your car; if means you can go into the heart of the wilderness and be content. Moreover, a quality sleeping bag lasts for many years. I've just retired a sleeping bag I paid $75 for in 1956. I estimate that I've slept in it at least 1000 nights (and like Sheherezade, there's a story for every one). So it cost me well under a dime a throw. Not too bad.

Even if you don't think you need a sleeping bag, or especially if you think you don't need a good one, I recommend that you get one anyway. Having a sleeping bag that enables you to experience the wilderness at its fullest will just naturally be an inducement to do it, whether or not you planned to originally. In other words, buying some kapock-filled piece of crap that you intend to use only in your car just traps you into staying with your car always. Buy the best bag you can afford and then be free to go anywhere at any time.

Down sleeping bags, each with their own features and advantages, are now manufactured by dozens of companies. Trying to sort thru them is a job, but one worth doing. Send for some of the catalogs from outdoor suppliers and read what they have to say about the factors influencing bag quality. Almost all manufacturers eloquently describe the parameters of sleeping bag design, and if you read a few of them you'll be able to make an intelligent choice. Some of the factors are quantity of down, type of down, type of bag construction, type of outside material, shape of bag, total weight, quality of construction, type and placement of zippers — and those are only the main features. There are also such factors as smell, taste, and sanitary disposal facilities. (Joke.) My own particular preferences run something as follows: The best. I prefer higher quality goose down over duck down, tho it costs more. I prefer a bag that has the full length zipper to allow for temperature control on nights that aren't so cold (my own bag — Bugaboo brand — also has a unique feature that allows the down to be shifted within the tubes from top to bottom to allow for temperature control). I prefer a modified rectangular shape — not a full rectangle, but still not as tight as the mummy. (It's more comfortable and makes the bag easier to use as a quilt when I'm not sleeping outdoors.) I prefer a bag that can be zipped to another for you-know-what (expanding to double my size at nite).

It's important to know that a sleeping bag alone does not provide protection from ground chill. This is because the down underneath you is compressed when you sleep and so does not protect you from cold underneath. A foam sleeping pad is much better than an air mattress. Air mattresses are heavy, need to be blown up and deflated, are forever leaking, and don't provide good insulation either (because of internal air currents). Foam mattresses are bulkier but never leak, are lightweight, and provide superior insulation and comfort.

TENTS Consider first whether you need one. In fifteen years of camping — including car-camping, backpacking, mountaineering, and vagabonding — I've yet to buy my first tent. Nevertheless, there were times when I wished I had one, and not just for keeping the rain out. They're also a Godsend for insect-ridden environments. Also, don't overlook the privacy that a tent can give you, especially in today's overcrowded campgrounds, some of which look more like pig farms than recreation grounds. There are, of course, other ways to solve the problem for which the tent is merely the most materialistic solution. Plastic or cloth tarps can easily be made into a variety of rain shelters, especially if the tarp has grommets and you carry some poles that allow rigging it in a variety of ways. In most locales, insects are not a problem, but where they are you can use insect repellant or head netting. As for privacy, you can strike out for places where privacy still exists, or just do your thing(s) anyway. A tent is a womb away from home, and like any other womb it isolates you from what lies outside its walls. Moreover, a womb costs money, takes time and trouble to set up and break down, and adds more pounds to your luggage, especially if you're carrying it on your back. Consider the hardships you'll endure if you don't get a tent or don't bring one. Then consider the extra freedom from equipment and greater challenge to your ingenuity if you don't have one.

If you still decide you want a tent, then (to repeat myself) the best place to start looking is in the catalogs of outdoor suppliers. They also describe and sell fly-sheet awnings, tarpulins, tube tents, ponchos, pole and pegs, guyline tighteners, and neat gadgets called Visklamps (for attaching guylines to plastic tarps). Examine the literature carefully and see what best suits your needs. Try to keep it simple, but don't waste your money by getting a tent without mosquito netting, without a waterproof floor, and without a separate fly sheet to make it waterproof. The right tent — that is, the one designed to keep out bugs, keep you dry, and be light enough to carry and constructed enough to last, will cost you around a minimum of $60 going on up to over $200. However, you can buy a two-man tube tent for around $3 so don't rush into buying a full-rigged tent simply for the glamor of it all.

COOKING GEAR First you need a fire source. There are two basic kinds of fires available to the camper. The first is the wood fire, the natural fire. The second is the stove, burning gasoline, butane, or propane. The order of mention is also the order of desirability. A wood burning fire requires the least equipment and gives the most rewards. It's not as efficient as refined-fuel stoves, but involves a ritual of wood gathering, fire starting, and expertise of use that appeals to the independent woodsman in us all. Unfortunately, the time is past when we can count on using wood as a fuel anymore. In some places at some times, wood is acceptable and abundant. These places and these times grow fewer and fewer. Most national parks now forbid natural wood burning unless you bring it yourself into the park. (We bought a supply of it in Maine which we strapped onto the luggage carrier and carried across country. One time, stuck in sand on a back road in Massachusetts the availability of that wood to put under the wheels was the only thing that got us out.) Of course you can buy Presto Logs when no wood is available. But even travelers into the back country are finding that all the wood is stripped or that there simply isn't enough to go around.

For this reason, all conscientious campers today should plan on using stoves that burn refined fuels. And don't forget to bring the fuels with you, either. The advantage is that with good planning, you'll never run out of flame. You'll be doing the ecological right thing and you can cook much more efficiently. There's no question that a wood fire is both slow and messy — it soots your pots and takes forever. So, it's easy to give up the glamor of wood fire for the utility of stoves, even disregarding the ecological implications. And, of course, this way you're still free to enjoy or use a wood fire where the supplies are ample.

So, of the two types of stoves, which is best? To my own mind, there's no question that the gasoline burning stove is better. The butane or propane stove is *inherently* better — less messy and less dangerous to us. But it only reaches its full efficiency if the fuel source is a relatively large container. Butane stoves with a big fuel tank are OK, but you only find these on large camping rigs. All the small stoves use propane cartridges which are a real pain in the ass to use. The fuel jets tend to clog because of internal dirt, mostly due to shoddy manufacturing. Even when that doesn't happen (which is frequently), as the cylinders empty they gradually lose pressure and the flame dies down accordingly. These problems never occur with gasoline burning stoves. They burn cleanly at high pressure, down to the last drop of fuel. The only disadvantage is that more care has to be taken with gasoline storage and in refueling the stove tank from your main fuel container. Nevertheless, my vote goes to the gas stove. The name Coleman has become synonomous in this country with the gasoline burning stove. These are efficient and reliable, but have always been surpassed in design by European manufacturers such as Primus and Optimus. Coleman stoves are designed for big and sloppy car-camping rigs. European models are much smaller, lighter, and more suited to all around use, outside as well as in the car.

POTS AND PANS Don't make a big deal of it. Use your household pots if you can, especially if you're just cooking out of your car. Backpackers and other weight-conscious types will need to buy a lightweight nesting set of pots. Beyond that you'll need some utensils, something in which to serve the food, and some biodegradable soap and scrubbing pads to clean up. Apply the same criteria as mentioned earlier for other equipment. Carefully think out your meals and determine exactly what you will need to cook, to serve, and to clean up afterwards. Add what is necessary, leave behind what isn't.

It's easy to go overboard on equipment, especially when you don't have much experience. It's true that the more experience you get, the less equipment you bring. In the wilderness, equipment is the equivalent of money. People make a show of it to hide their ignorance and fear. A better way is to start gathering your experience a little at a time, and buying only what you learn to be necessary thru that experience. See what other people are bringing and using, and don't be afraid to ask questions about how they're doing with their stuff. Just don't be overawed by somebody's super-duper spun magnesium wilderness crusher. Maybe it's just another jive gadget of the Industry.

The following is a list of things you might consider taking. It's just a checklist from which to make your own list, so don't you dare take all of these things. You'll be sorry if you do.

CAMPING EQUIPMENT LIST

COOKING EQUIPMENT

Bowls
Butter container
Can opener
Coffee pot
Cups (Sierra-Club type)
Dish pan
Dish towel
Fry pan
Firewood, charcoal
Griddle
Grill
Matches
Plastic bags
Plates (or Sierra Club cups)
Food containers
Pot tongs
Pots and saucepans, pref. nesting set)
Scrubbing pad
Soap for dishes (non-detergent)
Spatula
Stove
Utensils
Food (See lists in chapter 12)

CLOTHING

Bandanas
Gloves
Knit cap
Parka or windbreaker
Pants washable or Levi's
Sweater
Underwear
Sewing Kit
Belt

Hat, brimmed
Scarf
Shorts
Skirt, slacks
Socks, cotton or wool
Swim suit
Hiking boots
Moccasins, sneakers, or sandals

PERSONAL ITEMS

Hairbrush
Chapstick
Comb
Shampoo
Soap
Toilet paper
Toothpaste
Stash (?)
Smoking gear
Musical instrument
Watch
Metal mirror
Nail clippers
Nail file
Shaving gear
Sunglass, extra glasses
Toothbrush
Towel, washcloth
Birth controllers
Camera and film
Books, maps, guidebooks
Wallet
Cash
ID (driver's license)
Notebook
Pen/pencil

CAMPING EQUIPMENT

Sleeping mattress, air or foam
Air mattress pump
Air mattress repair kit
Binoculars
Candles, candle lantern
Canteen or bota
Chair or stool, folding
Compass
Clock or watch
Flashlite
Fuel bottle
Ground cloth or poncho
Hatchet
Lantern
Heater, portable
Lantern, gas
Maps
Matches
First aid kit (See chapter 15)
Backpack (See chapter 13)
Day Pack
Nylon cord
Pocket Knife (Swiss Army)
Repellant
Sleeping bag
Sleeping bag shell (winter use)
Portable sink
Tent or tarpaulin
Tent poles or stakes
Rip-stop tape (for fabric repairs)
Sporting equipment (don't forget a Frisbee)

First aid and medical matters are discussed in chapter 15, including a checklist of things to include. Backpacking advice and equipment is covered in a chapter all to itself, numbered 13 (for luck). The back of the book has appendixes listing other information sources about camping, equipment suppliers, park and recreation areas, and more.

FINDING CAMPSITES Anyone properly equipped for camping, whether traveling by camper, car, bike, cycle, or thumb — will experience little difficulty in finding places to do it.

First come the public campgrounds, under the auspices of civic and government agencies. These include campgrounds in all national parks and national forests; most national monuments, state parks, state forests, and state fish & game areas; and many city parks, county parks, and miscellaneous state and federal recreation areas. Other agencies with campsites includes the Corps of Engineers, Bureau of Land Management, Bureau of Reclamation, National Wildlife Refuges, and Indian reservations. Most of these public campgrounds are characterized by great natural beauty, adequate but not extravagent facilities, and moderate prices (from nothing at all up to around $3 per nite).

Then come private campgrounds, a booming category of campsites catering especially to the low-consciousness camper owning a 30-foot mobile turd, seeking a luxurious place to air it out for awhile. Private campgrounds are characterized by less beautiful surrounds; by luxury features like swimming pools and water-electric-sewage hookups; and by higher prices (generally from $2-$3 up to around $6-$8 per nite). In fairness to private campground owners, some of them are beautiful and perfect; others are total gross-outs and disgraces. Private campgrounds usually exist only wherever public campgrounds are too few or inadequate. In general, they live on the overflow, tho some of their business comes from the luxury-only campers.

Lastly come the "casual" campsites, which means parking yourself (and usually your vehicle) somewhere off the road, but not in any designated camping area. I recommend this kind of camping, but only to travelers who are aware of the ecological damage they can do, and take rigorous steps to prevent it. Casual campsites include stopping by the roadside at turn-outs and road-shoulders, parking on city streets and in driveways, following dirt roads and side roads to find remote spaces and clearings, pulling into fields and open country, and in general discovering your own private

hideaways. These casual campsites are characterized by a sense of stealth and paranoia; by
the fact that they're free of charge; and again,
by the danger of polluting the places you stay.

When casual camping, you always risk
being rousted out by the authorities for camping where you're not supposed to be (police
for cities, hiway patrol for roadsides, rangers
for parks and forests), by citizens for the same
reason (owners on their property, locals in
their locale), and by pranksters and hoodlums
for the hell of it. The resultant paranoia looms
large in casual camping, and makes it too
unpleasant for many.

The practice is feasible only if you have a
suitable vehicle — one that is small and drab
(easy to conceal); able to travel dirt roads and
byways; and self-contained (food, water, fuel,
beds, cooking). Bring equipment to get you
out of sand or mud when you get stuck. A
van-type camper or truck will do; also a motorcycle, bicycle, or backpack. Most big camping
rigs and Reckers won't.

The ecology of casual camping is simple.
Don't leave turds all around your vehicle, or
toilet paper or tin cans or any other refuse you
brought to the spot. Carry a portable toilet or
lidded can; or dig a latrine hole, and cover it
when you leave. Don't leave tire grooves and
oil stains on the ground; don't run down
bushes and trees, tear down fences and gates,
make open fires, and otherwise despoil it (even
when it's already been worked over by previous visitors). Respect both the place and
whoever "owns" it.

Many directories of public and private
campgrounds are available; some are listed in
Appendix 2 — USA Guidebooks. I found that
such a directory is quite useful because you
frequently won't know if there is a nearby
campground without it. Private campgrounds
usually advertise their presence, but public
ones don't. Also, you'll know in advance what
it costs, how big it is, what facilities it offers,
etc. However, a directory is hardly a necessity,
merely useful.

I sing the song of mississippi
alabama florida nevada
arizona chicago and
new york.
I sing about friends of the
road who share your heart
and come to know you utterly
and then are forgotten
almost utterly.

Meeting The Natives

They Speak Your Language

THE GREATEST SIGHT OF ALL Traveling thru America, you can see the greatest natural wonders on earth. You can also see the greatest unnatural wonders — the American cities and megalopolises. You can engage in every conceivable kind of activity, partake of every amusement known to man. And yet . . . having done these things, you can still miss the greatest experience of them all, if you fail to meet the Americans. As the land of America is characterized by diversity, so too are its natives. There is no end of contradictory hyperbole about Americans. Americans are the richest people on the globe, yet millions are poor. Americans are the most material people, yet among the most spiritual. Americans are the most friendly and generous, but Americans are also the most vicious, violent, and cruel. Americans dress well, and in rags. They are ultra-radical and ultra-conservative. They come in all colors. They come in all sizes, from seven-foot basketball players to three-foot circus dwarfs. They're liable to speak any language on earth in addition to English. Their cultural and ethnic backgrounds stem from anywhere in the world, and so forth and so on.

For all these differences, Americans are also the same. There is a continuity of characteristics that is so typically American. For the most part, these characteristics favor the casual traveler, the vagabond. They include a pioneer heritage of accepting you at face value, of judging every person as an individual, and a tradition of fair play. Other characteristics include generosity to a fault, and willingness to help in time of need. They include a great sense of humor. They include religious strength and belief in themselves backed by that strength.

But most of all, when you put these things all together, you come up with a person who is *interesting*. Your normal, everyday, run-of-the-mill average American, when you start to know him, is likely to be a truly interesting person. His life has been shaped and his character developed by diverse and powerful currents. As a result, when you discover Americans, you truly discover America, and of course, you gain insight into yourself as well.

The towns in NEVADA
    trailer houses
3 prs of jeans on the line
12 rotting cars in the yard
Sage-brush and tumbleweed
        garden

a woman inside
    nursing a baby?
    reading a magazine?
    waiting
        in the beautiful
        cool
        hidden

paradise of utter solitude
        waiting
in the brilliant white
        slant
slab
        of light
        Children for
            plants
and stars.
        I pass you by
and kiss your thin bony
        loneliness
good-bye.

Consider how many different kinds of Americans there are, how many life styles, how many alternative personalities are tolerated in America. Meeting the people of America is an endless journey in a vast landscape of personality, some of it fascinating, some of it boring, some of it ugly, some of it beautiful. The point is that the United States is an entire world in itself, a complicated, intricate, incredible world of people — the exploration of which can be a continuing source of energy for expanding the richness of your life.

MAKING A SOCIAL SURVEY What I'm recommending — what I'm insisting upon — is that you meet Americans when you travel in America. If you do this consistently you'll make your own social survey of America. Almost anyone you meet becomes a piece in a gigantic puzzle that takes form as you collect the pieces. The more Americans you meet, the more you get an up-to-date picture of America today. You may think you know America, but it's probably not the place you imagine from watching TV and reading the newspapers. Nor is any part of it the same as the last time you were there. It's still a puzzle, and the more pieces you fill in, the more colors it has, the more richness it offers, the more fun it becomes.

People always get you involved in something or other, and that's good. Involvement means energy exchange, or getting high on experience. For example, you arrive in a strange city but you have a contact — a friend or relative, whatever. Soon you're sitting in his or her home, drinking coffee or wine. If you show any interest, your friend will be happy to give you an insider's report on that city. You can learn what's happening, what's special, what's free. You discover what kind of place it is. You learn its advantages and disadvantages. You discover the best things to do and the things to avoid. In short, your friend is your guidebook, only much less dull. But you can also learn about things that will never be in the guidebook, and do it quickly and painlessly.

Frequently the person you visit may give you a guided tour, or direct you to a special sight, introduce you to other people, or fix you up with a date, or a fig.

But how do you do it? Who can you meet? How do you meet them? Where are all these Americans? Well, the wonderful thing about traveling in your own country is the lack of cultural barriers. Fraternization can be made part of any trip. Even backpacking in the wilderness you can meet other people on the trail and at the campsites (or bring friends). The same holds true for the bicyclist, motorcyclist, car-camper, certainly the hitchhiker.

You already have friends somewhere (come on, you must have at least one friend somewhere), you have your parents and relatives, and you have a set of miscellaneous misfits you know thru your work, your recreation, people you've run into here and there, stray acquaintances, and so forth. Let's look at these various categories because they represent a goldmine of potential contacts for the vagabond.

FRIENDS Have any of these? Think hard . . . Aren't there friends who you haven't seen in a long time, old high-school buddies, sorority sisters scattered God knows where, guys you knew in the service, work companions who transferred to another branch or left for a better job, kids who went off to school? Sure you do.

Looking up an old friend is a particular and peculiar joy. Soulmates you dearly loved years ago may now be boring fuddy-duddies. The creep you knew slightly and never liked too much may have blossomed into the world's greatest character. How great to find these things out now. Even where it's disappointing, it's still interesting to share in news and information, to discover amazing time warps and make explorations in the world of "if." In the same category is looking up old girl friends, or old boy friends. Meet their spouses, dandle their kids on your knee, hear about their lives. It's interesting, to say the least.

DESERT

NEVADA BY CAR.
17 JUNE 1972

Sign of the Times: Written in dust in the back window of a car in Jackson, Wyoming: FUCK MOM

RELATIVES Yes, we all have relatives, but do you really know them? If you're like me, you have lots of relatives you barely know, haven't seen in years, or may never have met. Usually, if I did know them, I knew them a long time ago, before I had developed into the person I am now. Or I knew them as stereotypes, without insight or interest in them as human beings. Uncle Jack was just like anybody else's uncle; Aunt Mary was the fat lady with lollipops in her purse. If you're now in the process of growing up (whether your age is 16 or 46), you might just be interested in finding out who Mary and Joe really were, not only then but now.

This kind of new look at old faces has special importance when it comes to your parents. Talk about stereotypes! Are you grown-up enough to see your parents as people just like anybody else, instead of gods or devils? Parents are just people (the same as you), who along the way have kids (like you), and problems and joys and good traits and bad. Think about the possibility of visiting your relatives and discovering their life stories and what makes them tick.

This approach to the familiar faces in your life is one of the hardest things you can do, and therefore one of the most rewarding. You have to be pretty straight with yourself, but it's such a trip to attempt it. The really surprising thing is how many of your relatives will open up to you if they believe you're sincerely interested in them. After all, they're as messed up as anyone else. They want to be understood, they want to be cared for, they want sympathy for their problems and recognition for their achievements. The difficulty I found is in convincing them you're interested. You have to repeatedly ask questions, disregard polite changes of subject, and other protective barriers. But once you get thru their defense system, stand back, because here comes a wave of humanity whose released energy can break down your walls of ignorance and apathy.

The week that I spent with my parents in Florida was one of the most informative, intimate, fun-filled times of my life. I went there with the deliberate intent of getting them to talk about themselves, something they seldom did before. I wanted to hear about their lives back in Poland, what America was like when they first came over, how they courted, how they had their children ... I deliberately brought my tape recorder because I wanted to record their stories for myself and my children; in short, I wanted to discover them as people. The results not only expanded my consciousness, but theirs. At first they were reluctant to talk. They suspected my curiosity. I tried to explain that my ignorance was a barrier to our relationship. Moreover, I was genuinely curious — their lives were totally unlike anyone else I knew. So, gradually at first, then with more and more ease, they began to fill in the gaps and answer questions; they began to paint a picture of themselves as people, immigrants arriving from Poland with little money, unable to speak the language. I heard fantastic stories of their first days in America, stories of suffering and prejudice, of back-breaking work for slave wages. I heard the story of how they saved their money stingily for a year during the Depression, and then blew it all on their wedding — hiring two bands and a hall, inviting 400 people and having a celebration that lasted for days. My mother told me about having her first child (which was me) at home, afraid but capable. There were stories about the early days of the bakery business, tales of life in the old country, of long ago parties and old courting swains, of friends and relatives killed by the Germans in the war, of social customs and practices now disappeared both in Poland and America. It was completely marvelous. We spent hour after hour, day after day, involved in conversations that had no previous counterpart in our relationship. It was a breakthrough of consequence for all of us.

Crossing this country
it is still possible
to fall in love with
wildly alive people
who recharge us with
their energy
and send us off on the road
    eyes bright
    delighted
    Alive

RELATIVES OF FRIENDS Speaking of relatives, you don't even have to visit your own. Your friends have relatives too, especially their parents, or their brothers and sisters. Looking them up is unusually easy and rewarding. You almost always see in the siblings of your friends some of the same characteristics, but also fascinating differences. You discover similarities that are cultural (such as manner of speaking), or parental (such as similar attitudes) or hereditary (such as appearance). Meeting the family of friends always tells you more about your friends, and makes you part of the family. If they're friends you don't know well, meeting the family will strengthen the friendship. It's also common for new friendships to sprout from within your friends' families.

The parents of your friends are usually people you wouldn't ordinarily encounter, usually because they're older or have a different life-style. Of course, those are excellent reasons to relate to them. Furthermore, older Americans are experts in the lore of latter-day Americana — its events, its attitudes, its consciousness. You ought to tap their knowledge and experience.

Parents of friends are easy to visit. In fact, you have a much better chance of receiving an agreeable welcome in agreeable surroundings then visiting just your average nobody. In the first place, you get a better welcome because most parents are somewhat out of touch with their children and eager for news or personal contact with anyone who can tell them about them. Parents often don't know their children's friends very well and are uncertain what their relationship is, so they assume you're a good friend or you wouldn't have come to visit (this isn't necessarily so, but they don't know that at first). From the standpoint of guest facilities, most parents have more house than they can live in, especially since their children left, so they always have one or two extra bedrooms. There's always room for you to stay, which is sometimes a problem when you visit younger people or people with large families. Finally, parents are further into materialism than most young people and they've spent their lives trying to build their estates. So they usually have a comfortable house, plenty of food, sometimes a swimming pool, and they can put you up in comfort and style without any personal sacrifice to themselves.

On our last tour of America we had some of our very best times with the parents of friends. These were certainly the most comfortable visits from the standpoint of physical surroundings in that we always slept in our own room, ate well, got to use the swimming pool, the boat, the car, the color TV set, etc. But beyond the mere physical comforts, we found that simply because they were older, these people were more far-out in certain ways than young people. The older generation is a treasurehouse of information and opinions, nonsense and wisdom all mixed together. Even when badly screwed up in their attitudes or ideas, they still want to understand what's going on, to be in touch with other ways of life. Even when you stand on opposite sides of the fence, so to speak, from the parents of your friends, it's understood by all parties that you're under a flag of truce for as long as you're there. This gives you freedom to openly discuss areas of conflict and to exchange information about each other's viewpoints. It almost never happens otherwise — that's the truce of friendship.

A special kind of communication takes place in these relationships. I think it's very important because it's the only kind that's likely to lead to any change of attitudes. It's during these heart-to-heart talks that we can truly penetrate the usual defenses that people put up. If you're a young person, speak for your generation in this situation. You can change the minds of older people more easily under these circumstances. As a friend of their children, people grant you both welcome and credibility. Don't ever forget that parents are people, too. Showing an honest interest in *them* instead of their *roles* eliminates the usual social superficialities and frees everybody to discover their real selves. It's exciting when people relate to each other honestly — it frees energy that causes change, and that's how to make this trip meaningful.

Off The Tape
INSIDE LAS VEGAS

Visiting with Mike's sister and her family, we found them to be warm and friendly people, even tho our lives are very different. It's great to be able to stop in a strange city, particularly a city as strange as Las Vegas, and be able to have a sense of home for a little while, to have a sense of this as somebody else's home, to understand how they think about it, to understand how they live here. Las Vegas is an incredible place actually, over a hundred thousand people, mostly centered around one industry — tourists. One of the world's greatest collection of services and sensationalism in staggering proportions. Immense amounts of money are exchanged, immense amounts of energy involved, enormous numbers of people passing thru, and yet for many people it's just home, just a place where they live, raise five children, build a business, make investments. Live their lives.

Las Vegas is a unique place, but it's completely American. Tour the casinos and examine the faces of the people that come thru. Watch them in their pleasures and their spending and see America revealed in the most naked way. American at its most money hungry, its most garish, and its most wide open. For this enormous symbolic bubble to be set in the middle of the great American desert, literally next to a great American technological masterpiece — Boulder Dam — is a marvelous irony.

I'm strolling in the evening dusk in the backyard of a tract house in Las Vegas. The perfection of the evening desert air has to be experienced. A black silhouette of the mountains ringing Las Vegas stands on the horizon. The sky is clear, the first stars are coming out, some crickets are chirping — it's a fine place to be.

FRIENDS OF FRIENDS Your friend's friends are frequently your own acquaintances. You may not know them, but have heard of them or perhaps they've heard of you. In either case, the door is already partly open. Friends of friends are frequently an extension of your friends, that is, they're about the same age or have the same background, the same likes and dislikes — there's something there already that made the friendship pull together in the first place. Therefore it's likely that you'll get along pretty well with them too. Generally you'll relate to these folks more easily than to most others because of these apparent similarities.

Young people nowadays give warm welcomes to vagabonds of all ages. The new generation just seems to be more friendly and open to everything, praise the Lord. Young people usually have much less in the way of material advantages then their elders, but in the balance they're much more likely to share it with you. Some friend of a friend of a friend may live in a small pad, but he is not uptight about offering you the floor as a place to crash, nor should you feel uptight about accepting it. These hip hosts and hostesses are usually the people with the best feel for whatever is happening and where the action is. They can introduce you to their friends and activities, and soon you have a scene. In fact, it's easy to make this scene most anywhere in America. Pay your way by not using people and being real.

OTHER CONTACTS Beyond these possibilities, there are the strangers you meet who become friends, whether for an hour or forever. They can come from anywhere, but common sources are travelers you bump into, chance conversations, accidental meetings, etc. There are also various kinds of clubs and directories you can deliberately use to meet people. I'll be talking more about these categories shortly.

HOW TO GET ADDRESSES The best way to meet people is to make the arrangements before you start the trip. The mechanics of it are simple. First look up all the addresses of eligible friends and relatives. Get telephone numbers! Very likely you haven't seen some of them for a long time, and don't have their addresses. So do some research: Write your parents and other friends.

Root thru your junk to find old address books and old letters, and make a collection. Next turn to your friends, to your parents and relatives . . . and start asking them for addresses. Let them know you're going on tour and want

reasonable but not outrageous effort; that is, I went thru all my old address books and I asked numerous friends for addresses. I didn't ask everyone I knew and I didn't press anyone. Yet when I started off on the trip I had several hundred addresses of people thruout America — in the big cities, in the countryside, little towns, big towns, in all parts of the country and about half the states. The addresses tended to group themselves around the large cities, which was alright since it's the large cities that one goes to anyway.

For example, you should have more addresses in New York City because you're more likely to go there than Troy, New York, and you don't want to pay housing costs in New York City if you can help it. Furthermore, New York City is an urban maze and you need whatever help you can get with it, someone who knows the region, someone who can give you tips and show you around.

Once started, I found that I picked up more addresses easily as I went along. Hitch-hikers gave me addresses, people who picked me up while I was hitchhiking gave me addresses; other hitchhikers I met on the road gave me addresses. People I encountered at campsites and tourist attractions were also free with these kind of contacts (and of course, not just addresses of people, but addresses of places to crash, things to see and do, etc.)

These things can get a little out of hand. For example, I asked a friend for some addresses, and a friend of that friend contacted me to lay some more addresses on me. These included her parents and some good friends of hers, but it also included the address of somebody who'd picked her up hitchhiking on the east coast, and the address of a friend of that driver who she never had a chance to visit. Now, if you care to run that little chain down, you'll find that she gave me the address of a friend of a friend of a friend of a friend, and neither of us felt this to be out of the ordinary.

to meet people. Tell them how you'll be traveling and in what direction (any direction, all directions).

You'd be surprised at how easy it is to collect addresses from acquaintances and relatives. In fact, they like the idea a lot. Second, you can bring news of them to these people, especially if you know them pretty well. Or you can act as a courier. What surprised me when I was requesting addresses was how even slight acquaintances frequently offered the addresses of their parents and friends. Gathering addresses for my three-month tour of America, I made what I considered to be a

An important tip about gathering addresses in this way is to ask for a little rundown on the person being listed; that is, some kind of thumbnail sketch so you'll be able to recall who that person is, and to help you judge whether it's worth going out of your way for later on. This little sketch should always include the relationship to the person who gave it to you (friend, relative, whatever) and just a little bit about that person so you won't walk in completely cold. For example, is the person male, female, married, perhaps what kind of work, and any personal idiosyncrasies like "hates strangers." One of my sources for addresses put in remarks such as "Linda: ecologist, good fuck." (Probably a better one than he is.)

Now your feeling at this time may be that this all strikes you somewhat weird. I mean, going to all this trouble collecting addresses. Well, let me justify it this way: First of all, it isn't very much trouble. The addresses pile up with ridiculous ease. Next, the people you meet thru these addresses will put an incredible amount of zing and energy into your trip. Someone you meet this way may change your plans and your life. Anything is possible, if you open yourself to it. That's what makes a vagabond. Finally, people you visit usually offer a place to crash or a meal or some direct service that saves you money, maybe a great deal of it. In fact, with enough contacts along your way, you can travel for practically nothing and have a great time doing it.

STRANGERS WHEN WE MEET Having the addresses is one thing; actually using them is quite another. In the first place, Americans tend to keep a certain reserve between themselves and strangers they meet, especially in these changing times. They're not likely to make a joyful to-do just because you knocked on their door and said hello. Next, almost anyone at sometime or another dislikes being imposed upon, dislikes being dropped in upon (with or without warning), dislikes relating to one or more strangers just as he was settling down to watch "Let's Make A Deal" on television. As you tootle down the highway, think about these problems, if you haven't done so already.

always accompanied by a fear that you may impose. The fear is necessary because it makes you sensitive to how people feel about your visit. Without it, you're not going to play the game of visitor very well. The rules require you to go back three spaces if the erstwhile host is hassled by your visit. It's a bum trip to pressure somebody to give you a bed or a meal simply because you showed up and wanted one. It's better out on the streets fending for yourself than getting anxious because you're bumming someone out.

On the other hand, you need enough confidence to actually stop by and find out what reception you'll get. In any case, you can be sure you've got something to offer in return for hospitality. As a vagabond, you bring a different and powerful kind of energy into people's lives for a while. You bring information about other places, you bring news of friends and relatives. You offer a willing ear to listen to their story and an interest in their

situation. It's important for people to have something to exchange, and the vagabond's stock in trade is energy. It's his main capital, and his barter is more than fair.

Wherever possible, give people a little advance warning that you may be coming. The best way is to ask the person who provided you with the address to write to say you may be coming, and approximately when. Of course, if the contact is your friend or relative, then you can do this yourself. If this kind of epistolary warning is posted there's no problem. In any case, try to telephone in advance — preferably a few hours. This not only puts them on "vagabond alert" but assures you they're home. It's also a first indication of their receptivity. Sometimes they'll say 'no'; sometimes you'll say 'no,' just from the vibes over the phone. Sometimes it's heavy.

Frequently, the address you seek may be difficult to find (for example, in a large city) or you can't get to it very easily (for example, if you're on foot or hitchhiking), or it may be in a little town somewhere off the main road or the interstate (requiring a considerable detour). In any of these cases, phoning ahead can tell you if it's worthwhile to visit or if anybody's home. It may be better to go ahead to your next address if you have one, or just fend for yourself. For these reasons, when you get addresses *always* get the telephone number as well. Lacking that, call up 'directory assistance.'

If you're an average person, it's difficult to screw up your nerve to make a contact, at least some of the time. This is particularly true if you don't know the person at all, if you don't know much about them because the contact is slim, or for whatever reason you need to make that contact (for example, maybe you had a horrendous day on the road and desperately need a haven or friendly face). Anyway, you call and it's liable to be awkward, but the first impressions are important. In my estimation it's necessary to be sensitive, to pick up vibes thru the phone.

People will usually be friendly and willing to see you. Occasionally, they'll transmit some reluctance but when possible insist on seeing them anyway. (I frequently found that people who were hesitant over the phone were extremely friendly and hospitable later on. I had simply misinterpreted them because of my own insecurity.) If people clearly don't want to see you, they'll let you know it. Don't push yourself on them; simply relay your message: Say hi from Uncle Mary — and pass on. (Or pass out.)

When you finally find their house and are knocking at the door, there's another moment of uptightness. The early minutes are difficult as you and the host try to make some kind of connection. The good intentions of most people being what they are, you'll find one, even when the original connection is poor. Frequently, the person who gave you the address soon drops out of sight altogether and the personal responses between you and your hosts are good enough to keep the whole thing going. Of course, this has to happen even when your contacts are good. You still must get along with the people you're visiting or it's no-go.

Characteristically, the people you're calling won't offer you a meal or a bed over the phone. If it happens that you are visiting and the meeting continues cool, make some polite bows and split. However, it takes a while for people to thaw out, even under the best of conditions, so don't be in too much of a hurry to rush off. Neither should you overstay your welcome. Just try to make the most of your point of contact whatever it may be, and hope for the best. Keep calm. Try not to involuntarily urinate in your pants. Don't start screaming for no apparent reason. Try to control your trembling. Don't take off your shoes as soon as you come into the house. Don't ask what's for dinner.

Exercises

SOCIAL EXERCISES

1) Have a day of silence. A speech fast is a wonderful way to learn to relate to people again. We tend to use words as crutches sometimes, actually inhibiting or preventing any real communication. Being silent with your friends or family will release a lot of energy into your social situation, sometimes too much. Being silent with attendants and other service types is also a trip, bound to make life interesting.

2) Superficial contacts with people are usually an energy drain instead of an energy input. To avoid this, try always relating to people as honestly as possible. Everyone gets involved in foolish conversations about the weather or other trivial subjects, and these are sometimes more annoying than edifying. The way to solve this problem is to direct the conversation into areas of reality . . . ask questions you really want answers to; give answers that are the truth, not empty noise. This serves to scare away bores and interest others. Meeting people isn't really difficult; the problem is meeting people you can relate to.

3) Sometimes in a tourist crowd or a campground, it happens that you become aware of someone whose appearance or actions appeal to you or make you curious. You say, "Look at that couple over there," or something similar. That's a sign that you should try to make contact with them. Usually your interest is merely casual, so your approach should also be casual. Just say, "Hi, I noticed that you . . . dibble dibble." At least you'll get some better impressions, maybe even a conversation. Nothing is lost by trying, but the initial interest is the indication that a quality contact can be made.

4) When meeting new people, and the conversation is lagging, ask people questions about themselves. Don't talk about yourself and your trip, except in answer to direct questions. Then steer the conversation back to them. After all, it's them you should be interested in anyway (you've already heard about yourself), and people do like to talk about themselves best. Really.

5) If you're traveling with children, let them lead social interference for you. Kids are the best ice-breakers in the world, bar none, because they are always direct and honest. We should follow their good example. The converse is also true: To meet someone with children, relate to their kids. Children are a joy to meet anyway, and can change a bad mood or release you from depression or boredom very quickly. That's because they're alert and full of energy; their energy can energize you when you're down.

6) Your fellow travelers — your family or friends in your car — tend to build patterns of relating to each other that become stagnant and dull after awhile. Experiment with ways of breaking down these patterns. If one person is making decisions about where to stop, designate someone else to do it, or do it by majority vote. Ask everyone, in order, to describe why they liked or didn't like some particular sight or experience. On long empty stretches of road, ask each other personal questions you've been curious about but never found the nerve or opportunity to ask before. Use your imagination to discover new aspects of each other.

THE GRAPEVINE This is the generic term for the information network that envelops the nation and is one of the traveler's staple sources for information, contacts, friends, sustenance, you name it. There's nothing formal about this at all. The Grapevine can pop up anywhere. It has to do with meeting people on the road. It has to do with talking to gas station attendants. It has to do with picking up hitchhikers. Frequently you can make contact with it at college campuses and student unions, underground newspaper offices, at dance halls and beer bars, by calling Switchboard numbers and free clinics. Absolutely everyone belongs to the Grapevine.

It's a kind of game. All you do to play is keep your eyes and ears open and ask questions. Don't be afraid of people. Always make contact with them. This applies to public officials too, particularly people like national park rangers, hiway patrolmen, museum guards, ticket takers and tour guides, etc. You'd be surprised how much information practically anyone has available for the curious questioner. Naturally other vagabonds, travelers, and tourists represent rich deposits of information about all the places they've been and the things they've seen.

In dealing with the Grapevine, it's always necessary to evaluate your source. Perhaps the people in America most open to meeting travelers on the road are other travelers. This is a truism of travel everywhere. Travel is a condition in which you naturally open yourself to the possibilities of experience so fully that you find yourself speaking to people you would never dream of talking to in your normal life. Wherever you see tourists or travelers it's commonplace to walk up to them without introduction and ask anything on your mind that falls within wide boundaries of civil decency. Typically, you start off by asking people where they're from, where they've been, or where they're going. And you ask them about how they're traveling, or how their camper is equipped, or the structural details of their backpacks, and then just go from there.

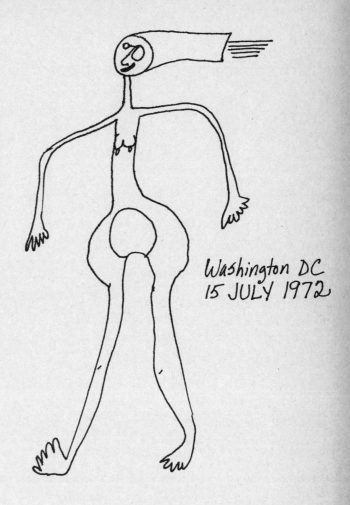

Washington DC
15 JULY 1972

Very often you can wind up trading notes or addresses.

For this reason, it's remarkably easy to meet other travelers in American campgrounds. This goes a long way toward livening up the typical American camping experience. Far too many Americans hole up in their campsites as if they were bivouacking on the slope of Everest. They crawl into their tents or campers as if there were a blizzard going, and you don't see any more of them for the duration of their stay. I've always found that people like being invited over to your campsite for coffee after dinner. Or, if you see a group of people around a campfire, it's relatively easy to wander over and be invited to join in.

HITCHHIKERS Whether you're a hitchhiker or a motorist, don't overlook the possibilities for meeting people that exist in this means of transportation. Hitchhikers, of course, depend on people they meet to give them rides, and every mile they travel means they're relating to somebody somehow. On the average, however, hitchhikers don't meet a full cross-section of Americans because so many motorists refuse to pick them up. And hitchers are no cross-section of America either. Nevertheless, anything is possible, and the consequences of meeting people are what hitchhiking is all about. All hitchhikers know this, of course. Any hitchhiker can tell stories of the spontaneous generosity and friendliness he's received.

What I want to concentrate on here is the reverse process — that is, the benefits for the motorist of picking up hitchhikers. These have primarily to do with energy. Hitchers have to be great or foolish to be out on the American hiways in the first place, and that already distinguishes them. They have a great deal of energy available to cope with the trials of the road, and when you pick up a hitchhiker you're going to get some of that juice.

Beyond that, hitchhikers tend to be young and free. They live honestly and speak truly. Their values are often strange to the middle-class American, and so they are spokesmen for their points of view. If you want to understand why young people do the things they do or believe in the things they do (and you're serious about finding out, not just throwing out a liberal smokescreen) then pick up a series of hitchhikers and ask them questions. As a group, hitchhikers are glad to talk about themselves, and can teach you quite a lot.

A good example is the hitchhiker I picked up on the road leaving Las Vegas. A young bearded man, he turned out to be a budding spiritual master, already quite advanced on the path of learning the ways of the earth. His particular gig was collecting herbs in the mountains of the southwest (and Hawaii, where he'd first gotten interested in herbs). At first he talked for an hour about Hawaii, and then gradually worked into the subject of herbs and God. He was a new kind of young American, making himself strong physically, mentally, and spiritually by taking a course of action that is purely individual, free, and self-reliant. He lives by collecting and selling herbs. He told us how many of the natural herbs are richer in food value and vitamins than anything you can buy. Dandelions, for example, are healthiest of all. Even mesquite can be made into a tea with healing properties, and sage as well. Nettle tea was his favorite, and he brews it strong to clear his kidneys. We shared his home-made loaf of bread, made with nuts and seeds. Meeting a man like this is exciting because he illuminates how someone can shape and control his life, despite his cultural influences. To us he gave knowledge, a spiritual sense, a surge of energy. This is not an isolated occurrence. Many hitchhikers are unusual people.

There are practical uses to which hitchhikers can be put, such as helping you drive your car, or keeping you awake with conversation when you're tired, sometimes even sharing expenses if they have some money. They are sources of information you can freely tap, especially useful if you're traveling on a budget. They know places to stay. They can turn you on to things to do, and maybe give you some addresses.

(The dangers of picking up hitchhikers are discussed in the next chapter.)

Off The Tape
HITCHERS' DIALOGUE

There's so many straights going down this road. Some big car will drive by and like you know that it's a Cadillac or a Buick. It's moving pretty slow down the road — you know that when it goes by you there's going to be in it some old man (no matter what his age he's going to be an old man), and next to him will be a chick with a bouffant sprayed hair-do, right? Now if she's old, she's going to have her face sprayed as well. (Laughter) They drive by real slow and they look at you and while they drive by you have the feeling that they're saying to each other, "They shouldn't allow people like that on the highway." (Laughter) "They ought to do something about that." I asked my friend on the highway, as we're sitting here drinking, and hitchhiking, I ask my friend on the hiway, "People don't pick us up, why do you think that is?" He says, "I don't know why, it would be good for all of us." And I say, "What if we were the kind of people who went in and raped and robbed these people who gave us the ride?" And he thought about that for a while and he said "They'd have to really be asking for it, for me to do a thing like that."

TRAVEL DIRECTORIES AND CLUBS Still another way to meet people is to belong to clubs that are intended to introduce people to each other, or which can be used for that purpose thru their membership list. For example, an organization called Traveler's Directory is "an international registry of hip travelers who enjoy meeting others everywhere, whether around the corner or around the world." The Directory was set up as a listing of people's names, addresses, telephones, ages, interests, and offers of hospitality to other travelers passing thru. It started in 1960, but is now suffering hard times due to over-subscription. Success may have ruined a good thing, or has at least delayed its regular publication. To get information about it, to find out whether it's still going, write to the address provided in Appendix 6.

The basic idea of listing people who welcome travelers across the country is so good that several other people are trying to do it, like Free Magazine and Black Bart's Outlaw Institute — also listed in Appendix 6. The Alternatives Journal — see "Communes" in Appendix 1 — also puts out an annual People Directory for the purpose of getting strangers together.

Right now, the best travel club I know about is The Globetrotter's Club, located in England. Any serious vagabond should certainly join this club, which mails a quarterly newsletter of the most up-to-date travel information all over the world supplied by the members. The accent is definitely for vagabonds, that is for travelers who are interested in the unusual, the exciting, and the inexpensive. There is a directory of club members, most of whom are Americans, giving addresses and offers of hospitality. If you know that you'll be traveling you can make an announcement in the newsletter and ask people to contact you with information or offers.

If you belong to any clubs or organizations whatever, and have access to a membership list, this can be a super source of contacts. Many clubs, fraternities, social and business organizations, warmly greet out-of-town members. Even without membership rosters, if you belong to clubs such as Rotarians, or Kiwanis, you can see if there are any meetings scheduled for the day or evening when you arrive in town. The city limits of any American town has a billboard with a patchwork of club symbols and meeting dates, showing you where you can make contact. An extension of this idea is to visit communes as you go across country, bearing in mind that many communes discourage visitors because their own existence is too precarious or too self-involved for outsiders. The Alternatives Journal has a directory of American communes, and it regularly lists new communes, old communes that have failed, and news and commentary about the state of communes generally. Highly recommended for anyone interested in communes or communards.

There are other off-beat ways of meeting people. For example, if you're a ham radio operator and have a mobile rig you can CQ your contacts whenever you need them. Just go on the air. The chances are you can work yourself up an invitation for a stopover at least, and maybe extend it into more hospitality than that. A citizen's band radio can be used the same way, in addition to picking up information generally. However, don't cut into other conversations and stay off the 'working' bands (6-8-9-14-15-21). The police guard channels are 6-9-14; state police use channels 8 and 21; frequently channel 15 is used by hotels and channel 9 for general information.

In some locales at certain times, depending on your vibe, it's still possible to find a meal and lodging by offering to work for it — that is, by doing chores, chopping wood, doing any kind of labor in exchange for hospitality. Of course, the prevalent paranoia is going to make this risky and you may get a lot of funny stares or curt refusals, but if you can hack that and keep going there's no question but that you'll strike somewhere. Part of the time anyway.

Finally, just laying your trip on somebody at the right time can also put you in contact

driving thru vermont 18 July 1972

with people and services. I've mentioned this already, but go anyplace where there are hip young people ... college campuses, free clinics, Switchboards, rock concerts, street fairs. Most likely you'll find something or somebody to help. If you do this, don't make it a ripoff ... make it an exchange. Give something back for what you get.

SEX POSSIBILITIES Sex and the male vagabond are in a funny relationship. There's the myth of the traveling man who sweeps over the countryside deflowering the girls in droves. But then there's the rocky actuality of the perpetual stranger passing thru, the man who never has the time to make any kind of deep relationship with people. The truth lies somewhere in between. The romantic nature of the vagabond captures the imagination for both men and women who are open to the attractions of a stranger. From my own sexual experiences as a vagabond, I would say it comes to something like this: Most of the time, I'm pretty horny and lonely . . . a man on the move with not enough time to really explore relationships, to feel intimate enough with anyone for sexual encounter. But some of the time, a special magic is at work, and a sexual experience becomes as inevitable as the sun rising. The truth is that you can never count on anything. Any sex that's worthwhile depends upon a real attraction between people who find some spiritual common ground whether it's for a little while or a long while. Simply getting laid for the sake of getting laid is not a particularly good trip and frequently leads directly to various energy bring-downs like having to lie to people, having to be lied to, getting involved in bad scenes, or just simply getting VD. Finding someone to couple with generally involves doing the same things you'd do anywhere. Be open to people, don't be afraid of them, seek them out, go where they are.

This applies to female vagabonds, too, but considering how sexually stereotyped the woman's role still is in most places, don't flaunt your liberation. Be sensitive to local customs. Incidentally, I've met some hitchhikers, both men and women, who have told me they met their true love while hitchhiking. Some said they were doing the hitching, some said they were doing the picking up. The reason this happened, of course, is that strangers who spend time together in a car get to know each other pretty well after awhile and find it easy to generate a sexual interest

after this deeper acquaintanceship. All vagabond travelers should carry birth control devices of some kind whether they're men or women. You never know. See chapter 15 for a full discussion of birth control and VD measures, for these are among the most possible of sex possibilities.

AMERICAN PORTFOLIO Here's a short sample of Americans — some of the world's great people. There are millions more ... go out and meet a few.

Philadelphia, Pennsylvania: This ebullient lady is Joanne Pratt — a friend of a friend. Her hospitality made the town a special place for us. Tho a 'matron' with teen-aged kids, her enthusiasm for life and her openness mark her as a new-consciousness American.

Omaha, Nebraska: Visiting with acquaintances Steve and Chris, I pose with all the neighborhood kids. It was a wonderful midwestern midsummer evening — a time for jump-rope, story-telling, guitar playing, and making friends.

Perth Amboy, New Jersey: My gentle lovable loving Uncle Henry Solecki with his grand-daughter and grand-niece. I only see him every few years at most, but each time I marvel at how human and good this man is. Uncle, I love you.

San Jose, California: One of my oldest friends (tho he doesn't look that old)—Jules, the Pearl . . . by any standard an extra-ordinary guy. Brilliant, funny, kooky—an almost vagabond who went straight.

Laguna Beach, California: Arley Ranger feeds a friend, a characteristic action by a warm and independent person I chanced to meet one day on the beach. She's the proprietress of the Funk Factory, a head shop right on the main street.

Birmingham, Alabama: My brother Lester obligingly identifies himself for the camera. An executive at the University, he nevertheless has maintained certain human traits that endear him to his vagabond brother: A sense of humor and a warm-heartedness that make him a special guy.

New York City, New York: In the inner sanctum of Random House, I palaver with the Ed.-in-Chief, Jim Silberman. Tho not your run-of-the-mill vacation stop, it only proves anything is possible for vagabonds. Despite his title, Jim is soft-spoken and unassuming.

Yuba City, California: A nameless street vagabond I met at an art festival. His friendliness and stories of bygone years told me he was a man of heart.

Isle of Palms, South Carolina: Jim Mathias, MD, a new-style Southern gentlemen . . . a gentle man, soft-spoken and tolerant, free-thinking and generous host. A pleasure to know you.

Big Sur, California: Some of the mellow people I met hitchhiking down that not-always-so-lonesome road. We had a stoned time . . . never got the names but here are their faces.

142

Rye, New York: Frank Heineman, a successful clothing-firm owner in the city, is the father of our dear friend Carol. He is an example of how parents could be if they tried: Wise but warm, sophisticated but human, well-to-do but generous.

Mt. Shasta, California: Rich Simonelli, who gave up being an electronics engineer so he could keep being gentle, loving, and spiritual. A student of everything, and a graduate human.

America By Car 9

Outwitting Your Auto

CARS AND ENERGY The automobile is a machine for energy release, and "America by Car" is an energy bath, a traveler's dream come true — the great American fantasy within reach of everyone. Cars in America are almost as common as carburetors, yet still have the power to excite us. Any road vehicle is exciting because it energizes us with the sensation of movement. Something new and unknown is always coming over the horizon, waiting around the bend, and the prospect turns us on. The countryside ever-changes, new sights constantly appear, others are being anticipated . . . This mystique of traveling applies particularly to car touring, because you are The Driver — you control your pace, your direction, your destiny.

The automobile is a machine for energy release. In fact, we often get in our cars and "go for a joy-ride" with no particular destination, just to be energized by the movement, by the sense of power inherent in controlling this release of energy. When we want more energy, we can either go to a different place or simply go faster (which is a way of changing the same place into a different place).

However, traveling by car is also fraught with problems and frustrations. First, the energy is released via an artificial device — a machine rather than a natural agent. We simply sit in the machine — we don't get any physical opportunity to experience the energy, or to use our bodies to integrate or absorb it. The result is a stagnation of energy, even a perversion of it. Often the energy is dissipated in useless activities like smoking, nail-biting, nose-picking, or worse things like speeding and risk-taking. After awhile, boredom sets in because there is no place to use the energy input. Travelers start blocking out the world and become oblivious to their environment. They lose interest in it because being interested means being energized, and they can't handle energy while locked up in a painted metal box. Ironically, they have everywhere to go but nothing to do.

Another source of frustration is that your artificial energizer — your vehicle — is restricted in its movements by roads and laws. Only certain paths are possible, mostly paved and policed. One stretch of interstate starts looking like any stretch of interstate, one road

CLICHES OF THE ROAD

Arrive Alive
Clean Rest Rooms
Speed Checked By Detection Devices
Your Highway Taxes At Work
Litter Barrel ½ Mile
Use Your Ashtray
Help Keep _____ Green
Historical Marker ½ Mile
Elect Archie T Wigger Coroner
Warning: US Government Property, No
    Trespassing
$25 Fine for Throwing Trash on Highway
Free Ice to Travelers
Speed Zone Ahead
Narrow Bridge Ahead
Keep Off Median
Road Narrows
Careful Driving Is A Civic Duty
Bridge Ices Before Highway
This Truck Pays More Than $3280 in State Taxes
Do Not Pick Up Hitchhikers. Do Not Stop
Emergency Stopping Only
The Children Ahead Don't Deserve to Be Dead
A Country That Runs on Oil Can't Afford to Run
    Short

looks like all roads . . . After awhile — an hour, day, week, and/or, month — the road loses its magic. It loses its energy; it becomes de-energizing . . . a rip-off, a demand, an agony.

Another serious problem with driving is that it insulates you from the world, and distorts your reality. Being in a car is like having an outer skin of metal. Your consciousness — your sense of yourself — expands to fill the car, actually taking its shape. You sense exactly where the left front fender is, and you keenly feel the tires rotating on the road surface. In a very real way, you *become* a car when you're in one, especially for a long time. Some people benefit by being cars (like racing drivers), but most of us don't make it too good as cars. Actually, people get off best by being people. But the consciousness of the car is powerful, and most drivers end up being completely controlled by their cars. Cars prefer high speed and continuous driving, and that's what they get. Cars never want to stop anywhere, so they seldom do. Cars like freeways better than back roads, and that's where they go. Cars don't like people, so they avoid them or honk at them; given any opportunity they kill them. Cars are heartless.

People in cars are really not people, but rather a special case of people-in-general. People-in-cars are cut off from contact, literally, with the earth and other people. They live in a special reality that is allowed to come in thru the windshield, but is not the same reality that exists outside the car. Hitchhikers know this most vividly: One moment you're cooly cruising down the hiway getting a reflection of the surroundings from inside the shell. Next moment, the car disappears and there you are, hot-flashing on reality. Stepping out of that box leaves you vulnerable, and the surroundings suddenly are overwhelmingly right there, heavy with life possibility. (Love is just a kiss away.) The energy impact of leaving a car can be psychedelic. Try it sometime.

Finally, this land of America is so vast that any means of traveling it becomes a gesture of futility if you don't understand its limitations and possibilities. Most Americans clog the hiways with their cars, but their brains and hearts are at home, or otherwise out to lunch. America is too big to just sit there on your ass, mile after mile, and expect something great to happen while you're farting thru your sateen seat covers. You've got to put some energy out to get some back. You've got to take side-trips — geographical, intellectual, physical, social, spiritual — side-trips are those pattern-breaks that get you stoned. Let's see what can be done . . .

DRIVING TO DISTRACTION Seeing America by car means that most of your whole trip will be spent behind the wheel. Some days you'll drive more hours than you'll sleep at nite. No matter how fresh you start, how alert or eager you are, the road just goes on and on and on until you turn weird with boredom or exhaustion. You can't appreciate the country if your enthusiasm trickles away as the miles tick off on the odometer. Here are some thoughts and suggestions for keeping loose, for vagabonding while driving.

SCHEDULES Did you know that "schedule" is etymologically related to "shit"? Well, it's true that timetables and itineraries, even day-to-day ones, are shitty obligations. If you recognize this beforehand, maybe you won't be enslaved by them. Traveling should be an attempt to slip away from obligations. Yet time and again, the "number one" road mania that brings you down is rushing from point to point on some "schedule" written across your brain. Do you really have to be in Albuquerque in 45 minutes, just because it's there? If you aren't in St. Louis tonite, does it mean you're no good? The victim of this mania really knows what's happening. He spots likely stops, rest areas he could pull into, scenic views at which he's like to set up the tripod . . . But he doesn't do it; he's afraid he'll "fall behind schedule."

That attitude is nothing more than inertia. A body at rest behind the wheel tends to stay behind the wheel. What you need is an energy shot to release yourself from this inertia. Here are some ways to do it.

the highway is for remembering
scenes from the past rise
            like oases
to relieve the endless snake-like
        white on black.
we are unseen as we ride
            thru space
bodiless machines
our motors drive us silently
we force a tunnel thru
            the wind
        it whooshes unheard
        to mark our passage.

SWITCHING DRIVERS Change drivers at forced intervals — for example, every 100 miles or every two hours. When you do, everyone in the car should also get out for a stretch, a few kneebends and deep breaths. If you're nodding at the wheel, here's a tested way to revitalize yourself. Look for some roadside slope covered with grass or flowers — some fantasy place you'd like to sleep. When you see one, stop! Make a dash for it, and throw yourself down. Sleep! You won't sleep very long, but the sensation of giving in to it — a few minutes of closing your eyes in bliss — will wake you right up. Try it.

ABOUT HITCHHIKERS If you don't have a substitute driver, try picking one up by the roadside. Actually, hitchhikers give you such an energy shot you won't need to leave the wheel just yet. Relating to a new person always turns your head around, and usually puts new life into your day.

People don't realize how much hitchhikers can do for them. In the first place, hitchhikers are out there on the road in a direct way, sampling life, testing America at its sources. You have no access to that experience unless you hitchhike yourself or pick up hitchhikers. Well, it's a lot easier to pick up hitchhikers than to do any hitchhiking yourself. In the comfort of your own car you can benefit from the hitchhiker's life. Ask them to relate their experiences ... ask where they've been, or what they've seen that you might be able to tune in on, especially if you're going that way. You'll also get a feel for another world of traveling, and you should trade notes because you're both travelers on the road.

The supposed danger of picking up hitchhikers is, of course, what prevents so many people from doing it. It's true that letting a stranger into your car can be a frightening business. In the sense mentioned before, your car *is* yourself: Allowing someone to enter is an act of love, especially difficult with a stranger. Yet danger threatens the hitchhiker far more than the driver. The hitchhiker is vulnerable and helpless ... a stationary target.

Occasionally desperados and bad men hitchhike as a last resort, but it's too dangerous for them to be so exposed, and they're more often in hiding than thumbing. In actual fact, hitchhikers are victims of crimes and murders committed by drivers far more often than the reverse. Prevent violence by giving a hitchhiker a ride.

HOW TO PICK UP HITCHERS First of all, don't feel guilty about not picking them up. You don't owe anybody a ride. Pick up hitchhikers only when you want to or need to, and when it's convenient to do so. For example, when it's safe to pull over to the side of the road. When you see one or more hitchhikers ahead, slow down a little. Look him-her-them-it over. Try to make some judgements based on your own background. You can always get some impressions from hitchhikers depending on how they're dressed, what kind of signs they hold, what the signs say, and their general appearance.

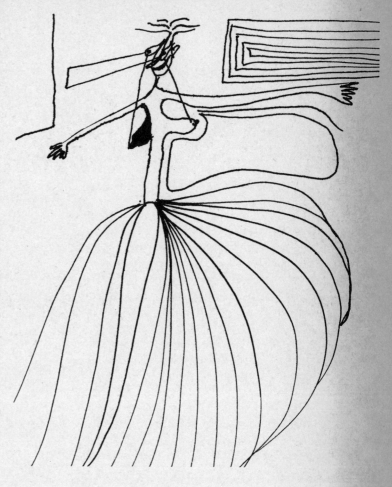

At this point you'll either be moved to stop or you won't. If you feel like stopping, you need to consider also whether it's possible to stop. Sometimes you'll be in the wrong lane on a high-speed freeway, sometimes there isn't space to pull over where the hitchhikers are (which is their own fault and something for which you shouldn't endanger yourself); sometimes by the time you've made up your mind it's already too late (in which case you should just go on).

Just because you've stopped doesn't mean you have to let the hitchhiker(s) in. You can still keep the door closed, or locked, roll down the window and have a little conversation — interrogation at the door. You can ask where they're heading, meanwhile getting further impressions. You can always refuse a ride saying that you're only going up the road a few miles. If you're not sure about how far you want to take a hitchhiker, you can always tell him or her you're going to a close destination. That way, if s/he fails to be entertaining you can let him or her off at the next town. I personally feel that hitchhikers have an obliga-tion to be interesting, to offer some kind of stimulation to the driver in repayment for getting the ride in the first place. If, for whatever reason, the hitchhiker doesn't deliver, it's OK to let him or her out.

Let me say this to allay the fears that motorists have about hitchhikers: My own experience time and time again has been that hitchhikers provide me with some of the best human contacts of the entire trip. Hitchhikers frequently deliver that plus quality that makes for memorable experiences. I say it over and over again, but it's true: People give you your best times on the trip, not places, and one of the best ways to meet exceptional people is to pick them up along the roadsides.

Off The Tape
LEE'S FERRY

Down here at the Colorado River in Lee's Ferry watching a Hatch River Expedition get started. There must be 80 or 100 people on about 10 boats. Giant boats, guides, everybody in orange life preservers. A scene of mass confusion, of mostly tourist-looking people, California types, families, children, not too many oldsters, boats loaded down with canned Pepsi and Coca Cola crates, the center portion of them with tarps lashed down, full of supplies. Folks get a last-minute briefing lecture just before they man the boats. It's a great scene, like a scramble scene — "pilots, man your planes; tourists, man your boats, we're going down to Phantom Ranch."

Right behind the boat launching ramp, I see my first trailer motel — a series of half a dozen duplex trailers of the mobile-home type. Also a trailer restaurant, a trailer campstore, a little mini-trailer gas station. All of these lie right next to the old Mormon Trading Post baking quietly in the sun. The stone buildings here, or the remains of them known as Lee's Ferry Fort are an ironic contrast to the trailers. Somehow the pioneers had time to build from stone. Today's modern society can only haul in tin trailers and dump them in place. Inside the trailer store at Lee's Ferry they're selling beer by the case, river-running hats for five dollars made in Japan for 39 cents. The place is jammed, they've got 10 and 12 people standing in line in this tiny store. Some business at Lee's Ferry.

SOCIAL INTERCOURSE Another way to make time pass is by talking. Big deal, you say. Well, you have to do it differently so it has some juice in it. This is what hitchhikers can get you involved in, but it can also be done quite deliberately at times. You have to turn to whoever is in the car with you and say, "Listen, I'm bored . . . let's talk about something or I'll go crazy or fall asleep at the wheel." Then you look at each other stupidly and say, "Well, what shall we talk about?" Look at it this way: You have a captive audience, complete privacy, and nothing else to do (driving takes up none of your conscious energy) — why not use this opportunity for some far-out relating? One time while traveling down the road bored, Stephanie livened up our lives by saying, "Ask me something you've always wanted to know about me but were afraid to ask." If you're traveling with people you're close to, intimate discussions and meaningful talks can be important energizers while traveling thru the desolation of automobile land.

SEXUAL INTERCOURSE This is for loving couples. For whatever reasons, occasionally you get sexually turned on in the car. Gratifying your sexual desires during a day's dull driving raises the energy level like a tonic from Zeus. As is well-known tho little discussed, making love in new surroundings noticeably arouses one's sexual ardor. (It's that ole energy release again.) In the car, never stopping, genital stimulation is an interesting, perhaps dangerous, distraction of the driver. Less awkward and frustrating is stopping by the roadside and going to the back of the van. Best of all are spontaneous sex picnics in the woods on a blanket, or in a barn or abandoned house. The joy of this love-making is in the openness of yourselves to each other and the feelings of the moment, the sudden release from the tension of the road, and the novelty of the surroundings. Together these things make for wonderful interludes away from the mechanized dreariness of the road.

WORD GAMES Well, how about word games then? We played "Ghost" and "Geography" and some visual recognition games. They were boring. No energy.

If you're traveling with children, these types of games may be occasionally interesting ... like how many dead animals can you spot, or who'll be the first to count up to 500 billboards, etc.... But in-th-car games pall rapidly, and you'll have to get those kids out of the car, the more frequently the better. Don't be pissed at them ... they're only showing better sense than you are. Follow their lead.

MUSIC LISTENING Listening to the radio, of course, is the standard way to keep boredom at bay, but it seldom works well because the transmitters keep going out of range, the signals fade in and out, the stations play strange unbearable tunes, etc. (But I did enjoy listening to small town commercials and the news). On our trip we had a stereo tape player and some tapes, and that worked out much better. At times it's clearly unreal: High speed, high volume, full stereo, windows closed. But at those times, the hiway represents a lesser reality, all there is in the world is its greatest rock and roll band, or Bach's greatest hits. You start to tire of your tapes, tho, so you should try to exchange them with other tape deckers you meet.

MUSIC MAKING Here's one of the richer joys of life. Making music is creative, emotive, crazy. If you already play an instrument, bring it along. Play to entertain the driver and yourself. When traveling by van, mobile jam sessions are possible if enough musicians and instruments are on hand.

If they're not, or you don't play, then try picking up a musician. Many hitchhikers announce their abilities with guitars in hand, and you should make them play a tune to pay their way. Whether or not you play, bring along a harmonica. It's a simple instrument and small, can be blown thru for amusement even if you don't play, and is handy when you meet someone who does.

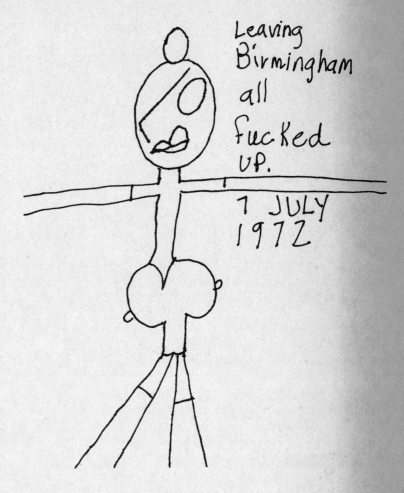

Leaving Birmingham all fucked up.

7 JULY 1972

MARIJUANA AND DRIVING As I write this, I think of the people who'll read it, and want to say something meaningful to everyone — I want hip dope smokers to say "Right on, smoke dope!"; I want non-smokers to relate to it without being threatened or angered; I want safety-conscious officials to not feel betrayed. After thinking about it, weighing the pros and cons, I am moved to recommend it as an occasional way of energizing the driving experience, for those who care to. However, I'm speaking to those readers who already smoke it, and am not encouraging its adoption by non-smokers. (Adopt new vices according to your own needs, not anyone else's).

On the negative side, marijuana unquestionably affects some driving skills — tho the medical evidence shows that you drive much better stoned than drunk. Also, 'grass' tends to make you slow down and take more care, not less. I occasionally drive while stoned and haven't yet had an accident while under the influence (which is more than I can say about driving behind alcohol or even driving sober). Nevertheless, for the sake of safety, don't smoke dope under demanding traffic conditions. The open hiway is safer, and anyway, that's where grass is most useful to relieve

boredom. One other negative note: A small percentage of grass smokers are made drowsy by it, even when driving. And some varieties of pot may make you feel that way even if you normally get energized. If you do get tired, stop and sleep it off.

Its positive effects include heightening your perceptions and stimulating your thoughts. Listening to music becomes a soulful experience; a discussion becomes uniquely animated; long trains of silent thought roll by in glorious splendor. The character of the landscape is more clearly seen, and felt emotionally. What can I say? When used in moderation, being stoned on good quality marijuana is an intensifier of life; if you like life, you'll like it even better stoned. I particularly enjoy driving at nite stoned, either alone or with the other occupants asleep. Just driving down that hiway and thinking and thinking and thinking. No boredom.

If you do drive while stoned, it's important to be careful while toking. Don't make it obvious that you're passing a joint from hand to hand amongst the occupants. Keep your dope well stashed, out of sight, not on your person. If possible, roll your joints in private so you don't do it in the car and so there won't be a litter of criminal evidence in case you're stopped. Grass is likely to be illegal for a long time yet, so don't get caught thru gross negligence. (Marijuana is also discussed later on in chapters 14 and 16.)

GETTING OUT OF THE CAR Getting bored? Getting tired? Get out of the car! There must be a nearby park, a rest area, even just a parking space. If you're on some barren stretch of hiway, pull over and sit on a fence. Pick some flowers. Photograph the view, photograph your car. Photograph your camera. Make impulse stops. Take a leak by the roadside or in the bushes. Pull over for a cuppa Java and a donut. Have a Kreme-Krud or a Bum Burger. Have a look at the stuff in the trading post, souvenir shop, or post card emporium. (I found some jumping beans.) When nearing a city with friends, telephone ahead — see if they're home, give them a decent warning.

Take a short hike every day, no matter where you are. When on the road this can be done by stopping each day at parks enroute. Most nature areas have self-guiding walks or trails to the points of interest. Almost every national park or national monument has a trail system designed for people who only have an hour or two to spend. These are ideal for midday jaunts to get the freeway out of your system, and move the sludge thru your bowels. Do the same thing in cities. Most large American cities can be seen, at least in part, on foot. Read chapter 13 about hiking for more ideas for short day-hikes.

Cycling is another escape from the car, and you can bring your own or you can rent them wherever you happen to be. More about this in chapter 11. Finally, to completely get yourself out of the car consciousness, staying with friends overnite is lovely because it gets you into a home (sweet home). Travelers are always around other strangers — in a car or in a campsite, hotel, restaurant … It's not the same as being with friends in their own homes — a complete change of pace that makes car travel more tolerable on a day by day basis.

Exercises

DRIVING EXERCISES

1) Live one day as if you had no car. If you're in town, take the busses or walk. In camp, walk all around … don't run any errands or sightsee in the car at all. Be stranded for a day. How do you feel? Helpless?

2) As you drive thru America, make a game of seeing how many automotive influences you can spot along the way. Get one of your kids to keep count of gasoline stations, garages, repair shops, parts stores, dealers, junkyards, motels, drive-in movies and restaurants, etc. Get a statistical feel for the influences of the automobile in different parts of the country.

3) Count how many animal corpses you spot on the hiways. See how many different species of animal you can identify. (In both totals, don't forget to add humans.)

4) Driving down the interstate on a day in which you have some time to spare, start an exploration by taking any off-ramp into an unknown region. Drive randomly for 20 or 30 minutes without looking at a map or selecting any particular way to go. See if you discover anything interesting. How does this kind of joy-ride make you feel?

5) When map-reading, we all occasionally notice certain interesting or comical names that catch our eye — of towns, natural features, whatever. We frequently say something like "Wow, I wonder what *that* place is like." Why not find out? Make a practice of taking just-for-the-hell-of-it detours for the slightest of reasons. It's a good way of getting some variety into a dull driving day, and there's always the chance of turning up something really interesting.

6) One of the values of good maps is that they'll show the low-grade roads and back roads, many of which will be short-cuts or alternate ways of getting somewhere. Try these once in a while, especially if you've been driving the freeways a lot lately.

7) On days when your car is being serviced or repaired in a strange city, don't wait for it in the Customer Waiting Room — get out on your feet and take as long a walk as you have time for, or hop a bus around town. A surprising amount of information can be gained in a pleasurable way about a place, even if you're in the suburbs or out in the boondocks.

ECOLOGY AND CARS The automobile, first-born child of a technological century, was a world-beater: It created previously undreamed-of personal freedom in all areas of human experience. It brought prosperity, mobility, a new morality, and a completely new style of life. In return, it's killing us. Violence, pollution, and ugliness are the dark cloud within the silver lining. It's becoming gradually clearer that Technology's gifts have their hidden price, and we need to find out that price before we clasp the glittering goodies to our cancer-prone bosoms. To own an automobile is to take part in and directly support the exhaustion of the world's resources and the poisoning of its life.

But we can't live without them: Automobiles are with us, in droves and indefinitely. They control our way of life, and hence, the way we think. Even the most extreme back-to-the-land communes and hippies still depend on automobiles, tho they use them more efficiently — for earnings as well as transportation, for housing instead of ostentation. The answer lies in that direction: We need automobiles and always will, but we must make them more useful so we can do with fewer. What we don't need are autos more powerful than needed, more polluting, more expensive, more specialized. We need autos that are simple, all-purpose, cheap, and clean. The concept of value needs to replace that of profit. This isn't politics but good sense; it affects the quality of our lives right now, and ultimately our survival.

There are some things you can do now, and they directly help you right now, as well as being ecological. First, buy a car that is as useful as possible . . . the more uses it has, the more efficient it is per dollar you spend, and the less overall ecological damage it does. (My version of the ideal car was described in chapter 7). Second, whatever you now drive, keep it in good shape so it'll run cleanly, safely, and indefinitely. Don't waste money and resources replacing it every year. Finally, be conscious of pollution and your contribution to it. Remember that you "Fuck the USA in your Cabriolet," so don't be too smug. You poison the air and earth with it, waste resources to make it, destroy animals and wilderness by using it, and create a runaway environment of exploitation around it — noise, traffic, parking lots, factories, red tape, pollution, materialism, injury, and death. You can still be one of 50,000 killed each year by it, one of 200,000 permanently injured, one of 2,000,000 hurt, or all three. That's some car you've got there.

AUTOMOBILE CLUBS Yes, OK. Useful for an extended tour of America, not too much the rest of the time. I recommend joining for the trip and dropping out later. You'll probably get your dues back in services. They're most useful in emergencies — if your car breaks down, if you need legal aid, if you get into trouble with the cops. Even without a disaster, they're loaded with useful information for the touring motorist, both before your trip and while at it. This is especially true of AAA, whose multitudinous local offices will give you detailed information about their areas if you stop in. Most automobile clubs are affiliated with garages for emergency road service. However, their affiliation with hotels, motels, and restaurants are a burn, tho their guidebooks are worth having anyway. Incidentally, I don't think I belong to an auto club at this writing, but I have belonged to AAA and NAC (National Automobile Club). Both were fine; the other clubs I don't know about at all. I have a (partial) list of them in Appendix 6.

INTERSTATES AND HIWAYS By wholesale blasting thru mountains and hills, filling in valleys and gullies, and paving over enormous stretches of open land, today we have the interstate hiway system. Over 40,000 miles long, serving 93% of American cities of 50,000 or more people, its intestines occupy a total area larger than Rhode Island. Interstates also happen to be about twice as safe as other roads in terms of death and accident rates. For the traveler on wheels, they make it possible to skim (scum?) over America, to travel long distances during their annual vacations. Now you can go from coast to coast, and back again in two weeks. Some vacation.

Nevertheless, the interstates fulfill their intended function, and I think they're necessary, even beautiful. The worst thing about the interstates is that they've given a tremendous impetus to the chain motels and restaurants, which provoke and prolong a mass consciousness geared to the lowest common denominator of quality. Besides that there isn't anything bad to say. They're actually ecological. Even tho they occupy a lot of area altogether, they still concentrate a lot of traffic in that area, reducing noise, pollution, and accidents everywhere else.

In the East, it's outrageous that some of the interstates are also toll hiways. They're all built with (primarily) federal money, tax money from the American people, and then in addition they charge tolls. Robbery! In some cases, like Interstate 95 north of New York City, there's no practical alternative route, so you're effectively blackmailed into paying these road costs. One day driving around in the New York-New Jersey area, I spent over $10 in tolls. It's things like this that make it hard to travel on $5 per day in America.

People say you can't tell much about the countryside while driving the interstates, that it's a poor way to see America. Well, we all know what they mean, but I don't think it's

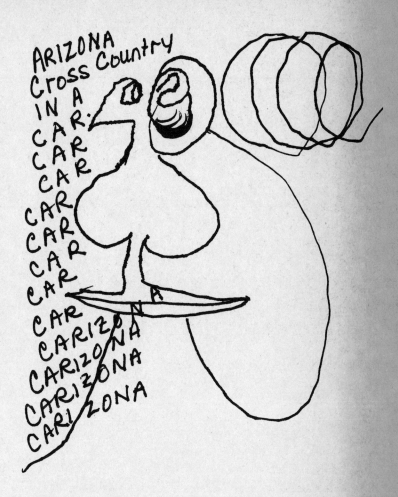

true. You can get a particular feeling for the American land when you drive the interstates. Driving at high speed begins to approach the vision of flying — you see the land forms of the earth spread out before you in a map-like projection. The speed and the straight-line character of the hiway give you a good sense of what the land is like — its shapes and colors. The scene changes more often because of your speed, and that keeps you more aware and interested in it. You zoom thru hillsides and see the rock or earth formations beneath the topsoil layers. You get panoramic vistas of wooded forests that would sometimes be impossible on a smaller road that followed the lay of the land. There were a lot of times I was thankful we had interstates, just for the view they gave.

SIGN OF THE TIMES

A large moving van passes us on the hiway, quite dirty and dusty. On the back of it somebody has written in the dust ANOTHER LOAD OF GO-GO GIRLS GOING NORTH. I actually spot this truck while driving past Climax, Michigan.

Off The Tape
AMERICAN HAND SIGNALS

People don't wave to you very much in America. About the only exceptions I've seen regularly are black kids in the south, and drivers of Volkswagon busses who motion to each other as they pass. Also, if you're on a rural or back road in the South or the West, farmers and ranchers will wave at you as you drive on by. If you like being waved at as a sign of friendship and acceptance, then the thing for you to do is to wave first. If you catch somebody's eye, wave at them. Most often they'll wave back and you'll get a smile too. If you wave at black people in the south, or probably black people anywhere, you may get the clenched fist salute in reply. Also, young kids passing in the backs of station wagons and the like will flash you the peace sign. Hardly anybody seems to give the finger anymore, a gesture which has gone into something of a decline in recent years. Certain Jesus freaks you may encounter on the road may give you the one-fingered sign, that is, holding up one finger to signify the one path to God. (A mistaken notion.)

BILLBOARDS There are other kinds of highway scenery, too, which include things like billboards. Most of the interstate systems don't permit billboards, at least not close to the hiway. Here and there, tho, you'll see them stuck back, way off beyond the right-of-way. And of course, there are always the gas stations around the interstates that have these enormous dirigibles of signs that float hundreds of feet above the ground on tall stilts so that you can see them a long way off. (That's a purely American touch. The Congress says 'no signs on the interstates' so now the gas stations make bigger signs further away.) Off the interstates there are some places where a veritable diarrhea of advertisements and billboards and neon plops on you constantly. (There are 300,000 true billboards in the country, and 500,000 more other-kinds of road signs).

It's surprising that there are still places where signs are used with great restraint, and some lovely places have few or no billboards at all. South Carolina is one that comes to mind, particularly in the countryside; Alabama is another. Some of the most annoying billboards to me are the ones repeated over and over again, sometimes hundreds of miles away from the presumed destination. Some Nevada gambling casinos use this technique: Wall's Drug Store in Dakota, Little America in Wyoming, and dubious attractions like Reptile Lands, Snake Farms, etc. The reason I don't like them, I guess, is because they're dictatorial — they don't give you any freedom from their message. This is a classic advertising technique — saturation is coercion. I remember one place in Florida that begins its billboard pitch some miles ahead, and in piecemeal cojoles you with everything from strange reptiles and exotic birds to rare animals, food and confections, cheap gas, free admission, free overnight camping, giant milkshakes — anything that might induce you to stop and buy.

Another type of American billboard: Nobody ever mentions it, but I don't mind pointing out that the roadsides and hiways of America are animal slaughterhouses. What an incredible carnage goes on out there! It's a

grotesque drive-in zoo of native American species, including our own. Identification is sometimes impeded by the rules of the game, which call for smashed skulls, disemboweled carcasses, shredded tissues, and long tell-tale stains down the pavement. There's nothing particular to be done; it's only a reminder of another hidden cost. The murdered animals on our hiways only symbolize the far greater numbers that died silently because they had no other choice.

BACK ROADS AND DIRT ROADS The interstates and toll roads may get you there but it's on the back roads and dirt roads that you really see America. Paved hiways extending over the horizon in boring straight lines are the main traveled and hence the least interesting routes. Try getting off into the back country via unpaved roads, and see where they lead. You'll be surprised.

The moment you're on a dirt road your whole consciousness of the country changes. You'll see everything around you in a more real way, a more sensitive way. You heighten your sense of distance and of time, because a trip on any dirt roads is always a backward step in time. You see a more primitive America, an early America that was slow and rural.

In New Mexico we went on dirt roads to approach various pueblo ruins. How different I felt to approach history slowly and bumpily, leaving a cloud of dust behind us, smelling the land and feeling its wildness. How much better than zipping up on an interstate and taking the exit ramp right into the pueblo ruins.

Another time, we were having trouble "finding" the Ozarks because all the hiways and paved roads were (g)littered with signs and billboards. There didn't seem to be much of Arkansas around. A decision to detour onto a dirt road got us what we were looking for: a view of the country the way it was, with quiet roads, farms, mountain hollows, hamlets nestling in the backwater of history. In one town we came onto the Tuesday morning livestock auction and flea market, with all the locals gathered around, visiting with each other, trading news, waiting for the auction. We bought an old hat, fresh fruits and vegetables, a pair of shorts, and "visited" with quite a few folks. Further on down the road we unexpectedly came on a place called Lost Valley, a primitive and little visited park. We hiked into an overgrown limestone gorge to a cave at the back end, then went on all fours to find a waterfall inside a hidden grotto. We lost the flashlite and the baby was screaming, but it was a great adventure, one we would have missed by staying on the paved road. While there we heard about a nearby swimming hole on the ole North Buffalo River. So, a little further on, on a hot Ozarks summer day, we went down to the crik with a bunch of the neighbors, ranging from little toddlers up to old galoots, splashed around and cooled off in real country style.

It's the back roads, the dusty country lanes where you find the sights and sounds and feelings of a vagabond's America. You'll meet here the people that you hoped to find; you'll discover an unknown America far from the pressure-cooker society. It's a rich personal experience. Incidentally, of the total road mileage in the United States, 4/5 is rural and about 1/5 is not paved. Or to put it a different way: the interstate hiway system mileage represents about 1/1000 of all the miles in the country.

SIGN OF THE TIMES

Gas station in Bucksforth, Maine: BP IS HERE — IT'S A GAS.

A NATION'S STATIONS

Ashland	Gasland	Chex
Redhead	T-Bird	Empire
Hep-U-Sef	Tulsa	Golden
Boron	Humble	Bi-Lo
Standard (Chevron)	Merit	Pathmark
Whiting Bros	Top Gas	Hi Test
American (Amoco)	Interstate 95	Sohio
Union 76	Scot	Total
Gulf	4M Gas	Freeway
Shell	Gasland	Beacon
Fina	Tri S	Best
BP	Potters	Clerk
Sunoco	Conoco	Zephyr
Arco	Lehigh	Skelly
Esso	Power Test	Red X
DX	Valu Gas	Holiday
Red Dot	Hesse	Transport
Douglass	Midwest	Mobil
East Coast	Double S	Citgo
Philips 66	Kayo	Getty
Deep Rock	Consolidated	R Gas
North Star	Seaside	Urich
Derby	Fast Gas	Sinclair
Kerr-McGee	Apco	Vickers
Husky	Sav-o-mat	Amerigo
Wheel Camper	Wilco	U Pump It
Maverick	Shamrock	Ronco
Golden Eagle	Stinker	Bronco
Hungry Onion	Sav-way	Richfield
Franko	Time	Leathers Oil Co

To find these back roads you'll need good maps of the vicinity you're interested in. Get the state hiway patrol maps, which are available free to tourists. Inquire about how to get detailed county maps, available for most counties in each state. Another good source is one of the sportsmen's maps sold at sporting goods stores (prepared for hikers, fishermen, hunters), which frequently show extremely fine dirt road details. And, of course, local inquiry is always worthwhile, even when you know exactly where you are and where you're going. It's a good trip to stop and ask directions a lot. That way you get some idea of the kind of folks living in this neighborhood. You'll find these conversations can easily be stretched out for great lengths of time and can prove to be the high point of the day.

USES OF GASOLINE STATIONS Buy gas at the cheapest price you can, because it's ecological to spend your money carefully. Many full-service gas stations are rip-offs, especially since you often don't get much service anyway. On the interstates, gas always sells for less in the adjacent towns, not along the route itself. It pays to shop around. Sometimes the price varies as much as 10 cents per gallon within a few blocks. With those savings, I don't mind if the attendants' uniform isn't up to military standards. Restrooms are another matter, but most independent gas stations maintain clean rest rooms, and you can usually tell from the way a place looks before you go in.

Providing toilets is the next most important function of gasoline stations (what if there were roadside toilet stations with one or two gas pumps behind the building?). Gas station restrooms are among the most useful rooms a traveler sees. In addition to "resting" your bowels and bladder, they can be used for physical refreshment, for personal cleanliness, hair grooming, clothes changing, sponge bathing, reading and/or writing graffiti, stocking up on condoms, and autoerotism. If you need a full-service restroom, then use a name-brand gasoline station. But if you just need to take a leak, go to your no-name independent who has a hole or two out back. Save the difference in what you pay for gasoline. Of course, you can use the full-service restroom without buying the gas, but this is sometimes complicated by getting the key from the attendant, or by the coin-operated lock on the door. (Fast coming up on the travel horizon are full-service restrooms attached to roadside rest areas and tourist information centers. These are always free and often the last word in modern-day defecatoriums.)

Gas stations are also places to get emergency help, maps, candy bars, cold drinks, lube jobs, local directions, and a few friendly words in the middle of nowhere or the night. Pumping gas is not one of your more great jobs, so gas station attendants are frequently eager to make contact with the motorists they serve, especially if you're from out-of-state. Try a little small-talk.

BREAKDOWNS Automobile breakdowns are examples of pattern breakdowns that release energy OK, but threaten people so much that they never enjoy it much. It just goes to show how tied we are to our plans and our cars. While you're frantically worried and energized over getting your act back on the road, note your sense of helplessness and frustration — it proves how dependent you really are. Next time try to be freer.

Meanwhile, you're broken down. Well, it's silly to think you can own a car and not have trouble with it sooner or later. It's like having a dog without dog shit. If you've got one, the other isn't far off.

So, know what to expect, and be prepared. Mainly you'll lose time and money (both are energy equivalents) in order to counteract the drain of free energy the breakdown represents. The time loss should be merely a bother, presuming you haven't scheduled yourself into a tight corner that has no room for Acts of God. Actually, the time you spend this way is rich in experience, and gets you fully involved in your surroundings. In that sense, breakdowns are good for you. But they also cost

Off The Tape
TROUBLE IN MISSISSIPPI

The gas gauge showed a little gas left, but suddenly the car just stopped running. I hailed down a kid on a tractor and got a lift into town — about ½ mile or so. The outskirts were a collection of shacks, then a few blocks of shabby downtown Americana. Hot and hazy sun, humid, no traffic. Mostly black people on the street, standing on corners or sitting in the shade on chairs.

Got a gallon of gas at a run-down service station; the attendant was a young man from LA. He had some relatives here, came back to Mississippi to escape the frantic city. But he hates being here now — "a terrible place" — hoped he could get away soon. I walked back to the car, put the gas in. It started but wouldn't keep running.

So back to town again. I tried telephoning a garage, but the public phone wouldn't take nickels. I asked a man standing by if he had a dime for two nickels. He shook his head and said, "No, we don't have nuthin like that around here." So I went inside a drugstore for change; they didn't want to give it to me because the phone didn't work. They were suspicious, but finally told me about the other public phone, a few blocks walk away. That one didn't work either.

I walked around some more, found the town garage. Well, they didn't work on VW's, but told me about a wrecker who might tow me into the nearest big town 27 miles away. Another man at an auto parts house, the only man who really tried to help me, came out and looked at the engine. But he was only a farmer who didn't know much about mechanics, and left. So I just kept trying to start the engine and soon it was running smoothly again.

I was only out of gas, but I guess some dirt had gotten into the carburetor and made the engine run badly for awhile. So that was that. Later on we stopped for lunch by the road. A flatbed truck loaded with young black men went by (two white men in the cab). We waved and got the clenched fist salute from all the blacks.

Stoned day in Mississippi.

money, as a rule. Set aside an emergency slush fund for this, or be prepared to basically rearrange some other part of your vacation. Owning a credit card is another way of taking up the slack in a hurry.

The biggest hassle involved is getting your car from the place where it stopped to the place where it can be fixed at some reasonable price. If you belong to any kind of automobile club then you'll have towing insurance that will get you to a garage. Auto club membership is worth having on a long trip, especially if your car is nearing its latter days. There isn't too much you can do about picking a reliable garage. Go to a dealership if you can, or to a AAA recommended garage, or do what local inquiry leads you to. The emergency service benefits of automobile club policies usually include mechanical first aid, towing to a garage (tho almost always to the garage that runs the towing service), tire changing, delivery of gas, oil, or water; battery service; and getting pulled out of ditches. Costs of parts and supplies are never included. Installation or removal of snow chains is never included. None of these services are supplied for heavy trucks, trailer, campers, or motorcycles.

Before you leave on your trip, have your car looked at or worked on to increase your chances of bringing it back alive. First get all the little stuff working: Make sure your wipers wipe, both headlights lite (upper and lower beams), headlites aim right, turn and brake signals work ... make sure you've got some brake linings left, check your tires all around, not only for tread wear but for gouges and tears. Get a good spare tire, jack, and lug wrench. Tune the car up before you go. Check out the voltage regulator and the generator (brushes OK), and put water in your battery (no one else is going to check it if you don't). If you've got a noisy muffler, do something about it now to avoid the inevitable ticket. Get an oil change and lube, maybe a new oil filter. Check your brake fluid level, transmission oil level, clean your cooling system if you've got one. Put a God's-Eye on the dashboard.

ACCIDENTS If you have an accident, first try to come out of it alive or unharmed. (In January of 1974, according to projections, the 2,000,000th American motorist will die in action — let it be some other lucky stiff.) Next give first aid to the injured and blessings to the dead. (See chapter 15 for first aid information and advice.) If necessary, call an ambulance and/or police. Get the names of witnesses. Do the usual information exchanges — names, addresses, license numbers — see the form reproduced here. If you have a camera, take pictures of the scene and the damage. Finally, praise God for whatever small mercy He's shown in the situation, and remember it wouldn't have happened if you'd gone hiking instead.

YOU SHOULD FIND OUT...

Who IS THE OTHER DRIVER?

Name_____

Address_____

Operator's License No._____

Who IS THE CAR OWNER?

Name_____

Address_____

Who WAS IN THE CAR?

Name_____

Address_____

Who WITNESSED THE ACCIDENT?

Name_____

Address_____

Name_____

Address_____

What WAS THE OTHER CAR?

Make_____Body Type_____

Year_____License_____

When DID IT HAPPEN?

Date_____Day_____Hour_____
                              (a.m. - p.m.)

Where DID IT HAPPEN?

City_____

Location_____
        (Street, Intersection or Landmark)

DESCRIBE WHAT HAPPENED:

DIAGRAM SHOWING HOW IT HAPPENED:

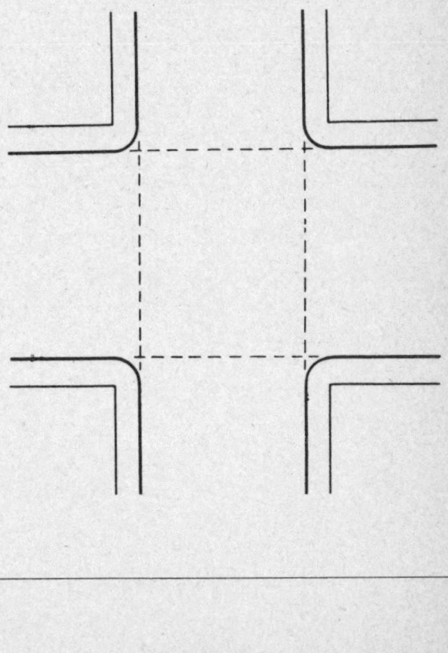

Off The Tape
PAYING FOR XEROX

It was in a New York town that a young woman with a learner's permit dropped a cigarette in her lap, lost control of her car, and hit us while we were waiting for a red lite. She also hit the car in front of us and a truck across the street. No one was hurt except the girl herself, cut lip, bleeding slightly, crying some. We spent a few hours at the police station — right next to the Life Saver candy factory and across the street from the Marvel Mystery Oil factory — filling out reports, seeing the inside of a small town American police station. The officer filled out reports for hours, didn't make any carbons . . . said that if we wanted a xerox copy of the police report we could either pay $3.50 or copy down everything on a blank form and sign his name to it, or anybody else's name to it. He wouldn't sign it because "who was going to check it anyway?" He explained that making out a police report at all was a favor conferred upon us by the department, because many police departments don't bother with them anymore. We wound up paying $3.50 for the xerox copy. The officer said it cost so much because tho the paper was only a few pennies, how was the machine going to be paid for? I said I thought that was what we all paid taxes for and he said, "No, look, you're from out of state, none of your taxes come here."

INSURANCE This is one of the biggest consumer rip-offs in existence, a self-serving industry with the power and money to say "Fuck you" to everyone including the government. If you're not insured, an accident that's your fault can ruin you financially, cause loss of license, or get you in jail. Despite the piratical rates, you should be insured if you can pay it, especially on a long trip. On the other hand, if you don't own anything anyway (you have no property to lose), your car is a clunker, *and* you drive very carefully — then live dangerously — drive without insurance. If you have a minor accident that's your fault and you're not insured, see if the other driver will accept a personal settlement. It'll be worth the cost to you because of the legal hassles it'll prevent.

PACKING THE CAR Packing for car travel is pretty easy. Except for some special items related to traveling by car, the advice is the same as for any other way to travel. First, take as little as possible. The place to be most canny about packing is your clothes. While actually traveling in your car you need little or none. That means you only have to dress for the rest of the time. The same for shoes — a pair of sandals or moccasins is fine in the car. You'll want to bring along a pair of walking shoes, maybe boots for heavy-duty hiking. If possible, take no more than two bags per person — a large one and a small one. The smaller bag should be a shoulder bag so that you can use it as an all-purpose carry-all for day jogs out of the car, for carrying cameras or lunch or guidebooks.

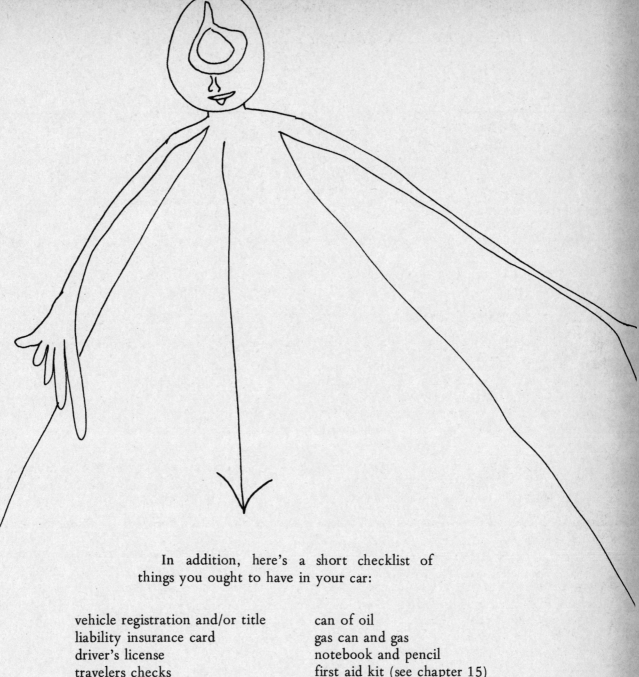

In addition, here's a short checklist of things you ought to have in your car:

vehicle registration and/or title
liability insurance card
driver's license
travelers checks
maps
guidebooks
paper towels or tissues
whisk broom
windshield cloth
emergency flares
flashlite
basic set of tools

can of oil
gas can and gas
notebook and pencil
first aid kit (see chapter 15)
medical guidebook (see chapter 15)
maybe spare change for tolls and
    telephones
a blanket to wrap around your feet
    when you drive old cars in winter
a vacuum bottle for hot coffee
harmonica or other instrument
a bag of fruit

Motorcycle Touring

10

Two-Wheel Wandering

MOTORCYCLING AS IT IS, by Norm Albers

DREAMS AND DRAMA Motorcycles appeal to the American hunger for mythic experience. We have a tradition of open-air heroes with wind-rush in their faces as they speed by on some juiced-up boneshaker — bronco, locomotive, cockpit, fire truck, or motorcycle. When technology advances to the point that the hero no longer gets wind in the face, he stops being heroic, and often even becomes the opposite. Take astronauts for example: Touted as heroes, everyone recognizes they're just well-trained businessmen — no wind in the face. Anyway, Americans don't go for heroes too much; they'd rather live the dream themselves than worship somebody else. In America everyone can be a hero. Why not? It's a free country, and that's where the motorcycle comes in. It's the perfect vehicle for free people.

It not only has the aura of drama, the physical sensation, the thrill of power *but* it's economical to operate, ecologically superior to any car, and because of the challenges and skills involved, is rewarding to an extent that non-riders can only dimly perceive.

The disadvantages of motorcycles are many, indeed, but usually don't mean much to the true bike addict; they only add to the adventure. These include danger, discomfort, and dirt. Bikes are expensive to buy, not easy to maintain, can't carry much, and tiring on the long distances. Still interested? If so, read on.

TYPE OF MOTORCYCLE At the outset, it's important to state that touring by motorcycle, for all its devil-may-care atmosphere, needs to be well-thought-out in advance. The place to start this thinking is right there in the machine, because the success of your trip may depend on the type of bike you ride. How well suited to your touring plans is it? The wrong bike will never give you the right tour. Here's what it's about:

A motorcycle basically imitates a car in that it goes fast, even tho it has much less power and only two wheels. What the motorcycle sacrifices in order to do this is a large margin of safety and comfort. Its characteristics and construction become crucial. In

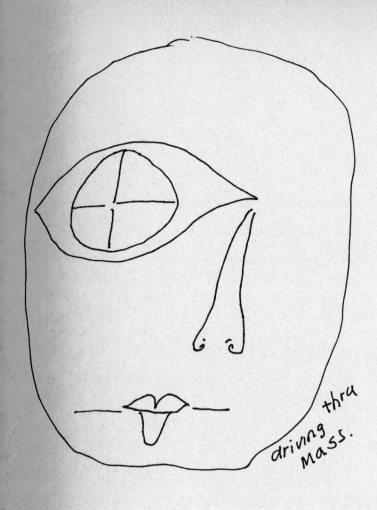

driving thru Mass.

Off The Tape
PERILS OF GETTING OLDER

In front of Independence Hall in Philadelphia we see some red-headed man of about 45 with a drum strapped to his hip and some kind of portable radio in front of his face and a big sign over his head saying **ALL MIGHTY MARTIN AND THE GRAND EQUIPMENT** (???) Can't tell what it's all about but he does a continual jig on the sidewalk, beating the drum, drawing a small crowd. Some passers-by say that he's been arrested once or twice. He's a local-color figure. A man going by excuses this behavior by saying "Well, we never know what we're going to do when we're older, do we?"

practical terms this means that the automobile driver can have a sloppy machine and sloppy driving habits without anyone knowing the difference — his margin of safety and comfort takes up all that slop. That margin isn't happening for the motorcyclist. For example, a passenger in a car doesn't matter, but on the bike the passenger makes a huge difference in performance, affecting speed, acceleration, balance, handling, and braking. Like, one bad tire blowing at high speed isn't just half your wheels; it's all of your stability. Like, a lite-weight bike straining at the freeway speed limits hour after hour isn't merely tearing up its engine; it's wearing down and bumming out its rider, too. You get the idea.

The fact is that the touring motorcycle needs to be right for the tour at hand, or vice-versa. What that means if you already own your bike is that you've got to pick a tour it can handle. A 250 cc street bike is OK for a fairly short tour without passenger, especially off the freeways. But it won't be either safe or fun for two riders to Fairbanks. If you don't yet own a bike, then pick and choose carefully so you'll get a machine that won't screw your trip one way or another. In no other kind of touring is this match between means and intention more important.

PRACTICAL FACTORS For long-distance touring, big and powerful bikes are not just *de rigueur* but *de only ting*. Big means heavy, because weight is where it's at when you're cruising. Weight keeps you close to the ground despite speed and bumps, weight keeps you tracking on a straight line despite wind and passing trucks, weight keeps you stable even loaded down with dunnage and partner. Powerful means high speed to get quickly from here to there, power means ability to pass and to pull on hills, power means efficiency that saves your engine, power means less vibration to keep your brains from scrambling.

Beyond those factors, your machine should be well-designed so that it's safe (brakes, suspension), reliable (reputation, availability of dealers and parts), and equipped for touring (windshield, good seats, saddlebags, etc.). It would be a blessing all around if it were also quiet in operation. This keeps you happy because you get to hear some of the rest of the world, and keeps others happy because they get to hear some of the rest of the world too. The bike should be put in top shape before you start out (tires, brakes, chain, mufflers, tuneup, lights, horn, etc.). Get it working before you get it on, or even before you get on it.

All this points to a new or late-model road bike of around 500 cc or more ... something like a big Harley, Honda, or BMW.

BUYING YOUR MOTORCYCLE Bikes cost so much because their speed and performance requirements are far more demanding than an automobile's, for example. So much power in such a small package puts great stresses on the frame, the wheels, the suspension. Engine and road vibration is a constant enemy trying to disassemble the machine. Every part has to be well-designed and well-manufactured to take the stresses, the vibration, the exposure.

These are also good arguments for buying a new machine. You know exactly what condition it's in, and that knowledge is basic to feeling secure on your machine when you're out there in the tules a long way from home. Being able to break in a new engine yourself is a great advantage for the potential touring freak, because that can have a major effect on the bike's future reliability. Dealers love to sell new motorcycles and will be glad to have you ride their demonstrator models. You can't get from a short ride all you'll need to know about the bike, but careful examination of the bike's features and its handling characteristics goes a long way in helping to choose. Other advantages are credit terms available and a warranty. The new bike buyer, incidentally, gets a lot to choose from — much more than the used buyer. However, the wide range of choice doesn't count a thing if you don't know about it. Don't buy till you've seen and compared numerous models and makes. Buy or subscribe to some of the numerous motorcycle

"Come on, you roving minstrels
And together we will try
To rouse the spirit of the earth
And move the rolling skies"

—Fairport Convention
Come All Ye (Song)

magazines for critiques of different models, or look up these reports in the library. See the list under "Motorcycling" in Appendix 1. Talk to owners of bikes you're interested in, wherever you happen to see them (usually around the cycle shops but often in the street, at gas stations and markets, wherever). The more you can learn from all sources, the more likely you are to come up with the right choice.

What about a used motorcycle? Well, it's not the same thing as buying a used car. For the same reasons that bikes have to be better built in the first place, they have to be better cared for and in better shape than your average good used car. A frayed clutch cable in a car is no big deal, but it can mess you up on a bike. And a bike that's been in an accident is hardly ever worth buying unless you're a good mechanic. The damage may not be noticeable when you buy it but is bound to cause trouble or disaster somewhere later on. Probably just when you're thinking how great to be a modern motorized vagabond, a happy dude on a healthy hog, and . . . CLANK, CRUNCH, etc.

Buying used should go something like this: First of all, no way to buy a new one? OK, then decide what kind of used bike you need to do your thing. Next, find out as much as you can about that style-model-type of bike. Ask, read, ride. That way you'll know what to look for and what to ask when you start looking at those bargain-priced jobbees in the want ads. Look for signs of accidents and repairs. Make a meticulous visual inspection. Also, check for rust, loose parts, other signs of poor maintenance. Run the bike. Ride it for at least a few miles over different kinds of roads to check shocks, handling, brakes. Bring somebody with you who knows about bikes, or that kind of bike. If possible, ride several of the same kind as nearly alike as possible so that you learn what's common to all and what's weird to one in particular.

If you do luck out with a new bike, pay attention to the manufacturer's breaking-in advice. This will generally consist of speed limits for certain mileage totals, and a maintenance schedule in the early life of your

machine. What's at stake is the top level of both reliability and performance as the machine grows older. To make parts wear right, friction must be reduced. This means good oil, frequent oil changes, smooth running, and warming-up the engine (to warm the oil) before blasting off. Excessive heat must be avoided, too. This means watching the red-line speeds during break-in and not overloading the engine by lugging or beating on it.

ROUTINE MAINTENANCE This consists mainly of routine oil changes, tuneups, and maintaining the bike as specified in the owner's manual that comes with a new bike. If you bought it used, get the owner's manual at a shop or write the manufacturer. Also try to get an authorized shop manual or unauthorized equivalent so you can learn to do some or all of your own maintenance (at least timing and valve adjustments, points and plugs). Besides that, periodically tighten down whatever keeps coming loose. Where possible, wire these things tight before you start your tour. Once on your

tour, regularly make close visual inspections and tightening sessions.

Breakdown-and-repair on the road is another matter, and as they say, "falls outside the scope of this discussion." However, carrying tools and spare parts is an absolute necessity. Even a total mechanical idiot will be able to diagnose certain problems (flat tire, broken cable) and can fix them if the means are available. The owner's manual will be helpful, too. The following list of tools and spares should be considered the minimum insurance.

Tools: Screwdrivers, regular and Phillips
      Crescent wrench
      Wrench set
      Pliers, regular and vise-type
      Spark plug wrench
      Test lamp
      Flashlite or penlite
      Electrician's tape
      Tire repair kit (and tire irons)
      Air source (pump or aerosol)
      Feeler gauge (for points, plugs, valves)

      Knife (penknife or camping knife)
      Owner's manual
      Small oil can
      Rag

Spare Parts:
      Bulbs (headlite, tail lite, etc.)
      Cables (throttle, clutch, etc.)
      Points & condenser
      Spark plugs
      Fuse(s)

If you break down and can't fix it, try to flag down another motorcycle. You'll get the most sympathy, and maybe mechanical knowledge. Otherwise hitchhike to town and/or help. Try to get the bike off the road and preferably out of sight. Lock it to a tree or pole. If you're traveling with a passenger, one of you stay with the machine. To help get a ride and maybe safeguard the bike, take off the front wheel and hitchhike with it in your hand. Take your valuables with you.

Off The Tape
HISTORY OF KNOTT'S BERRY FARM

Bill: I probably won't get the years right, you know.

Ed: It doesn't matter. I just want some general sense of it.

B: Well, Walter Knott is still living; the two Knotts are still living — they're both 83 years old. And both active in the business. In fact, I ran into old Walter about two days ago, yes, they're both on their feet still. But they opened their berry stand in 1920, like 51 years ago and not too many years later, he said "How about if we served up a few chicken dinners?" And she said, "Oh, OK Walter, but I don't want to go into the restaurant business." Yeah, famous last words. So on a Sunday (right, chicken on Sunday), next to their little stand they served 13 little dinners on her wedding china. And that was like 40 or 50 years ago.

E: Well you know, that's as classic an American story as you can get.

B: It is.

Jean: They are a true American pioneer story.

B: It's almost scarey how stereotyped they are.

J: They came in a wagon you know, literally.

B: Yes, they came in a wagon and a horse and the whole shot. And to this day they're that humble.

E: So what are the statistics now, how many chicken dinners did they serve per whatever?

B: Like today, nowadays. I think like their classic record is 6700 chicken dinners in a day that they've served.

E: I guessed that it would have to be something like that.

B: And they've had the same recipe for the last 30 or 40 years. Same menu is what I mean. They serve you, like, salad, the dinner, rhubarb, a little bowl of rhubarb, in fact rhubarb was the last grown item that they grew on the farm.

E: Is the site the same?

B: Heavens yes. This is why Knott's Berry Farm has not expanded, like Knott's Berry Farm of Florida or Knott's Berry Farm of NY. Because how do you transplant tradition?

E: Well, is any part of it still farmed?

B: No, the last part of it was stopped farming seven years ago.

E: Weren't they associated with boysenberries, wasn't that the original berry juice?

B: Right, Walter Knott is the developer of the boysenberry. Well it was developed by some guy named Boysen. And this guy crossed like a fudd-berry with a dingle-berry or something.

E: He crossed an elephant with a sweet pea and got the boysenberry.

B: Right, ha ha ha. He crossed a rooster with another rooster and he ended up with a very cross rooster. Ha ha ha.

B: So the eldest daughter said, "At the corner of the restaurant, could I put up a card table or whatever?" She started selling stuff, you know, probably needlework and whatever the people in those days had. So she ended up opening up a gift shop, which is now one of the most successful areas of the place called Virginia's Gift Shop. Well, by the late 30's, early 40's, people were lining up down there, and Walter Knott said "Let's give them people somethin to look at." So he started disassembling buildings in ghost town areas in California and Nevada, reconstructing them as exhibits. And by the 50's had developed Knott's Berry Farm and Ghost Town, and it was open to the public. Now we have become the third largest amuseument park in the world.

E: Who's ahead?

B: Well, I think we are slowly becoming fourth because the first one is Disneyland and then Tivoli Park, Copenhagen, and just to quote statistics, Disneyland was 10 million people; Tivoli Park, Copenhagen was about 7.5 million people a year; and then we do 5 million guests a year. But I think Disneyworld is going to knock Disneyland down to second and we will go to fourth.

E: Why is it that Knott's Berry Farm has become the third or fourth most popular amusement park in the world? I'm not sure why that's so.

B: Well if you want to go back to Economica 1A, you open to your first chapter, it says the best place to open a shoe stand is next to another shoe store, and the reasons that Knott's Berry Farm was the second largest amusement park is because they're nine miles away from the first largest amusement park. When I say second I mean second largest in the United States. We are what the old carnival guy would call the "blow-off." We're sitting next to the biggest, most successful big daddy of them all — Disneyland and we are reaping the benefits.

E: Well, I went to Knott's Berry Farm first, before there was a Disneyland. I think I'm one of the privileged few.

B: Why did you go?

E: Oh, Long Beach is such a dead town anyway. It was one of the attractions of the Long Beach area.

I remember when I went to Knott's Berry Farm. I was in downtown Long Beach — I caught a bus, just a sight-seeing bus or something, I don't remember. They were selling tickets downtown with free bus transportation or something like that. I remember driving way out thru the orange groves into this empty countryside, miles and miles.

B: How many years ago?

E: Oh around 1952.

B: Lord. Yeah.

E: But the feeling today is the same. I liked it then and I like it now.

B: Well, free parking and a buck and a half to get into the farm.

E: Wow, what a bargain!

B: Wow, what a bargain! That's true.

E: OK, we now go to the next step. I get a feeling but I don't know for sure, that Knott's Berry Farm has now gone through another phase with the opening of the entertainment center. Is that true?

B: Yes, actually I think we self-admittedly say that until about 1968 or 69 that we were a glorified shopping center in that we had the bulk of the income thru the retail sales and food service, and then we delved into the entertainment area. And in 1968 and 69, they were an influx of people who wished to live off the land, ha ha ha ha.

E: I don't understand that at all.

B: Well, the hippies came around, and uh, can we use that term?

E: Sure.

B: Right, And the long-haired communist left-wing bastards who were going to take over the world, ha ha ha ha ha . . .

E: I don't understand why they would come. I mean what could they get out of Knott's Berry Farm?

B: Well they felt, well, Knott's Berry Farm consisted of 150 acres of open land with lots of hiding holes and places where you could just kind of move in and sleep in an old covered wagon and they were just literally taking over the place and using it as a stopover, but unfortunately — they were seriously starting to eat the livestock. It was an actual farm. You know, let's start from the beginning. It was Knott's Berry Farm and they had livestock and chickens and goats and those who wished to be free-livers thought, well, God's word was that you should live off the land, so they thought well, let's live off this guy's land, and they were literally eating the chickens and cooking them on the curb, wringing their necks . . .

J: They were camping out, you know . . .

B: Yeah, it was a bad scene.

E: Well, what happened?

B: What happened was that they threw up a fence around it and charged a buck to come in and they kept out 99% of the people who were causing the problem.

E: So it's the hippies who are to blame for the admission charge?

B: Well, whoever they were, they were people who were unemployed and felt that somebody owed them a living, ha ha ha ha. And I think these type of people have existed since time immemorial.

E: Since 1966.

B: No, since 1968, that's when the wall came up. ha ha ha ha ha

J: 1776

B: But uh, so that's when the wall came up. So they said OK, slap a dollar cover charge on Mr. Knott's restaurant, and what evolved was a miraculous and unexpected source of income.

J: The family all this time had never realized that by putting up a gate you have five million extra bucks. It just sort of didn't occur to them until they had to do it.

E: So they have their lucky stars to thank the hippies. Why didn't they build a temple to the hippies? Using this extra money? ha ha ha ha ha ha

B: Somehow that doesn't make sense. ha ha ha ha ha. Temple for the hippies. ha ha ha ha ha. Because they've built one for everyone else.

E: Or a free health clinic.

J: Right.

E: Well, anyway, OK.

B: I think that . . .

J: I think we'd better forget the whole thing.

B: No, I think that probably their honor to the hippies is that they in essence treat them as equals. I mean the fact that they do let them in in spite of themselves.

J: I should say. You mean if they want to pay a buck they get in.

B: Yeah, if they want to pay a buck, but now it's a buck and a half. So they do treat them as equals and I think that is their honor to hippies . . . it's also "free enterprise."

E: I read in a guidebook, a guidebook to America, that Disneyland does not admit what they call "extreme hippies."

J: It doesn't matter if you're extreme.

B: Knott's Berry Farm will.

CLOTHES AND ACCESSORIES Clothes for motorcyclists are like motorcycles themselves in ways already mentioned before: they undergo exposure and stress that would rapidly disintegrate normal threads. It's not just wind and cold and rain, it's possibly being thudded about and ripped apart when and if flesh and pavement meet at high rates of speed. Specialized motorcycle clothing is not a frill for the sake of modesty, or even comfort, but a survival necessity.

Boots are essential. They permit you to crank the machine repeatedly without mashing your instep. They protect you from frostbite (literally) in cold wind and rain. In case of accident they gird your ankles and sheath your highly vulnerable foot parts. They greatly dampen vibration from the foot rests (the heavier the soles the better).

At the opposite end of you, a helmet is a requirement and is, in fact, a legal one in many states. Its major purpose, of course, is to keep your cute little bean from concussion and/or crushing when in striking or pressing circumstances. Helmets save lives a lot. Only a hardy fool is foolhardy enough to go without one. Helmets also greatly cut down engine and wind noise by covering your ears. For the touring rider who'll spend hour after hour sitting in the middle of his own noise, the ear padding in his helmet does an important job. (Almost 90% of motorcycle helmets tested by the National Highway Traffic Safety Administration in 1971 failed to meet performance requirements. The only eight helmets that complied with ANSI standards for shock absorption, penetration, and chin strap strength were the following: Bell R-T, Crager 60000, Fi-Pro, ILC 601, Falcon (701-52), Sterling Pro, Sterling Cougar, and Townley TB-310. For test results, write NHTSA, Washington, DC 20590).

Finally, all along the middle of you, between boots and helmet, should also be sheathed in protective clothes. "Protective" most certainly means clothes made of leather. Why leather? Because only leather meets all requirements for resistance to tearing, wearing, and puncturing under shock/stress; for sealing out wind and cold; for being pliable, flexible, and comfortable; for ease of care. No matter how loving of animal life you are, there is no substitute for leather garments while motorcycling. Jackets, at least, are a leather-only item; gloves, too. Pants can be otherwise, but should be leather-reinforced in the ass-end and the knees. Gloves should be gauntlet-type, so that they prevent entry of wind at your jacket sleeves. Neck should be mandarin-type to keep out elements of all descriptions. Zippers should be backed by wind-flaps, made of something that won't bind or rust, and be two-way opening for efficient ventilating on hot days.

We've now got all parts of you covered except the face, so let's get it shielded too. Goggles for the eyes are a damned good idea; just one piece of road gravel at high speed can really plug your pupil. Also, wind directly on the eyeball is uncomfortable at least, and unbearable for some. If it's raining, goggles are a must for eyeglass wearers, who otherwise are apt to go instantly blind, and won't even be able to get their tin cups out before wrapping around a pole. Plastic wrap-around face masks are another alternative, and more comfortable. They also shield the rest of the face, leaving nothing open to the elements. For those who must be in touch with the air in some way, try unzipping your fly.

One last bit: under heavy dust or dirt conditions, a bandana or handkerchief fastened bandit-style over the face is a useful thing to remember. (But take it off when entering any place of business.)

Another category of clothing is raingear, specifically designed for extensive wet riding rather than short stretches that your leathers can handle. These are made from weatherized nylons and cottons, and are usually worn just as rain outfits though the heavier ones can be used as general riding suits.

To price and/or buy motorcycling clothes, check the local dealers and ask well-togged riders. If you live in a big city, visit your local leather specialty stores. Clothes of the best quality can also be bought by mail-order. Write the following for their catalogs:

Bates Industries
701 W. Cowles
Long Beach, CA 90801

Wheels of Man
208 E. Wisconsin
Milwaukee, WI 53202

Herm's Leathertogs
701 Northampton
Easton, PA 18042

Top Gear
80 Pompton
Verona, NJ 07044

J Barbour & Sons
Simonside, So. Shields
County Durham
England

D. Lewis Ltd.
124 Great Portland
London W1A
England
(catalog 50 cents)

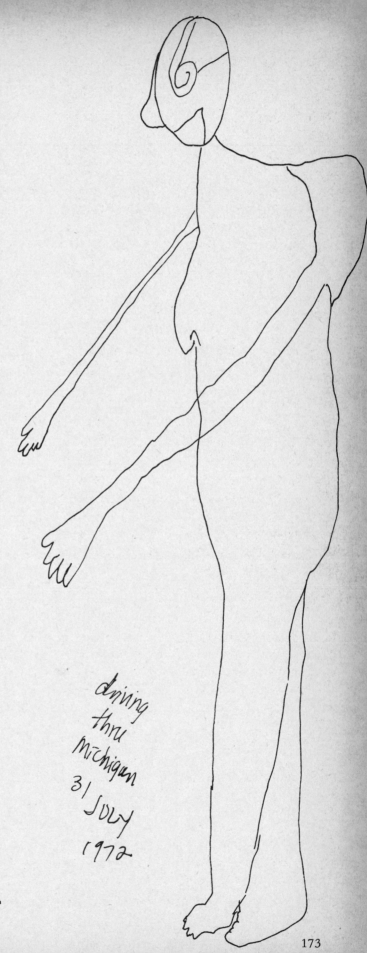

driving
thru
Michigan
31 JULY
1972

riding again
moving against the wind
faster than God intended
highway is framed
by well-ordered greenery
other lives speed by
too fast too fast
no chance for love
or length
just a quick touch
in time.
sky sky
night and day
sun
moon
time away away
day like month
month like minute
highway
high way
hi
way
Away.

RIDING TECHNIQUES This is where it all comes down real and hard. Right riding techniques reward you with pleasure and pride, and enormously increase your chances of avoiding accidents and spills. Wrong riding techniques make you tired, rob your fun, and make you dangerous to yourself and others.

First off, again, motorcycles are not cars. They call for greater skill, more knowledge, much more awareness. These are not liabilities of the motorcycle; they are in large part what make motorcycling so rewarding. Unlike the car, a motorcycle is not simply a way of getting somewhere — it is a way of getting somewhere with style and complete consciousness.

Consciousness is the key. Concentration on riding is what makes the ride fun and what makes the ride safe. When you lose concentration, you stop enjoying it and start becoming a menace. My most serious accident (fractured wrist, concussion) came while daydreaming at the bars, missing the stop sign and never even seeing the truck. A sad but common story.

Concentration is mostly ruined by being tired, either mentally (boredom) or physically (exhaustion). It can also be due to plain carelessness (lack of control or practice) or plain stupidity (dare-deviling or ignorance). Let's take a quick wheelie thru these.

Long hours on the road are boring. Everything suggested to cope with boredom in a car (chapter 9) applies here, only moreso. Being bored in a car is just being bored; being bored on a bike is dangerous. Motorcycle tourers should travel fewer miles and fewer hours per day than motorists. Plan on stopping often — to relax, hike, sightsee, loaf. Pace yourself by being map-conscious and destination-oriented.

Techniques of riding help both physically and mentally. Sitting upright is the best position for long-distance riding. This is much easier to do behind a windshield or fairing than without one, since you won't be leaning into the wind. Vary your position occasionally — lean on the bars, lean on the tank with your feet back, put your feet on the cylinders

(BMW), or roll bars or frame pegs if you have them, stretch yourself by squirming around, etc. Keep it brief — a variation, not a lengthy innovation.

No matter how you sit or what you do you'll eventually tire. By "tire," I don't mean saying "ho-hum" and feeling weary . . . I mean like Wipe-Out, sliding off the machine when it comes to a stop and being unable to stand up; like Wipe-Out, wishing you just had the strength to curse the day you bought it. I mean TIRED, man!

Touring that's too ambitious in scope or too tightly scheduled can do this, so one of the best riding techniques is to stop riding for a while. Schedule a few days off. Put something else you like between your legs for a change, something warm and beautiful. Maybe an enema bag . . .

Carelessness on the bike leads to total lessening of cares. Loss of control or lack of control can come from lack of practice in riding that particular machine. So learn all its

controls until they're extension of your hands and feet. Feel the weight and balance of the machine in your gut so that you instinctively react as part of the machine, and vice-versa. Learning to properly brake is a good example. Too much front brake alone, especially on slopes and bumps, will make you lose control, too much rear brake will lay you over, especially on slick surfaces. Try to practice driving using the brakes as little as possible; use the gears and watch your speeds.

Practice driving with your passenger before you leave. Make sure he or she makes all the same leaning movements you do, with both of you learning how to brake and corner as a single unit. Similarly, practice riding with your dead-weight baggage in place, too. Try some panic stops to see what shifts or wants to tear off; then re-do it till it's tight.

Everybody who owns a bike once in a while loses his better judgement and does something risky or downright crazy just for the sheer hell of it. Admit it. Of course, we've lost

Exercises

MOTORCYCLING EXERCISES
(Refer to "Driving Exercises" also, in chapter 9)

1) If you've been stopping and hiding out during rain, try staying with it for a change — assuming you've got some kind of rainwear.

2) If you've been riding in the rain as a regular thing, try luxuriating in a dry shelter instead. This is something you could get to like quite easily.

3) When taking shelter due to bad riding conditions, experiment with different varieties of hideouts: circumstantial like underpasses and trees; civilized like gas stations and stores; social like bars. Each has something to offer besides shelter.

4) If you're not already loaded, try picking up an occasional lone hitchhiker. Most hitchers appreciate the variety even tho they may not be dressed for the ride. Having someone else to relate to suddenly can change your head around.

5) When you stop for a break from the road, make a little trip out of it. After you've stretched out awhile, take a hike around. Climb to the top of a nearby hill, walk up a forest trail, stroll around the block. (Make sure your machine is locked up.)

6) Make a practice of talking to other bikers you see at campsites, rest stops, and restaurants. You'll pick up information and you'll also get energy from travelers who'll be able to understand your thrills and travails. Visit the motorcycle repair shops in the big cities for contacts and advice about what to see and do.

a lot of riders that way, but so it goes. You know what's involved and you know that curbing these tendencies is important if you intend to grow up someday. Think about it — a lot. And when you do feel cocky and too full of juice to keep from busting out, at least do it somewhere on your own. Messing with your own life is one thing; infringing on someone else's right to live is selfish and unworthy of any man (or woman).

The last bit of riding advice concerns awareness and keeping ready for instant danger in any form. Some examples: Sudden stops, crazy drivers, flying hubcaps, rocks or bricks in the road, potholes, running animals, grease slicks, puddles, beer cans, railroad tracks, large insects or birds in the face, mud splashes, biting dogs, etc. The list is endless, and can be added to when you least expect it. Stay alert, drive defensively, and learn from your close calls (you'll have 'em). Good luck!

PACKING UP Assuming you're going camping on the tour, look at the camper's checklist of gear found in chapter 7 (Camping) and in chapter 13 (Backpacking). The only consideration here is about how to carry the stuff. Weight distribution is more important than any other packing factor. The basic rules are 1) keep the stuff low, close to the center of gravity of the bike; 2) keep it balanced, left and right; 3) keep it balanced, fore and aft, if possible. Don't tie your pack up high on a sissy bar where it's just top-heavy dead weight. Reasonable alternative: get a frameless pack you can tie on a back luggage carrier or better yet, strapped onto the gas tank. Saddlebags are fine, but put some of the weight forward on tank bags if you can. Tank bags and other bags are professionally made by the following suppliers (ask for catalogs):

Great Outdoor Enterprises
4421 Hollister Avenue
Santa Barbara, CA 93105

MBI
Box 4171
Stamford, CT 06907

Your motorcycle dealer should offer various bags and carriers, and any camping supplier (Appendix 12) sells stuff sacks and such that can be tied onto the luggage carrier, tank, or frame.

Another storage possibility is using the spaces provided in the design of a frame-mounted fairing such as the Vetter "Windjammer" models. For a catalog, send $1 to:

Vetter Fairings
Box 927
Rantoul, IL 61866

WEATHER TO TOUR Touring is largely a summer business, and even then keep an eye out for weather. Some parts of the country get most of their rain at that time; others get occasional freak storms anytime. For the average rider, at least, rain means time to hang it up and hang out somewhere. Take a shot of luxury in a hotel, or catch up on your reading in a tent. Touring in wet weather is more work than fun, and more dangerous than not. You never know where rain will find you, so always be prepared for some of it by having at least a rain slicker or poncho handy. That way if you get caught with no shelter in really heavy weather, you can at least stop and hide yourself somewhere.

Cold weather is something you should naturally be dressed for anyway, so it's no hassle if not accompanied by rain or snow. Hot weather isn't any problem either, except possibly for sunburn if you strip down overmuch, or get frisky and risky enough to take off your helmet.

Wherever you go, leave at least a little room in your schedule for side-tracking due to weather. To find out how much, do a little research at the library or call the Weather Bureau. Accept bad weather as part of the overall plan of things. Consider ways to enjoy yourself anyway. For example, this is the time to hole up with friends and relatives ... a beautiful reason to stay another day or two. Or rain in the big city is a good opportunity to be a tourist afoot, taking the sights off the machine for a change, out of the perpetual hurricane.

If you do plan to ride in the rain, be prepared and take your time. Wet riding is a whole other way of riding, with its own special beauty and excitement.

THE FINAL SOURCE Sources of first-rate information about motorcycle touring have always been scarce and/or haphazard. With the publication of *Two Wheel Travel — Motorcycle Camping and Touring* (see Appendix 1 under "Motorcycling"), those days are gone but good. This 11 x 14 size book is a beautifully written bible of advice and information. Anyone contemplating a motorcycle tour should see a copy ... it's orange. If your bookstore doesn't have it, send $3 (price) plus $.35 shipping to the address in the back of the book.

THE FINAL WORD Traveling around America last summer I saw literally hundreds of motorcyclists touring the country, both men and women. Sometimes two on a bike, sometimes several bikes traveling together. I met them around campfires, I dug them on the hiways, I saw them from California to Carolina. It's a whole new wave of adventurers traveling the hiroad to America by living each minute in full. Motorcyclists are easy to meet and happy to trade experiences, so seek them out and make some new friends. Better yet, become one yourself.

Off The Tape
MOTORCYCLIST

Upon arriving in the campground at Zion National Park, we meet Norm, a physicist from Stanford working on plasma physics and nuclear power generation. He's riding a BMW and has camped here for six days. We quickly get companionable, later start eating and hiking together, and share the same campsite. We discuss his future in physics, vis-a-vis being a bearded long-hair, and decide he'd probably be better off following a music career tuning pianos and organs, than being a nuclear physicist. One of the reasons he's considering dropping out, and I think he'll probably do it, is because he can only work in his field for the government or the larger corporations. Either one would make his contribution dehumanizing, or work against humanism in the end. It's much better tuning pianos.

MOTORCYCLING AS IT IS
(Queasy Rider)
by Norm Albers

If there's going to be any rain or cold weather on your motorcycle journey (and there probably will be), weatherproofing is absolutely essential. You come to see the country, and you just can't dig it as much when you're shivering or damp or both. The first time I donned my rubberized $8 Japanese fisherman overalls and parka was in the face of a Nevada thunderstorm. What a thrill to be dry and yet feel the rain strike your body with the same thorough indiscrimination it shows in soaking the earth around you. Don't forget a good water-and-wind-proof cover for your pack, though, or you'll sleep in an indiscriminately soaked bag that night.

Cold weather, on the other hand, was not as mellow a scene for me. I awoke early one westbound June morning near Kanab, Utah and headed up toward Cedar City for a hot diner breakfast (a treat I can't resist every three or four days). At only five or six thousand feet elevation the morning air was chilly, but I was warm enough riding. It must have been soon after the turn west onto highway 14 that there appeared a large yellow sign warning the road was closed in winter at high altitudes. Since it was late May I didn't worry and headed down the road. Or rather up, passing a succession of signs reading off thousand-foot levels of increasing altitude. By nine thousand feet I was a bit chilled but I assured myself that at 9 am on a sunny day the air would soon warm. The elevation probably wouldn't rise much more.

It did, and through some of the most crystal mountain country I have ever seen. Above ten thousand feet the temperature went way below freezing and I got colder than I've ever been before or since. I stopped to stand around a few minutes and warm up but realized I was still just getting colder. It seemed best to continue over and down the mountain. The entire road is only forty-two miles long with beautiful pine and cedar stands near bare black lava beds, cold as the moon. Finally I descended to Cedar City, a tourist mini-opolis where a startled waitress didn't get to rest until well into my fourth cup of hot coffee. I tried to stir up a little conversation with her or anyone else, but no one could seem to handle it so I split, seeking warmer company with the outside. The place was American in the worse sense anyway: plastic decor, high curly hairdos on waitresses whose age might have left them a soft echo of beauty had they not tried so hard to hide it. Were their lives as bitter as their sagging facial lines suggested?

While basking and thawing outside I was pleasantly surprised when a short-haired fellow my age walked over and started a conversation. He was an Oklahoma geological engineering graduate on his first field assignment with a prospecting crew probing for iron (I had passed an old mine on the mountain — wish I'd been warm enough to stop and look around!) Being a drop-out graduate physicist, I felt I knew where he was at. Living in a motel room next to the diner, he hadn't had much interesting company for a while so we really got it on. As if to demonstrate our American cultural unity, he showed me his room and, once inside, pulled out a huge bag of Oklahoma home-grown. I was very happy to see my karma balancing out for the day. What's more we found out we both were named Norman. Now that's an experience which a Stephanie or an Ed probably just can't appreciate quite as much as we did, especially stoned in Cedar City, Utah.

There is a physical and psychological gestalt about motorcycle touring: good weather or bad, you're in the outside. You have a different perspective on enclosures since, excepting your body covering, you have none. The automobile is a motorized, enclosed space which a driver moves around for protected transport. Like a man on horseback, the cyclist is forced to relate directly to the environment on whatever terms he can arrange. When you first realize this, your psyche instinctively starts grasping for walls to define security. There are none but those you build or locate on the spot. But then you let go, realizing the outside is what you came for, and instead of contracting your consciousness to the bounds of a container, you let it out, out, dissipating into the majestic spaces and forms around.

You exhale the pent-up ego of civilization, the localized I, like a sigh. Unrestricted, you are conscious of much larger things and the mind exalts in its freedom to roam and play in unlimited spaces, Peripheral vision gives you continual awareness of the creative tension flowing between earth and sky. You breathe, and realize you are joyfully content. Riding through Nevada grazing lands, my new found road partner came to a sudden stop in the middle of nowhere, pointing to a huge cow with distended vagina and pink feet just emerging. There was no sound other than her lowing, telling the world of her creative passion. We watched as the earth received her child and the clouds blessed it.

Basics Of Bicycling

Invitation To Individualists

11

BICYCLING AS IT IS, by Gini Howe

INTRODUCTION Bicycling, after half a century of being relegated to the junkheap of history, is making a dramatic comeback today in the USA. In 1972 Americans bought 11 million bicycles, and altogether 80 million Americans now own bicycles. The reasons why are generally the same as those causing so many other "comebacks" such as natural foods, natural childbirth, outdoor activities, etc. The modern world, with its tensions, crowding, pollution, cynicism, has created a counter-culture that is resurrecting the values and ways of earlier times in order to synthesize the best of the past with the best of the present.

The bicycle is a beautiful example of this trend. It is an efficient and ingenious (because simple) way of converting muscular action into horizontal motion. The machine producing this conversion is small, light, inexpensive, quiet, non-polluting, healthful, and fun to operate. What other machine can make these claims?

It has virtually no inherent disadvantages. All its so-called faults are actually flaws in the consciousness of the user (for example, that it requires too much work) or flaws in its envi-ronment of use (for example, that it's too dangerous because of cars). The correct and advantageous use of the bicycle requires prac-tice and determination, but it is not a contrap-tion for muscle men only. It is literally the only means of mechanical locomotion that can be extensively used by anyone from childhood to old age — eloquent testimony to its sim-plicity and ease of use.

Its comeback can only be regarded as a sign of returning sanity to the mass of tech-nologically crazed society. Everyone has bicycled in their youth, and loved it. And virtually everyone has been weaned away from it later because it was "impractical," "danger-ous," and "foolish." What a crock that was. When we turned our backs on our bicycles, we made our first big mistake, opening the way for a succession of mistakes that strapped us (with safety belts, of course) onto the Tread-mill of Progress, leaving behind our innocence and health. Today, we're making another chance for ourselves. The pendulum of society is slowly swinging back toward its middle position, balancing the advantages of the past with the advances of the present.

BICYCLES DON'T POLLUTE

ON THE Beach in Florida

Today, bicycling offers its traditional values combined with modern improvements. Ten-speed gears, liteweight construction, and modern accessories and camping gear make it an exciting new vehicle for exploring both the world we live in, and the selves which do the living. Here's how.

TOURING VS. DAY-CYCLING There's a world of difference between taking a bicycle out for a day or for a tour, tho both are recommended experiences. The boom in bicycling has made it popular to tour by car or campers, but carry along one or more bicycles as a way of expanding the travel experience. For these part-time cyclists, this chapter provides useful information about buying, riding, and renting; and about car-carriers and other car-cum-cycling matters.

However, this chapter is mostly about full-tilt bicycle touring, which is far more demanding in all respects. Long-distance cycling is a pursuit for purists, for individualists who share some of the qualities of hitchhikers but are less gregarious and more disciplined.

Indeed, discipline is at the heart of bicycle touring, because covering a hundred miles a day on a bicycle for days on end is not something picked out of a hat or bought at an easy price. In addition to choosing the correct bicycle with top-notch equipment, it requires conditioning and self-control, a somewhat unreasoning desire for independence, and a kind of crazy courage to cope with the hostile environment of hiways and their horsepower maniacs.

The rewards, depending on the individual and upon luck, can be excessive, leading to delirium or ecstasy or nil, leading to dismay or disgust. Bicycle touring is not for everyone, clearly. I've known bicyclists who've sworn off touring altogether, after returning bruised, exhausted, and defeated. Others return with glazed eyes, mumbling praises. Let's see what's involved.

FUNDAMENTALS OF TOURING Successful bicycle touring requires the following ingredients:

1) A quality 10-speed (or 15-speed) bicycle, in excellent condition, with required accessories and paraphernalia.
2) Correct riding technique, perfected by experience and prompted by desire.
3) Careful planning and preparation, whether tripping individually or with a club group.

These are discussed in more detail in the following sections.

BUYING A TOURING BICYCLE Standing there in the store looking at the price tags, you may feel like saving money by buying a cheap bike, or maybe a 3-speed. But once you're out there, on your own, a long way from Mom and Dad, you'll be real glad you bought a top-quality name-brand touring bicycle with 10-or 15-speed *derailleur* ("de-railer") gears, dropped handlebars, and liteweight frame. It'll cost you (new) from about $100 to $300, and it's worth it.

Bicycles have power sources that need all the help they can get, and the way they get it is by efficient gears and by minimum weight throughout. Superior materials, design, and construction are needed to achieve liteness. The same goes for simple, reliable gears. Add these together and up comes Money. However, even small differences in performance or comfort are greatly amplified when measured over long distances, so buy the best you can afford.

Buy the bicycle at a bicycle store instead of department store. You'll gain the benefits of better service and a choice of proven fine makes, virtually all of which sound foreign because they are. Some of the good brands are Campbell's, Heinz, Del Monte — oops, I mean Peugeot, Gitane, Raleigh, Fregus, Legnano, Louison-Bobet, Cinelli, Mercier, Allegro, Bianchi, and Schwinn. Get as much information as you can by questioning bicycle owners and intently checking specifications in sales literature and advertisements. The guidebooks mentioned a little later and also Appendix 1 — under "Bicycling" contain chapters on evaluating and buying. Read one or more of these books for detailed information on criteria and testing of bicycles.

When you look at bicycles, tell the dealer you want a high-quality *derailleur* touring bicycle (no squirrel tails on the ends of the handlebars). He'll explain the differences among the makes and models, and his recommendations can generally be trusted. There are no "bargains" to be had because, in bicycles, the cost is commensurate with quality. But the differences among models will be important, and you may want a certain gear selection or type of tire. Quality of certain components, especially the *derailleur* (Campagnolo Gran Turismo is the best) and brakes (Weinmann and Universal are excellent).

Used touring bicycles can frequently be a genuine bargain, because owners of high-quality bikes usually lay a lot of TLC on them. As

ACADIA
National Park Brochure

"Have you ever tried doing nothing? Acadia is a good place to begin. First, find a rocky ledge or stony beach: Then sit down and relax. Things start to happen as your senses awaken to the scene around you. A gull sails up over the ledge with a sea urchin, captured from a tidal pool, in its beak. The urchin is dropped onto the rocks below, where its spiny, shell-like armor smashes; the gull, which has followed it to earth, devours it. Listen carefully for the chuckle of pebbles moving in surf. A wavelet gurgles in a hidden crevice, and, behind you, the breeze sings through a grove of spruce. The salt air smells good, and the sun is warm on your skin. Doing nothing on the shore is an art, a pleasurable experience — anything but a waste of time."

"Vacation time is precious and must be spent carefully. Why spend yours driving as far and as fast as you can? Instead, why not spend a few days here? If you have generally traveled the one way, the other may surprise you: it certainly leads to better understanding of nature: and it may lead to better understanding of self."

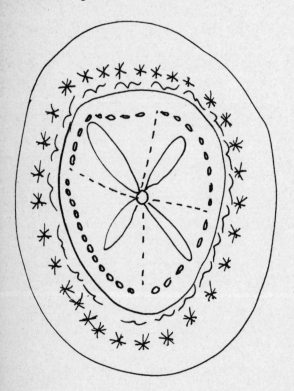

with new bikes, first familiarize yourself with model specifications and new prices.

Before buying any bicycle, even hot from the box, carefully insure your getaway by first inspecting it nut by nut. Check all nuts and bolts for tightness, brakes and cables for play and adjustment (and wear, if used), wheels for play and alignment, *derailleur* for alignment and adjustment, tires for type and pressures, spokes for tightness, frame for paint job. That little machine has so few parts that you'll sincerely miss them if a few fall off or fuck up because you didn't check them. Especially when the parts-dealer is far away and the handlebars are wrapped around your chin.

Fitting the bike to yourself involves frame size (most important); type and adjustment of handlebars; and seat (saddle) adjustment. Proper frame size means being able to stand on the ground comfortably with the bike between your legs. (Otherwise the cross-bar bashes you in the genitals when coming to stops.) Dropped handlebars (definitely *not* the flat type) are necessary, but of the several shapes available, pick one with a long enough straight portion on top to rest your hands side by side, the common touring position. The posture achieved by leaning over dropped handlebars allows you to put more muscle into the sprocket and lowers your wind resistance. At the same time, it forms a natural shock absorber for easier and more restful riding. Feels strange at first but rapidly grows on you. Handlebars need adjustment in stem length and drop angle, and handles should be taped. The dealer can show you.

The saddle should be of leather and quite narrow, no matter how likely it might seem to disappear up your anus. Remember your weight will be shared by arms as well as ass. The correct adjustment for saddle height has been scientifically determined by genuine ergometers to be 109 percent of inside leg length. That's the truth, actually. Get your dealer to adjust this.

Another item to consider is type of tires, there being two: tubular (also called "sew-ups" and "tubeless") and tube type (also called "clinchers" and "wired-on"). Tubulars are

standard equipment on most high-quality touring bikes, for they give smoother and faster rides. However, the liteness that provides these qualities also makes them more prone to puncture or damage, and their sewn construction more difficult to repair. Generally speaking, tube-types are recommended for use in the city and on rough roads or surfaces where they're tougher and easier to repair. Tubulars, however, are lite and flexible enough that you can easily carry one or more spare tires with you.

A final thing to check out when buying your bicycle is the range of its available gear ratios. Any good touring bike should have a selection ranging from 30 or 40 up to around 100. The lower the ratio, the lower the gear — the higher the ratio, the higher the gear. Simple.

RIDING AND TOURING TIPS Your touring machine consists basically of two parts: The chassis, which is the bicycle itself; and the engine, which is you. Both parts have to be in good shape, and well-matched to each other. To get the cycle in shape is a matter of inspection and maintenance; to get you in shape is a matter of training.

Like all organic engines, your body has a very limited capacity to vary its work output without breaking down. However, it does function quite well when maintained at constant speed, and this is the key to successful distance riding. Find a pedaling rhythm that you can keep up for hours on end without changing. This is called "cadence," and for most cyclists falls around 70 to 80 crank revolutions per minute.

Exercises

BICYCLING EXERCISES

1) Meeting other cyclists is an important source of information and especially energy. Try to talk to them whenever you see a touring bicyclist. They may also know about special bikeways and bike paths along your way.

2) Try hitchhiking with your bike, especially if you hadn't planned to. If you can't handle that thought, at least be open to accepting rides from the occasional friendly traveler who offers it without your asking.

3) Do get off the machine now and then so you can exercise some other muscles for a change. On hot sweaty hard-working days in particular, try dropping yourself into a nearby ocean, lake, river, or swimming hole. It's a righteous way to cool off.

4) If you meet some other cyclists and strike a chord, consider traveling along with them for a few days, wherever they're going. In cycling, there is a certain strength in numbers that makes for more fun, more energy, and greater safety on the road. Even if you're a loner-type, a little sharing can't hurt and you might like it.

5) Using a suitable directory, or by inquiring at local bicycle shops, get in touch with cyclists who live in the area you're visiting. Call them by phone — see what information or hospitality they can offer.

6) If you normally hide away when the rains come, try cycling as it pours for a change. Be prepared with slickers, but if the rain and climate are warm, just strip down to your shorts and have a shower at the same time.

Once you establish your cadence, you shift your *derailleur* gears where necessary due to hills and wind so that you keep the same cadence as much as possible. Thus your ground speed will vary depending on what gear you're in, but the engine works at the same rate all the time. This keeps the engine happy and reliable.

The way you change gears is therefore important. Always shift while pedaling, without breaking cadence, smoothly and just one gear at a time. Shifting way down when a hill is coming breaks cadence, and ultimately tires the engine. In general, anything that breaks cadence or makes your passage even slightly less efficient will greatly increase the chances of tiring you out over a long distance. For this reason, practice riding without wobbling and learn to steer precisely. Make every motion as smoothly as possible.

Vary the position of your hands on the handlebars for comfort/variety and for the kind of pedaling being done. Hands together on the stem is a common position of relaxation; so are hands placed just behind the brake levers. Moving the hands forward onto the brake levers arches you forward more and is a good power position for level riding or downhill coasting, as your hands are near the brakes. Placing your hands just below the brake levers is a work position, say for going uphill. The last position, with hands grasping the ends of the bars, pulls you forward as far as possible and makes the lowest body profile. Hence this is the most efficient work position for getting up to maximum speed (which incidentally, should be around 30 mph if you've got a grade and/or wind going for you).

The pedaling technique called "ankling" is also important in touring, and should be practiced until it's second nature. With the balls of the feet on the pedals (never pedal any other way), it means having your foot tilted up at the top of each stroke and tilted down at the bottom of each stroke. Thus your ankle is constantly swiveling up and down in synchronization with the crank rotation, smoothly and automatically. Your ankles act as levers which deliver more power to the crank without any increase in power from your legs. Efficiency is the magic word.

Those are the theoretical basics; here are some of the practical fine points. Foremost among these is to keep constantly alert around cars. In America, cars and bicycles usually share the same roads, and the mismatch is atrocious. Cars can make you commit suicycle: Stay constantly alert for danger anytime they're around. Here are some things to watch out for:

- Don't get squeezed up into the curb or wall by passing traffic; watch for tight places.
- Ride in straight lines to keep out of traffic lanes.

- Always ride with the traffic stream, never against.
- Watch parked cars for sudden pullouts or opening doors; watch driveways.
- Intersections call for wariness and slowing down, even if you have right-of-way. Try to make sure you're seen before entering. At dangerous ones, it might be best to walk across.
- If possible, avoid main routes and rush-hour traffic.

There are other hazards, such as oil slicks, sand on corners, pebbles and other objects to avoid, puddles and potholes, and sewer grates that can swallow wheels. Dogs attacking cyclists is not just a cartoon situation, but a common and dangerous occurrence. Cyclists' feet are usually unprotected and dog bites can cause fright, slashes, loss of control, or possibly even rabies. If you can't out-run or out-manouver an animal in pursuit or on a collision course, the next best defense is to carry some kind of dog-spray or whip close at hand. Don't hestiate to use it. You have every right, humanely and legally.

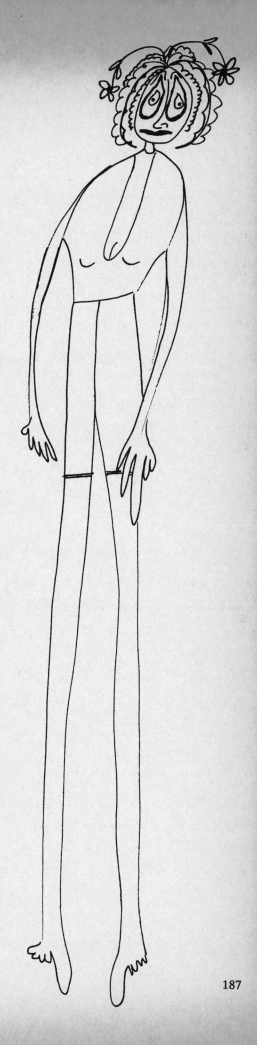

SAFETY ACCESSORIES Dog defenses are one type. Here are others worth considering. In the city especially, wearing a hard hat or helmet of some kind is advised. Lites are a necessity for any night riding, as well as reflectors and/or reflecting tape. The tape can also be applied to shoes and helmet as well as the bicycle. Clothing should be lite- or bright-colored, or wear one of those Day-Glo vests. Gloves are a good idea for better grip and skin protection. Goggles and bandana might be worth carrying for rain and dust conditions.

PACKING UP This refers to car carriers for transporting your bicycle(s), and also to carrying supplies on your bicycle.

Bicycle carriers for your car or camper are of two types: rear and top. Rear carriers are simple to attach and easy to use. The best known one is the "Bike Toter," available for $16 by mail from Box 888, Santa Monica, CA 90406, or your dealer will have an equivalent. It'll carry one or two cycles. A rooftop carrier will tote up to 4 or 5 bicycles, and can easily be made from standard cross-bar type luggage racks. Plans for making these are shown in most bicycle books or are available from the Bicycle Institute of America (see address in Appendix 1 under "Bicycling). You can also buy them complete from a supplier such as JC-1 Industries, 904 Nogales, Industry, CA 91744.

Loading your bicycle with bags and stuff has only a few basic principles: Take as little as possible (every pound means more work, fewer miles). Balance the load from side to side, and if possible, from back to front. Finally, keep the center of gravity low (put your heavy items in the bottom of the bag).

The bags themselves can be located in several places: rear-wheel packs (or panniers), handlebar bag, saddlebag, and a pack on your own back. For liteness, toughness, and water resistance, nylon is the best material, and all good bags should be made of it. Some of the best bags are made by Bellwether, which sells by mail order through many dealers, and also through Sierra Designs and their many outlets.

(Get catalog from Bellwether, 1161 Mission St, San Francisco, CA 94103, or Sierra Designs, 4th and Addison, Berkeley, CA 94710.) A sack on your back is not considered kosher for touring (it's tiring and increases wind drag) but a small one is useful for always keeping valuables and frequently used articles on your person.

EQUIPMENT Whether or not you're equipped for camping makes a big difference in what you bring. Camping means bringing (a lot) more equipment, but it's free in spirit and cost. But many cycling clubs and individuals tour extensively with prearranged lodging (hotels or private homes) in order to minimize both the equipment and the rigors. Take your choice. Many of the things I say about hitchhiking in chapter 12 apply to bicycling as well. This is also true of equipment lists, though there are many differences having to do with clothing and tools, for example. Here's my recommended equipment list.

CYCLISTS EQUIPMENT LIST
(Men and Women)

To Wear

Cycling shoes
Wool or cotton socks
Underwear & T-Shirt
Shirt, long sleeved
Cycling shorts (also swimsuit)
Belt
Visored cap
Bandana
Watch
Sunglasses & case
Swiss Army knife ("Outdoorsman")
Money belt or neck pouch (?)
Small daypack (?)
Wallet — cash, ID (driver's license), draft card (men), credit card(s), youth hostel card (?)
Wool mitts
Helmet (?)
Toe clips (?)

Clothes in Sack

Pants, washable (men) or skirt (women)
2 shirts or blouses, washable
1 sweater
1 light parka or windbreaker
3 bandanas
Cycling cape or rain poncho
Sweat pants
Sweat shirt
2 pair underwear & T-shirts
Levi's
Hiking shoes
Sandals or moccasins

Camping Gear

Down sleeping bag
Tent, 1 or 2 man (tube tent will do)
Nylon cord (50')
Stove, Svea 123
Fuel bottle for stove
Matches in plastic bag
First aid kit — aspirins
(See chapter 15) salt tablets
                 antiseptic cream
                 vitamins
                 surgical tape
                 thermometer
                 personal medication
Sleeping sack (?) — for Youth Hostels
Flashlite
Sun tan lotion
Insect repellent
2 Sierra Club cups
Spoon & fork
Bota or water bag
Sewing kit: safety pins
               needle & thread
               rip stop tape
Towel
Cook kit (?)
Candle lantern, folding
Spare food

Bicycle Needs

Tool kit: metric wrenches
               spoke wrench
               crescent wrench
               screwdriver
               pliers
Tire patching kit
Bike lock & chain(s)
Spare spokes
Spare brake blocks
Spare cables
Spare chain & rivet tool
Tire pump
Spare tubular tire(s)

Rear packs
Handlebar bag
Saddlebag

Personal

Toothbrush
Razor & stainless blades (men)
Barrettes for long hair, or scarves
Toilet paper
Soap & plastic container
Comb and/or hairbrush
Pocket mirror, metal
Condoms (men) or Pills, IUD, diaphragm (women)
Tampax (women)
Jewelry
Stash (?)

Other

Traveler's checks (?)
Notebook (good size — 5½x8)
Pen(s) and/or pencil(s)
Address book
Guidebook(s)
Maps
Reading matter
Camera and film (?)
Binoculars (?)

THEFT Bicycle theft has become big business. Machines are stolen by organized gangs, shipped by truck to distant cities, repainted and resold at great profit. Not to be outdone, individuals everywhere also just help themselves whenever they need bikes. It's bad enough having a large money investment in the bicycle, but if it's also your transportation and vacation, then having it stolen could cause you psychosomatic sinus attacks, or worse. Locks and chains are about all you can do, so do them without fail. To prevent theft of just a wheel, which also happens, use a long case-hardened chain that can be threaded through both wheels and the frame, and around a pole or tree as well. You can insure it, too — either on your homeowner's policy or your parent's, or with a special policy that costs about $10 a year and up, depending on the bike's value.

SHIPMENT AND HITCHHIKING Especially in the USA, many bicycle tours will start by turning your bike over to a bus, train, or plane for shipment somewhere. It's sensible to buy your bike and provision your tour at home where you can control the details, then ship it off. Shipping is not that expensive (seldom more than $15 even across country). Bus lines require bicycles to be boxed and shipped as freight, and you should send it off about a day ahead of you to make sure it gets there when you need it. The boxes can be cardboard, and you might as well include some or all of your panniers and bags.

Trains will take uncrated bicycles but that increases their chances of getting damaged. Costs are roughly the same as busses.

Airlines may or may not require crating, and may or may not be accepted as regular (free) baggage. Check with various airlines.

Hitchhiking with your bicycle is certainly a possibility, though your ride chances will no longer include VW sedans and motorcyclists. Nevertheless, depending on your luck, you can put together a tour covering a much larger area if you include hitchhiking in it. Blessings be upon pick-up trucks and flatbeds.

REPAIR AND MAINTENANCE Before you ever start out, familiarize yourself with your bicycle. Know how to adjust the *derailleur*, brakes and cables. Know how to replace a tire and/or repair a flat. Study the theory and operation of your bike, according to manufacturer's literature and a good bicycle guidebook. Get a list of authorized dealers for your bicycle, and thru bicycle clubs, try to obtain the names of club members you can contact enroute if you get into trouble, or just to say hello to. A source of this information is the *Bicycle Clubs Directory,* obtainable free from Bicycle Insitute of America, 122 East 42nd St., NY 10017. Lastly, carry tools and spares.

RENTALS For those who aren't into cycling, but who enjoy a little tootling around town or in the park, a rental bicycle may be the answer. It's almost always more fun than walking, more stimulating, and capable of covering much more ground. Costs per hour or per day are reasonable, and you generally get a three-speed, flat handlebar model that is no great prize but adequate. Bicycle rental shops can be found in all large cities and most areas frequented by tourists. If you don't see any shops, ask some of those people pedalling about, or look in the yellow pages, or ask at a local tourist information office.

INFORMATION SOURCES There are some excellent books available about bicycling. Some of them are: *Two-Wheel Travel: Bicycle Touring and Camping* (Tobey Publishing, 1972, $3); *The Complete Book of Bicycling* by Eugene Sloan (Simon & Schuster, 1970, $9.75), and *Anybody's Bike Book* by Tom Cuthbertson (Ten Speed Press, 1971, $2.95). There are now starting to appear bicycle touring guidebooks, such as *North American Bicycle Atlas* by Asa Warren (American Youth Hostels, 1970, $2.25) and excellent local guidebooks, such as *California Bike Tours* (Gousha Publications, 1972, $2.95). These books and others are covered in more detail in the Trips Appendix under "Bicycling," tho there are many more books appearing these days than we can list.

Florida, moist with the memories
of youthful times.
Nostalgia of the balmy night.
Tropical dreams tumble in a
plastic tumble machine.
No one unravels the past
it just lays
hot and heavy on the land,
steaming in the swamps.
Florida dreamer
eyes half closed
seeing visions with a
golden aura.
Florida, Lotus Land
Opium Kingdom
the air is a sweet narcotic
people rush like ants
to the feast.
Good night, Florida,
Good night.

Also listed in *Trips* are bicycle magazines and clubs. If you're thinking about a bicycle tour, consider going along on one of the club-sponsored ones instead of taking an independent tour. You're guaranteed companionship, encouragement, and assistance in case of trouble. It might be a good idea for your first bicycle tour — the one you shouldn't mess up. American Youth Hostels (National Campus, Delaplane, VA 22025) is the American branch of the international organization, and is into a lot of other numbers besides bicycling. However, bicycling is their major trip and they run sponsored tours for members, among other things. Their hostels in America number about 100, but are mostly in the Northeast. However, AYH is a fairly staid and moralistic outfit bearing as they do the Responsibility for the Youth of the Nation, etc.

The International Bicycle Touring Society (846 Prospect, La Jolla, CA 92037) is organized primarily for informal touring for its members ($3 per year). You get a schedule of "Huff 'n Puff" tours (none are camping tours), a membership list, and free information bulletins on request.

Arranging tours through a local club or with a group of cyclist friends is perhaps the best way of all. You already know some of the people, and you can arrange for the security of a backup equipment truck (known as a "sag-wagon") if you all want it.

Maps for touring will generally be the same old road maps you already use in your Chevy. However, they're less than ideal if you don't know the area, its terrain, and particularly the least trafficked roads. Try to get better, more detailed maps by writing state and local tourist bureaus, National Forest offices, etc. as applicable. Inquire also about county maps and sportsmans' maps that are frequently for sale in the region of interest. The most direct path to map and touring information is to write a bicycle club representative or member in the target region.

BICYCLING AS IT IS
by Gini Howe

One of the best ways to see the world, besides on your own two feet, is on two wheels. Pick the most beautiful part of the world you can — one that you really want to see completely. The West Coast, from California to Alaska is a good one. With no training (no jogging for weeks ahead of time, no long distance bike strenuousities, no running up and down stairs), my man and I cycled from Santa Barbara, California, to Skagway, Alaska, along Highway 1 and the ocean the entire way. Through rain, sleet and occasional snow, with enough sun and incredible beauty to balance it all off.

Our bikes are not $500 specials, but nice $100 Raleigh 10-speeds. Peugeuts and Gitanes are good. Once you've got the bike and your trip together, don't be tempted to throw everything in a backpack and take off. On our 2000 plus mile trip up the coast we noticed a lot of bicycle tourers sweating along under packs. We really wondered about this, having biked home from big shopping sprees with groceries in our backpacks, feeling super gravity bound and constricted . . . it's hot and you can't stretch your back at all. So. The answer is saddlebags. Let the back of your bike, instead of the back of you, take the load.

Into the saddlebags, put as little as possible — no more than 30 pounds and preferably less. Gloves, wool stocking cap, rain poncho (the kind that snaps on the sides — it doubles for your groundcloth), sunhat or bandana, shorts, jacket (down, preferably) and light sweater, polaroid sunglasses, a map and maybe a good book. Also swimming trunks or bikini (they can double as underwear) and mosquito repellent if it is that time of year. On top of the saddlebags fasten your down sleeping bag and light tent if you have one with those hooked stretchies. You may want to make another waterproof stuff sack for your sleeping bag to keep it extra dry in downpours. Be sure your bike has a good, comfortable seat. One thing you will get is saddlesore. No matter what, you will probably have crotch rot for the first week or so. Other necessities are: a canteen that clips onto the bike, bike lock, tire pump, repair kit, spare cable and toe clips or spurs. These help a lot on hills or mountains. You can use your toes to lift the pedals up, thus calling on a different and less tired set of leg muscles. You may want to carry more spare parts for bike sickness. Some folks carry extra spokes,

tires, tubes, derailleurs — the list goes on. But I've found that I'm never all that far from a bike shop. Besides, it's pretty easy to hitch with your bike if you have to. Anyway, in over 2000 miles we had only 2 flats and 1 broken cable between the two of us.

If you're a girl, be sure you don't get talked into buying a girl's bike, because your body is not going to like riding very far in that ludicrous Girl's Bike Upright position. When you run into headwinds or roar down hills you'll want to ride as low as you can on the bike. Lean way over with your head near the handle bars. This cuts wind resistance.

A word about shoes. A stoned salesman in Berkeley sold me a nice pair of Italian bike shoes for $15. Unfortunately they never did break in like he said they would. The first day out, after 30 pinched miles, I hobbled into a shoestore and bought tennis shoes. They were great and I still bike in them.

Two good books to read before you go are Bicycle Tripping by Tom Cuthbertson with many tips for riding and touring, and Anybody's Bike Book, also by Tom Cuthbertson. In a very readable manner, this one tells you how to fix things with good tips on the kinds of sounds to listen for and how to tell what is causing them. (When there is a loud crash, you have probably fallen off your bike. Quit drinking and clean up your act.)

Now you're ready to start. As far as road conditions go, you'll soon learn to get up as early as you can manage and start biking to get an edge on the traffic. California has an added problem with occasional freeways stuck onto the coastal route. If there is no other road, you can legally ride your bike on the freeway. Check first to see if there's a NO BICYCLES, etc., sign at the freeway entrance, or ask at a gas station if there's an alternate road. If there isn't (or if there is but it means you have to bike 15 or 20 miles out of your way) get on that freeway and ride like hell. At least there's a huge shoulder. (We rode one stretch of Southern California freeway at 5 a.m. in a downpour. Four cops passed us. No one stopped. If they had we'd have begged a ride.) However, on the plus side, California does have the best shoulders on their roads. As you travel north the shoulders — your cycling territory — get worse and worse. Oregon is fair, Washington is worse and Canada is just terrible.

So. What to do when those Nomads, Star Treks, Securities, Pathfinders and Travel-Eze complete with patios, boats and motor cycles hanging off front and rear bear down on you at 65 mph. Basically you want to slow these mothers down a little. (Those immense side mirrors can be lethal as the drivers attached often have absolutely no idea where or how far out they are.) As the threatening trailer or car approaches, try the wobble technique. The person riding behind should ride like a rank beginner. Swerve back and forth a lot. This will scare the driver of the car and usually slow him down considerably since he thinks you will crash at any minute. Or, if you are extremely brave, you can ride double. We've done it at times, but you should be able to keep up a good speed and be able to stand a lot of obnoxious horn honkings. This is, however, an excellent technique for riding in towns. But on the coastal route you won't get many of those as 3,000 is a big city.

Also, be prepared for logging trucks. We started running into them just north of Fort Bragg and never did run out of them until the roads ended. One day in Washington, just outside of Port Angeles, we counted 90 full and 85 empties. As soon as you see redwood and cedar bark laying like dead animals on the roads, you've run into logging trucks. Next you will hear them (jake brakes screaming down the road) a mile or two before they brush by you, usually far too close for any remote comfort. You will be both terrified and pissed. However. Resist the temptation to give the finger. I did once and barely escaped with my life. These are very mean mothers and they drive like hell and they are ENORMOUS. In fact I don't know what the answer to logging trucks is. You will have to decide for yourself whether to pull off the road and wait it out or what. It's worth noting that there aren't as many trucks on weekends. Just more cars.

As you start to get tired, you can change positions, if you are riding with a friend. When you ride fairly close together, the one in front breaks the wind for the one behind. An ancient method long used by migrating birds.

Be prepared for headwinds. One more good reason to start early in the morning is that at dawn it's pretty calm. Travelling north we seemed to hit more than our share of headwinds. Apparently most people bike south in the summer as the winds seem to go that way too and give you a nice push. You might want to check out a wind chart when you plan your trip. It's terrible to pedal as hard as you can to go downhill. Sure cuts into your daily mileage.

We did average 50 miles a day. That was with long lunch breaks, stops to admire the incredible beauty everywhere, and food buying excursions when we got to towns. You can do a lot more but 50 is a nice easy pace. We started around 7 am and then about two hours before sunset started looking for a campsite. Once we found one, we pitched our tent if the mosquitos, black flies or no-see-ums (vicious, almost invisible little black bugs that you can expect as you get into Washington and Canada) were out in force, or if rain threatened. Then we read. Then we ate. And slept. We never did pay for a campsite. On a bike you have the pick of the most perfect, most beautiful places in the world. Remember, you don't have a car to scream out "I am camped HERE." There are beaches. There are trees and forests. There are lakes. And if you don't have a tent, there are bridges to camp under. All you need is a flat peaceful bit of ground. Here is a good way to spot a place if the trees seem pretty dense. Look for smaller, different colored growth. This usually indicates an old dirt road that is now overgrown and out of use . . . a perfect, flat campsite. You can wander back in as far as you like. Roll out your sleeping bag and get dinner going.

We carried very little food. Each day or so we'd buy crackers, cheese, nuts, fresh fruit and vegetables, wine, milk or whatever. We didn't have any cooking equipment with us, which meant no hot food. However, this provided us with a good excuse to stop in at an occasional cafe. But. It would be cheaper in the long run to carry a light stove — a Primus or Optimus — and a small, light cooking pot. With a Sierra cup and a spoon, your bike kitchen would be complete. Also, if it's summer, there will be plenty of free food, easily spotted as you bike along. Blackberries, thimbleberries, salal berries, miners lettuce — check Euell Gibbons and Stalking the Wild Asparagus.

Now. What to do when it rains, because it probably will. Often we just kept on riding. When rain riding, your gloves should grip the front of your poncho from underneath. Keep your hands on the handlebars, thus pulling the poncho forward, creating a little protective overhang for your peddling legs. This keeps legs and gloves relatively dry. The back of your poncho goes over your saddlebags. However. There seems to be almost no way to keep absolutely dry. Waterproof leggings don't breathe and you break out in a dripping sweat which doesn't solve a thing. So, if you don't anticipate a laundromat into which you can throw everything to dry, you may want to find a pleasant pub, a museum, or a library. Libraries usually have a nice bonus — luxurious johns with no one to rush you and HOT water, which most of the filling stations you will be frequenting do not.

About hills and mountains which do abound on Highway One and the West Coast. The highest climb was between Rockport and Leggett, California, where Highway 1 cuts over to 101 and climbs 3000 feet in the process. We got up this mountain with two brief stops, mainly because it always seemed as if the top would be just around the next bend. A few ideas for getting your body and bike mentally and physically up a hill or mountain. I've found that if I repeat some simple thing over and over to myself, mantra style, my mind goes off the stiffness of the climb and lands somewhere else. (On this particular mountain I alternated between an obscure 50's tune Tan Shoes and Pink Shoe Laces and Hare Krisna.) For a more physical aid, stop at the bottom of the hill and down as much honey as seems feasible. This will give you a nice energy rush. Brush your teeth right away though, because straight honey goes right to cavities. The main thing to realize is that no hill or mountain is impossible. Gear down and try to resist the temptation to get off your bike and walk, because that just makes it worse. Go as slowly as you want, keep moving steadily along and remember the soaring flying ride DOWN that always awaits you at the top.

A few words about the route we took. Basically, we just followed the Coast all the way. Through California and Oregon, then across the 4 miles $1 toll bridge at Astoria and on into Washington. Then straight north on 101, through Humptulips (which we were told is an Indian word that means can't pole it up the river) and up the Olympic Peninsula. At Port Angeles you can catch the ferry to Victoria on Vancouver Island in British Columbia, Canada. This island is amazingly beautiful, and excellent bike touring country. As you get further north, mountains, wooden bridges and clear clear streams and lakes start to happen. The road runs out at Kelsey Bay. Here $30 will put you on a 330-mile non-stop cruise to Prince Rupert. Your bike rides free down there on the car deck with all those cars that have paid $60 apiece. The ferry — a beautiful, Canadian one — leaves Kelsey Bay at 1:30 p.m. or Prince Rupert at 12:30 P.M. and in summer there are sailings northbound and southbound on alternate days. From September 23rd on there are two round trips weekly, with a 25% fare reduction from October to mid-May. This is a 20-hours-plus ride, so be sure you bring your own food. Ferry food tends to be expensive. You can crash in great comfort on the deck in your sleeping bag, or in one of the lounge chairs inside along with lots of other people who don't want a cramped

stateroom either. If the weather is good, this ride is spectacular. Mountains and dense forests come right down to the ocean. Also, it's a comfortable break from cycling and gives you a chance to lay out on the deck in the sun for a long time. And there are showers on board.

At Prince Rupert you get off, explore the town, stock up on food again and find a place to camp while you wait for the ferry to Skagway, Alaska, to leave. We met some fine people who invited us for dinner and let us spend the night in their house. This was convenient as free campsites in P.R. seem a little hard to come by, though there is a $1/night park on the hill above the city.

Your next ferry ticket will cost $42 if you plan to go all the way to Skagway (Indian word meaning Home of the North Wind), which is as far north as the Inside Passage goes. The Alaska State Ferry system has 4 "luxury vessels" that operate 6 days a week in summer. You can get off at the various towns en route . . . Ketchikan, Wrangell, Petersburg, Juneau, Haines. In fact, you can spend a day or two in them if you like. This ride, over 22 hours long, is really stupendous. If it's clear, you'll see incredible mountains, glaciers that come down to the water, icebergs, whales, porpoises, leaping salmon and wilderness thick everywhere. There are 20-foot tides to watch, too.

But, there are hardly any roads, so you won't be doing much biking. It is handy to have your bike with you if you get off to explore a town, because the ferry often docks about 5 miles outside the town.

We spent two weeks in Haines, in a very nice free, official campsite right on the water, complete with free firewood. Here we did a lot of hiking and met a lot of people. Incidentally, there is some fine West Coast Indian art still alive here . . . wood, bone, metal and totem carving and weaving of Chilkat blankets from mountain goat hair and cedar bark. We left our bikes with some friends and hitched up to Whitehorse in the Yukon. Came back on the old 1900 White Pass narrow gauge railway. This trip from Whitehorse to Skagway costs $20 and includes a big feed midway, at Lake Bennett. It covers the 1898 gold rush route and is really a fine train ride complete with deserted log cabins, lakes and spectacular high mountains. Or, from Skagway, you can hike the famous gold rush route, the Chilkoot Trail, to Lake Bennett. Take a light pack and sleeping bag and plan on 2 or 3 days. This is a great trip with little cabins to sleep in and all kinds of interesting stuff dumped by the old gold rushers along the trail. You could take the train one way.

Now you can pick your way home. We took the ferry back to Prince Rupert and then took the train to Jasper, Alberta. Canadian trains are nice and inexpensive. Again, your bike rides free, but you'll have to take your gear and saddlebags off. (Apparently one avid cyclist had a 150 lb pack on his bike last summer and the train loader cracked his back heaving it into the baggage car.) In Jasper we met a couple who'd biked the entire Aslaskan Highway, from Anchorage to Jasper. Neither of them had ever done a cycling trip before. It took them 3 weeks and they said it was fine . . . a little dusty, being a dirt road, and a little bumpy which caused their kidneys to act up a bit. But a beautiful trip. Incidentally, Jasper has a fine free campground for folks hitching, backpacking or biking, about a mile from town. A very communal and mellow place, full of good vibrations.

From Jasper we took our bikes on the train to Vancouver. We've lived in Vancouver over a year now, and next to backpacking and hitching, our bikes are still our favorite means of transportation. Once some long distance bike trails start to happen, cycling would move up to my number one favorite. But now, especially in Canada, narrow or non-existent shoulders and a surplus of rushing cars take a lot of peace out of the beauty. Maybe if some people start switching over to bikes for long distance trips . . . maybe if they start feeling the beautiful openness of the country and the people as they peddle along (people can talk to you as you ride by, people invite you to stop in.) Anyway. It's a beautiful, cheap way to travel.

You see lots of animals as you bike quietly by. Sounds all hit you. Smells just knock you out . . . wild lupine and roses, redwoods and cedars. You ride into all kinds of natural phenomena. I remember a California day when baby spiders were ballooning in a fantastic migration. Our bikes and hair were soon covered in delicate white web knittings. Once I woke to find a deer standing over me . . . elk prints all around. From my bike I've watched sea lions play, a red shafted flicker feeding her young, an eagle spread low, a turkey vulture landing in front of me and an ant lion.

Best of all, you can stop whenever you want, instantly, and check out each new piece of beauty.

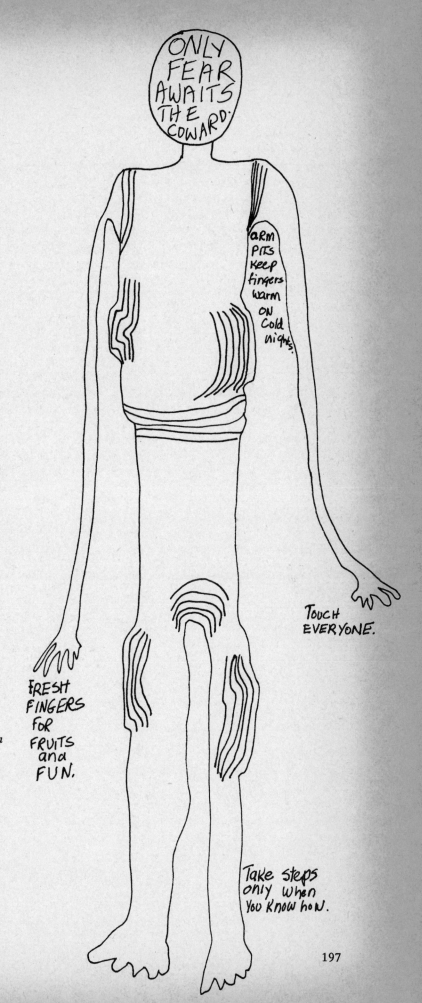

197

Adventuring By Thumb

12

The Complete Hitchhiker's Guide

HITCHHIKING AS IT IS, by Mac Groben

THE DREAM Just as travel is a dramatization of life, so hitchhiking is a dramatization of travel. It breaks down even deeper norms and releases even more energy. Hitchhikers, like all adventurers, vibrate with this energy. It makes them sensitive and alive to their experiences, and attracts others to them. Of course, handling this energy is difficult: The more that things are random and unexpected, the more you need to improvise, the more you fully use all of yourself in the business of being. But then one day on the road, you suddenly realize that you're having the time of your life. You feel the energy of the universe flowing right thru you. It's the dream come true.

The dream of hitching goes something like this: "With my dusty pack on my trusty back, I travel for free across the wide spaces of my native land. I think people are beautiful, and I trust them. As a result, I meet many friendly folks who give me rides and food and places to stay. But I also give and share the little I have. I help the drivers I meet by taking the wheel, telling my tales and listening to theirs. I honor Nature and the land by not polluting as I go. As a hitchhiker I see America with clear eyes,

its good and bad, and I listen closely to its rhythms. Finally, I arrive at my destination wiser for my experiences, knowledgeable from my travels, warmed by the new friends I made. I am the dream hitchhiker." Believe it or not, most hitchhikers are pretty well described by this dream — young, idealistic, friendly, open-minded, interesting.

Hitchhiking as practiced today is a healthy mass-reaction to America's current preoccupations with safety and security, money and materialism, police and paranoia. Today's travelers are saying HELL NO to these soul-shrinking forces, and they're putting their faith on the line and their packs on the road to prove it. They want freedom and adventure, and traveling by thumb is made to order — it's unpredictable, it's cheap, and it's about people. The widespread notions of its danger and illegality only make it more attractive.

THE REALITY The reception being given to these new rebels is the same as that meted out to rebels anywhere else — apathy, hostility, repression, arrest, and violence. Hitchhikers are a special category of poor people, distinguished

JUICE

Juice yourself up
with all the
Acid juice they've got
go faster than sound
to put it all together
Zoom to heaven.
love fuck kiss
all the inside lips of paradise.
speed thru
smoke soar
red comet
ride
high
punch
shoot
Combine it
refine it
crush it
hold it

then give it all away.

by their vulnerability and their rebelliousness. In America, hitchers qualify as prime targets for absolutely everyone with an ax to grind — legislators who self-righteously pass anti-hitching ordinances, policemen who see criminals everywhere, disturbed citizens who use violence as a form of expression, and all too many ordinary citizens so frustrated and dehumanized by their society that they are either hostile or apathetic to the fate of their children.

"Look at that crummy deadbeat up there trying to get a ride. Who the hell does he think he is? I work hard for a living and bums like that have nothing better to do than loaf on the highway, wanting me to stop and be mugged. I oughta teach this guy a lesson and run him over, goddamned commie creep. Of course, that chick with him is something else. Bet she'd blow me for a fiver... Well, I'll be damned — it's my daughter and her boyfriend."

The truth is that as a hitchhiker in America you'll be stared at by some of the meanest looking people in the world. (Weird people in their world looking at a weird person in another world.) It's likely you'll be shouted at, harassed, asked to move on, threatened — all this in addition to the long waits, discomfort, depression, boredom, anxiety, and uncertainty.

It's a heavy load to carry for your average everyday fun-seeker. And that's the point. Hitchhiking in America is not for everybody. It's long on paranoia and short on comfort. It's pressures can easily distort the experience, or warp your vision of America. For example, you tend to rate a place mostly on whether you got a ride there or were hassled. You wind up hating places — anyplace — that you would have loved in other circumstances. The arduousness and the challenges frequently use up so much energy that hitching is not worth doing, at least for some people.

Despite everything, the number of hitchhikers grows year by year. More and more motorists are discovering how vital and good-hearted these vagabonds are, and how exciting their world is. Their new hopeful consciousness

— of sharing and trusting strangers; of traveling as a way of living clearly, freely, and cheaply — is an idea whose time is coming. Meanwhile, is it for you?

REQUIREMENTS FOR HITCHHIKING What does it actually take to go hitchhiking? Who should do it and who ought to shun it? Here's a profile of a modern American hitchhiker.

Character. A hitchhiker should be a character with character, because hitchhiking is a test of who are are. Character has something to do with deliberately choosing the better way over the easy way. To do that and make it, you may have to pull out all the stops. Being on the road is a challenge to become a whole person . . . you should be confident in the face of doubt, tolerant when victimized by the weakness of others, tough in order to endure the physical hardships, flexible enough to go with the changing fortunes of the road. You also need a sense of humor to ward off the ever-threatening cynicism.

Hitching is a test of humanity, because you'll see people at their best and their worst. It means opening yourself to people in the face of frequently damaging evidence. Some people will crap on you and laugh. Somehow you must live it and forgive it. Most people will simply ignore you, and that can be even harder.

Being on the road means learning to "be here now," taking each moment and extracting whatever it has to offer. You'll stand countless hours in dozens of places, struggling with the mysteries and miseries of reality. Gradually a feeling of contentment and fullness can be reached, no matter how forsaken and weird your situation may be. If it's a skill you want to acquire, then hitchhiking may be for you.

Shortage of Money. Lack of cash may open your heart to hitchhiking where spiritual arguments fail. Dig this: Even in the plutocratic USA, you can travel just about anywhere on $1 to $5 a day. The cost variation depends mostly on your style of travel — that is, comfort requirements, traveling companions, and such. You save money directly, of course,

"I'm a-standing on the corner in Winslow Arizona
Such a fine sight to see.
It's a girl, my Lord, in a flat-bed Ford
Slowin' down to take a look at me.

Come on baby
Don't say maybe
I've got to know if your
    sweet love is gonna' save me.

We may lose an' we may win
Tho' we will never be here again
So open up, I'm climbin' in

So take it easy

Well I'm a-runnin' down the road
Tryin' to loosen my load,
Got a world of trouble on my mind
Lookin' for a lover who won't blow
    my cover
She's so hard to find . . .

Take it easy
Don't let the sound of your own wheels
    make you crazy
Come on baby
Don't say maybe
I got to know if your sweet love
    is gonna save me

We got it easy
We oughta take it easy"

—by The Eagles
Take It Easy (Song)

by getting transportation for nothing; but you also save money because hitchhiking is a life-style in which finding inexpensive food and lodging becomes second nature. It's based mostly on meeting people, so you also invariably undergo great social adventures as well. All this comes from the advantage of not having too much money to start with.

Abundance of Time. The more time you have, the stoneder it gets. A few weeks hitching on the road gives you a heavy charge and can get you across country or over a short tour. But a summer's tour will really do it to you, and you can't possibly come back the same person you left. No way. Serendipity is the hallmark of hitchhiking, and it takes time for that to get itself together in the right sequences. Why not take time before it takes you? Remember, time is always here; it's we that pass.

Health is Wealth. Or, to render the wisdom in its homey fullness, "Good Health is the Only Real Wealth." Amen and thank you, Dr. Bronner. Yet, it's true. Hitchhiking requires you be physically tough and resilient, again to an extent depending on your particular traveling motif. Tarzan need not step forward; he isn't called for. But the uncertainty and irregularity of hitchhiking is at times disturbing or unsettling. You'll get rained on occasionally, wind-blown a lot, sand-blasted and smogged-on, sun-burned and frozen. You'll be stiff from sleeping two hours, then stiff from standing three hours. On the credit side, you intensely experience the weather and the spaces around you. It's heavenly to feel gusts and puffs of zephyrs lightly stroke your skin; to watch tall clouds fall slowly by.

Your chronological age has some importance, but the limit is at the lower end, not the upper. Older hitchhikers are seen far less than young 'uns, but it's not a matter of ability so much as life style and enthusiasm. Not many older people (like, over 40) hitchhike, but it just isn't their style anymore. It could be, tho, for older people get rides without extraordinary difficulty.

Stuff. A certain minimum amount of good-quality stuff is necessary: A light pack, sleeping bag, canteen, extra clothes, boots, etc. (There's a detailed list later.) Beyond the practical, you'll need some political baggage: ID especially, and other paperwork like money and maps. The police around the country will want to inspect your paper carefully (more about this shortly.)

And that's what you need.

DANGERS OF HITCHING

Everyone has heard all about the kinds of dangerous hitchhikers there are: murderers, groupies, tramps, deserters, poets, pimps, musicians, runaways, dealers, thieves, hippies, communards, gurus, Reds, flower children, lunatics, gamblers, narcos, junkies, smugglers, saints, spies, whores, homosexuals, artists, convicts — practically everybody I know.

They're all out waving their thumbs, and they're not just testing the wind. How dangerous are they? Well, all those desperados put together are not so dangerous as the people who give them rides. In fact, hitchhikers are victims of violence far more than drivers are. Even so, the number is small compared to the number of hitchhikers. But there are rapes, robberies, beatings, and even murders once in a while. There are police arrests, fines, and jail. But that's where we're at as a country, and violence and injustice victimize not just hitchers but everyone at random. Hitchers are more exposed, however, and do run somewhat more risk. That's the way it is.

What can you do to protect yourself? First of all, few people are out for trouble, and it's foolish to expect the worst or fear that possibility constantly. Expect the best from people and you'll usually get it. Next, even if you do get a ride with someone who seems wayward, remember there are many borderline personalities who are kinky but seldom dangerous: eccentrics, neurotics, misfits, drunks, addicts, half-wits, delinquents, pranksters, and so forth. These fellow-freaks may make you uncomfortable, but try to relax and relate to them as best you can. Frankly, many rides come from

Off the Tape
PYRAMID LAKE

I'm sitting on Enchanted Beach at the north end of Pyramid Lake. It is, I think, one of the most enchanted places I've ever seen. The lake is some kind of incredible aqua, not like a normal lake at all . . . Looking across its expanse I see a range of treeless mountains — every shade of earth tone. Overhead a few puffs of clouds are painting shadows on their bare faces. A few ducks are off shore, very close in, looking over once in a while. Behind me on the north end of the lake are what they call the Pinnacles — a series of very jagged, vertical outcrops that are not to be seen anywhere else around the lake. An unearthly moonscape. There are some sand dunes around, and right in them is a geyser. Turning around, leaning on one shoulder, I can see steam rising from the geyser with one of the pinnacles as a backdrop. There is no sound anywhere. The sky is clear overhead — clear blue. The sunlight is brilliant everywhere, but there's a wind coming from off the lake that makes for perfect weather. The perfection of this place at this moment is captivating, even stunning. To think I hitchhiked here.

I was speaking with a ranger earlier and he said that the Indians whose reservation this is have no water rights to it and more and more water is being taken away from the Truckee River which feeds the lake. The level of the lake is gradually dropping. A big battle over water has been joined but the ranger thinks the Indians are going to lose and the level of the lake is going to keep dropping and gradually this will become a dry lake — drunk up by Reno, by the farmers for irrigation. As it now stands, the lake is only 1/40 of its prehistoric size. These pinnacles right on the shore of the lake are old lava fumaroles — the shapes are positively organic. Rounded, hot bubbles rising up a cliff face. This must have been a sacred Indian place. I can imagine spirits coming out at nite to dance by the shore, by the eerie shore.

I'm sitting right in the hot bath now, looking up toward the geyser. Pyramids all around me, lake all around me, blue sky, sun beating down, in a hot bath naked and alone. Too far out. Some kind of paradise. A little moment, but it's high.

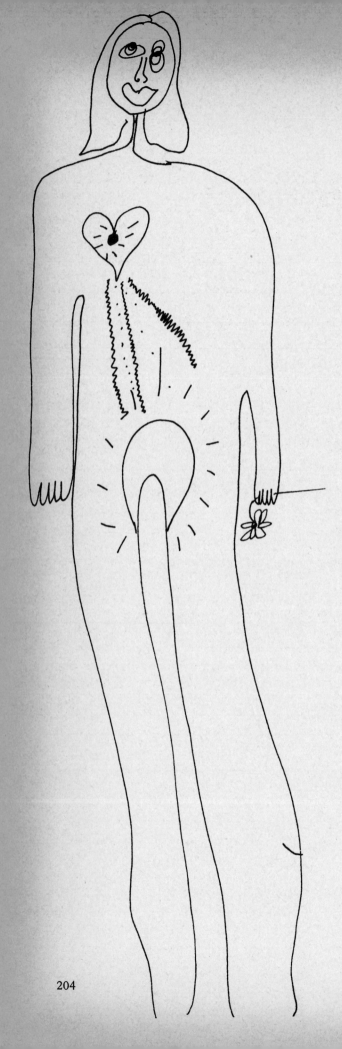

people who feel so alienated generally that hitchhikers are some of the few people they can relate to. They may be looking for a temporary diversion or a few friendly words. Of course, if they threaten trouble in some way, you need to firmly resist their trip. Call them on it, or ask them to let you out.

As in all hitchhiking encounters, the social interaction between you and the driver is crucial. There isn't much useful advice to be given about this. Play it by ear. If you sense trouble coming, don't panic. It's usually possible to talk your way out of trouble or out of the car. The vibe you project is important. If you seem like someone who can take care of yourself, the situation will probably turn out to be a case of bluff or empty talk or someone deliberately trying to rattle you for amusement. Keep cool.

When male hitchers are hassled, it's usually by belligerent drunks or speeders. Ask to be let out. Very rarely, some "macho" or "redneck" troublemaker may try goading or insulting you. Unresponsiveness on your part is probably the best reaction. Stay as peaceful as you can.

Rape. For female hitchhikers, the danger of rape is real and not to be scoffed at. Many rape incidents involving hitchhikers are not even reported. First of all, to avoid being considered as a sex object, try not looking like one. Don't hitchhike in provocative clothing (filmy dresses, tight sweaters) or strike sexy poses by the hiway. Believe it or not, there are still a lot of cavemen types who think hitchhiking girls must be nymphomaniacs on the prowl, so don't give them too much encouragement. Disguising your gender is unnecessary, but dressing in (so-called) men's clothing (pants, shirt) is a good idea all around. Not only less provocative but more comfortable and practical.

Always avoid hitching alone if you have any choice. Another girl is better; a guy is best. Hitching at nite raises the odds for rape, so avoid it. Before jumping into a car, get an impression of where the driver is at by asking him where he's headed, or at least eyeball him carefully. If your first impressions aren't good,

don't hesitate about passing up the ride. Tell the driver you're not going his way. The vibes are particularly important if the car has two or more guys in it, and no women.

If you're in the car, enroute, and the driver starts making sexual advances or sexual conversation, ask him to stop or let you out. If he won't do it and keeps coming on, get out if you can at a red light or other stop. Hail a cop if you see one. Be ready to split if he becomes violent. If you're obviously about to be raped — especially if he has a weapon — try whatever last-ditch efforts the situation calls for (your choice): Stall for time, promise him a later date, say you've got VD, scream, struggle, grab the car keys, honk the horn, whatever. If nothing avails — remember that getting raped is better than being killed. Stay alive for a better day. Carrying a weapon isn't a good idea unless you know how to use it expertly. (If you hitchhike a lot, or are planning to, maybe you should take some courses in self-defense or really learn how to use a basic weapon like a belt knife. That's pretty heavy, but so is rape.) Carrying a weapon isn't a good idea unless you know how to use it expertly. One of the best preventives is to hitch with a well-trained dog.

Accident Prevention. Machines are a more certain source of danger than people. The possibility of being struck by a passing vehicle greatly increases for anyone who hangs around roadsides all the time. For this reason hitchhikers should take measures to make themselves as visible as possible. Wear bright clothes, carry a sign, or station yourself so your profile can be seen against the background or sky. This also increases your chances for a ride. Don't turn your back to traffic. Don't step in the traffic lanes to attract cars. If there isn't room to stand on the shoulder, or there isn't space for a car to pull off the road, move to another spot.

Other Dangers. The police are not exactly a danger of hitchhiking but if you're doing something illegal or undesirable and they come along to arrest or hassle you, then we can consider them as dangers. Unfortunately, hitchhiking is illegal in a lot of places (see ahead). So the police sometimes will be out to stop your lawbreaking ways. Mostly they only ask you to move on, after they've checked your ID and perhaps run a computer search of the records to see if you're wanted.

MINNESOTA IS THREE HUNDRED MILES
by Alice Rogoff
(A Talking Song, with Steady Strum)

```
E              B7          E
Minnesota is three hundred miles.
E                    A7         E
Now we ain't poor but we ain't rich
              A7    E
so we started out to hitch.
E                  A7       E     A7
As the day grew older our feet grew colder,
          E       E      A7
as the road grew wet and slicker,
                              E
we started to get less rides less quicker.
E                          E
Then out of the rosy-fingered sunset
          A7        E
came a hundred to one bet,
A7         E     E  A7        E
peaches and cream, the hitchhiker's dream,
          A7        A7       E
a regular homer, the California Roamer.
E            A7
Now we said: "Where ya going?"
```

Finally, there's the biggest danger of all, and also the one most frequently encountered: Once you start hitchhiking, you're in danger of opening up a world of experience that forces you to change. Most people don't like to change. That's partly why you find so few "successful" people hitchhiking. And so few uptight people, and so few older people. They can't afford to risk this danger. Too bad for them.

THE HITCHHIKING WOMAN Sisters, don't let the rape rap on the previous page scare you out of trying it. Hitchhiking offers your sex everything it does the others, even tho you are second-class citizens. Maybe you should hitchhike for that reason alone — to break down the barriers by a personal effort. It is well-known that women get rides more easily than men. Even tho the reason for this is basically sexist, the result nevertheless is easy hitchhiking. Women can count on traveling more comfortably and swiftly than their male counterparts. Therefore, if you feel confident you can take care of yourself, hitchhiking becomes reliable as well as interesting. Many people that pick you up are people you'd like to know anyway. They're probably young and either ex-hitchhikers or part-time hitchhikers themselves. Many women I've talked to feel that the best place to meet men socially and sexually is while hitchhiking. It certainly beats meeting men in bars, where the rape incidence is higher and the clientel less interesting.

LEGAL ASPECTS Hitchhiking is technically legal in most of the United States tho you'll hear a lot of advice to the contrary. Every state has the right to pass its own laws regarding hitchhiking. Frequently cities and towns will pass their own ordinances about hitchhiking as well. The way most of the hitchhiking laws are written, it is illegal to stand in the road and solicit a ride. Almost universally, what this means is that as long as you stand on the shoulder of the highway, that is, off the paved portion, you can legally hitchhike. In only eight states is hitchhiking technically illegal, and these are:

Arkansas
Connecticut
Delaware
Maine
Nevada
New Jersey
North Dakota
Wyoming

(Washington state is frequently mentioned in various sources as having anti-hitchhiking ordinances. This was true until 1972 when hitchhiking was legalized.)
However, I've seen many hitchhikers in all these states, whether legal or not, and I've hitched in some of them myself. The best parts of the country in which to hitch, generally speaking, are the west coast, the northeast, the north central states, and the southwest.

The technicalities of legality don't mean too much, however, because this is what actually happens: In most states the cops take upon themselves the right to hassle you if they feel like it. Police thruout all the states frequently (sometimes invariably) stop hitchhikers for questioning and checking ID. Hitchhikers are seldom arrested unless they are breaking some other law as well or unless they have no money or ID. (Sometimes the cops just want to play mean sons-of-bitches.) If you are arrested for a hitchhiking violation, you will generally be fined from $10 to $25 and let go with a warning.

In all states, hitchhiking on freeways, interstates, and toll roads is illegal. This always refers to hitchhiking on the hiways themselves and not to standing at the entrances. These are always marked by signs saying "No hitchhiking" or "No pedestrians" and so long as you stand in front of this sign you are legally OK. However, the police may order you to move from that location if they think you're a traffic hazard. Frequently the traffic at the entrance road is so slight that you'll be tempted to venture onto the freeway itself in order to get a ride. If you do, you better hope for a ride before the next patrol car comes along. In a few states, the police will overlook

```
E                A7
Now he said: "I've got no way of knowing."
E                A7        A7
Now we said: "Where ya headed?"
E                A7             E
and he said "After the white line":
E                A7
Now we said, "In which direction?"
E                    A7          E
And he said, "In mine, mine, all mine.
E
I've been to California and back,
    A7        E       A7       E
but where I'm going and where I've been
    A7      E
I don't keep track."
E                        A7        E
He drove us to the North coun-tree,
E          A7     E        A7     E
passing thru Ames to Emmons and Albert Lea.
E                    A7           E
He left us in Hopkins after many a mile.
E
He left us to wander down the Mississippi
    A7          E
or up the blue Nile.
E                                  A7      E
He left us with a bottle of wine and a great big smile.
E     A7      E
The California Roamer.
E          B7          E
Minnesota is three hundred miles.
```

Off The Tape
DOWN THE COAST

There's a bird below flying over the white surf, a wave breaks over her. The surf is so brilliant, so alive, looking down on it through a curtain of trees, bushes, looking down on the surf beating in, beating on the rocks, once again it's far out to be here wherever this is. Just the world, I guess, somewhere in the world, I guess.

The sun came closer and closer to setting. It got much colder. I put on one jacket, and then I wore my wind breaker for the first time. My traveling companion was Steve Murphy, from Brooklyn, with whom I'd been drinking and smoking and hitchhiking the day thru, tho I just met him today. We prepared to sleep out, but he didn't have any wind breaker. He started to sweat the rest of the day. He was going all the way to Lompoc which was still a long way off. We walked back and forth and just before the sun went down into the ocean a car stopped.

So we met Eddie, a guy from Switzerland who'd been working and traveling around the United States since last November. He was going all the way to LA, so we got Steve close to his destination before dropping him off. The rest of the drive down to Santa Barbara was pretty uneventful, except for picking up a girl who'd just been propositioned by a guy who gave her a ride. When she said no, he said "Well, get out then."

We stopped at a coffee shop on the way and had some coffee and I bought some French fries, and that was my first expenditure of money since I left San Francisco a few days ago. Later on we left the girl off, and then Eddie and I came down to Santa Barbara. Just before we got in I gave Anna Fontana a call, and that's where we are now. She was delighted to see us. She ran outside and was waiting for us on her street corner as we drove up to show us where her house was. Her man Roland is asleep. She made us a midnite meal of pork chops, french fries, green beans, two flavors of ice cream, coffee, cookies — the first supper I've had in two days and all here seems pretty good.

this, but not in most. Hitching anywhere on the freeway proper is always a clear violation of the law and they'll nab you for it.

Wherever you hitchhike you are almost certain to be stopped by the police at some time or another (in some states you'll be stopped several times per day) and ordered to produce identification and sometimes money or other signs of ability to pay your way (traveler's checks, credit cards). It is absolutely imperative that you have identification and some money when you travel. Identification is more important than money, because sometimes they won't ask you about your money. However, traveling without ID is a no-no, and they'll hold you for investigation. If you're a minor, a notarized letter from your parents or guardians giving permission to travel will help prove you're not a runaway. A letter from your local police station stating you have no police record there is also a handy piece of ID. Traveling without money may result in being arrested for vagrancy. To beat it, always carry at least $20 on your person.

WHO TO GO WITH In hitchhiking as in most other things, two heads are better than one, but one of them better be female. To be female is to be blessed when it comes to getting rides; therefore if you are already a female, congratulations. You not only get more rides, but the statistics show that you'll be healthier and live longer than your male counterpart. If you're a male, accept my condolences and do the best you can. In hitchhiking, doing the best you can means traveling with a girl. A male-female couple is unquestionably the best hitchhiking combination. The girl gets the rides, the man protects the girl (presumably), and couples make a much better social impression on all concerned — ordinary citizens and police and potential troublemakers too. A couple is "respectable," and respectability is a good thing to have going for you when you're hitchhiking. Two girls traveling together will get lots of rides, but unless they

are particularly self-sufficient, they're a double-bubble of sexuality that has drawbacks on the road. Two guys hitching together can make it OK, but should expect far fewer rides. Too much latent masculine violence. However, if the men turn out to be boys, that is, they're youngsters, then this objection diminishes.

In all cases, when two people hitchhike together they create a space problem, and they'll be bypassed by people who would have picked up a single hitchhiker. Another disadvantage of double-thumbing is the high likliehood of friction with your traveling partner. Personal relations are always more difficult at times of stress, and when you're hitchhiking stress is often high. Even if partners are well-suited to each other, some disagreement and discord are almost certain. Don't dwell on it. Being able to share the rewards of the road is a compensating joy.

Traveling alone is the end-all trip. You're the freest and the fastest, and it puts a lot of space in your head. It's just yourself and the road and nothing in between.

MONEY You've got to have it; the only questions are how much and in what form. Back in chapter 4, I talked about travelers checks and credit cards. The only further remark for hitchhiking is that they're even more important here than in other means of traveling. Other kinds of travelers don't get hassled because everybody assumes they have money. But everyone assumes hitchhikers are broke, hungry, and dangerous. Credit cards are good because they imply solvency, and they're your insurance for getting out of a jam. And they're safe to carry because in case of loss or theft the maximum liability is $50. Travelers checks are OK, especially if you carry them but don't use them. In other words, start off with enough money for your trip, but then bring along a few hundred dollars extra in travelers checks for show money and just in case, for your emergency slush fund. This money could bail you out on a bus if the going gets rough, prevent a vagrancy fine, or pay for unexpected "extras" along the way.

Off The Tape
FRANCESCA

A point of indecision. I could call to Laguna Beach and see if I could raise Edie's sister. But that would cost 40 cents, I find out. So, to save 40 cents I decide to go back on the hiway and try to get closer to Laguna Beach, and then call Edie's sister. By this time the sun, which has been beating down on me (my nose is very red by now, sunburned along the face) goes down. It's just dusk. After about a half an hour, during which I wonder whether I'm going to make it at all, I get a short ride down to the coast hiway, which I accept because it is going to simplify very much getting a ride to Laguna. The driver — John, a student at Long Beach State — says if I can't get a ride he shares a place in Seal Beach with a few other students, and I could stay there with him. So I say, I'll see how it goes.

I get down to Seal Beach and get back on the street again with my pack, ready to start hitchhiking when this exotic girl walks by and says: "Where are you going?" So I tell her to Laguna Beach. "Well maybe you should stay here this evening, there's a party just up the road and I could give you some names and you could get in free." So I said "Well" and that decided me to stay in Seal Beach and stay with John tonight. So, now I'm getting ready to eat dinner at John's. He has four room-mates, three guys and a girl. (I'd give their names but later on I lost my address book.) He's cooking Cornish hens for his room-mates and his girl; I went out and bought some wine. All is groovy. There couldn't be a better place than here right now.

MUSIC. Well, here am I at the party and at the dance. It's a completely crazy youth scene. Teen age kids, really young. Far out kids tho, far out California teenagers, 15 to 20, really freaking out, getting wild-assed drunk on 3.2 beer, falling all over each other, hugging and kissing, ass-slapping, jumping up and down. MUSIC. The crowd is going into a frenzy. One thing I'm surprised at — no dope here. The whole event, incidentally, is taking place in some huge quonset huts not too far from the beach, I guess in what used to be an area of sand dunes. I'm outside right now, taking some air, looking thru the night air. I guess that's a PGE power plant off to the left. I count one, two, three, four, five and off to the right several dozen oil derricks. And the ubiquitous power lines that pervert this part of the country. That's about all. Power lines, power plants, oil wells — completely industrialized landscape and here in the middle of it is the youth that it produced, doing their number. MUSIC.

Well I'm leaving the Marina Palace now. I feel I'm 10 or 15 years too late. While at the party during the dance, I saw the girl who had told me about it in the first place. She went outside for a breath of air. I went over to her and I spoke with her for a minute. She seemed one of the most beautiful women I've ever seen. I asked her if she would like to dance and she declined, said she'd gotten too sunburned that day — she's fallen asleep in the sun. A little while longer and she excused herself and left. That was the last I'll ever see of Francesca. Francesca Cum or something like that. Seeing her leave made me feel sad. Somehow the old sadness of wanting to be everybody, wanting to do everything, wanting to see everything, wanting to be every girl's lover, wanting to see every place in the world, wanting to know every experience. Feeling inadequate, small, human, mortal, frustrated and sad. (On the other hand, doing the best I can is pretty interesting.)

HOW TO HITCHHIKE "Shucks, there ain't nothin to it" — but there are some things worth knowing about if you haven't tried it before or if you haven't thought about it much. Let's thumb thru some of them . . .

Place is Paramount. First of all, find a place with some traffic. (That's right — no cars means no rides.) Sounds stupid, but I've frequently seen hitchers standing on some road with little or no cars on it, while just a short distance away is a main-traveled road offering much better odds. Having a map is the surest way to beat this problem. Gasoline company road maps are usually the best, and easiest to get. Find out where you're going, find out exactly where you are, and figure out what's the best route in between them. Sometimes there are several routes. Studying your map and using your noggin may save you hours of time on the road. Another way to dispel your ignorance is simply to ask the best way from here to there. Tell your informant that you're hitchhiking because his advice may be different if he knows that.

Now you're on the right route. What next? Pick a place where you can easily be seen by approaching motorists. The further off the better. This gives someone a longer time to decide about your ride, and also keeps you from getting killed by someone that never saw you. The place should also have room for a car to pull over. Picking a spot endangered by the traffic flow is a terrible choice. You'll probably be better off somwhere else.

Other considerations relating to place: How comfortable is it? Is there some shade from the sun, something overhead to shield out rain? Is it a place where you can spend a couple of pleasant hours if you don't get a ride? If the few pleasant hours gradually turn into an unpleasant day, how close is it to someplace to sleep, someplace to get food?

Your spot is the most important thing in hitchhiking success.

Appearance. How you look (your vibration) is the next most important thing. Part of your appearance you can't help. That is: whether you're male or female, whether you're one or two, whether you're young or old. As far as clothes, my own experience makes me think you should dress for the road and never mind dressing for drivers. Skip the suit and put on jeans and a durable long-sleeved shirt. Wear boots, because hiking is half of hitchhiking — you'll walk plenty, frequently in strange or rough terrain. A hat is important, wide-brimmed for summer sun and rain. You should also have a pack and sleeping bag. Put this together and how do you look? Mostly like a vagabond hitchhiker rather than an office worker or college boy or girl. The matter of long hair is moot. I think it doesn't make too much difference anymore in *most* places. Everybody is used to longhairs and there's no longer a prejudice about giving rides. Except in the Rocky Mountain/Plains states and Southern states. Even so, it doesn't warrant cutting your hair or avoiding these places. Just bear it in mind as a possibility. Wear your hair back or under your hat, if necessary.

Aside from that, the only important advice is to keep neat and clean, no matter how you dress. Men, shave as often as necessary to keep from looking ornery, or travel with a beard or a moustache, but if you do shave, do it often. Everybody keep your clothes dusted off and looking clean as possible. When they get grimy or start to stink, change clothes and wash the first set in a laundromat, or by hand in a stream or tub.

Women should dress the same — jeans, shirt, boots, hat. Of course you should have a skirt in your pack but it's too impractical and sexy for the road. Likewise make-up. Wear your hair anyway you like, but if it's long tie or tuck it in; otherwise it'll be blown around by the wind and passing trucks. The same thing, of course, applies to long-haired guys.

Carry A Sign. A sign with your destination lettered on it is always useful, sometimes necessary. At interstates or freeways, you'll frequently come to an on-ramp which feeds traffic in any of several directions — north, south, east, west, up, down, and maybe more. Use a sign here to indicate which direction you want. Do this any time confusion might exist

Off The Tape
THE GOOD LIFE

Here in New England, in New Hampshire, in a small town, in this idyllic old American countryside we see a new American life style. Lenny and Elise have traveled all over the world, they've lived in Italy, they've lived in Cornwall, they've lived in Ireland, they've lived in San Francisco, and now they're back to their home in New England. Lenny is an art teacher and he will be able to continue being an art teacher, he thinks. He's going to combine it with a life style that includes his own life on the farm. He's a kind of gentleman farmer, but not for the sake of the farm so much as for style, for the sake of self-involvement, for the sake of independence from a style of life which suffocates the individual. Like so many other new Americans he wants to be free from the kind of materialistic dependency that our old American society has nurtured in its citizens. The old way taught us that however much money you made you had to spend it all to support an ever growing level of consumption.

And the new way is to consume as little as possible, to make as much as you can with your own hands, to grow as much of your own food as possible. If you can be independent, then you don't need to be a producer in an industrial society. You can be a creator in a creative society. But just as he does not want to be a slave to technology, neither does he want to be a slave to the land. The idea is to find the balance — a reasonable balance. It's not a total negation of materialism. But neither is it a negation of the land. It's about soul.

Lenny prefers living in America for many reasons. He thinks Europe does not offer enough material for the artist to create, for the inventor to work his mind. America's richness of materials catalyzes a fecundity of ideas, generates a zoo of people. The trick is to let the materials free you, not enslave you.

about your direction or destination. It's up to you to straighten it out for the motorist; he's unlikely to stop to ask you in which of several directions you're going. Even where unnecessary, signs are useful for the following reasons: they make it easier to see you, especially if you hold it out toward the motorist as he nears (the movement increases your visibility); also the sign provides additional information about you, and hence makes the motorist feel he knows you better (try adding something like STUDENT, HELP, or HARMLESS to the destination).

Whatever you use for a sign, make it readable and wind resistant. Signs are useless if written in pencil, and they'll soon rip to shreds if they aren't fairly stiff. I advise buying a *wide-tipped* felt pen and then scrounge pieces of cardboard for the signs. Corrugated cardboard can be found anywhere in America on short notice, frequently just lying by the roadside, or at any market or store. Start with a piece in your pack, and then keep an extra piece there so you'll have it when you need it. Fold it once to stiffen it further. Write your destination in large letters, the larger the better. Sometimes it's better to write a compass direction (NORTH) rather than a city destination, or OUTSKIRTS, or DOWNTOWN.

City Hitching. Unlike Europe, most American cities are OK for hitchhiking in or thru. American bus systems are so bad (or non-existent) that hitchhiking is accepted and practical. However, some large American cities do have good subway or bus systems (New York for example) and there you'll do better with public transportation. Other cities (LA in particular) have such intricate freeway systems that a bus may be the best way to thread the maze. To help you get thru a strange city, by all means get a map at a local gas station — and ask about busses.

Nite Hitching. Hitchhiking at nite is feasible but not particularly fruitful or comfortable. You'll get fewer rides, be colder, have less to look at, and be more likely to get waylaid, checked by the police, or maimed by a motorized drunk. If you do hitch at nite, make absolutely sure you can be seen — under a street lamp, in front of a gasoline station, or on a brightly lit street. Gas stations, coffee shops, and diners are good places to hitchhike because you may have a chance to speak to people as they come in or go out. You'll always get more rides when you approach somebody directly and introduce yourself face to face rather than at 60 miles an hour. This is true at all times but at nite it may be your only way to get rides.

Food and Water. In America's open spaces and long stretches, it is still possible to get stranded and literally die from exposure or lack of food and water. In any case, it's easy to find yourself alone and surrounded by mile after mile of nothing, and that nothing includes food and water. If you don't carry your own at all times, I guarantee you'll be unhappy somewhere along the way. Always carry water. Make a practice of filling your container every time you're around a gas station, whether you're on foot or in someone else's car. Make a practice of carrying some (non-perishable) food in your pack — can of tuna or sardines, hunk of cheese, couple of oranges, bag of peanuts, etc. Avoid candy bars (they melt), soft fruit (it squashes), or anything in a glass container.

(In the picture here, the wine bottle was given to us a moment before, and we wasted no time in downing it. Prosit.)

Hitchhikers partake of the most wretched diets known to man. You're so anxious to thumb rides that you either hurry thru meals or skip them altogether. When you've got a ride, you'll frequently skip a meal to suit the driver's schedule. Much of your diet comes via the vending machine — candy bars and soft drinks. When you do get a hot meal, it probably comes from some greaseburger joint more likely to nauseate than nourish you. All this is OK for awhile, but on a long trip, you better watch your diet lest you suddenly collapse at some point, or simply succumb to some strange malady. Over and over again you hear about hitchhikers who get sick enroute for reasons they don't understand. But if you examine their diets, the amount of sleep they get, the conditions of stress, exposure, and weather to which they're subject, you wonder why they're not sick more often.

This food syndrome is worsened by the fact that food is the hitcher's most expensive item. Transportation is free, and you usually sleep for nothing. So that leaves only food. You're tempted to skip eating so you can travel completely free. This is false economy. I would say this: Get one good meal a day and you'll be fine. Try to make it the evening meal, and as often as possible try to get it home-cooked. Get it at a friend's house, or at the house of someone who has invited you to stay, or cook it yourself over a campfire, or have a full meal at a decent restaurant. Eat all your lunches out of your knapsack, restocking at the supermarkets, and stay away from garbage-food. For ease of refreshment at all times, carry a bota or canteen filled with plain water, wine, or whatever's wet. Strung over your shoulder or tied onto your pack, the bota is always handy for gulping.

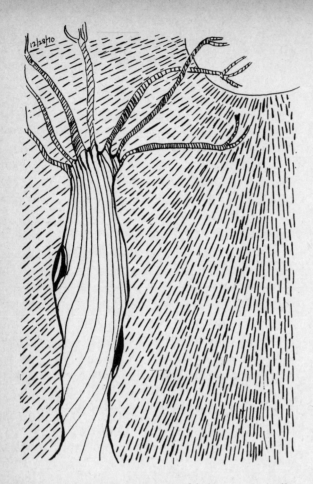

WHEN TIME DRAGS Hitchhikers naturally get impatient waiting for Destiny to snatch them off the roadside and into their next adventure. Yet so much of your time is spent at the roadside that you should think of better ways to use it than getting impatient. How do you make *tempus fug it?* First of all consider its constructive uses. Is there a store nearby to restock your food supply? Is there a faucet to replenish your water supply? Is there someplace you can get a map? If you have a map, do you know where you're going? What's the best route? Study your map to answer all questions you have about the next leg of the route. Is your sign ready to go? Should you make a new one? Is there any sign material nearby for next time you'll need one? Check your address book. Is there anyone you know around here that you should call? Is this a good spot to call ahead to your next contact down the road, if any? Feel like writing a postcard? Is there a post office to buy stamps? Are there any other supplies you need that you

can buy here? Is your pack secure? Is everything tied on and strapped in? Is there anything you need now out of your pack or anything you can put back in while you have the time to properly stow it? Do you have to take a crap? Is there a toilet around? Can you stock up on toilet paper here? Is there a place to wash your face and perhaps shave? Should you take the time here for a bite to eat? Or to wash your clothes in the laundromat? Hell, maybe this is a good place just to stay awhile, for the next day or two and take a break from the road. And so forth.

Next, after you've considered these actions and you are finally standing there with nothing else to do, what now? How about tuning in on what's happening around you? It may not seem like much, but just stand there awhile longer and you'll feel the rhythm of the place, absorbing it thru the pores of your skin. No one is likely to bother you now, so you have the privacy and the time to review your trip, and to plan ahead. If you're traveling with someone, it's a great opportunity to talk about anything and everything, throw stones, crack jokes, and just skylark around. In small towns especially, it's pretty easy to strike up a conversation with someone like a passerby or gas station attendant. They'll be curious about you anyway, so why not satisfy their curiosity and remove their lingering fears about who you are? It's smart, too, because once they feel relaxed about you, they can help you a lot. For example, they might find a ride for you, or talk someone into giving you a ride, and they may just may offer you a meal or a place to sleep. None of that will happen if you don't make the first step by starting a conversation.

Boredom is one thing, but how do you handle being freaked out? Getting discouraged is one way it happens, getting sick is another. Feeling alone, getting hassled by citizens or police. Being rained on and miserable, being frozen and miserable, finding you've lost your wallet, finding you've shit your pants, finding that everyone is staring at you and laughing. Maybe you have a bad day, or two bad days in a row, or three bad days in a row. Maybe as many bad days as it takes to make you collapse, and then suddenly you collapse. What do you do? Get off your ego and remember you're not unique. Whatever is happening to you now has happened to hitchhikers somewhere before. They handled it or got thru it and so can you. The right thing to do in a situation is whatever seems right to you. Once you're doing something — anything — you're already getting on top of the situation. If you can't stand being someplace, get the hell out — catch the bus, walk out if necessary. Hole up somewhere where you can sleep it off. Crawl into a sewer or your sleeping bag. If all else fails, Lose Consciousness! (Sleep is the best way of doing this.) Tomorrow is a new day.

WEATHER WORDS Almost all hitchhiking is done out of doors. It's necessary to say that because people forget that being outside means preparing for whatever Mother Nature dishes up. The truth is that people have no idea what it means to be outdoors all the time because they're used to living indoors. Folks, it just ain't the same. The solution, by courtesy of the Boy Scouts: "Be Prepared". The main problems you'll face are sun, heat, rain, cold, wind, glare, and some associated outdoor things like insects and dirt. Proper equipment and accessories are the answer in all cases. Wear your main defenses: Hat (wide brim) for sun and waterproof for rain; long-sleeved shirts with collars for sunburn (you'll need some kind of sun lotion too); and if the wind comes up, a liteweight, water-repellent windbreaker (one that can be closed at the wrist, neck, and waist.) As it gets colder, wear sweaters beneath the windbreaker — first one, then another. If it gets colder yet, wear a second shirt under your first shirt and a scarf around your neck. Likewise pants — wear a second pair under your first. Depending on how cold it's going to get, bring gloves or mittens (remember that standing in one place reduces your circulation, so your extremities — like fingers, toes, nose — will get colder than usual). For hard rains, bring a full-length poncho to go entirely over you and your gear, especially for those times

when you're stuck out there with no shelter whatever. Sunglasses for road glare are a necessity. For high dust conditions or a dust storm, breathe through a bandana tied around your nose and mouth. Of course you'll have boots and a couple pairs of woolen socks. If you didn't bring gloves in an emergency you can use a pair of your woolen socks. (To avoid cramps, first take them off your feet.)

Hitchhiking is something for all seasons. Naturally if you know you'll be in winter conditions, you'll dress accordingly. However, it's always wise to carry some cold-weather gear, even in summer, especially when crossing mountainous regions, because out-of-season storms can prove serious if you're unprepared. Even at mild temperatures, wind or rain can chill you quickly. In short, it's better to carry around a few extra ounces of wool than freeze your ass.

Sleeping Outdoors. This is the customary mode for hitchhikers, and with proper equipment is no big thing. Don't consider traveling without a good sleeping bag, preferably unobtrusive in color for camouflage in populated areas. To go under it you'll need a ground cloth of some kind — your rain poncho will serve. To go over it (only in case of rain) you'll need a tarp or tent of some kind — a tube tent will serve (this is just a large tube of plastic big enough for you to crawl into out of the rain). You'll need a long (50') piece of nylon cord to string the tube tent up (using poles, trees, or other supports). In bad weather, sleep indoors or in a protected location if you can find one. In the country, look for barns, sheds, abandoned buildings and farmhouses. Lacking that, sleep under bridges, overpasses, tunnels, or in culverts. In the wilderness, look for caves, overhangs, dense trees, or just string up your tarp or tent. In cities and towns, look for buildings under construction or otherwise empty, gas stations, city parks, freeway ramps. You can even sleep dry inside or underneath abandoned cars or trucks. Be prepared for occasional run-ins with insects, animals (especially mice and dogs), and people.

BAGGAGE AND CLOTHES Since I've been talking about things to take, let's just get to the whole megillah. A couple of points and then comes a road-tested equipment list for hitchhikers.

Backpack. How are you going to carry your stuff? I recommend taking it in a backpack without a frame, and I'll say that again: a pack without a frame. Lots of people and various guidebooks, recommend a rigid frame pack for hitchhikers. That's bad advice — a sign of inexperience or inability to learn from it. Most travelers either know from experience or have figured out that a pack should be sturdy, well-built and able to carry a fair amount of weight. But there's much more to consider yet.

Here's what I think, based on using packs for hitchhiking, backpacking, mountaineering, rock climbing, and hauling: For hitchhiking, the pack should be frameless. Frame packs have numerous disadvantages. They weigh more and they add rigidity — which means that you can't get them in or out of cars easily (or trunks or other storage spaces). You can't flatten them out or roll them up when you're not using them. A frameless pack, however, can be stuffed into the back of a car or at your feet or in the trunk and it goes easily thru a car door. While waiting for a ride, its a comfortable seat — a useful piece of furniture instead of a tangle of aluminum rods. When a frameless pack is empty, it can be rolled up and put out of the way or used as a pillow, or flattened out underneath you to keep you off the ground. The kind of pack I like has a waterproof inner shell that extends the pack when pulled inside out. This inner shell can be used in one of two ways. When loading the pack, it increases the volume of space available. Then when the pack is empty it can be slipped over your feet as an emergency "elephant's foot", and the extension pulled out over your knees. Finally, it can be flattened with the inner shell pulled out, and it's long enough to serve as a shortee ground cloth.

People sometimes say a frameless pack won't carry enough weight or is uncomfortable. Well, if you've got so much in your pack that you need a frame to carry it, then you're carrying too much. All your road goods should go lightly into a frameless pack. Second, whatever your bag weighs, it won't be on your back all the time. In fact, it's either going on the car seat beside you or on the ground in front of you as you hitch. The only time you carry it is while hiking thru a city or for overnite hiking in the woods or mountains. If possible, the pack should have side pockets to make it easy to get to the things you use most often. The bottom of the pack should be reinforced, ideally with leather so that it takes a lot of scraping along the ground, so that it can be set down on wet ground or even into puddles without soaking the contents. The shoulder straps should also be padded for comfort.

Where, you might ask, can you find a pack like this? Well, it doesn't exist but there are two packs that come close. One is an English pack (BMB) sold by Recreational Equipment Company (see address in Appendix 12). It's called the Cairn model and sells for about $18 plus shipping. This is a liteweight, extremely rugged and well-built pack that has all the features but one: side pockets. It does have a leather-sheathed bottom and a complete inner shell that extends outwards. It also has tie-rings on top for attaching other things (bota, loose clothes, sleeping bag). If you added your own pockets (and padded the straps), it would be perfect. Another rucksack I've seen like it is made and sold by Sierra Designs (see address in Appendix 12) and it's called the Summit model, selling for about $28 plus shipping. It weighs a little more but does have three outside pockets. It's well-built and has a leather sheath on the bottom, padded shoulder straps, and a partial inner shell that expands it an additional six inches if desired. The only disadvantage is that the inner shell isn't full length. The pack, with shell extended, is only 26 inches instead of about 36 inches for the Cairn pack. Both of these are truly all-purpose sacks and highly recommended.

Now besides your rucksack, you need one other smaller shoulder sack. This is the one that never leaves your side, for in it should be your valuables such as money, camera, maps, guidebook, and lunch. The best bag I've found for this is an army-surplus ammunition bag, about 1 square foot in size with one inside pocket, a top flap, and various strap arrangements for carrying it over your shoulder, on your waist, or in your hands.

I think it's important to carry just two bags — your large rucksack and your small shoulder bag. If you're carrying a guitar, a camera around your neck, and a bota bag over your shoulder, and whatever else, sooner or later you're going to leave something somewhere, probably in a vehicle. Jackets, sweaters, hats are some of the things that hitchhikers consistently leave behind in cars. I've done it myself and it leaves me cold. Make a habit of putting everything into just those two bags and then keep them on your consciousness at all times. That means if you take off a coat or you take out a camera or your bota or waterbag, as soon as you're thru with it, automatically put it back into one of the bags. Then you won't worry about losing things.

Sleeping Bag. Buy the highest quality you can afford; it's one of the best investments you can make. $100 is not too much to spend; it will repay you many times over in comfort and could even save your life. Of course, it should be down-filled. Also, the shell should be heavyweight nylon, not lite weight — it adds a little more weight but the bag lasts much longer before the down starts to squeeze thru, and it resists tears and snags much better. See chapter 7 for a longer discussion of sleeping bags.

Poncho. This is your all-purpose piece of waterproofed cloth. It serves as a ground cloth when sleeping out, emergency shelter, or make-shift tarp to throw over your baggage. The army type is cheap and heavy; the nylon types are light and expensive.

Bota. This is a Spanish wine bag and its collapsibility is its best feature. You can also buy plastic water bags at an army-surplus store.

Pocket Knife. The Swiss Army type is far and away the best and most useful, tho it costs about $15. Of its many models, the one I've found most useful over the years is called the "Outdoorsman", with two knives plus can opener, bottle opener, scissors, wood saw, leather punch, file, corkscrew, toothpick, tweezers.

Flashlite. My most hairy use of a miniature flashlite was after getting picked up by a guy whose car had a burnt-out generator and a dead battery. To keep from freezing, we drove 70 miles thru the Rocky Mountains at nite without lites on winding roads, using only the penlite I pulled out of my pack. By holding it out the window and shining it on the center stripe, we were able to stay on the road and make it into the closest town. Flashlites are handy. A must if you're sleeping out. By the way, reverse the batteries when you're not using it or you're almost sure to discharge them inside your pack. Or tape the switch.

What follows is an all-purpose equipment list based on the idea that you'll hit some cold weather, but it's not meant to be a winter touring list. If you know that you're going to be restricted to hot weather touring, cut some of the cold weather items.

HITCHHIKER'S EQUIPMENT LIST
(Men and Women)

Personal

Toothbrush (handle cut off)
Razor & stainless blades (men)
Barrettes for long hair, or scarves
Toilet paper, small roll
Soap and plastic container
Comb and/or hairbrush
Pocket mirror, metal
Condoms (men) or pills, IUD
    diaphragm (women)
Tampax (women)
Jewelry
Stash (?)

Survival

Poncho
Down sleeping bag
Tube tent
Nylon cord (50')
First aid kit — see chapter 15
Sun tan lotion
Insect repellent (Cutter's or Off)
Flashlite, small (AA batteries)
Book matches in plastic bag
Sierra Club cup (use as cup or plate)
Spoon (use as spoon or fork)
Bota or water bag
Sewing kit — safety pins, needle, thread
Svea 123 gas stove (?)
    (one burner for beans, soup, coffee)
Spare food
Candle lantern, folding

Clothes in Pack

Pants, washable (men)
    or skirt (women)
2 shirts, or blouses, shorts and
    long-sleeved
1 sweater
1 light parka or windbreaker
2 bandanas
Wool socks
3 pr cotton socks
Gloves
Wool cap
2 pr underwear & T-shirts
Jeans cut short (for swimming and
    sunning — women use bandanas
    for top)
Moccasins, sandals, or tennis shoes

To Wear

Hiking boots, rawhide laces
Wool socks over cotton socks
Underwear and T-shirt
Wool shirt, long-sleeved
Pants or jeans
Belt
Jacket or coat, liteweight
Brimmed hat
Bandana
Watch
Sunglasses & case
Swiss Army knife (Outdoorsman)
Money belt or neck pouch (?)
Wallet — cash, ID (drivers license),
    credit card (s) (?), letters
    of reference (?)
Frameless pack
Shoulder bag

Other

Traveler's checks (?)
Notebook (good size 5½x8)
Pen(s) and/or pencil(s)
Guidebook(s)
Address book
Maps (Road Atlas is best)
Reading matter
Felt-tip pen, broad
Clothespins (2) — to dry clothes
    on pack
Piece corrugated cardboard
Harmonica
Camera and film (?)

PEOPLE YOU MEET Hitchhiking is about people, and therefore you should try to understand them and, if possible, become one yourself. When a person stops to give you a ride, s/he's decided to become involved with you in some way. You should understand the reasons why s/he did this, because you'll both have a better ride that way. People don't stop for you purely out of charity. They want something from you. Sometimes they're just bored or curious; they need an energy shot from outside and you're the one who can give it to them. Other people feel guilty about passing up hitchhikers, usually because they used to hitchhike themselves when they were younger or they hitchhike now, and they feel they owe some debt to the people who gave them rides in the past. Sometimes they want something tangible; they want you to share driving, for example. They may want you to talk or to listen, or perhaps just sit there and provide company. Or they may want to rape you. For that reason don't just get in the car; say Hi, and fall quiet or asleep. Find out who your benefactor is. Find out where s/he's going and what makes him or her tick. People are fascinating but you have to prime the pump a bit by showing you're interested in them. Once you're done that, you'll find that just everyday people can be amazing. Occasionally, when strangers get together in the right kind of environment (and a car is that kind), they can communicate with unusual intensity.

Of course, trying to relate to drivers also makes them feel better about picking you up, and hearing what they say about why they picked you up will make you feel better about it too. After all, you're both pretty nervous at the start and until you each get some idea of who you are, your ride is in jeopardy and so is your enjoyment. A friendly driver is a good thing to have going for you. S/He may go out of the way to help you — for example, when you get to town s/he may drive you to a particular address, to a bus station, offer you a meal or place to sleep, or try to find you some kind of accomodation. It always pays to make friends with a driver.

Off The Tape
NEVADA

Some quick impressions of Nevada from an all-nite hitch: Nevada is a place where men have tried to fill the void, have tried to fill the spaces with a sense of bigness to match the open spaces. The little towns are explosions of neon in the night. Gas stations boast of being the largest with 25 pumps, all of them empty in the nite.

Spirit of wide-open enterprise, of wide-open gambling, wide-open women, wide-open spaces. Everything is wide open, anything goes, everything is extravagant, gawdy. Anything is possible. Nevada is a neon dream made possible by the desert lonliness.

The barrenness of Nevada is in such contrast with the riches it has produced from the earth. Virginia City is another example of the same thing — people searching for wealth in the most barren spot in the world. The incontruity of what they were doing was the inspiration for their flamboyance. Reno and Las Vegas are contemporary examples of the same kind of phenomenon. People coming to find wealth, and, as if to make up for the incongruity of coming here to do that, feeling bound to do it with a grand display, to do it garishly and boldly, as if to say — look, this may seem stupid to you, but it can't be stupid because we do it so completely.

Homosexuals. Sometimes the drivers offering rides may have in mind some kind of homosexual liaison, altho nowadays this has gone out of fashion. Overt homosexual advances were a fifties trip because times then were so repressive for homosexuals. With today's greater freedom, homosexuals seldom proposition hitchhikers anymore. Nevertheless it still happens. If it does, don't be upset. Maybe it might arouse your interest (not necessarily sexual). Most "normal" men and women don't meet homosexuals in their daily lives, so you could consider it an opportunity to learn something about this "aberration". When I was a hitchhiking sailor in the 1950's I frequently got rides from homosexuals and found they were good company and seldom offensive. I was a teen-ager then with little sexual experience. After meeting several homosexuals on the road, I decided it would be beneficial to have some homosexual experience myself, and on two occasions I did. The experiences were neither great nor terrible — just another trip, interesting and educational. I didn't regret them, then or now, because I found out something I needed to know — that I had some homosexual curiosity but it wasn't very deep. It's important for men and women to face their homosexual sides, rather than be afraid or suffer guilt. If you can do that, you're better equipped for any kind of sexuality — hetero, homo, bi, or a . . .

Types of Drivers. As a hitchhiker, you can't predict what kind of people will pick you up. Nevertheless, on the average the hitchhiker tends to meet only certain types of people. This is because so many Americans refuse to pick up hitchhikers under any circumstances, severely limiting the range of types. The people that do befriend hitchhikers fall into one or more of the following categories: Young people, students, adventurers, salesmen, workers, servicemen, drunks, poor people, petty criminals, and various other miscellaneous minorities. The people you'll seldom meet are the well-to-do and the middle classes. This exemplifies again that it's possible to hitchhike thru America and not get a representative view of it. The hitchhiker still has a distinct affinity with the lower classes. This isn't bad; it's just unrepresentative. The fact is that most hitchhikers are poor. Naturally the people most likely to give them rides are other poor people — that is, people who have some sympathy for their plight, who know what it feels like to be poor. Today this situation is changing as America slowly realizes that poverty is not the only reason someone would want to hitchhike.

FREIGHT HOPPING Most people think that riding the rails, crossing the country on a freight train, was something done only during the depression of the 1930's. But the freights are still running and people are still riding them. In fact, many farmworkers depend on them to travel where the work is. Freights have long been associated with hoboes and tramps, but there's no reason why they can't be used by hitchhikers too. Incidentally, here's how the difference amongst hoboes, tramps, and bums has been defined. "A hobo is a worker on the move. A tramp is a non-worker on the move. A bum is a non-worker who stays in one place."

This information comes from an acquaintance of mine, Dave Beedon, who's done a lot of freight hopping and written a pamphlet called "A Psuedo-Sophisticated Guide to the Art of Riding Freight Trains — Based Mainly on the Experience of One Person Who Has Hopped Many Trains and Digs It". Freight riding is technically illegal, of course, but in practice few freight train riders are hassled or arrested. Freights are also uncomfortable, cold, wet, and noisy. Being around trains is also a dangerous business for accidents are frequently mangling or deadly. You can also get locked more or less permanently in empty box cars, and your relationships with other freight riders need to be approached with some caution and a great deal of sensitivity. Like anything else, riding the freights involves a body of knowledge and in this case it's difficult to obtain.

A Poem For Ed While He's
      Traveling
(written on the night before you left to vagabond)

This is the crucial day
and it's like all the others.
It is today.
Your smile was like eternal sunshine,
your touch like lapping water:
it entered my arm and was
absorbed into me.
Parting lovers
like mirror reflections
but the mirror is gone for awhile.
I pass my hand before my eyes
to signify the passing of time.
I close my eyes
and bless you
and the road
and all the people you will meet.
I lay back on the soft cushion
of our time together
and know that it is time for
      new beginnings.

Have a joyous and uplifting
      journey, Ed

and come back to the warm,
   healthy heart of
      your family.

Dave's pamphlet is an excellent way to that knowledge if you're interested in riding the freights. It covers every aspect of the trip, including how to minimize the dangers and hassles; rating each different kind of car (such as boxcar, flatcar, gondola, etc.) for comfort, concealment, scenery; how to get information on freights; how to catch a freight on the run and so forth. You can get this pamphlet from David Beedon, 1204 East Glendale Avenue, Milwaukee, WI, 53211. Send $3 or 4$ to pay his Xerox and mailing costs.

AIRPLANE HITCHING I've never used this method of hitchhiking except when I was in the Navy. It's now being done by individuals who approach private pilots and ask if they can get a ride. The technique in both kinds of hitchhiking is the same. It's based on person-to-person encounter and on finding out when and where the planes are leaving. Go to a private airfield and try to spot someone getting ready to fly his plane. Sometimes you can find pilots filing their flight plans at a control tower or desk. Sometimes you'll see them gassing up, sometimes you'll see them untying their planes. Ask them if they're flying out and would like a passenger. Sometimes they'll say yes, sometimes they'll say no. I read in the newspaper that it can be done quite successfully (especially by women) and is one of the greater ways to hitchhike. Also you don't worry as much about meeting any weirdoes this way. Pilots don't tend to grab-ass too much — it's unhealthy.

INFORMATION SOURCES Your primary sources of information while on the road will be maps and personal encounter. On hitchhiking adventures it pays to carry an atlas in your pack, something like the big Rand McNally Road Atlas. It not only provides road routes but camping information, park locations, terrain information, city maps, and tells where the colleges and universities are. All of this vital information is useful to the hitchhiker. The other source of information is the grapevine; that is, the word-of-mouth information network. The grapevine tells you how uptight the

cops are in this state or this town, where are the best places to catch rides and the best streets to get out of town, where's a good place to eat, where you can crash, what things there are to see and do. This kind of underground information will help you again and again, so make contact with it as frequently as possible. Always talk to other hitchhikers you see on the road. Ask them where they've been, where they're going, if they've had any trouble. Let them know your situation so they can personalize the information to your needs. In the same way, approach other than hitchhikers too — the drivers who pick you up certainly may have some useful tidbits for you; gas station attendants, storekeepers, waitresses. When you're traveling thru *terra incognita* everyone is a landmark. To read more about it, look in Appendix 3 for some hitching guidebooks and also at some of the other information sources. Good luck.

HITCHHIKING AS IT IS
by Mac Groben

I discovered hitchhiking about 2½ years ago, and so all of my experiences reflect the current state of affairs here in the U.S. of A. The only knowledge I have of how things used to be is through reading Jack Kerouac, who wrote that he gave up hitching in 1956 because of too many gungho state cops and prohibitive laws. He'd surely roll in his grave if he knew what it's like these days. Sometimes I wish I'd been born a little earlier.

Since my discovery that all you need to travel is a thumb, I've hitched cross-country eight times, plus innumerable excursions in between, Minneapolis to New Orleans, San Antonio to Bangor, and on and on to the point where I have a hard time remembering them all. Here's some of what I've found, arranged in no particular order.

Legal Prohibitiveness (on the interstate highways): These are the worst: Colorado, Washington, Wyoming, Nebraska, Connecticut. The cops will bust you 90% of the time no matter where you choose to stand. Hitchers are arrested, period. Fines $25 – $90 (Wyoming). The only way to beat it is stop at the border and wait for a ride all the way through, or if you're trapped in the state, solicit rides at the Howard Johnson's type of road-side restaurant, and do the old rest-stop hop across the state (you also have to do this on the NY thruway).

In most other states it's OK to hitch as long as you stick to entrance ramps, and, if it's a toll road, if you stand in front of the toll booths. If you're feeling devil-may-care or in a rush, you can stroll down the ramps to where they plug into the highway, so you achieve maximum visibility. However, if there is a sign proclaiming "No Pedestrians", better not go beyond it. Such signs usually mark the boundary between the safe zone and forbidden territory.

These are the best: Arizona, New Mexico, Texas, Louisiana, Alabama, Mississippi, Utah, Nevada, Oklahoma. I stand right out on the highway and never been arrested, and yet I've seen many state troopers drive right by. I hear now that Arizona is cracking down a bit.

I ought to add that with each successive summer, the horde of people taking to the road by thumb increases mightily (for this reason summer is my least favorite time of year to hitch; I try to stay in one place and wait for everyone else to go back to school), which in turn creates a greater and greater paranoic response from the cops. Each year the laws get progressively harsher. Therefore, any list like the above is subject to rapid change. State police programs to "clean up the highways" (of vagabonds) are often instituted overnight, and you may find yourself busted in a state you've previously hitched in with great ease. It's really quite a dilemma. Although it's good to see so many more people enriching themselves through travel, the reaction it evokes from the police is making the situation very much of a drag. I think quite seriously of leaving the country.

Technique. I am a devoted hitcher of the interstate highway system. I know people who shudder at the idea and refuse to use them because the risk of arrest is higher, and also you sacrifice the asthetics of leisurely meandering for a speedy passage. It just depends on what you prefer.

I always use destination signs. There are many reasons for this, phychological as well as practical, and I'm sure you know them too. I carry a 12 x 18 artists' pad and a black magic marker, and make them up as I go along, flipping from one to another as I progress.

Instead of making only one sign with my final destination on it, I print several with the names of intermediate large cities. Hitching from NY to San Francisco, I start with a sign for Chicago, then Des Moines, Salt Lake City and finally SF. A lot of people who pick me up tell me that they wouldn't have stopped ordinarily, but they saw my sign for Hawaii, and by god that's just exactly where they're headed for. And needless to say, there are a lot more people headed from NY to Chicago, than all the way to California.

Perhaps a few words should be said on the technique of actually soliciting rides. I try to communicate and appeal. Instead of standing frozen, sign held immobile, eyes glued on some distant point, I seduce each likely-looking car. It takes more energy,

223

but it can be fun and it also pays off. As a car approaches, I make eye contact with the driver (and for this and other reasons I never hitch wearing sunglasses), fix a winning and amiable smile on face, and move sign around as the car passes, much like a bullfighter with cape. Hah toro! The idea is to let the people know you are an individual human being, not some nameless vagrant, while also assuring them of your friendliness and amicability. This is quite a lot to accomplish in a couple of seconds, but it seems to work.

Unless I am in a bad spot, or I've been waiting 6 hours and memorized the bill board advertising chewing tobacco across the road and need a change of scenery, I turn down offers for short lifts, say 50 miles or less. I keep telling myself that the big one, my long ride, is out there somewhere, and he'll come eventually. He almost always does, though at times it means a bit of a wait. Waiting doesn't bother me as much as it used to. I groove on wherever I happen to be ("Wow, here I am in Dennis, Oklahoma. Unreal."), and the idleness is conducive to roadside philosophizing and reflection. The total simplicity of the situation can be so cleansing and clarifying. And you just can't beat the rush you get when a car finally stops, going 500 miles in your direction, and the driver smiles, hands you a lighted joint and turns on the tape deck.

I remember waiting one hot, late summer afternoon on an entrance ramp to route 80E in Sacramento, with two other guys. After about an hour a car stopped, and the driver said he was going about 10 miles down the road. I turned it down but the other two got in and left. After another 2 or 3 hours, and a few more short ride offers, a car stopped, going all the way to Salt Lake City. Boom: The big pay off (we also passed the other two guys stuck a little way down the road — the fucker wouldn't stop).

Equipment. Needless to say, my packing equipment (sleeping bag and backpack) is my luxury. I have bought the best I could afford, and never regretted it for an instant. The hazards and hardships of life on the road are rigorous enough so that, were it not for a warm place to sleep and a comfortable load on my back, it might tend to become unbearable after a short while. I have lived on the road for lengths of up to six months, and the discomforts which ended these ramblings were not physical.

Other Stuff(which I carry, some of it I even use a lot):

1. Road Atlas — one of my most important possessions.
2. Nylon Rain Poncho — grommetted corners: doubles as ground cloth or fly sheet.
3. Space Blanket — amazine device, actually works; good for everything except wiping your ass. I recommend them.
4. First Aid Kit — nothing, absolutely nothing worse than being sick while traveling, especially if by yourself. No sympathy, tender loving care or chicken soup
    contains: bandaids, gauze bandages, adhesive tape, ace stretch bandage, antiseptic eye ointment, iodine, snake bite kit (no shit), thermometer, aspirin, Lomotil and Darvon.
5. Water Bottle.
6. Vitamins (multiples and 500 mg C's) — let's face it, eating while vagabonding is a chancy business at best, and have you noticed the lack of organic food stores on the highways? Ya gotta get dem minerals and whatnot somehow. It's also a good idea to carry your own.

Food (unless you like eating at Stuckey's). I don't carry canned foods because they are a lot of extra weight and water, so I try to concentrate on dried edibles like:

- *dried fruit (raisins, apricots, apples, peaches and more)*
- *nuts*
- *protein beans: soybeans, peanuts*
- *sunflower seeds*
- *granola (excellent stuff)*

This is by no means intended to provide a complete diet, but in a pinch it helps.

Assorted Sundry Info. *An oasis in the desert: When that dragged-out raunchy feeling sneaks up and begins to pull you down, and you'd like a bath, a good meal or the company of people, all you have to do is check your road atlas for the nearest college or university, and make use of their facilities. You can clean up in a dormitory bathroom, maybe sneak into the cafeteria or at least buy a meal at the student union, check out the girls who will surely dig the adventurousness of your ways, and maybe even someone will offer to put you up for the night. Colleges are great rest-stops for the weary traveler (at the more conservative ones you can expect to be stared at like some Martian being).*

Getting around cities: *When you find a city blocking your path and you have no desire to stop there, you have to get ready for a little work. Frequently you may find yourself in a car that is headed for some city you have no wish to visit. You just want to keep going. Most large cities are surrounded by a labyrinth of expressways and freeways, which can boggle the mind of the innocent hitchhiker, and on which thumbing can be a death-defying chore, as well as very risky arrest-wise. So, to avoid all this, I ask to be let out 10 miles or so from the city limits, and I wait for a ride from someone who is going clear to the other side. Of course, sometimes it can't be avoided, and you find yourself dazedly wandering around some urban maze. Although I'm proud to say I've hitched all the way through L.A. on the freeways, the best thing to do is get a bus that will take you to the outskirts. In L.A., if I'm headed north for instance, I'll grab a bus for Santa Monica and resume hitching there.*

Dealing with cops: *At some point, you may find yourself reflected in the shiny sunglasses of a state trooper who has taken an interest in your presence on the road. My general rule of thumb is be polite (not obsequious) — acting wise-ass or hostile will get you nowhere, except maybe to jail. And remember, hitching is illegal almost everywhere, so you're probably breaking some law by doing what you're doing, even if you don't know it. The cop may search you, and for this reason I don't advise carrying anything illegal (although the hollow tubes of my pack frame are a place they never look). If your identification is out-of-state, you have a certain immunity, as you can plead ignorance of their laws. I always carry my defunct student I.D., and tell the cop I'm just a harmless school-boy on vacation, seeing America. I also emphasize that I'm merely passing through the state, as quickly as I can. It all seems to work; I've been stopped a lot, but arrested only once.*

Well Ed, *there's a lot more that could be said, but I've written my fill. I've tried to put down the important stuff, the things you learn with experience, which cut down on mishaps, mistakes and bummers. Of course, If you expect a fool-proof, smooth-as-silk trip you might as well not go, or better yet, buy a Mustang on time, get a gasoline credit card, and Holiday Inn yourself across the country. The sheer unpredictable hapazardness of vagabonding provides the high. In a culture where the biggest risk we take is switching brands of deodorant, tossing yourself out on the road does such amazing things to your head. Give life a try, take a chance. "You only go around once in life," as that Schlitz commercial quips. So many people I know make such big plans, and end up talking and dreaming it all to death. I say, kick out the jams and do it! It's a high I'll never forget.*

Hiking And Backpacking

The Final Solutions

13

INTRODUCTION Why walk, when you can ride? This once-popular slogan, delight of mad-men admen, now only shows the extent of the speaker's ignorance or brain damage. As yet another example of today's new national consciousness, Americans are unquestionably on the path to rediscovering their feet. Walking is more than just a means of transportation between chairs, automobiles, and toilets. It's what distinguishes us from the animals, and is what our bodies were made to do. The human frame is a machine designed for walking, not for standing still and sitting down — things it does less well.

Walking is healthier than any other common human activity, and more enjoyable than all but one or two (your preference). Its been proven one of the best exercises for fitness and weight-control; excellent for digestion, respiration, and circulation; a profound tension-reducer and mental stimulator. Somehow we already all know these things in our bones; acting on it is what we need, and what this chapter is about.

There are basically two types of serious walking: day-hiking and backpacking (overnite hiking). The distinction is of duration primarily, not of kind or quality, but duration does tell.

Day-hiking requires little planning and can be done by anyone anywhere. Yet, considering the minimum investment of time and effort involved, day-hiking offers rewards too extravagent for any traveler to bypass. Since it's so easy to do, only the next few paragraphs are concerned with it.

The remainder of the chapter devotes itself to backpacking, which requires more expertise and equipment, but rewards its devotees with satisfactions that verily make the gods groan with envy. If you chuckle and doubt it, it only means you haven't done it .. Read on.

DAY-HIKING OK, so you're not a backpacking type (at least not yet). Why should you take day-hikes? (By which I mean hikes not longer than a day, and usually much less, say an hour or two.) Well, let me put it this way: you're crazy if you don't.

It doesn't matter how you're traveling — automobile, camper, motorcycle, bicycle or hitchhiking — you absolutely *need* to walk or you'll go crackers with boredom and/or frustration. All mechanical means of travel except cycling require you to sit still. "Have all the fun you want, but don't move." Some fun. Man,

you need a break! You need activity in muscles as well as mind, and a hike for an hour or so is the way to go. Even bicyclists, who don't need the exercise, can use the change in pace.

I'm not just fancifully word-mongering on you. Boredom and fatigue on the hiway can be deadly, especially for motorcyclists and motorists. People who don't leave the hiway voluntarily for stimulation sometimes leave it involuntarily from lack of stimulation. And what about your health? You may love to move that car, but do you like to move your bowels? A heavy-duty hiway freak who never stops for exercise gets constipated within a few days (peristaltic paralysis), and after about a week will be bloated as a blivet. Sitting in or on your vehicle, hour after hour, day after day, is as unnatural as astronauts. Even they get space walks, and so should you.

Get out of that metal mother at least once a day for a mile or more of legwork. Soon you'll be looking forward to it like a junkie for his fix, only this one is righteous. Hiking gets you

intimately in touch with the air and the earth — you can fill your lungs with fresh prana and dig your toes into the clean dirt of Papa Brahma. To greatly amplify joys of this kind, bring along one or more field guides to identify flora, fauna, and geology. There are many such books identifying everything from algae to weeds. Also trees, wildflowers, animals, birds, ferns, fish, shells, insects, mushrooms, butterflies, snails and even stars. Many of them are listed under various headings in Appendix 1 — *Trips*. Nature hikes will provide both serious photographers and just plain camera-toters with some of their best photographic opportunities.

HOW TO BEGIN? Walking is an acquired taste, like beer and football and monogamy and other good things. You force yourself to try it; it's not all bad. You try it again and dig it a little. Soon it happens again, and you learn more about it and like it better. So it goes. One day you're hooked, and you're better off. The main thing is being open to trying it, and being open to what changes happen as you do it. This little paragraph is for the grumps who "don't wanna do nuttin", not even stop the car to take a few steps. Mama, lean on him.

DAY-HIKING NEEDS You only need a few things. Like shoes. Wear shoes, especially anywhere. On trails with rocks and stuff, you need something sturdier than street shoes. All travelers should have good quality, comfortable hiking boots. That's *all* travelers. If the terrain is easier, street shoes or better yet, moccasins.

Next, a daypack, which can be a knapsack or any small sack with a shoulder strap. Your larger pack is OK if you already have one . . . no need to carry two. The daypack carries a canteen or waterbag, lunch, fruit, maybe camera or binoculars, guidebook or trail map, and is a place to stash a sweater-shirt-jacket you may remove as you warm up. If you're going a few miles, also consider a small first-aid kit with aspirin, tape for sudden blisters, insect repellent, sun tan lotion. If it's threatening rain, add a poncho. The pack is also nice for collecting specimens — rocks, shells, flowers. Bring sunglasses and/or a brimmed hat. If the day is cold, gloves and scarf. Finally, for those daring devils who smoke marijuana, I'll pass the tip that it can bring literally wonder-ful encounters with nature on short hikes. Being high outdoors is a new dimension in experience. (If the suggestion makes you nervous, forget I mentioned it.)

Add lastly, time. Don't rush through your hike, even though your mental schedule allows but 14 minutes for a stop. This is your life. Where do you want to spend it? On the freeway?

WHERE TO HIKE Traveling anywhere thru America nowadays, you'll easily find places to hike. But you want special places, spiritual places to refresh your soul as well as uncramp your ass muscles. They abound.

Parks are the mainstay of the hiker, and these can range from the grandeur of national parks and monuments to the humble sweetness of small municipal greenswards. Some sort of dedicated parkland lies along your way each day in America, and these are among your best hiking arenas. Formal parks were all originally preserved because of some special quality of beauty or form or history. Often there's no way to appreciate those qualities other than by walking. Large parks always have existing trails, self-guiding nature walks, naturalist hikes, historical loops . . . These are worth seeking out.

If no park is at hand, certainly some pleasant stretch of seashore, meadow, prairie, farmland, woods, riverbank, hilltop or canyon cannot be far off. But remember where you started from, so you'll get back without the state police searching for you. (Leave a note on your car.) To find such regions, turn off the interstate hiway for some likely-looking byroad. Then pick a path to explore, perhaps one which promises a special place to spread your lunch.

American cities offer less than European ones insofar as walking opportunities, to put it with extraordinary mildness. Yet even the worst of these human jungles and industrial junkpiles possess some clearings of space and greenery, of historical interest, or urban uniqueness worth exploring on foot. Indeed, large portions of a

few cities such as New York, Washington, and San Francisco are a walker's delight. And smaller portions of many cities should only be seen on foot. To find where to hoof it in unknown cities, inquire at tourist offices. Lacking that, look for the large parks on the city map, for the chic downtown areas, for the "old town" (if any), for the well-known historical or cultural "quarters" (if any).

HIKING TECHNIC Hiking is different from walking, especially if you don't even walk very well. Most Americans don't; they're out of practice. To hike, here's what you do.

First, open up your stride; take longer steps. See if this doesn't feel better than just dragging your feet listlessly through the dust. A brisk stride is about 100 steps per minute, and you can cover a mile in 20 minutes without difficulty at that pace. That same pace means 3 miles per hour, which is a normal pace within reach of most people. Any pace that suits you is fine, of course, but the easiest in the long run is one that is steadily maintained. It's like bicycling again, in which your body works best at constant energy output.

Let your breathing be your guide. If you start to pant or huff, slow down. On uphill grades, don't work harder; simply shift gears way down. If you want to go faster, it's OK as long as you can maintain breath control. Don't race, then collapse. Take it evenly and gracefully. For more serious walkers, and for people who are curious how far they go, a pedometer is recommended. Most outdoor outfitters sell them; see list in Appendix 12.

BACKPACKING PHILOSOPHY Backpacking carries the idea of outdoor hiking into the realm of wilderness exploration. Hiking gives you a taste of Nature; backpacking means becoming part of Nature. Human beings are biologic organisms . . . highly evolved animals. Sometimes we pretend otherwise by sheathing ourselves in chromium or other coloration we think appropriate to our "elevated" station.

As a society we've shown no mercy for the natural world because for centuries we declined to be included as part of it. "Man is divine, Nature is dirt", was the motto. (That's the motto with me; what's the matter with you?)

Today we're starting to understand that it really goes something like: "Nature is divine; man is part of Nature; thus (and only thus) man is divine also."

Backpacking is a way to bring you "home" at last. A final solution. When you get out there in the woods without your automatic garbage compressor and discover the gleaming constellations while lying on your back deep in the forest, then you get a feeling of your place. Try discovering in person how big a mountain is by standing on it; better yet, feel the raw energy and choreographed pageantry of a storm breaking on a mountain chain. It may seem out there, if nowhere else, that the turmoil and busyness in the world of humans — all that squiggling about and thrashing we do in the name of Civilization and Progress — is just an irrelevant game . . . just some miscellaneous energy fizzling around. The real importance of human beings is that we're related to the mountain and the storms; we're all part of a wild and wonderful state (no, not West Virginia) whose totality is nameless and unknowable. So let's relax and stop jerking-off so self-importantly. Let's glory in Nature. Big comedown: Let's go backpacking!

Aside from cosmic events like metaphorically shaking God Almighty's hand, backpacking offers direct personal rewards. The work you put into it (the sweat and the aches) and the skills you develop by doing it (camp-cooking, crouch-crapping, etc.) give you a sense of confidence that goes deep. Holding down a job or knowing how to heat up TV dinners doesn't do it somehow. It's important to learn how to travel in wilderness on your own, self-contained and free. It's not just manly . . . it restores you to your natural self. It's necessary.

ECOLOGY AND BACKPACKING This may come as a surprise, but: Backpacking destroys the wilderness and needs to be curbed in some way soon to prevent ecological disaster. We've come to the critical point in our history when the sheer volume of people piling into the wilds is turning them into the tames, and polluting them, at that. Of course, backpacking is the least polluting of all means of wilderness entry, but in certain wilderness areas the woods are literally full of backpackers. A few years ago, the Muir Trail in the Sierra Nevada was a lonesome walker's paradise — empty and lovely. Today, any stretch of it during the season looks like an endless refugee column (which it is) or a mass migration of hunchback monkeys.

Starting now, backpackers need to be more careful about where they tramp. Not everyone can go to Yosemite or to the Tetons anymore. To be non-polluting isn't enuf; you've got to be scarce too. Start fanning out to other parks.

Off The Tape
OVERFLOWING SINK

People are great, but too many people are a drag. The problem was well expressed by a national park ranger I talked to. "The problem in our national parks is simple — too many people in too small an area. It's a population problem. People are not confronted with the population problem because they have their own little two acres somewhere, but when they come out here and try and compete in the national parks for campsites they begin to realize the problem. Maybe the national parks will make people realize that we've got to solve the problem at its root. We've got an overflowing sink and we're still trying to mop up the floor. The water is overflowing and we're not reaching for the plug or the faucet to turn it off."

Off The Tape
CAMPING IN THE TETONS

Ed: This is what you meant when you said Madison Avenue is taking over? Madison Avenue is selling the dream story even tho its obsolete.

Ranger: Right — they're going toward selling stoves, equipment, whatever they can. Take rock climbing — well, once just a few people did it, now rock climbing is an ego trip for a lot of people. Read any climbing magazine that's coming out now, they look like National Geographic. The days of just going out backpacking are limited in areas like this. There *are* places you can go. I'm confident I can always find places where I can go without any reservations. I personally like to stand around a campfire but I know that this is not the place for it. America is really sad in its education about how to camp — I'm not speaking of the boy scout type — a camper can carry everything on his back in 30 pounds or less, and that includes a gasoline stove, lightweight tent, gear — it's expensive but uh . . .

E: But aren't you also talking about a consciousness that is conservation-oriented? To love the land so that you can go places a lot of people won't be, for example?

R: But see, if everybody does it, that's the reason the Tetons have suffered so . . . There's a drive in people, and if they find or discover a neat place, they want to tell everybody they can about it. There were people making movies at Wind River last year and they didn't even walk in, they took horses, they took 400 pounds of gear and nine horses to carry their equipment, took two weeks to make a movie, and took it back to California to show their buddies. And a lot of books are coming out, and climbing magazine and guides. I've written for a couple myself and I won't write for another one. I used to write for magazines, and I just quit. I refuse to write any and I'm cancelling my subscriptions.

E: Because you find yourself put in the position of perpetuating the rape?

R: There is a rape of America going on, that's for sure. For instance, at Holly Lake, there's five camping permits issued with reservations in advance because we feel this is the number of camping permits this lake will hold for one night, and I went up there, oh, a month ago and cleaned out 29 firesites there and the next week I found ten more — and this is the kind of overuse we have. They come in here and we say, sorry we're full for two weeks and they say, OK and they go camp anyway. A guy was in here a while ago, was horrified. He had a reservation and seven people came and set up camp in his campsite that night, and there was horse excrement all over the trails and at the campsite. This is the second complaint in that area this week. We caught some people throwing their garbage into the bushes, at Marion Lake. At a group campsite the other night, they left their fire burning, they cut fir bough beds, they left a whole sackful of garbage in the camp and this was a group of Boy Scouts.

E: Boyscouts?

R: The Sierra Club took 40 horses to Lake Solitude a few years ago. This is the Sierra Club. There's another thing that's going on — people join a club and they think they're saved. It's like joining a religion — they can commit all the sin they want. The worst offenders I've seen are the so-called hips, the young people, the earth mothers, whatever you want to call them, young people who claim they already know this stuff . . . There are so many. I mean it's really fashionable to be hip or whatever. It's also fashionable to go hiking. You can go in any drugstore and get an aluminum packframe, a gas stove, a climbing rope in most drugstores now. There's a big chain in Denver, like a value mart or government mart or whatever they call them where you can get anything at discount prices. And Swami belts, and your other climbing aparatus. Bring in your swami belt and our professional mountain climber will compare it with ours, and there's no comparison. They sell carabiners, they sell these rock shoes that look like rock shoes and they're really felt or suede things that are imitation and you get blisters 2-2½ miles up the trail and they fall apart. Sold down the drain on this stuff.

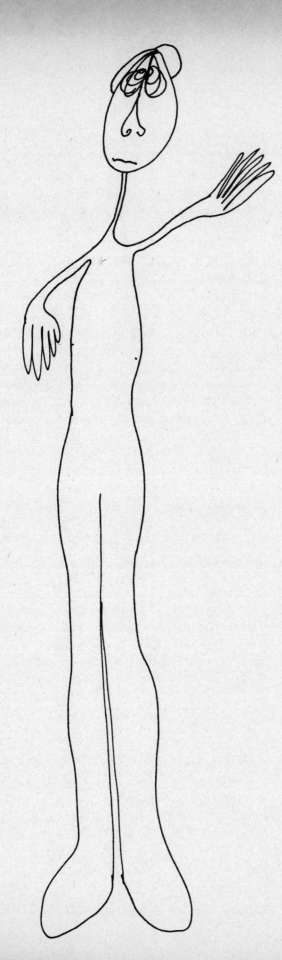

E: Mountaineering has been co-opted also.

R: Yeah, it's worse than the skiing craze, and the thing is, we're really suffering. Snow skiing, you can ruin the snow, chair lifts of course destroy certain areas, but at least the snow is a little less damaged. Back packing . . . you know, I don't take pictures of mountains anymore, I take pictures of people's garbage, I take pictures of campsites. There's 30 chopped-down trees at Lake Solitude, once probably the most beautiful lake in the United States. We had to close it. People couldn't believe it. Why? And I say, haven't you noticed when you were out there last? Haven't you noticed about the trees that have been chopped down? I mean, there's literally 30 or 40 trees in the area that are chopped down. There's not one limb in the reach of hand or axe, you know they just limbed all the trees as high as they can reach. They limb the whole thing if they can climb up 'em. In fact I caught a guy the other day, climbing up a tree and he limbed as he went up and couldn't get back down.

E: How does this make you feel as a ranger? What do you feel . . . this must get pretty discouraging.

R: I'm just getting hard core about the thing. I issue citations. Three years ago I used to be nice and say please take your dog down to the end of the trail. He'd get around the corner and give me the finger. And this year I found some people at the highest lake in the park with a dog and without a camping permit. He did have a stove and I thanked him for that and gave him a $5 citation, which is nothing, and let him stay the night even. They gave me phony names and addresses and were joking about it to some other people — that's how I found out about it. There were four of them, so at $1.25 each they sold their integrity down the drain. And what I've done since then — if I find a person with a dog on the trail I give them a $10 citation and I walk them down, hand in hand. If they don't have any ID, I take them down and put them in custody, put them in jail if necessary until they get ID, because I will not mess around anymore. It's the back country that's at stake. There was one man with an Irish Setter up at Inspiration Point the other day, yet there were dog signs posted on all the trails. People want us to take the signs down because they're "negative" — but they don't think that garbage on the trail and horse manure is negative . . .

233

YAMAHA HAS A SOLUTION

"The last time you went camping, you swore you'd
    come back in a week . . .
But next week turned out to be three or four years
    and it isn't quite the same . . .
That grassy spot for your sleeping bag is a sales
    office for a subdivision . . .
And it's kinda hard to fish with those water skiers
    going by every two or three minutes.
So where can you go now?
Well, maybe to a Yamaha dealer.
He's got some trail bikes that are sorta like time
    machines.
They'll take you up and down a few hills to a place
    that's just the way it was four or forty years ago.
And the great thing about a Yamaha is that once you
    get where you're going, you can be sure you'll
    get back.
That is, if you want to come back."
    (Harmonica in the background.)

Go to lesser known wilderness areas and national forests, especially. Wherever you go, use some logic—ego-logic. No more wood fires in many regions; no more bough-beds anywhere. Deliberate policing action by everyone to help stop the unconscious creeps who don't care. Crimes in the wilderness include tree-cutting, littering, trail-busting, careless fire-making, hole-digging, and certainly using off-road vehicles such as trail bikes in places they're not supposed to be. We're at the place now that everyday citizens need to actively start defending their wilderness, because if we wait till it starts defending itself, we're all goners. It used to be good manners and too much trouble to protest as somebody chopped up a campsite, or some idiot came charging by on his trail bike, but those days are over. Somebody has got to lay on those people, and for their own good too. Backpackers have a responsibility not only to avoid littering, but pick up other people's litter and educate others where they can. This hard-nose attitude eventually will work its way upward to all areas of ecological threat, and we can now see an awakening citizenry all about. The backpacker right now, though, is at the first line of defense — the wilderness.

Permits are now required for backpacking and camping in all National Parks, Forests, and Wilderness Areas, and reservations are being taken in some areas, the same as hotels. It's a sad pass, but it's real and we've got to accept it and abide by it.

Writing a chapter like this, urging people to go backpacking, urging people to use the National Parks in any form, may seem to be a lapse of consciousness. Is this another rip-off guidebook with only money motives and no sense of ecology? Maybe, but I don't believe in a campaign of silence, of hiding our national treasures in hopes they'll last longer thru less usage. The problem is first one of education, that is, of everyone knowing what's at stake and not pissing in the drinking water anymore, so to speak. Next, we need more space for re-creating ourselves, and more preference given to wilderness values. This has to come from willingly forsaking or modifying some of our materialist desires to make room for better use of what resources are left.

All this is happening now, but not without desperate struggle. The battle is being joined more fully every day, and no one can avoid commitment in the end. The squeeze is on; the old battles the new, and where do YOU stand?

FUNDAMENTALS OF BACKPACKING Your equipment stands between you and the wilderness. The less of it you have, the closer you approach the wilderness. In a lovely book entitled *The Backpacker* (see Appendix 1 under "Backpacking") the example is given of Tibetan and and Chinese yogis who traveled the wilderness with only their faith, a cotton cloth, and a bowl. They knew the wilds up close, living mainly on light and enlightenment.

John Muir is another, closer example of the same kind of freedom from equipment. He brought a bag of meal, a cup, and a blanket, and a notebook to record his rapture with the Sierra, ". . . the Range of Light, the most divinely beautiful of all the mountain chains I have ever seen." But nowadays, no matter how flipped out you get over the mountains, you'll need a minimum of equipment.

There are three basic equipment requirements: Food to keep you nourished, insulation to keep you warm and dry, and a pack to carry your food and insulation needs. And, of course, you'll need your camping permit. Beyond those basics, you'll want some equipment for personal comfort, distress, route-finding, and experience maximizing. Finally, a certain amount of technics will prove beneficial, and may even keep you from stupidly killing yourself, or worse yet, from harming the forest in some way. Let's examine these needs and technics.

BACKPACKING FOOD A great to-do is made over foods for backpackers, but the basics are simple. First, your food should be real food, that is, nutritious. Next, it should be liteweight and/or low in bulk, which points to dehydrated (dried or freeze-dried) foods. Preparing it should be easy, and lastly, it should taste good so somebody will want to eat it. These requirements suggest planning your diet in advance.

Planning means writing out a list of food for each meal on the trail, (including snacks), then adding up quantities into a shopping list. See Food List ahead. After buying it, then pre-package it for trail use. More about this shortly.

Breakfasts should be simple and quick because you'll frequently be preparing them under chill, clammy, or dark circumstances and anxious to get on the trail. Cereal is a best bet, either hot (Wheatena, oatmeal) or cold (granola, Familia). Mix in dehydrated milk, raisins, wheat germ for energy and flavor boosters. Start with fresh oranges or orange juice crystals. For more leisurely breakfasts, powdered eggs and biscuits, or pancakes and honey go down well. For drinks, teas prove superior to coffee and offer much more variety. Cocoa or Bosco-type chocolate or carob drinks all make sipping-good early-morning treats. Pre-mix the dry incredients (for example, chocolate, milk, sweetener) at home.

Lunches are munches. At home, mix up a batch of Gorp, the generic term for any trail snack consisting of munchable morsels. Typical incredients are nuts, raisins, M&M's, dried fruits, granola, coconut shreds, and seeds. ("What foods these morsels be.") Supplement this with bread and jam/peanut butter/honey from squeeze tubes, maybe some cheese. Breads should be dense pumpernickel types or maybe wafers like pilot bread. Candy bars in the pocket give you an energy boost in between meals, but try a sesame-seed bar, a fruit bar, protein bar, or a mountaineer's treat like mint cakes.

Dinner's the time to relax and leisurely prepare the culinary adventure of the day. However, you'll frequently be bushed from exertion; uncomfortable from cold, wind, or rain; hampered by darkness; or simply too starved to last long without food. So don't attempt multi-course stomach-stoppers. The main-dish approach is recommended — a stew, perhaps preceded by soup and followed by hot drink. Packaged stews and one-dish meals are fast and particularly good at high altitude where low boiling temperatures prevent cooking of foods like beans. However, "homemade" stews taste better, usually, and more "real", They also enable you to vary the ingredients (stew does get boring) from day to day. Rice is a good stew base. You can use minute rice, or better yet, cook up a batch of brown rice and/or barley at home, then dry it on a cookie sheet in the oven at low heat. Bring along a selection of dried vegetables, bouillon cubes, spices, dried mushrooms, freeze-dried meats, soup mixes, dehydrated onions, soy beans, and a few fresh foods (carrots, garlic) to make up your own version of the Stew That Won The West.

I think all suppers should start with a quick cup of soup or bouillon, which frequently ensures you'll live until the main course is ready. Other supper ideas are cheese-base dishes like noodles and cheese, or rice and cheese, with anything added that smells good or tastes right. Soy beans provide as much protein as meat and can be eaten alone or added to stews. At home, soak them overnite, then roast at 350 degrees till brown or fry them.

Salads can be made from fresh ingredients brought along and sometimes foraged. Fresh alfalfa sprouts can be made enroute if you make a clear plastic bag with a netted hoop so air can get in. Desserts are commercially available but not necessary, at least not with every dinner. Stew some dried fruit for a hot late-night snack; eat any left-overs in the morning with breakfast.

Miscellaneous food tips: Do all your measuring and packing at home, using clear poly bags, plastic screw-cap jars, and refillable squeeze tubes. Remove all possible outer boxes and such to save weight and space. Pre-mix all dry ingredients that will go together anyway later on.

Outdoor equipment suppliers usually stock dehydrated and freeze-dried foods, both full meals and individual items. However, there is some question whether freeze-dried foods can be properly digested by the body, and they are more expensive than any other type of food. Natural food and health stores are good places for dried fruits, nuts, seeds, grains, flours, teas, oils, etc. — also vitamins, high-energy candies. Supermarkets wil provide soup-mixes, noodles, powdered milk, cocoa, etc.

BACKPACKER'S FOOD LIST

Meats: Dinner dishes with meat (dried and freeze-dried), numerous freeze-dried steaks, chops, patties. Freeze-dried additives: Chicken, beef, ham, meatballs, meat bars, bacon bars. Beef jerky. Spreads: Chicken salad, ham salad. Dry sausages, salami.

Vegetables: Dehydrated potatoes, corn, peas, beans, carrots, etc. Freeze-dried potatoes, dried mushrooms; flaked onions, tomatoes, celery, etc. Fresh carrots, sprouts, garlic, cucumber, onions, mushrooms.

Fruits: Dried or dried-and-honey-dipped apples, peaches, apricots, etc. Dried cocktails, minces, cobblers, and sauces. Fresh oranges, apples. Fruit bars and biscuits. Raisins, currants, figs, dates, prunes. Coconut shreds.

Beverages: Powdered orange, grapefruit, tomato, pineapple. Powdered milk. Freeze-dried orange juice, coffee. Instant coffee, tea, cocoa, chocolate, carob. Teas: Regular and herb varieties. Wyler's fruitades. Shakes in various flavors. High-energy protein drinks and broths. Bosco.

Soups: Dried and powdered, various. Bouillon powders or cubes. Noodles to add.

Dairy: Eggs, powdered or freeze-dried. Canned butter. Yoghurt and kefir. Powdered milk, freeze-dried cottage cheese. Cheddar cheese spreads. Fresh cheeses: Swiss, cheddar, parmesan.

Breads: Mixes: Cornbread, biscuit, gingerbread. Biscuits: Pilot, trail. Health breads: Rye, pumpernickel, wheat, etc. Scandinavian wafer breads and crackers.

Spices and Sweets: Salt, pepper, herbs, soy sauce, Miso, sugar, brown sugar, honey, chocolate, high-energy bars, mint cakes. M&M's, candy bars. Jams and jellies.

Other: Beans, especially soy beans. Nuts: Almonds, peanuts, walnuts, pecans, etc. Seeds: Pumpkin, sesame, chia, sunflower. Grains: Brown rice, barley, oats, cornmeal, wheat germ, etc. Fresh-caught fish; fresh-picked herbs. Vitamins: Especially water-soluble vitamins such as C. Mixes: Pancake, bread, biscuits, sauces. Cereals: Wheatena, Familia, granola, oatmeal.

FOOD PREPARATION Wood fires are passé; everyone should pack a gas or cartridge stove. If wood is abundant, use it for an after-supper or late evening social and psychedelic centerpiece. Incidentally, keep sleeping bags and clothes clear of sparks if you do this.

But cook on the stove. I've tried both kinds — the gas burning ones (Primus, Optimus, Svea) and the butane-cartridge type (Bluet). I'm for the gas burner, of which the Svea 123 is a classic of reliability, small size, and effectiveness (I've used my original one for 15 years so far on hundreds of outings). Gas stoves usually require priming and are noisy, but they work beautifully anywhere, and you're not lugging empty cartridges afterwards (just a fuel bottle). The cartridge models burn well at first, then peter out as the cartridge empties, making them slower and easier to blow out.

As for pots, the Svea 123 also happens to fit beautifully in the center of the "Sigg Tourist" kit of nesting aluminum pots. My cook kit is as old as my stove and looks like its been used as a clapper in a belfry, but it's still serviceable as long as I keep pounding out the dents and burnishing the soot layers. The stove has just one burner, of course, which is why one-pot meals make good sense. This stove-

and-pot outfit will hold up to four hungry backpackers at bay, but a second outfit could be appreciated by them.

To eat with, I recommend carrying just two Sierra Club cups (stainless steel with wire handles) — one to drink from and the other to eat from, or vice-versa. One fork, one spoon, a bandana to wipe your mouth, and toilet paper to wipe your ass completes the cook-kit requirements altogether.

Cooking tips: Fill up your stove with gas each meal; it'll prevent having to refill while the stove is hot and the food gets cool. Bring one of those mechanical pot holders to prevent burned fingers and spilled chow. Clear the area around the stove to prevent fires in case it tips over. Speaking of which, it's easy to kick over your supper, and is a particularly depressing mishap for weary and hungry trail-hoppers. Make a flat solid base, preferably off the ground.

Wind conditions can greatly affect the efficiency of your stove. The windscreen on the Svea-Sigg combination is a good one, but under severe wind conditions it will help both the stove and its owners to huddle close around. This applies to mountaineers above timberline, mostly, and other campers without natural shelter or good luck.

INSULATION This includes clothes, sleeping bag, and tent. The chief clothing advice is the same as always: Take as little as you can. Build your wardrobe on the theory of adding thin garments as it gets colder, not of taking heavy coats. Remember that during the day, you'll be keeping warm by walking. During the night, you'll be sleeping in your down bag. Thus, your chief need for warm clothes comes at sunrise and in the evening. But at sunrise you'll be moving around breaking camp and preparing for an early start, while at evening-tide you'll have your supper fire to keep you warm (maybe).

Here's the clothes I recommend: Wear blue jeans and a long-sleeved shirt, tho on days when you feel sporty, wear just shorts and a T-shirt. Wear a hat (for sun) and a bandana (for sweat). Outdoor underwear should be the fishnet type — its both lighter and warmer than ordinary underwear. Bring an extra shirt, a sweater, and a good windbreaker-type parka (with hood). If you expect cold, add long underwear, a down vest or jacket, gloves, and a knit or balaclava pull-over cap. That's basically it except for footgear.

Boots are obligatory, of course, with Vibram soles. Plan to spend around $25 for a medium-weight high-top boot. Wear two pairs of socks — cotton next to your skin and wool next to the boot. This keeps your feet warm if it's cold, cool if it's hot, let's them breathe away moisture, reduces the likelihood of blisters, and feels quite comfortable. Wear these socks while the boots are fitted; break in the boots by wearing them around the house or on shorter hikes. If you expect some rain in the sky or snow on the trail, waterproof the boots with something like Sno-Seal or Leather Seal. Get rawhide laces if the boots don't already come with them.

A sleeping bag is next. This is your womb away from home. It gives you warm if not wet dreams. No other item of equipment is more important, because it's what enables you to call "Time Out" when you're wiped out. If you can't sleep warm when you're tired or sick or discouraged then you may as well cash in your beads and report to the glue works. For my money, a down-filled bag is the only way to go, and damn the dollars. It's among the most necessary things you can own, right up there with your Tibetan prayer-wheel and autographed copy of the I Ching. Details about packing and buying one are given in chapter 7. Use it with a pad beneath (like black ensolite) to prevent ground chill, and a ground cloth beneath that to keep the whole sandwich from damp and dirt. Air mattresses are too heavy, forever leaking, and a drag to both pump up and push down. Use the ensolite pad instead: for weight and space saving, make it a short one, by the way, for your head to hips only. Put some clothes under your feet.

Next is your tent. In many parts of the country during summer, you won't need anything but a tube tent. This is simply a polyethylene cylinder 9 feet long and 8 feet in diameter, weighing just over a pound. There's also a two-man version with a 12-foot diameter (2 pounds) but two people can sleep in the one man version on an occasional basis. (The most efficient way to do this is sleeping head-to-feet.) Put your sleeping bag(s) inside the cylinder and hold the top up by stringing a nylon cord thru it (tied to nearby trees). The ends remain open to let air in and body-moisture out. Rain generally won't come in since you're several feet inside from the openings. If you expect rain, position the tube so rain runoff won't pass thru the tube, or scoop up some protective earthworks at the entrances (demolish in the morning).

If you decide you do need a tent because rain can be counted on, there are many lite-weight ones available. I can't advise; I've always found a tube-tent or tarp-with-grommets adequate. Plastic tarps (cheap) or nylon tarps (durable) are extremely useful pieces of things because they can be configured into all shapes of shelters if you have enough nylon cord and trees along. (Take 50' anyway — it only weighs a few ounces.) More about tents in Chapter 7.

OTHER STUFF Before I get to the full-fledged equipment list, I'll make a few miscellaneous remarks. Pocketknife should be one of the Swiss Army models and I prefer the "Outdoorsman" as mentioned earlier. This has scissors, tweezers, toothpick, hole-punch, blades, can-opener, wood saw, among others. Useful? Yes. Don't bring a hatchet — not needed.

A candle-lantern is a neat thing if you like to read, or see the person you're speaking to. The folding Japanese jobs work surprisingly well.

First-aid kits frequently are worth their weight in blood alone. Its contents depend on your trip, both the objective one and the subjective one. The one I've listed is a fairly complete one; you might want less. See chapter 15.

Fishing gear is optional. If you're into it, great. They stock all the rivers and lakes everywhere with fish, and fish are a fantastic supplement to your freeze-dried diet. I've personally never been able to get into it, but I intend to keep trying. For beginners, a good fishing primer is listed in Appendix 1. Your gear should be as compact as possible: Several-piece rod, reel, line, leader, hooks, sinkers, and salmon eggs and/or spoons. Have a bout with a trout; go fight a fish; put a mullet in your gullet; kill a carp; kiss a bass on the ass . . .

CHOOSING A BACKPACK Many schools of thought here, with (most) everyone agreed on the need for tubular frame, but lots of variations as to division of space in the pack, number and location of outside pockets, sleeping bags above or below or inside, etc. Buying the right pack, I'd suggest, is a matter of defining your needs, shopping around at one or more specialty stores with salesmen who know what they're talking about (which lets out all department and discount stores), and buying what feels right to you. A rucksack (no tubular frame) may be OK for shorter trips but I go for the heavy-duty capacity of a well-designed pack with aluminum or magnesium frame, several outside pockets, and no interior baffles for the most in packing flexibility. Padded shoulder straps and a strong waist-belt for heavy loads are recommended. Frames and parks are not cheap but they last for years. As with all outdoor equipment, the best equipment you can buy is generally the cheapest in the long run, and the most comfortable even in the short run. The total weight of your loaded pack has a lot to do with your enjoyment of the trip. For women, try to keep it under 30 pounds even on a long outing; men under 40. On one trip I went in with a 72-pound load and it was OK, but that's masochistic if not macho.

BACKPACKER'S EQUIPMENT LIST
(Men and Women)

To Wear

Hiking boots, rawhide
   laces
Wool socks over cotton
   socks
Underwear & net T-shirt
Hiking pants, cuffless
   (jeans, twill pants,
   knickers)
Wool shirt, long-sleeved
Belt
Brimmed hat
Bandana
Watch (?)
Sunglasses & case
Swiss Army knife
   ("Outdoorsman")
Wallet (?)
Backpack
Canteen or bota

Other Clothes

Cotton shirt, long-sleeved
Sweater, wool pullover
   or down vest
Parka/windbreaker
Bandana
Wool socks, 1 pr
Cotton socks, 3 pr
Wool cap
Underwear & T-shirts, 2 pr
Shorts
Moccasins
Clothespins (?)

For colder weather, bring
   along long underwear
   (or leotards), gloves,
   down jacket, down
   booties.

Survival

Poncho
Down sleeping bag
Tent, tube tent, or
   shelter tarp
Nylon cord (50 ft.)
Sleeping pad, ensolite
Sun lotion
Insect repellent
   (Cutter's or Off)
Lip salve
Flashlite, small
   (AA batteries)
Compass (?)
Matches in watertight
   containers
First aid kit:
   Band-aids & compresses
   Surgical tape
(Also   Moleskin
see   Salt tablets
Chapter Aspirin
15)   Snake bite kit (Cutters)
   Vitamins (?)
   Antiseptic cream
   Personal medication (?)
   Codeine (?)
   Antibiotic (?)
Sewing kit:
   Thread
   Needles
   Ripstop tape
   Safety pins

Personal

Toothbrush & powder or soda
Razor & stainless blades (men) (?)
Barettes for longhair, or scarf
Toilet paper
Soap & plastic container
Comb and/or hairbrush
Pocket mirror, metal
Wash cloth (?)
Birth controllers (?)
Harmonica (?)
Stash (?)
Camera & film (?)

Food

1½ to 2 lbs per day (adults)
Plastic bags
Rubber bands
Plastic squeeze tubes(?)
Plastic containers (?)
Sigg pot set
Svea 123 stove
Fuel container & fuel
2 Sierra Club cups
Pot gripper
Fork & spoon
Scouring pad (Tuffee)
Salt shaker (?)
Spatula (?)
Mixing bowl (?)

Other

Field and/or trail
   guidebook(s) ?
Notebook, sketchbook (?)
Pen(s) and/or pencil(s) ?
Trail map(s)
Reading matter (?)
Candle lantern, folding
Camping permit
Fishing permit (?)
Folding shoulder bag for
   day excursions (?)
Fishing gear (?)
Mountaineering
   equipment (?)
Pedometer (?)

MORE HIKING TECHNICS The advice earlier on how to walk applies with a backpack, only moreso. Keep a steady pace, uphill or down, step out in long strides on the level. Formal rest stops shouldn't be too long or too frequent, about 5 minutes every hour. A few moments to catch your breath now and then is OK, but if you find you need long or frequent stops you're pushing too hard. Slow down and set a pace that makes you look like a paragon of stamina. On dusty trails, try to lift your feet to avoid raising dust for those behind you. If possible, make camp early. Pick out your evening's destination according to the terrain to be covered, strength of party, time of start, and weather. Altho you can walk 3 miles an hour on level ground, most backpacking country is seldom level for long and your pace may be affected by altitude and trail condition as well. Figure 2 miles per hour for average mountain trail walking, and progressively less as more altitude is to be gained. Generally speaking, 5 or 6 miles is an easy day once you're in condition, and 8 to 10 miles is a full encounter with the trail.

For relief from that dead weight on your back, move the shoulder straps over a half an inch once in a while, or hook your thumbs under the straps, or support the weight from the bottom of the pack with your hands. A tump line (a pack strap that goes around your forehead) also works to relieve the weight on your shoulders.

Solitary hiking in the back country is wonderful but can be dangerous. A companion is always recommended for getting help in case of fluke accident or snake bite. If you do travel alone, make certain you let the local rangers know where you're going and familiarize yourself with direction-finding, first aid technics, and distress signaling. (Three of anything means distress — mirror signals, whistles, fires.)

CAMP MAKING Stop early so you can fully explore an area for the best camp and still have time for a daylite dinner, or at least daylite beginning. Some of the criteria for site selection are closeness to water and wood, ground slope, exposure (to wind, rain, sun), safety, privacy, and attractiveness. If you're wood-burning, use an existing fire-site if possible. If there isn't one, clear the area all around (within range of burning cinders) and pile some rocks. Don't build fires under trees. Keep the fire small. When you break camp, break up the fire-site if you made it. Always try to camp without leaving any signs of your presence. Smooth out the ground; fill any holes; rescatter the ground cover. Before leaving any camp, douse the fire with water beyond hope of re-ignition. Fires can smoulder underground on humus and spontaneously re-ignite hours later. This happened to me once when I was younger and smugger, and the guilt of having been responsible for a woods fire (fortunately small and containable) has since made me a confirmed water-douser.

Pack out all garbage that won't burn in the fire, especially cans and foil. Pick up other people's trash to the extent you can; it doesn't take much effort and you become, even in a small way, a modern-day hero. When defecating outdoors, scoop out a little hole for your contribution and cover it afterwards with earth or a rock. Save your toilet paper for burning in the campsite. Avoid using detergents for dishwashing. One bar of laundry soap serves fine for personal and laundry use as well as dishwashing.

CROSS COUNTRY Leaving the trail systems for the open country in between is exciting and challenging. It's lovely to think you may even be in a place where no human has ever trod before (unlikely, but possible). Cross-country travel requires a good map and excellent judgement. Below timberline, it's often unrewarding or impossible because too much bushwacking is involved. Pick a likely route based on the topographic map; once started, try to eyeball the route from high points. Be alert: Watch for designated landmarks such as lakes and streams; watch out for canyons you can't climb out of or cliffs you can't descend. Kick your way across snow slopes. Always

Exercises

BACKPACKING EXERCISES

1) If you always stick to the trails, plan a cross-country hike of a few hours or maybe overnite. Leave the freeway of the mountains — the trail — and venture into the trackless wilderness. But be prepared with maps, food, water. Cross-country hiking is a brilliant example of the vagabonding idea brought to the backpacking experience, provided you don't leave behind any signs of your passage. Be extra helpful with fires, destroy all evidence of your campsite, scout your routes. The feeling of freedom and adventure is intoxicating.

2) Climb a mountain. Pick an easy one if you haven't done it before, or a harder one if you dare. Regional guidebooks can tell you all about the severity of the routes. Remember that most mountains are simply a long upward hike, with no hazards involved at all. But the experience of it, of standing on the peak after having earned it, is unforgettable. Vagabonding at its best.

3) Bring a field guidebook along, and see how many trees, birds, flowers, whatever . . . you can identify on your trip. If possible, don't collect anything or disturb it. Just being able to recognize what's there will enormously deepen your experience with it.

4) For a day or two or more, try seeing how little equipment and supplies you can use. Try to cut down on clothes, shelter, food, fuel, matches. It'll give you a survival sense and be good training (for good living).

5) Deliberately plan hikes as far away from main-traveled trails as possible. Contact national park and national forest offices; ask them to suggest lesser-known routes and campsites more likely to be solitary.

watch your footing, particularly on rocks or scree — step on the larger rocks. Take along a roll of ankle binding in case of sprains. Sometimes cross-country routes are marked with man-made rock piles called "ducks"; these usually indicate the safest routes.

SLEEPING Picking your spot determines whether you'll be attended at night by the sandman or the bogeyman. Get a level spot, or the most level possible. (Head goes uphill if there is a slope.) Choose rocks or trees to provide shelter from the wind, and tie points for ropes. Sand or loam is most comfortable, but remove any sharp stones and pine cones first. Scoop out a hip hole (but fill it when you leave). Spread out your poncho, then your sleeping pad and clothes under your head and feet. Shake and lay out your sleeping bag well before bedtime so it will have time to loft. If you're using a tube tent, try to place it broadside to the prevailing wind. When sacking out, put your boots nearby, a flashlite in one and your eyeglasses in the other. If the night is cold, put on your pullover cap.

Sleeping outdoors in perfect comfort doesn't usually happen immediately. The ground doesn't yield to your shoulder, unknown sounds in the night menace your serenity, and the moist chill of wilderness air keeps you stirring at first. But after a few nights at most, the pattern of exercise during the day and relaxation at night starts working to condition your body and head into the state of amazing euphoria that is the hallmark of the backpacking experience.

Sleeping at high altitude gives most people some insomnia at first, but it is important to understand that you can get rested anyway just by lying quietly and relaxing your body. Don't fret about staying awake; your body is getting what is needs if you relax and think good thoughts.

Off The Tape
EMERALD POOL

A great day of hiking and beauty and adventure. First to Emerald Pool, a muddy little patch of water in an incredible setting. We hiked up a box canyon with towering red cliffs on all sides, after a steep climb to a grotto with a small waterfall, which was spectacular in its own right. We looked down upon the upper pool which is directly under the foot of the back cliff, the most sheer cliff. A trickle of water trailing off from up above, a 1000 or 1500 feet above us. Only young people around — five or six. Various of us took our clothes off and went into the water, which was icy cold.

Talking with the others, I found out they were from all over the country — east and west. It's always the same — new-consciousness people are always able to meet and talk with great familiarity, to exchange information about life styles without fear. One told about having been up here the week before when there were some Mormons here with their daughters. One was 11 years old and was whipping frogs until told to stop by a long-hair there. Later the long-hairs went nude bathing and the parents told their daughters to hide their eyes, but they peeked anyway.

CHILDREN AND BACKPACKING I started taking my daughter Jan on backpacking trips about the time she started walking, and she grew up as a frequent trail habitue. However, it ain't easy. She never got really crazy about it until she could start building some stamina and a more sophisticated interest in the outdoors, both of which began to be clearly evident at around 8 years old, and increased steadily thereafter. Until then, we didn't get much cooperation. Little kids hate the discipline of trail-walking, tire and lose interest easily (especially going uphill), and have to be watched to keep them from danger and getting lost (give them all whistles around their necks). Once in camp, they're great. (Take along a favorite toy.)

Plan on giving them frequent encouragement, rest stops, piggyback rides (even on already pack-laden backs), nap stops (best combined with a long lunch stop). They should have their own shortee-size sleeping bag, and a tiny cloth pack of their own. Some parents simply find it's too demanding, and leave the dears at home for that first vulnerable decade.

In the second decade, you'll still have some problems, sometimes because they're too stoned on energy to stay on the trail or keep manageable. Kids and teen-agers are the worst practitioners of trail-busting (short-cutting the switchbacks, usually in a way destructive to the slopes and the trail). This is the time to start teaching them the rudiments of trail manners and ecological principles.

Alternatively, there are such outdoor opportunities as the base-camp trip and the burro trip. Both types are sponsored by outdoor clubs such as the Sierra Club or can be independently arranged by one or more families. A base-camp trip is one in which you hike a few or more miles into a designated camp area, then stay as long as you like or the food holds out. The sponsoring club arranges for packing in the gear, or you can pack in your own gear, or arrange with a pack station to do it for you. The kids only have to handle the hike in and out, and the rest of it is an outdoor camp that the kids will love, especially if there are other kids there (the more the mellower).

If you want a moving trip, then you can rent burros by the day or week. Burros are marvellous animals, gentle with kids (and almost as good with grown-ups). They'll free you of all or most of your load, and the kids can ride them when they're tired of hiking. The best way to learn to use and appreciate them is to take a club-sponsored trip first. You'll learn all you need to know about packing, feeding, and living with burros, all under the tutelage of an experienced leader. After that, if you want to monkey with donkeys, you'll have no trouble. Burros are fascinating creatures, each with a distinct personality and its own idiosyncrasies. Kids adore them. On one of our burro trips, we even had a surprise burro birthing, which didn't seem to bother the mother at all but thrilled the kids.

HEALTH AND FIRST AID The first few days are the most troublesome, mostly with mundane matters like leg muscles stiff, shoulders sore from pack straps, feet sore or blistered, sleep interrupted, mountain sickness, and other such aggravations while acclimatizing to the life of the trail walker. After the initial shakedown and readjustments, you'll be sucking that mountain air like fine wine and pounding your chest like King Kong run amuck.

Blisters are common the first day or two, and need immediate attention. Cover any tender area with moleskin, whether or not it's blistered. If it has, first pop and drain it, leaving the skin in place. If it gets too painful to walk in your boots, switch to your moccasins until it heals.

Mountain (altitude) sickness hits just about everyone in the high country, but in varying degree. Acclimatization cures the ailment, but headache, nausea, vomiting, and weakness may happen first. Try to take it easy. Don't eat if you don't feel like it. Drink plenty of water, take salt tablets and aspirin, then wait it out.

As insurance, it's a good idea to carry a well-stocked first-aid kit, and a booklet like "Mountaineering Medicine" (see Appendix 1) on how to use it. True distress on the trail is rare but you'll feel better knowing how to cope with most varieties of it.

Insects and sunburn cause a lot of discomfort, too. Mosquitoes at nite can frequently be avoided by proper choice of camp location. Stay away from breeding areas near stagnant waters, and camp where you get a prevailing breeze off a lake or slope without mosquitos. A smudge-fire at night will keep mosquitos away. Sunburn at high altitudes is almost certain without a sun lotion or glacier cream and brimmed hat. Protect your nose. Sunglasses, especially on snow are necessary to prevent temporary blindness.

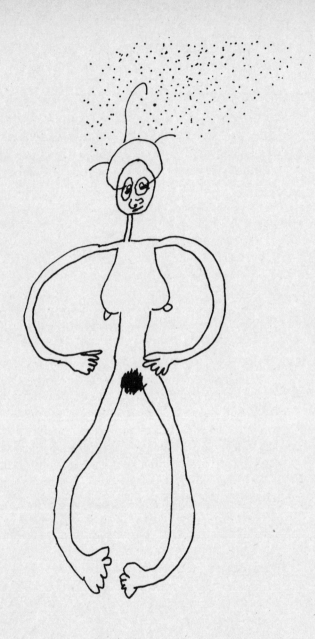

When I get old and thin
          skinned
crinkling in the wind
I want to walk in autumn
          air
thru tree lined paths
on the shore of some
clear lake
and let my mind
grow still
and let my body move
as high it can.
I'll be damned
if I'll always be a setting
in some old rocker
sweatered against even
indoor cold
remembering
remembering
while my eyes grow veils
and water trickles
down
my parchment skin.

INFORMATION SOURCES Look in the *Trips* Appendix under "Backpacking" for book lists, outdoor organizations and other information sources. Look under "Maps" for map sources and their addresses. Look at Appendix 12 for a list of outdoor-equipment shops. Places to go backpacking are listed in various other appendixes (7 thru 11).

Staying Awhile

Ways To Live And Work

14

FRUIT HARVESTING AS IT IS, by Joe Gaspers

INTRODUCTION Like the old joke about hitting yourself with a hammer because it feels so good when you stop, so part of the vagabond life is staying somewhere awhile. No one appreciates home like the vagabond, or can judge better where to settle or who with, because being on the road develops a critical faculty for places and people. Somewhere in America's endless tangle of intermingled Hells and Heavens, you may find your own private Purgatory or Paradise. Indeed, who deserves either one more than the vagabond?

So this chapter is for the vagabond at rest. It starts with a look at "dropping out" and offers some hints on how to do it. You find out after you travel around enough that the bonds on your life are usually self-imposed. By dropping out you have "nothing to lose but your chains." Then there's a section about working, about what you can do to survive whether you're on the move or settling down. And then there's a little bit about ways of settling down, such as the farm life and the communal life. (Appendix 1 – *Trips* – also has a lot of listings under "Working," "Communes," "Spiritual Centers," while Appendix 2 – *USA Bookshelf* – lists "Soulbooks for Americans.")

DROPPING OUT Being a vagabond means you've already dropped out. A vagabond is a tourist drop-out, that is, a traveler no longer willing to be plucked. You've "checked-out" from the TI's scheme to exploit your vacation or your travels. You've decided to live your own life story, not, the version some dildo businessmen want to lay on you for the sake of their bank-accounts. Sure, you'll make your own mistakes, but you'll make your own triumphs too. At least you'll get to feel real.

Dropping out of a joyless life as a wage-slave or corporate monkey has much the same rewards. Working free of the system, for yourself, gives you back your reality and your energy. You might wind up doing the same kind of work for less pay, but the new sense of yourself – the joy of living – makes up for everything else and then some. Your present boss won't give you your pension until you're too old to enjoy it, your freedom until your head is too messed to appreciate it. Meanwhile, you stand at the production line or sit at your desk, watching your life ticking away on your wonderful new waterproof electronic wristwatch with the latest style mod watchband. Nice.

"Catch a ride to the end of the hiway
And we'll meet by the big red tree.
There's a place up ahead an' I'm goin'
Come along, come along with me . . .

There's a place up ahead where I'm goin'
Just as fast as my feet can fly.
There's a place up ahead where I'm goin'
Leave the sinkin' ship behind.

Come on the rising wind
We're going up around the bend."

—Creedence Clearwater Revival
Up Around The Bend (Song)

The American job situation is way out of balance. At one time, jobs provided by the system did two very good things: they satisfied our material needs (paid the bills), and they gave meaning to our lives. But the system got out of touch with reality when it decided to harness technology towards achieving a higher level of materialism. Today the system is trying to make us rich, but in the process is removing the meaning of life (demeaning it). In exchange for your labor, the system promises you a big house before 65 and a big hospital afterwards. You do silly work for high pay while your body and brain turn to mush if they're not needed "on the job." You get no time or space to find yourself, be yourself, and develop yourself. You get to develop only what parts of you the system can use, and usually those parts aren't your best ones anyway. You gradually turn into a trained freak instead of a whole human being.

Society wants specialists —people trained to do only one thing because it's more "efficient" and hence more "profitable" for everyone. But where is the profit when the specialists are only half-humans, stunted with animal consciousness? Much of their potential humanity is not merely undeveloped but purposefully atrophied because the corporations and the factories don't need it. Things that are necessary for happiness, such as individuality and independence, have no use on the production line. People with these characteristics are either weeded out or retrained.

In return, the system tries to make you "happy." It says, "Here, you work for us and we'll make you rich and safe." But happiness doesn't come so mechanically. Happiness comes from being given the opportunity to become as human as you can. To work merely for things, for security in our old age, is to suck away the quality of life. The fully lived life requires only a modicum of gimcracks and guarantees. The fully lived life seeks challenges that unlock the potentials of the individual. The fully lived life means being free to find your own answers.

Of course a certain minimum of goods and services is required. We all need food and shelter and clothing. We need care when we're ill. We need protection from violence. And blah, blah, blah. What we do not need is a system that seeks to conform and control us for the sake of greater manufacturing and marketing efficiency. Individuals need a balance of freedom and security: Freedom releases energy that makes life rewarding; security binds energy that gives life its structure. Today our system is unbalanced — it leans toward security and away from freedom — it's unrealistic patterns are hoarding energy that could give us a higher quality of life.

If society is failing in its obligation to make you happy, you have to take the responsibility yourself. Dropping out is a way of asserting your own humanity and developing it so that you can be happy. Happiness is not a goal in itself but a byproduct of living fully; of becoming a generalist instead of a specialist; of trying to do as many things as you can, learning as much as you can. It doesn't matter how "smart" or "talented" you are — there's no need to compete. That's what you escape by dropping out.

Off The Tape
TALES OF A PANZER MECHANIC

This morning I had the radio exchanged on my VW and met Willie, a German mechanic who has been with VW since it started in 1932 in Wolfsberg, Germany. He was assigned there by the German army to help make VW's, then transferred to the Third Panzer division and sent to Russia. As he said "It was a good thing I was a mechanic or I would have been dead a long time ago." He was twice captured by the Russians but upon interrogation they found out that he was an expert and needed him to repair their own equipment. But he walked away from their lines both times and got away. Toward the end of the war in 1945, air-dropped leaflets promised good treatment for Germans who surrendered, but they had to cross a certain bridge over the Inn River in Austria, by one o'clock in the morning. By the time Willie got there the bridge was flooded and half down, but he commandeered a big German half track and was able to cross it anyway. He got over to the American side and turned himself in. He wound up in Salzburg where he spent several months as a prisoner tho he was free to wander around town as he liked.

He was quick to assure me that he never fought the Americans. He went thru Poland and was on the Eastern front during the whole war. He went into Poland in 1942. I looked at him and thought perhaps this man was one of the soldiers that starved and murdered my relatives then. Certainly he was around while the soldiers crashed their way across the north European plains in the Blitzkrieg. As a matter of fact, he was one of the men that put Blitzkrieg on wheels.

And here is now — nice, happy, round-faced, German mechanic, telling me that German goods are better than Japanese, but still a completely solid American citizen. I enjoyed being with him. America is so full of literally outlandish people like this — immigrants, expatriates, people whose personal history spans all the world and finally comes togehter here in America.

The Past ←   → The Past

HOW TO DROP OUT The most important ingredient for a successful drop-out is the desire to be one. If your desire is strong enough, there is no barrier that can ultimately withstand you. This maxim has been proven true, time and time again. Dropping out can be very difficult, depending upon the individual and upon the circumstances. But if you determine strongly enough to find another way to live, then you can do it. It's really as simple as that.

Dropping out is a process, however, not something you accomplish with a declaration of freedom, as your new life immediately begins. Dropping out is something you make a beginning at and then try to improve as time goes by. In the beginning, you can't know all the problems you have to face. Your consciousness is still back with what the system drummed into your brain these many years. Most Americans simply do not know how to fend for themselves anymore. They've spent years in training for college or work, for becoming specialized cogs in the giant wheel. Their thought processes have been controlled and channeled into seeing only the benefits of the system, while rationalizing the evils. Their drives to be independent and individual are the frequently short-circuited or crusted over with fear, or fallen into total disuse. So many of us are afraid to take any chances, to work for less money, to work longer hours, to live without our chrome-plated gadgets. We want the easy way, we want the secure way.

To begin the turn away from this brainwashing, try to listen to your inner voice, the inner voice which is your own and which speaks for you and you only, whoever you are. The inner voice knows exactly who you are, and it knows what you need. However, it's gotten small and squeaky from being locked up. To hear it again is to embark on a long journey of self-discovery. To drop out is to work at becoming whole — the task of a lifetime.

"SOME DECEMBER THOUGHTS"
by Irv Thomas
—Outlaw Institute Newsletter

"What do I do if I drop out?" This question seems to be the common obstacle. Those of us who have "dropped" reply that you don't *have* to do anything, but that's not an adequate answer to people whose lives have been built on structure and feel the need for it.

The problem, I think, is that we confuse plan with purpose. Sure, everyone needs a sense of purpose in their lives. This is something that's inside of us, in whatever form or direction it just takes. We don't ordain it, it just *is*. The plan is something we shape or construct around it. The plan, in effect, says "This is how I will pursue my purpose," like a road map.

But any road map assumes that we know the geography, and this is where we mislead ourselves. Because we're talking about unknown territory — the future — and *nobody* knows that geography. If you're crossing unknown territory, you have only two guide lines: your general direction, and the landscape that the eye can seen. A plan cannot reasonably take any more than that into consideration.

In pursuing your present stagnant life, you think you can see the entire landscape, as if from a mountaintop, and it's composed of a lot of dangerous pitfalls: Ravines of insecurity, sheer drops of ill health and other misfortunes, and a vast desert out there of old age. And you're very busy gathering all the supplies and equipment you'll need for those hazards. But nobody stands on such a mountaintop. That landscape is constructed of bits and pieces from what *other* people have experienced. And in your fear of their disasters, you think you can plan for every contingency, but that's absurd.

You have today. You don't know if you'll have tomorrow, and even if you have it, you have no idea what it will be like, or what problems and possibilities it will present for you. You don't even know how you'll feel when (and if) it arrives. If you try to structure tomorrow, you only succeed in binding yourself to today, and isn't that, after all, your present predicament?

The structure of your life — the only structure you need — is a continuity of purpose. And even that is not the same as constancy. It means, simply, that there is a meaningful thread from one day to the next."

Knowing What To Do The practical side of dropping out primarily concerns making enough money to survive while you do the things you want. Most "stay-in" workers have no real idea of what they would like to do if they dropped out. For so long we've done what we thought we wanted to do but it was really what the system wanted us to do. If we free ourselves, we frequently find that we are confused. Our inner voice is silent or seemingly silent. The solution is: Don't wait for your inner voice — do something now, regardless. The solution is to attempt the nearest job at hand, to take the closest opportunity to drop out, whatever it might be. If it doesn't work out for you, then that's the first step toward knowing what *is* right for you. Stepping the wrong way frequently steers us toward making the right step afterwards. The experience of trying to find your own way, no matter how confusing or dispiriting or unsuccessful, in fact always works to educate you and put you on the right path. Don't be afraid of uncertainty; don't be afraid to act because you're not sure the action is right. If it isn't right, you'll find out. If it is right, you'll find that out too. In either case, you'll find out. And that's what is crucially important — you must be the one to find out for yourself, in person. No one else can find it out for you. That is the essence of true education and of becoming a whole person.

Money Matters. Here are some practical tips on survival while you're trying to find out. Most important: How much you earn matters much less than how much you spend. The trick to successful dropping out is in reducing your living expenses. This automatically means you can survive on lower earnings. Food and housing are your primary expenses and there are many ways to lower them. If you have any money in the bank to start off with, use it to buy some income property. For example: buy a duplex apartment house, live in one half and let the rent from the other half pay your mortgage. Or buy a store with a house attached. Live in the house and either rent out the store or become the proprietor of the store.

Since we live in a capitalist society, it's always possible to put your capital to work, I mean truly to work, not to increase your security or to increase your material holdings, but to lower your living expenses. Most Americans use literally all of their capital for material holdings and security. Meanwhile, the real capitalists, the ones who employ them, use their capital for making more capital. This is something you can do with your capital also. Drop out: Become a capitalist.

Years ago I bought a two story building with an abandoned store below. (I borrowed the down-payment.) By renting out the quarters upstairs and converting the store into a place to live for myself, I enjoy a rent-free house. At a time when my income was virtually nil, which was most of these years, this advantage was a crucial factor in my survival. Another way to reduce expenses is to live communally. All this means is sharing costs among several people and need not imply any social, sexual, or religious interaction. However, many people who share the rent with others find their lives greatly enriched by sharing themselves too.

Yet another way to lower your living expenses is to buy a truck, a bus, a van, and to live in it after modifying it for that purpose. Many cities now forbid parking overnight on city streets, but it's easy to park your van in the country on privately owned land. Buy the land yourself, or get permission to use from your friend who owns the land, or from a private owner to whom you pay a minimal rental. Older busses and vans can be bought cheap. (The book, *Roll Your Own* gives some hints on how to do this. See Appendix 2 under "Car Camping.") Finally, there are mobile homes which can be bought used for very little and hauled to your own little piece of land in the country. As used by almost all Americans, a mobile home is an aesthetic disaster. This has to do with the consciousness of the occupants and not necessarily the structure itself. By painting or re-finishing the thing, making structural modifications, and throwing out or not using the usual trashy American furniture and appliances that are supplied with mobile homes, you can have a reasonably nice looking and comfortable place to live at moderate cost. The same thing also applies to house trailers, which are cheap, livable, and can be modified into something not too embarrassing.

Food Savings. As for food costs, there are many, many ways to save. The basic approach is to re-examine your diet and see what you need to live. Like, you don't need much meat or you don't need any meat at all. Soybeans are far cheaper than meat and pound for pound contain more protein. Buy your produce at farmer's markets or at wholesale grocery outlets. Eat more grains, and seeds, and legumes. And buy them in bulk. Join a "food conspiracy" if there is one in your area, or if there isn't one, start a food conspiracy. This is just a group of people who pool their money to buy food at wholesale prices. Volunteers are needed to buy, haul, distribute, process orders,

and divide the food up into individual portions, but these labors are alternated and in fact do not make many demands on your time. And of course food stamps are easy to qualify for and go a long way towards reducing food expenses. I was on food stamps for three years during the time that my earnings were so little, even tho I owned property at the time (the rent free house above). This is perfectly legal, by the way.

Is It Worth It? During those three years of doing what I wanted to do (being a photographer and a vagabond) I made very little money and suffered a lot of anxiety. However, my expenses were so low that I needed very little. I paid no taxes (meaning I gave no economic support to the system either), lived quite comfortably when I was at home, traveled all over Europe and America several times, made great strides in both personal and professional development, and had a wonderful time doing all these things. Whereas for fifteen years previous to that, I had worked for various corporations at big salaries, never had more than two weeks off a year, never was very happy, felt a continuing sense of personal frustration in my life and in my work, seldom traveled, and no matter how much money I made it never seemed that there was enough. What do you think? Which way was I better off?

WORKING Working can be a good trip. It is the heart of the Christian ethic, and there's nothing wrong with that as far as it goes. The problem arises when your work is not personally rewarding or subtracts from you in some way. Working is something you should like to do. No activity in life challenges us more than our work. It requires or should require maximum utilization of ourselves in all ways. If in fact it does this, then we know it is a priceless activity and we are happy doing it. On the other hand, if we look upon work as drudgery, or something that steals our freedom, or as a necessary evil . . .then something is wrong. For most Americans, of course, something *is* wrong.

Americans, known as the hardest workers in the world are increasingly hating their work. Moreover, they're also afraid of their leisure. A horrible human trap is being set up: People hate their work but make a lot of money doing it. Then, in their leisure time they spend their money, which they don't enjoy either. They buy packaged fun — things and tours. But they don't necessarily get anything out of their trips — they just spend money. They follow the dictates of the Travel Industry (and the Leisure Industry, the Entertainment Industry, etc.). In the end, everyone becomes some kind of robot — a robot on the job, and a robot on vacation.

What should be happening is something like this. What you do with your life is your work. Your work should be indistinguishable from your life. Those people who do enjoy their leisure, probably do something with their time that other people would look upon as work. For example, they build furniture, and they go hiking in the mountains, they participate strenuously in sports or active hobbies, etc. Many of these people could probably make a living from their leisure time activities if they lost their fear of taking the step.

In this section, I'm going to look at possible ways to make a living, whether you're on the road or whether you're staying awhile somewhere. Some of these ways to make a living are simply means of corraling a few dollars so that you can keep going when you're broke. Others are ways of establishing yourself in a region, and building a life around the work you do. The list I'll offer is by no means complete — it's intended only to stimulate your own thoughts on the subject. Some of these jobs are not necessarily pleasant, nor are they something you'd want to do for any length of time. They're just a means of making a few dollars so you can go on with your vagabond career. But even doing things you don't like to do has value. You find out about another way of living, about other values; you discover where the wrong steps lead, and that gives you information about the right steps.

You never know — something that seems distasteful or pretty weird at the beginning just might turn out to hold a hidden key to a future windfall or pathway of some sort. Life really is unpredictable despite our best efforts to make it otherwise. It's more rewarding and realistic to accept the unpredictability and flow with it, than to force experience into tightly sealed boxes that it keeps busting out of anyway.

ODD-JOBBING   Odd-jobbing is the vagabond's standby and is frequently as much a source of adventure as money. It means being willing to do whatever comes along for the sake of a few dollars, and frequently involves being clever and opportunistic so that you can realize a profit without too much drudgery. One of the mainstays of odd-jobbing is selling. Most odd-jobs, in fact, involve selling either miscellaneous goods or miscellaneous services and can be done almost anywhere. For example, you can sell newspapers in many cities — vendors of underground newspapers frequently are in demand but over-ground newspapers will also hire vendors on an odd-job basis. Selling newspapers is a great way of meeting people and of feeling out what a place is like. (This, of course, is true of most odd jobs.) There also are newspaper distribution jobs or advertising distribution jobs. In large cities, check the want-ads for handbill distributors. Look in the Yellow Pages for distribution companies. These companies usually hire men (women?) by the day.

There are miscellaneous things that you can sell either on a door-to-door basis or, if that's prohibited or too much of a drag, you can set up a roadside booth or maybe just a table next to your parked truck. Sell wildflowers you've collected, firewood you've gathered and chopped, stones you've collected. At Christmas time, sell mistletoe and holiday wreaths you've made. There are many things like this that can be gathered for nothing or near nothing, and which frequently sell very well for a good profit. Any place there are people you can sell things. If there's a beach nearby you can sell beer there or home-made sandwiches. I heard of some guys who sold Frisbees on the beach on week-ends and cleaned up. Your imagination is the only limit on things you can sell at a profit.

Services are certainly a good commodity. This includes gardening, lawn mowing, tree trimming, and hedge cutting. This is an excellent prospect for door-to-door inquiries. In the same way you can offer services for any kind of miscellaneous labor or handyman activities. Remove trash, clean houses, do miscellaneous painting and repair. If you have your own sign and brush kit, you can offer to repaint existing signs that have faded out or are peeling. This is easy work because the signs are already laid out and represent a minimum amount of labor. Going from door to door offering to paint house numbers on the curb is another good gig requiring only a stencil and a spray can of paint. Then there are babysitting and child care jobs and a variety of jobs that require minding the store, guarding the gate, answering the phone...to jobs that simply require a warm body around.

Odd jobs are most frequently obtained by direct inquiry, but always scan the local bulletin boards, or place ads there if you have somewhere you can be reached. Always ask anyone you encounter if they know of a job or a little work to be done. It's amazing how many people have heard of a few hours work here and a few hours work there that nobody seems to want. In fact, I've met people who subsist entirely from odd-jobs, working only when they need the money.

ARTS AND CRAFTS This is a big step up from odd-jobbing and requires the development of a marketable skill. Nevertheless, to be a free-lance craftsman is one of the best ways of making money while leading a free life. In the past few years, the demand for hand-crafted goods of all kinds dramatically increased and thousands of creative and free-thinking craftsmen are filling the demand. Actually, the demand was created by craftsmen who dropped out and investigated new ways of making a living. They found that there was a

Photo: Howard Harawitz

Off The Tape
MEETING MY PAST

It seems incredible that I was once a junior executive in the electronics industry — I can't imagine anymore what was on my mind then, that I could work that way for 10 years. I guess nothing worthwhile was on my mind — I was unconscious, like so many people I see around me today. What makes it strange is that I can see so clearly now how completely unrewarding it was. My hours were regular and boring, I took no real pleasure in my work, and all there was in my future was more of the same. I was well-paid, of course, but what did it mean? I was comfortable but I wasn't free. I had more money than I needed, but what else did I have? I was reminded of that time again when I met an engineer at Disneyworld, for it turned out we used to work for the same company. But I left it, and eventually the whole business. He left it, too, but went on to Bendix. His hope was to work abroad someday in one of their overseas divisions — he'd been trying to get transferred to Spain for years.

It was ironic because I'd wanted to go abroad, too — but like him, all my good pay, security, and comfort wasn't enough to get me there. So I quit — gave up my silly salary and hateful job —and went abroad, to Spain, where I lived for awhile. Poor but very happy . . . and I stayed abroad a year. Later I went again. And then again.

Now, years later on a summer's tour of America, I meet this engineer, this symbol of my past. He stayed with it, and he's *still* trying to get abroad. Ah well. In the meanwhile, as he himself said to me, he's got Disneyworld, where he comes frequently. How fitting.

opening

to

the plunge

to ———> greatness

you can be
who you are.

waiting market for hand-made quality goods because Americans have become so tired of machine-made products. Some of the best-selling crafts at the moment are leather work, pottery, jewelry, and macrame. All of these crafts are relatively easy, can be learned rapidly, and you can begin selling them from the start. I have sold at craft festivals for years, witnessing and being part of the crafts renaissance in America. The people I've met who live by their handcrafts and wits run in the hundreds, exemplifying every possible approach to dropping out. They sell anything imaginable, and here are some to give you an idea:

stone hash pipes	incense holders
carved wood toys	ceramic buttons
tie-died clothes	custom sandals
batik scarves	dress designs
enamel jewelry	driftwood tables
wire earrings	stained glass
decorator clock faces	hand-made dolls
far-out furniture	hand-made rag paper
personalized stationary	exotic knee patches
dream analysis	funky mobiles
palm readings	laminated cutting boards
horoscope readings	health bread and cookies
handwriting analysis	leather book covers
thumb pianos	chop-sticks
candles	knitted caps
embroidery	woven belts

For the pure vagabond, jewelry crafting is probably the best trade because it requires the smallest inventory of tools and materials and they are the easiest to carry around. Selling it requires only a small velvet drop cloth that can be laid across a table or on the ground to display your wares. Leather work and macrame are not far behind in these regards. Leather belts, pouches, purses, are easy to sell and make and carry around. The same holds true for objects in macrame. Pottery making requires a home base, or at least access to a studio with a wheel and kiln. However, if you have a home base and can make an inventory of pottery that you carry on the road, you can make money selling it almost anywhere. This applies to all other crafts which require a studio. Make the stuff in your studio and then

pack it in your truck to take it on the road and then sell it whenever you need money. I met one couple who traveled all over America making creative dolls from bean-bags and scraps of cloth. They traveled by truck and set up shop wherever they happened to be, driving into a town square, by the side of a road, on a college campus. Selling hand-crafted items is a great way to meet people as well. It's easy to make contacts for things you need, to make friends, and to get information about other opportunities in the area. The best places to sell are wherever there are either tourists or students. Tourists have the money to spend and students have the enthusiasm to buy even

when they don't have the money.

Art festivals have become a regular feature of many cities and towns, sometimes sponsored by merchants, sometimes civically, or both. These are great marketplaces to sell crafts as well as arts. To find out more, contact the local Chamber of Commerce or read the listings in local art magazines and newspapers (for example, WestArt Magazine lists the major west coast art festivals).

Of course, artists can also sell at art festivals and on the street, too. Art includes photography (which was my gig — selling prints and seeking portrait commissions), oils, etchings, drawings, sculpture, whatever . . .

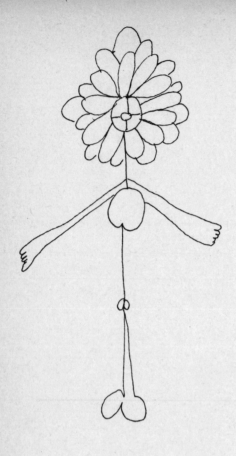

SKILLS

The next category of job opportunities also involves skills. Auto repair, for example, is a standard underground service for sale. With garage mechanics so expensive, business can easily be found amongst bargain-hungry motorists. My car is always worked on by Jim Koch, a bushy-haired philosopher-king/VW mechanic and friend that I originally met on a city street-corner where he was holding up a sign saying, "VW Tune-Up: $5." Jim doesn't make much money but he needs even less, and in the balance I would say he lives a richer life than most.

Direct advertising is frequently the best way to advertise your skill. Simply make a big sign and hold it up on the road telling whatever it is you can do for people. Appliance repair is a similar service and can be sold from the street, placing ads in bulletin boards or shopping newspapers. Furniture repair or furniture refinishing is another. Anyone who has any skill at all with carpentry, plumbing, or electricity, can easily get all the work he can handle in most American communities. The rates for skilled union carpenters, for example, are so strange that people can easily be convinced to give you the job instead. A few years ago when I was broke and needed work, I heard about a small plumbing job in which someone wanted a gas dryer and washing machine installed. I accepted the job, which brought me two days work. This eventually led to a whole series of other benefits. The woman who hired me became my girlfriend, found me a place to live, and I've stayed in that neighborhood to this very day. A skilled job of this kind usually leads to another. Most of the work comes from referrals and the only hard part is getting the first few jobs. After that, you frequently get all the work you can handle. If you have a welding outfit or can do sheet metal work, then you have a passport to money anytime you need it, asking around at small businesses, farms, garages, gas stations.

For women especially, cooking and sewing jobs can be found if you're into "women's work." You can advertise clothing repair and

Off The Tape
NEW AGE SHINING BRIGHT

"Spirit is around me like the rainbow around the sun." (sung)

That's the sound of a banjo, two guitars, two flutes, a violin, harmonica, drums, people with sticks, dancing, singing, here at Mt. Shasta, California. Impromptu party of some of the local free people. It's another traveler's bonanza, something which we just happened onto while visiting Rich, my old friend and former electronics engineer, now a dropped-out carpenter on the hill.

"We are Love, We are Light, We are the New Age Shining Bright."

patching, or if you're a really good seamstress you can manufacture clothes for sale or small items of clothing such as belts, ties, scarves, hand-bags, guitar-straps, embroidered things, knit caps, and so forth. Or the women can do welding and carpentry while the men sell tie-died T-shirts. Sell pies, cakes, and cookies on the street or door to door. Do your thing. Virtually any skill you possess can be marketed somewhere. It's only a matter of finding the customers and building the confidence that you can do it on a regular basis to supplement your income or survive entirely on it.

PERFORMING By this I primarily mean performing a musical instrument, but it can also mean dramatic performances or lecturing. Even if you can't play an instrument very well, you'll be able to make some money as a street musician. Musical talent is not the chief requirement here, just the balls to do it. Street musicians can usually gather a crowd by simply doing it. If you're ready to move on an instant's notice when the cops appear, you can do pretty good at it. A team works best — have one person play while the other circulates thru the crowd with a hat. Places to play include downtown streets, city parks, street fairs and festivals, tourist gatherings of any kind, or places where people are lined up waiting for a movie or other amusement. College quads, student unions, and other student gatherings are also excellent places, and again this is an excellent way to meet the folks.

If you happen to be a really good musician or a group of musicians traveling together, it's possible to get gigs at local clubs and bars by auditioning. College towns usually have one or more local beer joints or folk-music-type clubs that take walk-in talent and pay something, at least a meal and whatever you can collect by passing the hat. Sometimes cash on the barrelhead.

It might seem that lecturing is a pretty far out gig, and indeed it is — but it's possible. A friend of mine is planning a motorcycle tour and he's taking along three slide-illustrated lectures that he's prepared about life in California to show at schools and clubs while he's out in the sticks. He told me that he's not doing this so much for money, but as a way to meet people. He says that traveling has proved to be a lonely business for him, and this solves the problem.

FORMAL EMPLOYMENT Of course, you *can* get a regular job. In your case, it would help if it were only part-time or for the holidays. Many kinds of jobs are available to job seekers hanging around for a while. The Christmas season offers opportunities for selling behind the counter of a department store and the like. Frequently, no sales experience is necessary, but your appearance is important. Working at the post office during the Christmas season is another good bet, but this requires applying some time in advance and taking the Civil Service exam. However, these things aren't really that complicated or difficult, and one great advantage of working in the post office is that you meet the most incredible collection of freaks from long-haired hippy weirdoes to the most outrageous short-haired straight weirdoes. The government says it does not discriminate against anyone in hiring (except ex-convicts), so appearance and dress don't matter too much for this work.

Then there are numerous job agencies that specialize in short-term employment or in casual labor. The first is well-known and includes Kelly Girl, Manpower, etc. These people all look for experienced, skilled employees, and appearance usually counts too. However, many "heads," especially females, easily meet these qualifications and can land short jobs without any trouble. Knowing how to operate a typewriter, transcriber, key punch, accounting machine, or any other office machine is always a plus when applying for these jobs. More and more of these same agencies are branching out and finding short-term employment for other than secretarial types, too, including programmers, engineers, technicians, what have you.

At the other end of the placement agency spectrum are agencies that arrange casual work. These pay daily and aren't particular who they arrange jobs for. They usually offer hotel or kitchen work, cleaning jobs, and miscellaneous day labor. You'll get the minimum wage plus food if it's a restaurant. The agencies, of course, get a commission on placing you but it's usually possible to arrange for your own work later on at the same place without paying the commission. Casual labor can frequently be obtained by walking in off the street too, asking if they need dishwashers or doormen, as the case may be. ("Working" in Appendix 1 also lists some of these agencies in NYC.) Casual jobs of this kind are also available thru information clearing houses like Switchboards, the YMCA or YWCA, Traveler's Aid societies, and, of course, frequently in the want ads of local newspapers.

Then there's the whole area of summer jobs which can mean anything, anywhere. Be a camp counselor at Lake Minnehaha, be a cafeteria waitress at Rocky Mountain National Park, punch cows for the Bar X in Montana, drive the airport limousine for the Grand Hotel, or work on a road gang for the Bureau of Highways. These jobs cover the map, but in most cases you must apply well in advance, frequently competing with lots of others (students). There are some useful sources to aid you in your search. The first is probably your college placement bureau. See what leads and advice they might have. There's also the annual *Summer Employment Directory of the United States* listed under "Working" in the "*Trips*" Appendix. Other job-finding and work-idea books are also listed there. For state and government jobs, write directly to the offices involved. For national park jobs, write to the Director of the national park you're interested in. Do it as early as possible. Your letter shouldn't be longer than one page, and if you think it would be useful or necessary, add a one page résumé to the letter. Tell what job you're applying for and where you heard about it, tell why you'd like the job and why you should do it. The résumé should include personal data, information about your education and work experience, and some references. It would be a good idea to include a stamped return envelope for the employer's reply or application blank. Also give the dates that you're available for work.

Service jobs for religious groups or other organizations are another possibility. If interested, write some of the following addresses for their booklets on summer service opportunities:

United Church of Christ
Pottstown Rural Delivery 2, PA 19464

American Friends Service Committee
160 North 15th Street
Philadelphia, PA

Advancement and Placement Institute
169 North 9th Street
Brooklyn, NY 11211

National Council of YMCA's
291 Broadway
New York, NY 10007

National Student YWCA
600 Lexington Avenue
New York, NY 10022

To find out about applying for summer jobs in federal agencies, write the US Civil Service Commission, 1900 E Street NW, Washington DC 20415. Another source of information for government jobs for students in the US Department of Labor, Bureau of Employment Security, Washington DC 20210.

If you're planning on trying to find work in Hawaii or Alaska, there are some places you can write in advance. In Alaska, summer is the peak season for jobs in mining, fishing, lumbering, and construction. Contact the Employment Security Division of the Alaska State Department of Labor, Box 3-7000, Juneau, AK 99801. For information about other types of skilled and professional work, contact the Alaska State Employment Service, located in any of the larger cities. To find out about government jobs, which usually require an examination, write to the US Civil Service, Alaska Branch Office, 247 Federal Building, Anchorage, AK 99501. The state of Alaska has many workers who leave the lower 48 each year to try and find higher paying jobs in one of Alaska's several outdoor industries, but frequently the jobless rate soars. Prices of everything in Alaska are higher by about a third and housing is scarce.

In Hawaii, most of the people are employed either by the government or by some tourist-related activity or business. If people think you're only passing thru it will be much harder to get a job. I've also heard that hippies are resented on the islands. To find out about jobs contact the State of Hawaii Employment Service, 825 Mililani St, Honolulu, HI 96813.

Something else for the vagabond to consider is becoming a harvester or picker. In many parts of the country, particularly out west, farm labor is freely available to anyone who wants it. Most of it is damned hard work, bent over all day under a hot sun. Laborers travel from region to region, following the crops, usually in beat-up cars and sometimes by riding the rails. To get information about this, contact any local office of Farm Labor Information. Most farming towns have an office, with the address given in a big sign on the outskirts of town. My good friend Joe Gaspers, master of all trades, has written a report on fruit harvesting in Oregon to give you some idea of what it's like (at the end of this chapter).

SIGN OF THE TIMES

A billboard just outside of Kanab, Utah saying DROP OUT NOW: PAY LATER: A "public service message" sponsored by a local electric company.

"I like the system which lets a man quit when he wants to, and wish it might prevail everywhere."

—Abraham Lincoln

"Only a hobo but one more is gone
Leaving nobody to sing his sad song
Leaving nobody to carry him home
He was only a hobo but one more is gone"

—Bob Dylan
Only A Hobo (Song)

YOUR OWN BUSINESS Finally there's this whole area of going into business for yourself. For example, if you own a truck you can go into the hauling and moving business. If you'd rather keep clean, there's typing term papers and manuscripts, editing and writing jobs that you can get by placing ads in school and other newspapers. You can even start a business as a tour guide for your local attractions. Simply work up a spiel and place notices in the vicinity of the attractions, or walk up and down and canvass for business.

You can clean and remove trash. You can gather and sell lumber. If you're interested in photography and more or less stable, start a studio or become a street photographer. Photograph tourists whenever they congregate. There's a whole range of photographic jobs involving the ego business. Photograph performers and musicians, for example, and sell prints to the fans or to the performers themselves. I know a photographer who goes out to the stock car races and photographs the cars from the center of the track. Afterwards

DEALING DOPE Speaking of businesses, here's one of the easiest ones to get into and one of the hottest. Lots of people find themselves tempted to sell some grass, especially, or maybe hash. The next step is Coke and pills. Even assuming that dealing was a good deal, which I don't think it is, it isn't a good deal for the vagabond, that is, for the traveler whose knowledge of the local scene is probably non-existent. He may start selling his wares in a hornet's nest of narcs or informers or uptight people who might turn him in. Newcomers are always viewed with more suspicion, not only by natives but by the local police as well. It's much harder to get away with anything if you're just passing thru, because you're under suspicion all the time. I don't recommend it at all. The few dollars you make doesn't justify the paranoia and risk, and may bum out your trip. If you're holding a lot and plan to sell a bunch, then you're heavy into dealing and not really making a pleasure trip at all. You're not a vagabond, but a businessman — and your business is going to crowd you.

Making marijuana available is something that friends should do for each other, not something to be done as a business. You should never buy from or sell dope to anyone who you don't know well. Old-consciousness Americans like nothing better than to nail somebody selling dope. In some states any amount of marijuana found on your person is good for ten years in jail, sometimes without possibility of parole. Now, there's something that can put a crimp in your vagabonding plans. Stay clean, or at least don't sell it.

he sells the prints to the drivers. Similarly you can photograph people where they work, sell them pictures of themselves on the job. Go to athletic fields and photograph the little leaguers. Photograph athletic teams and sell prints to the players, to their fans. Someone with a Polaroid camera and a good spiel can surely sell instant prints anywhere that people gather — at parks and beaches, tourist attractions, picnics, wherever your imagination leads you. My fruit-harvester friend Joe (who I just mentioned) now has his own business making folding massage tables for studios and individuals. After a few months working out their design and construction, and making contacts, he's now got a nice one-man business that he works at just 2 or 3 days per week.

Then there's Jacob, a poet and professor who also sells sandwiches in the financial district of the city. He makes custom super-duper sandwiches like you can't get from the sandwich-route drivers, then sells them at premium prices to stock brokers, lawyers, publishers, and other elite technocrats.

STEALING Well, if you can't deal dope, should you steal? Stealing nowadays goes under the euphemism of "ripping-off" and certain kinds of ripping-off are considered OK. For example, if you rip something off from a corporation, it's OK; if you rip something off from a large supermarket, from any kind of mass marketing organization, it's considered perfectly cool by some. But I disagree. For some time I went along with it and said,

"Yeah, those corporations and outfits steal from the people anyway, so why not steal from them? Their crimes are much larger than any I could commit against them." That may well be true, and I tend to think it is. However, the larger truth is that stealing always hurts you more than it helps you. The act of stealing, even if it's only pencils from the office, a can of tuna from the supermarket, getting too much change back from the cashier — all tend to lower your estimation of yourself. Some part of you brands yourself as a petty thief, and over the long run messes up your consciousness.

Looking back over the things you've stolen, which of them are still with you, which of them have increased your wealth so much that it outweighs knowing you're a thief? If you don't think this matters much, looking at it the other way: A person who goes out of his or her way to be strictly honest does not make that particular self-judgement. S/He knows s/he's an honest man or woman. It doesn't take long before s/he begins to take pride in it and even becomes righteous about it. Now get this: That righteousness represents strength and it represents power. A person who truly works at being honest is a person to be reckoned with. S/He develops a sense of worth and clarity of mind that over a period of years becomes a very positive and powerful force in his or her life. What did s/he do to get that strength and that force? Actually, s/he didn't do anything. S/He merely did not steal on those relatively few occasions s/he had the chance to do so.

In other words, you can get that kind of righteousness for absolutely nothing. Just be honest and you'll automatically start becoming strong behind it. Then it begins to feed back into your head, and you reap unforeseen rewards. On the other hand, the average person who steals now and then never steals much. S/He never really gets anything for the effort except a bad sense of self, way down deep, working unconsciously to keep that person morally weak.

Light I have seen bouncing off the mother-granite Light in the sky and in a running child. GOD is The Light. Me, a dark child, rested on the banks of the YAMPA RIVER and received the Light. It healed my dissatisfied demon, raging in the center of Me. This is for YOU who wonder if there is any healing.

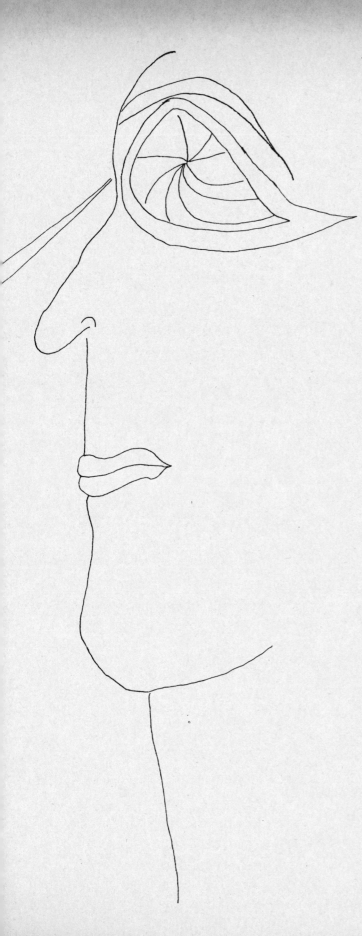

Not only that, but there's the risk of getting busted for it. It's a stiff price for a little piece of shoplifting in a department store or a bottle of mayonnaise in a supermarket. I've witnessed a supermarket bust, and I've known one person it happened to. First comes the police trip, usually ending with getting booked and fined, or maybe let go with a warning. But the main penalty is what happens to the head and ego. You go thru a heavy guilt and anger trip because you find out you're a petty thief. Like, it's right there for you to see, and you don't like what you see.

By contrast, how much groovier to simply be honest all the time about everything. Being honest with people flips them out and leads to all kinds of good things. Don't take my word for it. Try it and see. Become scrupulously honest about money and things, and note carefully what it starts doing for your head. The good trip and moral strength you get into more than make up for anything you could have stolen.

Finally, stealing is proof positive that you're still locked into the system. Most people in the system want security and material things, but they put their positive energy into working for it. People who steal are just as much into the system, wanting security and material things, but they put negative energy into it. Either way the system has you by the balls, and your energy should be directed toward breaking free of the system, not in getting tied up in one of its messier side-trips. Free yourself of the *whole* thing. Stealing is a bad trip because it robs you of your humanity. So is working at a job you don't enjoy, for the same reason. You should avoid both of them, not by any effort of will, but as easily and naturally as flowers open to the sun. If you get into that kind of good place, where you know what counts and you learn what things really matter, you find that people are more important than things and you stop thinking about honesty and about stealing. You simply do the right thing without any reasons. That's getting way out there. Yet we're all capable of it, or at least we'd all be better off by leaning a little in that direction no matter what our life style is like.

BEGGING Well, again what can I say? I don't dig it. Street begging brings down everyone associated with it. It's a low trip because it's a way of not facing the challenge of being broke with your best energy. You slip into a place of negative energy, instead of attacking the problem with your positive energy. If you're really broke and in need, you're feeling angry and helpless. It's a rotten head to be in, and the head is not going to be improved by trying to wheedle money out of strangers on the street. They're gonna get uptight. If you're not uptight already, they're gonna make you uptight. It's an exchange of bad vibes. Put your energy into thinking of other ways you could turn some money in return for your energy or time. It's that same kind of head trip again. If you beg, somewhere in your head you subtract from yourself by letting it sink in that you're a beggar. If you turn some money by some effort of body or brain, you re-enforce the idea that you're a person who can make your own way, and build confidence in yourself. When you beg, you lose that confidence. It hurts you more than you're helped by the spare change you get.

SETTLING DOWN Buying a piece of land and moving to the country is the dream of many Americans today. It offers escape from the rat race, from pollution, from city tensions and crime, and most of all gives you the opportunity to work with your bare hands and full resources to make an independent life for yourself. However, like all the other standard American dreams, this one is in trouble too. The booming increase in the price of rural property all across the nation is one of the most notable and depressing phenomena of recent years. Most of the land is being bought up by corporations and speculators, then by city people who want country property for a cabin or other recreation purposes, and finally by expatriates from the urban barrens.

If this is your dream too, now is the time to start looking if you haven't already. To raise the money, consider going shares with a group of people on a piece of land where you can live communally. If you don't have the money, it's frequently possible to lease a small farm. I know one group of people who've occupied a formerly abandoned farm and are renovating the ranch house by arrangment with the owner. In this case the owner was so glad to get someone to work on the house and occupy the farm that he charges them nothing at all. And the farm is within an hour's drive of San Francisco.

The best area of the country is the one that works for you. To find out where this is, I recommend taking a vagabond tour of America, visiting all parts of the country that interest you as a potential place to live, work, and possibly buy your own land. As you travel, stop in at real estate offices and local chambers of commerce to get detailed information about land prices, cost of living, and information about the local life-styles. To get free catalogs of country property, write to one or more of the following realty agents:

United Farm Agency
612 — 47th
Kansas City, MO 64112

Strout Realty
Box 2757
Springfield, MO 65803

Statewide Realty
Pyramid Life Building
Little Rock, AR 72201

Go to the library and look at an American atlas for details of weather, rainfall, population distribution, crop capabilities, and so forth. Also, look up articles in or subscribe to the *Mother Earth News*, Box 38, Madison, OH 44057. This magazine is probably the best single source of information related to buying and living on the land, dropping out on the strength of your own efforts. It gives you the information and encouragement to follow it thru. Two very interesting books that cover this area of how to do it on the land are *The First Time Farmer's Guide* and *How to Live in the New America*, both by William Kaysing (see details in Appendix 2 under "Farming.")

COMMUNES By a commune I mean a group of people, unrelated by blood, mutually agreed to share something in common. This may be a living space, land, food, or whatever. Other names in common use are collectives, cooperatives, intentional communities, and experimental communities. There are various kinds of communes, depending upon their particular structure or orientation: Religious, ideological, hippie, group marriage, service, and youth communes. These are the divisions used by Dick Fairfield in his book *Communes USA* (see Appendix 1). Dick is a friend and one-time neighbor of mine. His various publications are probably the best source of information about communal living in America. He is the founder of the Alternatives Foundation which publishes a fortnightly report called *The Alternatives Journal* (also in Appendix 1 under "Communes"). He also publishes a semi-annual book called *The Modern Utopian* with each issue concentrating on some aspect of modern communal living. The 1972 edition is *Utopia USA* and is a complete look at the American commune in virtually all of its aspects. The price is $3.95 in your bookstore, or can be ordered directly from Dick at the Alternatives Foundation in Los Angeles. Some other books about communes are also listed in Appendix 1.

There's very little I can personally tell you about communes: I've never belonged to one. However, my ex-wife and my daughter Jan belonged to the famous and ill-fated Harbinger Commune near Middletown, California. Founded on utopian ideals and mystical faith, Harbinger was typical of many communes of its period. Its members extensively experimented with drugs, and believed that survival, individually and communally, would come from faith alone. It didn't happen that way, and eventually the commune came to an inglorious end upon the forceful and simultaneous insistence of the police department, the health department, and the narcotics squad.

Off The Tape
FINDING THE FARM

Coming into Summertown, we didn't know the way to The Farm, so we pulled over to where these two old men sat in front of a house. One of them came over, an old geezer with no teeth and said: "Why, sure I know where Stephen Gaskin's farm is. You can't hardly miss it." And he proceeded to give us a fairly complicated set of directions and after he got thru he said "They's always drivin' down this road here, and if you see one of them just follow him." It was somehow implicit in his statement that "they" would be easy to recognize — there would be no doubt about it if you saw one of "them." So we started out down the road following his directions and we came to the first road where we might possibly turn off, and we pulled over to the side of the road. A car behind us slowed down and as it passed us the guy honked and shook his head and waved further on down the road. Then he led us on a little further and pointed at the dirt road where it turned off. And that was just because we had out-of-state license plates — they automatically knew that's where we wanted to go.

More communes fail than make it. In fact, it may be true to say that no communes make it at all, at least on the basis of survival thru time. Even those communes in existence for more than a few years, have only a handful of the original members left, if any at all. None of this is intended to discourage future communards, only to indicate that electing the communal life is a difficult path. In looking for a commune, or perhaps in starting your own, your should try to find out what other communes have gone thru, why they failed and why they worked. This is the main value of reading the available literature. *In order to succeed at communal living, you need to know what to expect out of the experience beforehand. Some means of organization is needed to insure that the members of the commune work toward its collective goals. Finally, flexibility is needed so the commune can adapt itself to changing conditions.*

Communes have a great deal to offer. They can cure loneliness. They provide ways to solve personal problems thru interaction and group analysis. They are an acceptable and effective means of showing resistance to the system, of demonstrating that alternative life styles are viable. Finally, they are practical: They make it possible to live economically and ecologically — reasons which frequently make communal living not a goal in itself but something done incidentally on the way towards other goals. In any case, the communal experience is one that raises the level of emotional and personal contact of the people to its highest possibilities. That's why American young people have flocked to it —they're disgusted with the coldness of human relations that characterizes our system.

Communal levels of human contact may cause over-amping (getting zapped with too much energy). Even so, the risk may be well worth taking. Whatever else may be happening, communes are focuses of energy and life, and those are good things to experience.

A COMMUNE OBSERVED Here's a look at the one commune we visited — Stephen

Gaskin's Farm in Summertown, Tennessee. Stephen is a modern-day religious prophet with a following of nearly 500 people who live on a farm they bought together, partially from the proceeds of Gaskin's book *Monday Night Class* and partly from the personal assets of the people themselves. It's a collection of mostly young people dedicated to old-fashioned virtues and to God, living lives of surreal beauty and charm on 1000 acres of Tennessee hill and woodland.

Yet they lead lives of stringent self-denial. For example, their diet includes no meat or dairy products. They live in tents, busses, and temporary structures, rising early for long days of hard work in the fields. But they all emanate a richness of belief in God and in themselves and in their leader. They believe in old virtues — marriage and having babies at home, of loving your neighbor and helping your neighbor. Visiting the farm in some ways is like returning to the past. However, modern farming methods are used, they publish books, pamphlets and advertisements on the Farm; they have a security guard system; they have a motor pool (the tractors run 16 hours a day in shifts). The Farm also has its own rock band that tours and makes records.

Nevertheless, on The Farm itself one sees the women in long skirts, pulling wagons behind them filled with water jugs and children, and the men in straw hats and beards. Affection is openly given and warmly received. You are greeted lovingly, without exception. People ask your name and talk to you, want to know about you, freely tell you about themselves and their lives. Almost everyone goes by their full formal name like Richard instead of Dick, Stephen instead of Steve, William instead of Bill: An old-fashioned way of showing respect.

Behind all of it lies the powerful personality of Stephen Gaskin, whose philosophy is expressed actively in the lives of everyone there. And verbally in the mouths of everyone there. They revere him almost as a diety, and like to tell eye-witness stories that prove his higher powers. Stephen, in fact, spends most of his time as a guru and administrator, busy with schedules, problem-solving sessions, moving here and there about the farm, advising, instructing, inspiring.

Off The Tape
AMERICAN GURU

Guide: "We make a decision about what's going to be done and he tells us how to do it. He's like concerned with interfacing with the world outside, interfacing with each other and he tells us how to do it."

Stephanie: And what does he do in the band, does he play?

G: He's like the astral mirror of the band. He engineers the band. He doesn't play any instrument. He integrates energy. He's like an energy focus.

S: Does he do that on stage?

G: He does that with the band.

Ed: That's pretty far out. Like he must have to move in some way.

G: He dances, he just like pays attention and integrates everything that's going on. An idea of what he can do is like he told the story once of how he went to a Grateful Dead concert in SF stoned on acid and he walked into this rock and roll hall and there was a cat who was on a violent ripoff trip off in the back — he was like being really violent and there was lights happening around him and all the energy in the rock and roll ballroom was concentrated on this cat back in the corner. And Stephen like saw that and went over to him and drained him astrally, like telephathically, and took all that juice and flung it at the Grateful Dead. And the Grateful Dead just came on, you know, and just started playing really loud and got really stoned and the cat petered out. He's really good with energy.

E: On an individual basis, like you, as a typical guy, what is your relationship to him?

G: I work at the gate so I get to see him pretty often. As far as how often do we get feedback on how our energy thing works, I don't know, we see him every now and then.

S: You mean you go to him when you're in trouble.

G: Sure, he's our confessor too among other things. We go in and we say, we've got this on our soul and . . . I'm really learning a whole lot about him. I started off, and he was my teacher and I've been coming in closer to him and closer to him, and I really feel him be my friend, like somebody I can just relate to, and just say Hi. At one end he's really human and a man and at the other he's just infinite. That's pretty far out.

Sunday mornings he leads sunrise services following a 45-minute meditation in an open field, everyone facing the sun as it comes up over a series of wooded ridges. Stephen goes off to lecture frequently at nearby universities and makes publicity tours for his books. His philosophy is thoroly expressed in his book *Caravan*, (see Appendix 2). The Farm proves that that kind of vision can work. It's an American fantasy becoming real.

Here are some facts and figures about The Farm that may be of interest to readers of the book *Caravan* and of people interested in details of what one commune is like (as of Summer, 1972). No smoking, no drinking allowed. LSD is forbidden, but natural psychedelics and marijuana are permitted. If you start living with a woman, you're automatically engaged; and if she becomes pregnant, you must get married. Stephen performs the marriage and is legally licensed in Tennessee. There are some "four-marriages" on the Farm and one "six-marriage," which is Stephen's own. The couple is the basic unit of the commune, and couples themselves can marry other couples, hence four-and six-marriages. These multiple marriages are like other marriages in that they are intended for life, and are not entered into lightly. All babies born on The Farm are delivered at home by teams of midwives, and they've had about 50 babies so far. (Their very first newborn fatality occurred while we were visiting.) When you come to live on the farm you turn over all your possessions and assets to the Farm, including your car, money, property, anything you have. Incidentally, these rules of living on The Farm are called Agreements.

A construction program is underway: There's one apartment house called the Adobe House that has six couples in it, each with a private bedroom with loft, while everyone shares a central living area, kitchen area, and sundeck. There's one house for a four-marriage and three or four other dwellings, all beautiful and creative structures designed by an architect who belongs to the commune. The rest of the members so far live in tents, busses, or miscellaneous shelters, all of which are comfortable. Other buildings constructed so far include the bath house, which was the first building built and a beautiful piece of architecture which is being copied by the state in a local park; a community kitchen where the field hands eat during the day; a newly constructed laundry; a giant dome-shaped community hall and kitchen under construction; and miscellaneous outbuildings. There's also the original building which was there when The Farm was bought, called The House, and is used as a school, information center, office, and book distribution warehouse.

Stephen is 37 years old. Altho a semi-diety, everyone knows him personally and has no particular awe of him but rather a warm admiring friendship. They believe he is doing what he was meant to do, but they know he needs all of them to help him do it. In this sense no one feels any less important than Gaskin, and in fact there is a common feeling that he is sort of slave to their will. Gaskin himself has no money or assets. His books consist entirely of transcriptions from his lectures and the profits are shared equally by everyone in maintaining the farm. Gaskin is thus dependent on The Farm and its members for all his needs.

Sexuality on The Farm is a curious business because there's scarcely a trace of it; the atmosphere is almost asexual. There's a tight morality structure but a complete sense of security, honesty, and trust. All personal possessions are always out in the open, and there's no fear whatever of theft. Everyone makes a special point of always telling the truth, yet with utmost friendliness and compassion. In fact, "compassion" is one of the key words on The Farm and one heard many times each day. Women on The Farm are responsible for the spiritual leadership of the couple or family group. The man is instructed to learn from his woman and follow her in matters of spirituality. If he becomes too egotistic or doesn't respect the woman's leadership, Stephen orders him to move into what they call "the rock tumbler," which is a bachelor's tent. The erring gents then stay there until their rough edges are rounded off. Interesting . . .

FRUIT HARVESTING AS IT IS
by Joe Gaspers

In Hood River Valley, Oregon, the fruit harvest begins around August 15 and runs on into late November. Bartlett pears come in first, followed by DeAnjou pears and then apples. There is usually at least a week — sometimes longer between Bartletts and DeAnjous and another week between DeAnjous and apples. This week or so in between each type of fruit is perfect for tripping around the area and also rests your sore back and neck. Picking pears and apples is hard work. A full bag of pears weighs around 50-60 pounds. The ladders are usually 12 or 14 footers. It takes about 30 trips up and down the ladder to fill a "bin." Growers pay from 5 to 7 dollars a bin. It varies from orchard to orchard depending on the yield. When the fruit is small and yield per tree is low the price per bin is higher. There is generally a lot of discussion among all pickers concerning the relative merits of one orchard's prices compared to another.

The "genuine" veteran pickers who know the valley and return year after year usually find an orchard which consistently has "good" trees with lots of fruit. The greenhorn who isn't in the know has to stumble around from orchard to orchard taking whatever jobs he can find. Once you have worked for a grower he will probably hire you again. I found the growers to be very mellow people. They depend on the pickers to get their fruit down, so most of them treat you gently. If you stick out the season —even if it's only one part of the season like all the Bartletts or DeAnjous — they will probably add on a bonus to your pay. My friend Sue and I found our first job after over a week of waiting and searching. We arrived right between the Bartletts and DeAnjous so we had to wait a week before they started picking at all.

The valley is about 18 miles long extending from the mouth of Hood River and the town of Hood River to the town of Parkdale. Mt. Hood — highest point (11,235 feet) in Oregon — looms in the background. It's always a surprise to look up from the top of your ladder (across acres of fruit trees) and see a snow-capped mountain only a few miles away.

The fruit ripens first down close to Hood River, so picking starts there and the activity gains momentum as more orchards ripen further up in the valley towards Parkdale. During the first few days there aren't many jobs available so it's best to find a place to hang out until more orchards start to pick. The only way to get a job is to go from orchard to orchard inquiring. It pays to return too, because there is a large turnover.

We asked everyone we met about jobs. Just about everyone will gladly give you some advice — good or bad. We were very near to giving up but our luck changed and we found a place to stay at an orchard in Parkdale that had not started picking yet. We had started asking about empty cabins — just for a place to stay. We got a hot shower and slept in a bed (first time in two weeks). The next day we investigated another orchard that we had heard was going to start picking that day. Our luck held and we were off and picking. There were no cabins available then so our boss rented the cabin we had stayed in the night before!

The next 6 days we just picked pears and learned about good trees and bad trees. The trees were mostly bad — on some days the two of us barely made two bins all day. He paid us $7 per bin, but it was very frustrating trying to pick trees that hadn't been pruned properly or just plain didn't have many pears to pick. In a good tree you can bring down a full bag every trip you make up the ladder and you can pick the whole tree from only six moves of your ladder, or so says one old-timer I talked to — "Why, 'Speed-ball Bailey' down the road picks 12 bins a day easy!," I kept hearing. I picked as hard as I could and got only four one day.

The older fruit pickers tell many stories of heroic picking feats. Anyway, we got to know our landlord while we picked in the first orchard and he hired us to pick for him when he started. As it turned out we had two days off in between. I spent one of those days at a gas station giving my Volksie a quick valve job. The second orchard was a little more inspiring — we did have a little more experience but the trees were more well-cared for and consequently had more fruit which was easier to get to. Also we lived right in the orchard along with the other pickers and got to know them better than our fellow workers at the other orchard. Everyone was friendly — although there were a few prejudices towards hippies and Mexicans, but very mild by most standards.

Our cabin, one of four, was a 10 x 15 shack (obviously not built by a carpenter) with an old wood cook stove, a bed, and a table and two chairs. Funky in the loosest sense of the word, but we spent $2 of our hardearned wages at one of the many local second-hand stores and decorated it with curtains over the dirty windows and a few pictures on the brown walls. It was actually very cozy — we spent several rainy days inside. I baked bread and even canned some pear honey — a tasty concoction of pears, sugar, pineapple, and coconut — the recipe for which we got from the wife of our boss. For those who are into it, there is lots of free fruit for canning. All the fruit that falls or gets dropped to the ground is left to rot because it is bruised, but it is perfectly okay for home-canning. Canning supplies are easy to get — everyone does it.

Our second employer paid us a bonus of 75 cents per bin because we stayed through the DeAnjou harvest from beginning to end. He also had apples but we were anxious to move on. I've heard that money-wise, it is more profitable to pick apples than pears. The reasons being that apples are red (except Golden Delicious) and therefore easier to see and generally grow thicker on the trees. Golden Delicious apples are very fragile and therefore trickier to pick but usually pay more per bin so it evens out in the end.

The work gets monotonous and hard, and the pay sometimes seems not to be worth the effort, but the orchards and surrounding country are fantastically beautiful. By late September the snow starts creeping down the slopes of Mt. Hood, changing its features day by day. Find an orchard with a view of the Mountain and nothing else will matter. Your life will slow down, surprisingly, even though you might spend your days hustling up and down your ladder. An orchard is a very magical place — it has a quieting effect on your soul.

I have rested here
and must remember
to leave behind
gentle vibrations
tho i've struggled here.
It is night now
Tomorrow on the road
We say good-bye to you,
        Strangers
who we never touched.
There are no tears.
I must leave behind
only gentle vibrations
for this chaotic place
for this dying
        silly
        love lost
        lonely
        alone
        place
and for all who i never
        saw here
here are the kisses and
love we couldn't give.

Birmingham, Alabama

HIPPOCRATES

Medical Matters

From Band-Aids To VD

15

FIRST AID
AUTO ACCIDENTS
OTHER ACCIDENTS
ILLNESS
NATURE'S PESTS
INSECT PESTS
ANIMALS
PLANTS
BIRTH CONTROL
VENEREAL DISEASE

Accidents, illnesses, and miscellaneous infections such as VD occur anywhere, of course, even at home in bed. But for the traveler, medical matters are frequently complicated by the strangeness of the environment, distance from a doctor, and ignorance. This chapter covers the most common medical matters affecting vagabonds.

FIRST AID All travelers should carry a first-aid kit designed to meet the needs of their particular situation. The contents of the kit will be different for motorists than for mountaineers, for example. You should have some basic knowledge of first aid, either in your head or in the form of a book or pamphlet accompanying the medicinal goodies. For motorists, car-campers, and bikers, I recommend either the *Emergency Medical Guide* or The Better Homes and Gardens *Family Medical Guide* whose first-aid section is the best I've seen. For backpackers and outdoor types, try *Mountaineering Medicine.* (See the *Trips* Appendix under "Health.")

Any first-aid kit should include at least the following:

Adhesive compresses (Band-Aids), selection
Square compresses (2" to 4")
Roller bandage (1")
Adhesive tape (½")
Insect repellent
Aspirin tablets
Antiseptic ointment
(Scissors and tweezers if you don't have a
    Swiss Army knife)

In addition, you should add as many of the following items as indicated by needs and storage space.

Snakebite kit
Vitamins, B-complex and C (500mg)
Chapstick
Oil of cloves for toothaches
Salt tablets
Thermometer
Antihistamine for colds, insect bites
Antibiotics for infections
    (prescription item)
Poison ivy tablets or lotion
Diarrhea potion
Antacid tablets
Spirits of ammonia
Petroleum jelly
Baking soda
Sterile cotton
Prescription pain-killer
Alcohol, isopropyl
Eye ointment
More bandages and gauze dressings
Large triangular bandages
Tourniquet
Antiseptic soap
Baby oil
Motion sickness tablets
Needle
Special medicines
Safety pins
Whatever else you fancy

Whatever items you take in your kit, learn how to use them in caring for at least the most common ailments: Cuts, burns, blisters, splinters, bites, infections, etc. For example, there's no need to check the temperature of a wound by inserting the thermometer into it. (Your finger will do just as well.)

AUTO ACCIDENTS Unfortunately, there is an appreciable chance that your physical integrity will be violated as a result of an auto accident. For example, your left kidney may be perforated by a 1969 Ford muffler, maybe still hot. What can you do to prevent it? Here are some quick check-points.

* Get your car together before a long road trip. Bad tires or brakes, bum wipers, steering shimmy, all that . . .are stupid reasons for getting creamed.

* Seat belts and shoulder harnesses aren't used much but they do drastically cut the injury rate. Put them on at least once in a while; maybe you can gradually build up to a psychological dependence on them (take them to bed with you and strap in).

* Drivers cause most accidents. Not cars. So learn to drive. Stay awake. Auto accidents happen when the driver is tired and/or falls asleep. There's something weird about how people keep driving even when they know they're weaving around, how they'll play risky games at the wheel. It's something about human nature, but you ought to try to fight your poor judgement if there's something you want to keep living for. The best drivers are the ones who have learned to correctly judge their own driving and adjust it to the particular circumstances — like actually stopping if they're tired, at least for a jog or a nap; or slowing down in bad weather; or yielding up their precious egos by yielding the right of way; or not following too closely when and if they realize it.

- Drinking we also know about. Half of all hiway fatalities are caused by drunk drivers. Smoke marijuana instead; it probably isn't safe but it's far better than booze. (I've never even come close to having an accident when stoned, but on a few occasions I have forgotten my destination.)
- If you see an accident coming, GM engineers say you can reduce the impact severity (up to 80%) by doing the following: fold your arms; lean forward, place arms on the wheel (driver), dashboard (front passenger), or on the back of front seat (rear passenger); then cradle your head on your arms. Fully 70% of all auto injuries involve the head, so the idea is to keep it from getting banged around.
- Treatment of victims is a doctor's business, especially if the injuries are obviously beyond the curative powers of band-aids and aspirin. Put your efforts into getting help. Don't try to remove unconscious victims from a car except in cases of imminent or actual fire. Where bleeding is profuse enough to endanger life, attempt to stop it with dressings, direct pressure, or tourniquet. Keep the victim warm and quiet till help arrives.
- Motorcyclists should always dress for danger, with boots, leather clothes, and helmets. Put plenty of reflectors and reflective tape on your machine. Bicyclists do the same.

RESCUE BREATHING
Infants and Small Children (Through Age Four)
DO NOT WASTE TIME—SECONDS COUNT

1. Place child on back; lift neck and tilt head back—do not force. (Quickly REMOVE any noticeable FOOD or OBJECTS from mouth).

2. Encircle both mouth and nose with your mouth and blow gently to make chest rise (expand).

3. For INFANTS, use only puffs (an adult blowing very forcefully may cause damage to a baby's lungs).

4. Continue 20 breaths per minute without stopping.

5. If chest does not rise (expand), hold the child with his head down, pound firmly between shoulders; resume gentle blowing.

HAVE SOMEONE CALL A DOCTOR IMMEDIATELY

U.S. DEPARTMENT OF HEALTH, EDUCATION, AND WELFARE
Public Health Service

RESCUE BREATHING
Adults and Children (Five Years and Older)
DO NOT WASTE TIME—SECONDS COUNT

1. Place victim on back; lift neck and tilt head way back. (Quickly REMOVE any noticeable FOOD or OBJECTS from mouth).

2. Pinch nose closed, make airtight seal around victim's mouth with your mouth and forcefully breathe into victim until chest rises (expands).

3. Continue breathing for the victim 12 times per minute without stopping.

4. If chest does not rise (expand), roll victim onto side and pound firmly between shoulder blades to remove blocking material. Also, try lifting jaw higher with your fingers. Resume rescue breathing.

HAVE SOMEONE CALL A DOCTOR IMMEDIATELY

Division of Emergency Health Services

☆ GPO : 1969 O—351-635

OTHER ACCIDENTS Some of the sudden emergencies that could arise are wounds, fractures, drowning, respiratory obstruction, electric shock, burns, poisoning, gunshot, or even nuclear incineration. Obviously you can't be prepared to handle all of these problems, at least not simultaneously, but the more you know about emergency treatment the better. Certainly some basic knowledge of artificial respiration, splinting and bandaging, etc. could prove important. Bring a medical guidebook and supplies if your travels take you away from professional help.

However, accident prevention is something everyone can work at personally. Good judgment is what prevents accidents, and is the super-trait we should all try to develop. Life is a kind of obstacle course whose challenges are neither predictable nor short-lived. If we rise to the challenges instead of retreating from them, we find that we slowly develop a sense of judgment that makes the course both less dangerous and more interesting to run. Good judgment means weighing in each action what is to be gained against what can be lost, and finding a workable balance. It means not being in too great a hurry if that causes carelessness; not over-exerting yourself if it causes loss of alertness or strength; it means sometimes taking risks, but calculated instead of foolish ones; it means considering external circumstances like weather and internal circumstances like emotions. Most accidents are not acts of God, but examples of poor judgment.

ILLNESS Traveler's illnesses usually result from a switch in pattern or environment, releasing negative energy. They typically include diarrhea (certainly a release of negative energy), constipation, nausea, headache, sunburn, muscular soreness, insomnia, fever, and other upsets in your otherwise easy routine. Most or all are self-curing, but can also be avoided with proper care or mitigated with proper treatment.

Diarrhea is frequently a response to change, and nothing more. Change in diet, change in pace, excitement, fatigue . . .loosening up all over may temporarily loosen your bowels too. Lighten your diet and perhaps try a bum-stopper like Donegal. Don't worry about drinking the water in America. Occasionally staphyloccocal or salmonella food poisoning may be the trouble, especially when accompanied by nausea and abdominal pain. (The major sign is when several people who ate the same meal get sick.) Salmonella, the more serious of the two, also has a bonus of chills and fever. Meats (especially coldcuts and hamburger), dairy products, and poultry products are the most likely sources. Buying and preparing your own food is one means of prevention especially suitable for campers. Food poisoning can be quite severe, and medical attention may be required.

Constipation is usually associated with sedentary travel, especially if you continue to eat your normal rations of Creamed Gook and Fried Munch. Peristaltic paralysis after a while makes you full of shit and no fun at all, so work it out by regular exercise like afternoon hikes and evening platter-pushing.

Nausea when traveling could be from motion sickness, or a side-effect of fatigue and stress. Lie down; relax. Take a pill for motion sickness. If you're driving, and nausea combines with headache, dizziness, ear-ringing, or heart-pounding, you might be getting poisoned by carbon monoxide. Stop the car; get fresh air immediately.

Headache is again one of those non-specific ailments that could come from practically anything, but usually associates itself with fatigue and tension. Aspirins, relaxation, neck-head massage, and local heat are effective treatments singly or jointly.

Sunburn is of course easily prevented by the interposition of opaque objects between you and the center of the solar system. That sounds difficult, but actually isn't. Wear a hat and long-sleeved shirt in the sun. Pants too. Bandana. Use a sun lotion on hands, face, and nose. For high-altitude hiking, use glacier cream, which totally blocks the sun's rays. If you do get a bad burn, or even blisters, soak or bathe the burned area in cold water, apply a burn ointment (a baking soda paste works well) and compresses, drink lots of fluids, take aspirin, and rest up in the shade.

Soreness, tenderness, sprains, aches, bruises are all minor protests of a body unused to work. Relief is obtained by doing more of the same for a few days. In the meanwhile, local alcohol massage, aspirin, and rest should make it bearable.

Insomnia is self-curing. Relax. Get a good night's sleep.

Fever can mean anything except that you're well. I like to carry a thermometer with me in order to discover whether or not I have a fever when I feel rotten. It's very frustrating sometimes to suspect that you're sick but have no objective way to prove it to yourself. Traveler's fever usually results from colds, influenzas, infection picked up from being overly cavalier about basic needs of the body. Poor diet or no diet, overexposure to rain and cold, inadequate sleep and the rest of that syndrome, just naturally make you sick after a while. If possible, find a comfortable retreat from the road and wait it out as best you can. Aspirin, cold-relief tablets, antihistamine tablets might help. Prescription antibiotics will eliminate the fever if it doesn't leave by itself.

NATURE'S PESTS Insects, animals and plants can all bite you, and at least some of them will. The trick is to keep their appetite at the level of annoyance rather than ruination.

INSECT PESTS Insects are everywhere. In fact, they far outnumber all other living things both in quantity of species and members of species. Only two types of creatures are growing in number on earth — humans and insects — so it is inevitable that they cross paths all the time. (The inconvenience is only temporary. Scientists point out that the cockroach is the most successful species ever evolved on this planet — it's the oldest still around — and is certain to outlast humankind.)

In the meanwhile, we're still here and need protection from the more disturbing varieties such as mosquitoes, flies, fleas, ticks, chiggers, bees, hornets, spiders, scorpions — to name the most common pests.

Mosquitoes For people outdoors a great deal, like hikers and campers, a good insect repellant is necessary, and during swarm times, probably inadequate. Long-sleeved (thick) shirts and trousers are important, and in certain areas and seasons, a head net may be required. All tent sleepers should have insect netting on their tent. Many car-campers waste huge sums on built-in appliances for their vehicles but forget all about netting for their doors and windows.

On this last trip I started off without netting for the car. It was in the Ozarks that mosquitoes put the fear in me. So, at Ft. Smith I asked at the VW shop if they sold any prefitted netting for our bus. The man said, "No, we don't have anything like that here. I guess you need it in California." What a laugh that was. I went to a department store and bought a 5-sided mosquito tent (which was all they had), intending later to cut it up and tape it over the windows when needed. We camped that very night at a recreation area along the Arkansas River under dark clouds. We started supper but drops began to fall and we retreated into the car just about sunset. Then commenced the wildest storm of our trip — almost continuous lightning bolts illuminating a river of vertical water, while winds buffeted the car like a carnival ride. It was entertaining for a while, but the problem was that we had to keep the windows closed. Soon it became unbearably hot and humid inside, and I discovered that mosquitoes aren't bothered by rain at all. There was a cloud of them around the car waiting to come in every time any window was opened even a crack. In a short while we had 30 to 40 mosquitoes inside — a whole squadron — biting while we sweltered. I got out this mosquito tent and while fighting off the bugs, started cutting it up to tape over the windows. I got hopelessly messed up in the folds of the netting, finally cut out a piece too small, then another one that the tape wouldn't hold because the inside surfaces of the car were beaded with sweat.

Meanwhile the storm goes on, the mosquitoes are pouring in. Stephanie is trying to kill them with a swatter. The baby is screaming frantically. The lightning is flashing, thunder and rain fill the night, we're crazy with heat, sweat, and frustration, angry at each other, exhausted. Everything is underfoot in the car, the netting spread over everything, nothing can be put outside because of the rain. All in all, a nightmare. I should have arranged for netting beforehand, yes?

Bites from other insects such as *spiders* and *scorpions* can be prevented by sensible cautions as to where you thrust your hands and feet. Campers should shake their shoes out in the morning.

Ticks are 8-legged little buggers about ¼ inch long that are found most anywhere, but commonly are first seen on your skin, into which they've burrowed their heads. They can carry any of several diseases. Remove them by dabbing with oil or applying some heat to their rear ends. The idea is to get them to back out under their own steam. If they don't, remove with tweezers, not fingers. Treat the wound with an antiseptic. It's a good idea to inspect yourself frequently for ticks or better yet, have someone else do it. Shake out your clothing frequently.

Chiggers (also called "red bugs") are another very common bug, actually arachnid, related to ticks and spiders. However, they're too tiny to spot unless you really look close. They burrow into your skin, which inflames and itches like crazy. It's like a severe mosquito bite that unfortunately doesn't go away. Treat the bite with alcohol to kill the bug and wait until the itching stops — unfortunately not for about 4 or 5 days. Preventive measures include repellent, alcohol rubdowns, keeping exposed areas covered with clothing.

Incidentally, the effects of insect bites can frequently be alleviated by taking antihistamine tablets. External aids to relief are ammonia or baking soda solutions.

ANIMALS Dangerous ones include snakes, marine animals like jelly fish and sting rays, and the larger ones like bears.

Snakes are naturally disliked by most folks, but the poisonous varieties are relatively rare. Nevertheless, all back-country travelers and hikers should carry a snake-bite kit as a matter of course. Even if bitten, the vast majority of people recover (about one bite in 100 is fatal), even with no treatment. There are several types of kits available, and you should be familiar with the correct use of yours before it is needed. Incidentally, the cut-and-suck method is now considered by many authorities to be of slight or no value. The most important treatment is to keep the victim quiet. After that, apply a constricting band, tightening only until the first pain is felt (do not cut off blood circulation). Bring the doctor to the patient. If possible, refrigerate the wounded area with *fresh-water* ice or a spray-on refrigerant while waiting for the doctor.

Avoiding snakes is easy if you know about their habits and habitats. They travel mostly at night, and rest during the day — usually in bushes, brush, or foliage. Don't plow through the bushes if you can go around. Where ground cover is scarce, snakes will rest near rocks, ledges, logs, etc., — so always look where you put your feet. Wear boots, trousers, and long-sleeved shirts. Putting your hands in the bushes, under a rock, on a blind ledge are all poor practices, especially since hand and finger bites (also face bites) are more serious than foot or leg strikes.

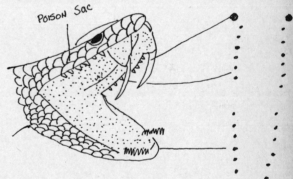

All poisonous snakes have fangs that leave two distinctive puncture marks, in addition to other teeth marks in parallel rows. If the fang punctures are present, the snake bite is venomous and treatment must be given. All poisonous American snakes (except the very rare coral snake) can be recognized by a pair of pits on the head — deep cavities lying between the eye and nostril on both sides. Also, they all have upright (not round) pupils in the eyes. See what they look like in a museum. If someone is bitten, don't waste time chasing the snake. Start treatment immediately.

Stings from marine animals such as rays, catfish, and others can cause painful wounds. Remove the stinger and suck out the wound; soak the limb in hot water. Another ocean swimming hazard is the jellyfish. Usually a jellyfish is not sighted but its presence can sure be felt. One wrapped around my chest when I was in my teens, and I remember the pain quite clearly. Serious cases may require hospitalization but in most cases, treatment to relieve the pain is all that's needed. Apply dilute ammonia water or vinegar, then Epsom Salts.

Bears Outdoorsmen usually encounter bears only when they're stealing food. Always keep food out of reach, preferably suspended from a tree branch with a rope. Bears think nothing of tearing a backpack to shreds, literally, to get a candy bar or soup package. Don't leave garbage lying around your camp and avoid spilling food on your sleeping bag. If you come upon a bear, just ease away or around it (don't run). Usually it'll mosey off first anyway. If a bear enters your campsite at nite, let it be. It'll wander off by itself. In grizzly-bear country, you should put a bell on yourself or your pack so you'll never take a bear by surprise. A startled bear is the one that tries to kill you. If it knows you're coming, it'll always clear out.

PLANTS The most troublesome are poison ivy, poison oak, and poison sumac. Learning to recognize and avoid them is the best course of action. Wear covering clothing. If exposed, immediately wash the affected areas with soap and water. If you know you're susceptible, carry along a relief ointment, prescription pills, or antihistamines. There are immunizing pills that work successfully for some people. Try them first.

Unless you have a good field guide and experience, it's not too wise to start eating all the wild plants you suspect are edible. There are over 700 poisonous plants in America, including many common plant varieties. It's best to learn to identify edible plants under the tutelage of an expert. Some guidebooks to edible plants are listed in Appendix 1 under "Herbs and Plants."

Other Bites All animals living in their natural state should be left unmolested. If bitten by an animal, the chance of rabies is present — more than half of all cases result from bites by wild animals. Any warm-blooded animal may transmit the disease, but the most common are bats, then racoons and rodents. Leave wild animals alone, especially if they appear abnormally tame or behave peculiarly.

BIRTH CONTROL Vagabonds, especially teens and twenties, should think about how to prevent the production of unwanted little vagabonds. Contemplating the possibility of sexual encounters while traveling is part of the fun, whether or not the sex actually happens. However, it frequently does, and birth control is thus an important matter, especially for female vagabonds. However, birth control is not solely the woman's responsibility. Men should routinely carry condoms (rubbers) as part of their traveling kit, and routinely use them.

It's a blessing all around when women use birth control methods, but never take it for granted. If you're about to convene sexual congress and you're a man, ask about birth control matters before plunging in unawares. If you're a woman, it's especially important that you be prepared, either by using some birth control method, or by insisting that the man use a condom. (If necessary, carry your own for free distribution.) The reason for all this, of course, is that the world already has a sufficiency of people who owe their existence to cold-hearted fucking. Even too many from warm-hearted fucking. Have a care. Respect your lady by not thoughtlessly impregnating her. Respect your baby by creating him or her as part of a loving plan, not as a vagabond's accident.

Women today have a potent arsenal of sperm-fighters at their disposal: The pill, which is easy and reliable, but distrusted; the loop or IUD which works well and can now be successfully installed in non-mothers; the diaphragm, which is somewhat awkward; and foam, which is messy and not altogether reliable. Also the rhythm method, which doesn't work too well despite the Pope's approval. If you anticipate sexual vagabonding, avail yourself of one of these methods. Otherwise, keep either your fingers or your legs crossed.

THE Hand OF the EYE . Seeing feelings BLOOM

CHILDBIRTH

This is not a suggested vacation activity nor necessarily a vagabond adventure. It's just a way of directing your attention to our last book, *Two Births* which describes in words and photographs the home delivery of our daughter Sierra, and the home delivery of Ona, the daughter of our dear friends Eugene and Janet. We think this is an educational book, an inspirational book, and we hope you'll read it when and if you're ready to have a child. Or when you're ready to rediscover your own birth. Really.

Two Births, Janet Brown, Eugene Lesser, Stephanie Mines, photographs by Ed Buryn, Random House/Bookworks, 1972, $3.95 paperbound ($6.95 hardbound).

VENEREAL DISEASE (VD) This not only hurts in your groin but injures your self-esteem. Total prevention of VD is easy: Abstain from sexual relations and dirty toilet seats. However, to rephrase and pun the old saw, "Abstinence makes the fond grow harder," so what about us indulgers? It's still easy to avoid VD if you pay attention to basic personal hygiene. The most effective VD preventive is the use of a condom, especially for gonorrhea, commonly called "clap." (A syphilitic chancre may lie outside the area covered by the condom and hence still transmit the disease.) If you don't use them, at least perform the following ablutions Men: As soon as possible after sex, take a leak (to cleanse the urethra of VD germs) and wash externally with soap and water. Women: Douche with vinegar or other mild solution (soap tends to wash out the normal bacterial flora you need).

Good judgment in your choice of sex partner used to be one of the main preventives but people on the move frequently can't check out their new friend's references, and with today's more relaxed sexual mores, they wouldn't matter much anyway. The fact is, however, that VD has reached epidemic proportions. Young adults are especially susceptible, and vagabond travelers certainly need to be aware of the dangers and take all recommended precautions. The nicest people in the world frequently have VD; someone's personality is no indication of their social diseases.

Symptoms If you do get clap, here's how to tell: Men will experience burning urination and a pus discharge from the penis from two days to a week (usually 3-6 days) after sexual contact. Women generally have similar early signs but not always. Their later sign will be pelvic inflammatory disease (PID) which causes acute abdominal pain and/or discharges. The primary sign of syphilis infection is a hard painless sore or chancre at the site of germ entry, usually the genitals or lips, but perhaps anywhere on the body skin. This appears from 10 to 90 days after exposure, but usually

within 3 weeks. The chancre may go unnoticed, and disappears by itself with no treatment. The secondary symptoms appear a few months afterwards and typically include a general body rash and mouth sores. The disease is still easily curable at this point.

Treatment If you suspect you have VD, the best place to go is the Public Health Department of any large city you happen to be passing thru. The service is always free, or near free, so don't be afraid of cost. If you have VD, they'll treat it or refer you to a doctor who will. There are no hassles or embarrassments in public VD clinics. I've gone lots of times for checkups, and have always found the experience interesting. I only had clap once (from a dear and unsuspected friend, I might add) and it was easily cured in a single treatment at no charge. Free clinics are another place to go, but most will refer you to the local public VD clinic anyway. Private doctors, of course, are another source of treatment but will charge you for their time and shots, of course. Don't skip a checkup if you have the tell-tale signs. Since untreated VD can ultimately lead to sterility, disablement, or death, it's crazy to avoid treatment, particularly when it's so easily cured at no cost.

Many cities across the country are establishing Sex Information telephone services that answer inquiries about anything at all having to do with sex. This is another source to check out if you have any questions. Ask the local operator if there is such a service in their area. At this writing, the cities with such services include San Francisco, Seattle, New York, Boston, Newport (Rhode Island), and Chapel Hill (North Carolina).

<u>Lice</u> A related subject is "*crabs,*" or pubic lice. These little nits are commonly the souvenirs of sexual intercourse with a stranger. (However, they are also easily picked up by sleeping in strange infected beds, so even celibate travelers can get them.) If you start to itch a lot in the pubic region, strip down and do a survey of your private parts. (Contemplation of the navel is called omphaloskepsis; I don't know what contemplation of the pubes is called.) Examine carefully what appear to be freckles or tiny spots, especially if they move when disturbed. To get rid of them, make a stop at a drugstore and ask for a topical treatment like Cuprex or Pyrinate (the latter works real good). Crabs are embarrassing and uncomfortable but easy to get rid of (usually just one treatment does it). Your clothes and bedding have to be laundered too.

Head lice and body lice are rare in America but can be picked up by habitually sleeping in lousy beds and not bathing. Treat with the same stuff as for pubic lice.

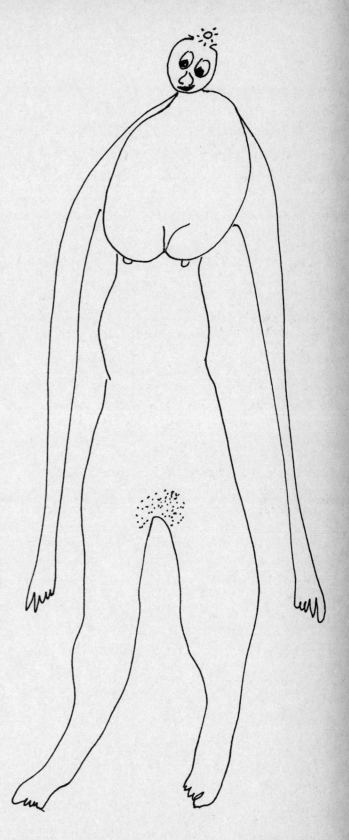

Terminal Topics 16

Miscellany And Conclusion

DOPE AND THE VAGABOND Marijuana is probably here to stay. Its illegal use has increased rapidly in recent years. As an issue it primarily concerns young people who use it both as a tool for expansion of consciousness and as an act of rebellion against the established order. Vagabonds therefore have a natural affinity for marijuana inasmuch as they use travel as a tool for expansion of consciousness and, in some measure, as an act of rebellion against the established order. It has often been said that travel is a drug and, indeed, so it is. It changes patterns, releases energy from patterns.

However, I'm only concerning myself here with the practical aspects of marijuana: using it, buying it, selling it, growing it. There's nothing intrinsically wrong with marijuana use other than that it's illegal. As I currently understand it, there are no side effects proven to be damaging, while the positive effects are generally viewed as beneficial. The main value of marijuana use is the feeling of euphoria and of relaxation that follows. Since we live in a society that is characteristically full of tension and notable for its disapproval of pleasure, it

isn't surprising that marijuana should become popular as a kind of counter-reaction. However, overuse or dependence on it can become an extreme position also. Hopefully the future will see an amelioration of both extremes into a reasonable middle view.

Meanwhile, the main practical consequence of using marijuana is its illegality. You should carefully weigh whether using marijuana is justified in certain parts of the country. Vagabond travelers such as hitchhikers and motorcyclists—as well as anyone who is youthful, long-haired, or bearded—are widely supposed to be marijuana users. If you fall into any of these categories, you're automatically more subject to spot-check and searching than other travelers. Therefore, carrying marijuana with you ("holding") may be a substantial risk. If a police search leads to the discovery of marijuana on your person, you certainly face at least great inconvenience and more than likely a trial and subsequent jail term. Jail sentences of ten years are still being meted out for first offenders in parts of the country, while in other parts multiple offenders dealing large amounts serve minimum time or go free.

The situation is extremely messed up to say the least. The best advice I can give the user is to carry only a small amount if you carry any at all. Stay alert and be ready to dump it or swallow it at a moment's notice. Generally, bringing your own isn't necessary because wherever you go you will discover someone who's got some if you want it. Of course, you should be leery of buying it from a stranger. If possible, don't buy it at all. Smoke somebody else's or bum a little to take with you. If you do buy, make it only a small amount. As a general rule don't buy from anyone who you haven't seen smoking it. Buying from one person in a large group of smokers is also pretty safe. Use your own intuition. If for any reason it doesn't feel right, simply don't buy. There'll be another and better opportunity along shortly.

Selling dope, except to close friends and relatives, is not recommended. In the end it's only profitable for professional dealers, since in that case the rewards are presumably worth the risk. But for your average penny-ante dealer, you're taking substantial risks for trivial rewards. Forget it.

Growing your own is the best possible source of supply. If you take proper precautions, you reduce the risks to practically nil. Also, by artificially controlling the growth environment and thru proper selection of seeds, it's possible to grow more righteous dope than you can buy. Of course, it requires a stable scene, but we all have that at one time or another. The best place to grow marijuana is in a completely controlled environment, completely away from windows or gardens where it might be spied and reported by nasty neighbors. Basements, closets and attics are all good places. Several books are available which describe the cultivation of marijuana in detail. See Appendix 1 under "Marijuana."

In many American states, notably in the midwest and the south, marijuana grows wild by the roadside. Under another name hemp—marijuana was, of course, grown as a commercial crop in the United States for many decades. The advent of manila fiber long ago killed the business, but many of the plants go marching on. The trouble is that most of this wild hemp is very low grade stuff for smoking and won't get you off.

POLICE AND THE VAGABOND There's a natural affinity between the policeman and the vagabond, but it's not a particularly good one. Anyone who's traveling in a carefree way, enjoying himself on little money, is obviously an object of suspicion for any good old-fashioned policeman anywhere. There are various police statistics to point out how many hitchhikers, for example, turn out to have criminal records. But we never hear about the immensely larger number who don't. Vagrants are also generally considered to be dangerous criminals, and in practice not much distinction is made between vagrants and vagabonds.

When stopped by police for any reason, you should be cooperative and respectful, but also ready to stand up for your rights. Most policemen in America are doing the best they can at what is a frustrating and occasionally dangerous job. It's their business to be suspicious and it's up to you to make them change their minds. Behind a protective armor of uniforms, guns, helmets, sirens, badges, and coldness, they're anxious to be related to as people. Hostile or sadistic cops who can't be reasoned with at all represent a minority; they're not characteristic of the average American policemen. If you do get a bad-ass, you have to play it by ear and do the best you can.

Identification: Policemen are friendlier if you can prove to them that you're really you. So, always carry ID, and the more impressive, the better. Everyone should carry a driver's license or some other unquestionable piece of identification such as a student ID card, passport, or other official-looking document with your photograph on it. Men should carry their draft cards or discharge cards to prove loyalty to your country and obedience to your draft board. For hitchhikers, especially, a letter of reference from some respected authority is a useful thing to carry. For example, a statement from your local chief-of-police saying you have no criminal record is a nice thing to be able to show the cops if they stop you. If you're a minor, a letter from your parents may keep you from being suspected as a runaway. The letter should give a phone number for authorities to call. The next kind of official-looking paper to carry is called money. In case you didn't know it, a checkbook doesn't count for much while you're traveling. Travelers have a difficult time cashing checks anywhere. Credit cards are excellent: No one with a credit card can be completely un-American. One of the main uses of money while on the road is to prevent you from getting jailed as a vagrant. Vagrancy is one of the catch-all charges that police use to punish anyone they don't like. Of course, it can't be applied if you have the money (usually about $20). Loitering, the other blanket charge, can be avoided by not standing in one place. If you have no other means of transportation, at least walk.

APPEARANCES Trying to keep yourself looking neat and respectable is a good idea, but isn't necessary in most places. The country is full of horror stories about how long-hairs are waylaid and shaved, about how bearded hippies are mistreated and fucked over, and certainly there is some basis for these stories. But the practice is not so widespread as the rumors would have you believe. There are literally thousands and thousands of long-hairs crossing the country at any given moment in a variety of ways, and only the tiniest percentage are hassled.

Remember, there are also tramps with flappy trousers, drunken down-and-outers, seedy characters minus arms and legs. There are strange-looking straights with facial tics, suit-and-tied uptights, tie-dyed groovies, sport-shirted louts and polka-dotted angels, cowboys of all ages and descriptions, hikers with packs and boots, fishermen with hooks in their hats, and lizard-skinned matrons with helmets of teased-and-sprayed hair. They come in all colors of clothes and skins, they come in all

kinds, these Americans. Everybody belongs, more or less. Whatever you look like, there'll be places where you feel more conspicuous and less wanted than others. If so, stay low and hang loose. Don't shout insults and spit on the floor. Act normal. It'll be OK.

The heart of the American tradition is to take people one at a time for what they are, and not what they seem to be. Most Americans still practice that kind of tolerance. The rednecks and low-brows who go out of their way to trouble strangers are the real freaks in America, and usually are psychologically insecure people. They are messed up but they are not the mainstream of our society at all. On the other hand, don't expect to receive any medals for your long hair or beard. It's safe to say that wherever you go, you will meet people who are sympathetic to you no matter how freaky you look. You can usually spot them because they'll look something like you. All travelers, no matter what their style, come in for a certain amount of suspicion from the authorities and from natives too. The traveler is always seen as a potential trouble maker, simply because he's a stranger. The suspicion is aggravated if he looks like a stranger or acts in ways different than the locals are used to. For that reason, vagabonds with packs, with beads or beards, with run-down vehicles with psychedelic paint jobs, with motorcycles, are all somewhat more liable to be stopped and interrogated by police, and to generally attract attention wherever they happen to be. You should expect this as a consequence of trying to assert your independence. Freedom is not easily won. There will always be someone questioning your right to it, or making it harder for you to exercise it. Even in America, a land supposedly dedicated to freedom, it doesn't come easy. However, bear in mind that even with the recent growth of fascism in America, we are still much better off than most of the world. The truth is that Americans still enjoy more personal freedom and show more tolerance toward each other than virtually anywhere else in the world. Really.

Off The Tape
MARY RAINO

If you want to see America the way it was, if you want to see the beauty and richness of a culture we destroyed — the Indian culture — if you want to see the Southwest at its very finest, then Santa Fe, New Mexico is the place. Here's where Indian culture, Spanish culture, Mexican culture, American culture, the climate, the look and feel of the Southwest, the romance of the old days, and a contemporary flowering of the arts, all combine. Even filled with tourists, it's beautiful. The tourists somehow rise to the level of Santa Fe, rather than bringing it down as they usually do. The museums are among the best in the country, certainly the best in their specific areas: Indian culture and Southwestern history and artifacts. The chief museum is located in the central plaza downtown, the center of the town's social, historical, and cultural life and is the oldest public building in America, dating back to 1610. A visit there should suggest to you that the Indians represent one of America's great human resources, one of its richest historical chapters, and some of the finest

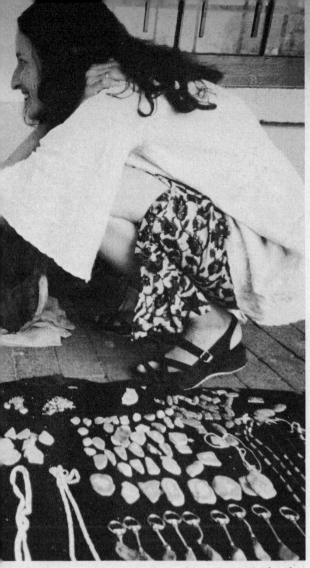

artists in the world. The city has obviously fought, with notable success, the incursion of commercial interests into the downtown area. It has retained a flavor from another time and place as well as can be done in contemporary America. It's far from perfect, but it's the best we have and all of America is richer for it.

One of our really high experiences here in Santa Fe was meeting Mary Raino, an old Pueblo Indian woman, one of the many here who spreads her beads and turquoise stones underneath the breezeway of the Palace of Governors facing the plaza. We took a liking to a necklace she had and came back four times during the same day, interspersed by meals and museum visits, to see if we could bargain her down further. We ultimately got the necklace with only 10% off but the experience of dealing with her, of finding out something about her, was a rich human adventure. We photographed her with our baby, and she wound up in the end throwing in a free loaf of bread for us. We thought she was great and I suspect she wound up liking us pretty well too. Everybody felt pretty good about it, and Santa Fe is the kind of place where that kind of feeling can happen.

THE AMERICAN INDIAN No book about America, no trip to America, can bypass the American Indian. Their influence is everywhere. There is hardly a place in American that does not have some Indian names, some Indian history that is associated with it. More than half our states are named after Indian tribes or words. The white man may have replaced the Indian in all surface aspects, but the influence of the American Indian is profound, and can never be wiped out. As you travel thru America, you'll be reminded again and again of your Indian heritage. By seeing Indian artifacts, museums, and Indians themselves, it becomes apparent that there is a great disparity between our culture and theirs. Indian life really was richer in its beauty, its style, its beliefs. Everything they made was practical and yet beautiful.

Become aware of the Indians is, without exaggeration, the most important thing you could do on your trip to America. I learned in traveling around America that I had been denied real knowledge of the Indians, and especially their message for contemporary America. Meridel LeSueur says that the Indians are not only our past but our future as well. They had no word for religion in their vocabulary because everything was religion, every action was a religious action, everything was endowed with religious significance. Today, America and Americans are at the start of a great new spiritual era. The Indians represent what we may yet become. One of the very best books about Indians, called *Indians of the Americas,* by John Collier, Sr., the first humanitarian head of the Bureau of Indian Affairs (and father of John Collier, Jr., a teacher whose influence completely changed my own life), said the same thing. Despite our best efforts to destroy the Indians thru acts of genocide, their value for us is the message they kept intact despite their tragedy (which is also our tragedy). Their message is to keep faith with God as He is revealed in the earth and the natural rhythms of life.

Off The Tape
INDIAN LOVE SONG

We visit a young white couple — lawyer and teacher — living on an Indian reservation in New Mexico:

Ellen: Yes, I think there is outright hostility. I quit my teaching job because of hostility. I didn't want the job because I thought a Navajo should have it, tho Paul can't really quit his job because there is no Navajo lawyer. But basically I think all the Navajos, deep down — and not so deep down — you know, everyone we know is hostile to whites. And it's healthy, you know, it's a healthy attitude. There's no hostility towards an individual. I think there are some Navajos who really like us; the hostility is just toward white people in general. I think they see white people as someone to rip off. You know, like at the Grand Canyon, they rip off white people who buy beads from them for three times what they're worth. Right now the unemployment rate is 70%. If every job that was held by a white person were held by a Navajo you'd still have a 40% unemployment problem. Actually the children now, this generation is the first generation that will be educated. And something is going to explode when they're ready. You know, a lot of them are really proud to be Navajos — you know they're not being sent away like previous generations. There's a lot of focus on the whole culture and stuff. And when they get out of school and can't find a job, something is going to happen.

Ed: But they want jobs within their own tribal area?

Ellen: Yeah, they want to stay. But there aren't jobs, there are a lot of jobs that could be created, but there are a lot of white people who shouldn't be here. Obviously there aren't enough jobs anywhere. As a result there's a big alcoholism problem. And the land is ruined.

Ed: Why is the land ruined?

Ellen: From over-grazing and no water. In 10 years, they predict the land is not going to be able to support any sheep. And another thing is that Navajos are just not very together. If they were more together as a people they could probably do a lot more things, more cooperative ventures.

Some understanding of Indian history and Indian culture will reap huge dividends for the traveler. Start by reading and studying so that you will bring knowledge to the Indian sights, villages and museums, and the people themselves. One reason for reading and learning about the Indians is to reduce your guilt. Unquestionably, the average American feels unconsciously guilty for what was done to the Indian nations in much the same way as Germans feel guilty for what they did to the Jews. There's so much false pity for the Indians inspired by guilt that it destroys the possibility for relating honestly to them or their culture. This effectively shuts you off from not only the Indians, but from America and yourself, too. What I'm saying is that deeper knowledge of the Indians is a requirement for finding out who you are as an American.

American Indian culture was incredibly diverse, much more so than ours today. For example, it included five hundred languages, and even more life styles and beliefs. What they shared in common we're only now coming to appreciate. The most significant Indian wisdom was living harmoniously with Nature. In the end this will turn out to be the most important ability of all, and we need now to turn to the Indians as our teachers.

Appendix 1 under "Indians", contains a list of Indian information sources. Find out about these amazing people and discover their trails and monuments as you travel to America. You will be amazed and moved.

BLACK TRAVELERS It would be pretentious, or even racist, of me to say much about black travelers because I'm neither black nor beautiful. I can only say that for the first time, black people (formerly known as Negroes) are starting to have the freedom to travel. If you are a black reader, I can only urge that you take the opportunity to see your country and accept the fact that you will still encounter occasional prejudice and inconvenience as a result of the color of your skin. No one can honestly deny that we live in a racist society, yet it is true that things could be far worse. They have been much worse. The need to travel as a quest for self-identity applies as much to black travelers as to anyone else, perhaps even more so. You should see as much of America as you can to get a realistic picture of your country. You will find much cause for despair, but some for hope as well (which is just what everyone will find). The country is changing, a new consciousness is coming. Certainly there is a new black consciousness, a pride in being distinctively different. Black people are trying to explore the difference, instead of trying to be like everyone else, which was patently impossible. We should recognize that people will always be different from each other, and concentrate instead on how much we're alike. Welcome to America.

Off The Tape
KAYENTA

We made several stops in Kayenta for our first real taste of Indian culture. We stopped in the cafe at the Kayenta trading post, and in a smaller store. The Indians have faces of incredible character. It's like being in Mexico. Their skins are dark, lined. The women and children wear long bright velvet skirts and jackets, blouses with long sleeves. Bright blues, bright reds. Here on the reservation they run everything. They clerk the stores, they're behind counters. I gassed up at a cheap dusty station on the outskirts of Kayenta, run by an Indian. His kids were inside, surrounded by hanging fan belts, watching an all-American, whitey program on TV, a situation comedy.

KAYENTA

The Indian women sit
outside the trading
company
on a bench in the shade.
They are wearing
green velvet shirts
and long layered skirts
and silver and turquoise.
They don't look at me
when I smile.

OLD GLORY

"Hello, remember me? Some call me **Old Glory**, some call me the **Stars and Stripes** . . . more than one aggressive nation has tried to haul me down, but they all felt the fury of this freedom-loving country . . . What has happened? I'm still the same old flag . . . But now I don't feel as proud as I used to. When I come down your street you just stand there with your hands in your pockets and give me a small glance and turn away. When I think of all the places I've been — Anzio, Guadalcanal, Battle of the Bulge, Korea, Vietnam — I wonder what's happened. I'm the same old flag but now I see children running around and shouting as I pass by. They don't seem to know who I am. I saw an old man take off his hat and then look around. He didn't see anybody else take theirs off so he quickly put his back on. Is it a sin to be an American patriot any more? . . . Well it won't be long till I'm on your street again. So when you see me, stand straight, place your hand over your heart. I'll be waving back."

signed/ 188th Tactical Reconnaisance Squadron, Arkansas National Guard

In the last few years, travel agencies specializing in black travel have appeared. I have no quarrel with this phenomenon, but at the same time I think that black travel agencies tend to perpetuate the same evils as whitey travel agencies. The TI wants money from blacks as well as whites. Dollars are not prejudiced. Remember that travel agencies are in the business of selling services and not experience. They are out to make a profit. Travel agencies will tend to book you into expensive hotels and expensive tours that guarantee you security, guarantee you a certain buffering from the most obvious kinds of prejudice. But nothing will guarantee you from prejudice because it still exists. If you travel on your own as a vagabond you'll still find prejudice, but at least you'll save yourself a lot of money. You'll also have a much realer experience, one that will mean a lot more to you. Incidentally, there is a black guidebook to America—Appendix 3—*USA Guidebooks.*

THINGS TO BUY As you travel thru America, you will be made aware by various advertising technics of regional specialties for sale. For example, Indian crafts is one broad category wherever there are Indian settlements. Other offerings include petrified wood in the southwest, antiques and scrimshaw in New England, blankets and quilts in the Ozarks, sombreros and blown glass, baskets and rocks, not to mention edibles like Georgia peaches and pecans, New England maple syrup, Florida oranges, regional produce all over. Some of this stuff can be bought at a good price, and frequently it can't be bought anywhere else. For example, you won't find shops selling scrimshaw (carved whalebone) anywhere else except around New England. It's not really bargains you're looking for, but a good time. So plan to stop and see local shops and roadside stands. Browse what they have; see what you can bargain for. No matter where you go in America, somebody is always selling something and it's a mistake to drive by with your nose in the air. Get in there and whale!

TIPS FOR FOREIGNERS Altho I've traveled abroad extensively, when it comes to talking about America to foreigners, there isn't much I have to say. The mechanical differences of culture relating to money and mail and transportation services and things like that are relatively minor. You can pick them up easily and enjoyably, so I won't go into that. These kinds of things are well covered in some guidebooks described in Appendix 3. Most visitors to America are students, but whether or not you're a student, it's a good idea to stay close to American students. They have far more interest in foreigners than most Americans and are in a position to give you the best money-saving advice about places to stay, to eat, and other matters.

For a foreigner, unquestionably the most interesting thing about America is Americans. Meet as many of them as possible. Meeting them is quite easy, but understanding them will prove challenging. Americans are contradictory people, not only because of their diversity but because of certain contradictory elements in their cultural and group personalities. On the one hand, they're over-friendly and hospitable. On the other, they're distant and impersonal. Tolerance is an important prerequisite for traveling in America. It's easy to misunderstand Americans and to be insulted by them. They are only a partially formed people and often are strangers to themselves. Most Europeans who stay awhile come to love America and Americans, but it does not happen immediately. Foreigners are usually very impressed at first, then disillusioned, and ultimately won over as they come to understand what is actually a most complex but quite human personality. Welcome.

DOCUMENT YOUR TRIP. Any kind of experience, even the most mundane, is worth recording in some way. When preserved it grows rich thru further analysis and examination. Much more depth can thus be obtained from all experience. But travel experiences, especially, should be documented in any way that is possible for you. The best ways are always the most personal. Thus, keeping a journal or diary in which you record your most personal impressions is a way of attempting to understand what is happening to you and represents a record that you can look back upon later with the benefits of hindsight. I recommend that all vagabonds take a journal with them, even if you've never done so before. Keeping a journal is a habit that pays rich dividends for minimum effort. Your journal does not have to be all in writing. Put postcards in it, paste in theatre tickets and other souvenirs of travel, make places in it for snapshots, do drawings or sketches if you feel like it. Use it any way your imagination leads you to. One of the great benefits in keeping a journal is not in the fact that you can read it later, but that it clarifies in your own mind what's happening to you while it's happening. By making some attempt to sort out your experience in real time, you get more out of it. It's that simple, and it works.

Photography is, or course, another way, and probably most popular of all. Don't knock the camera as merely a tourist accessory testifying to a plastic consciousness. Looking thru the viewfinder is a visual discipline that makes you see things better. It also forces you to relate to your subject. Whenever possible, don't photograph things that are already on postcards; simply buy the cards. Photograph what is meaningful to you, like people you meet, traveling companions, and special sights. The combination of a journal and photographs is the best way to maximize your vagabond experiences.

For serious photographers, I recommend a good 35 mm camera with two lenses, a wide-angle (24 to 35 mm) and a short telefoto (85 to 135 mm). A fast black and white film such as Tri-X affords the most flexibility in all shooting situations. Color film is more expensive and requires more critical exposure, so I don't recommend it. You should think of photographs as energy fragments. They enable you at some later time to reconstruct whole energy fields from which you can draw fresh energy and fresh conclusions.

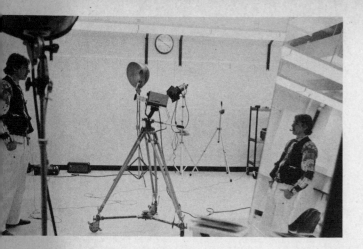

Off The Tape, Tape & Tape
VAGABOND GOES TO SCHOOL

In Laguna Beach I looked up Ron Sukenick, a spacy and sophisticated dude who's written some great and very funny novels with titles like *Up* and *Out* and teaches a class at the Irvine campus of the University of California. He interviewed me on videotape for his class:

Ron: It's an interesting situation because Ed is now on his actual vagabond tour, and in fact you're writing your book.

Ed: Yes, this is one of the major experiences of my book right now.

R: So what this means is that we're in Ed's book, Ed of course is in Ed's book, and I'm in Ed's book....

E: And you're all in my book.

R: Yeah, right, so we're all in this book and on top of that, or in opposition to that, Ed is also in our tape that we're going to make in the performance of our class.

E: Media reality is a new kind of reality that's never happened before — it gets to be very confusing.

R: What it suggests to me is that in other words you're making something up that we're going to be in and we're making something up that you're going to be in.

E: Right, and it's further confused by the fact that, for example, I can photograph you while this is happening.

R: Why don't you do that?

E: Yes, I will. I had thought of doing that.

R: When we get these two versions it might be interesting when Ed's book comes out to get a copy of Ed's book to see how you are in Ed's book and of course you'll see the tape and know how Ed is in our performance. Question is: Which version is the truth?

E: Right. It's further confused by the fact that I'm recording this also on my own tape recorder.

R: Oh that's terrific. (Laughter)

E: It's right here in my pocket. In other words, we're all completely interlocked in some strange way.

R: But also it brings up another interesting thought, which is that we're in the process of making several different versions of this conversation. There's gonna be the version in our performance, the version in your book, the version in your tape recorder. And then there's the actual version now as it's happening. Which however, is perhaps the least tangible. Since it's completely imbedded in our experience it's the one that's least available.

E: Certainly the one we have the least control over because it is the real event and it's the only one that's not predictable.

R: That's true and it's also the real event and is the only event that in effect you can't think about.

E: Well, this gets into my line . . . The real event then is a certain kind of learning experience and there's no substitute for the real event. The outgrowth of this real event — whether they are on video or aural tape or in my camera or written down — can be used in more structured kinds of learning. But there is a kind of learning that comes from experiencing the real event and that's what I write about, that's what my books are about, that it's only in learning to come to grips with reality that you can get a certain kind of sense of self, and a certain kind of your sense in the world and you can do that by traveling, for example. That's a traveler's reality.

R: Right, okay. Well, the only thing is I wonder is with all the versions, do you really think there is a real event?

E: Um.

R: Because I mean obviously it's something that happens, but it occurs, it passes and it's gone.

E: Well, perhaps that's irrelevant. Perhaps. I don't know. I hadn't really thought about that before, uh, I think that events themselves, whatever their nature, can be structured any way you like. Somehow it's the end product — what does it mean? We all know that events take place, we all know we exercise certain control over them, but they really have no meaning, they're irrelevant except as they mean something.

R: Right, but the meaning is something that we make up. In other words, it's another version. In fact, — and we haven't talked of this yet — we speak of this event as it's happening, and the reality — we can make a further analysis — that is, it's not only the version of our performance in your book, but there's also the version as we go along that I have in my head and you have in your head, uh, and the very fact that I don't know you very well. In a sense, I'm making you up, and same thing, you're making me up. So just as we have the video version, the tape version — we each have our own versions. So it seems that the further we look the more the thing that we call reality is dissolved. And we're left only with a series of versions. So, I guess what I'm really getting at is that when you start using electronic equipment maybe what you begin to get is a focus on what reality really consists of, that is different versions that are running through our heads like video film running through a camera.

E: Well, I think that reality events are some kind of energy concentrations and to the extent that when you tape them or record them or play with them with media tools, those are energy concentrations also, and that's why they can simulate events or be events in themselves because they, from an energy definition, they are as real as events are. So I like to think about the world in terms of energy, and even in terms traveler's energy. So, it seems to work from that. This idea of defining your world as you go is very real to me at the moment. Because I find that people want me to play certain roles as I travel, they want me to play a certain travel role and they respond to me in ways that they define and I respond to their definitions of me. Sometimes I resist that definition, sometimes I accept it, but as I move thru time and space there is ahead of me an energy wave that transforms the world as it comes into contact with me. So that I make my world at this interface between my energy boundary and the world. And I think everyone does that, so we all are surrounded by an energy boundary and within that boundary we make up the world as we go along. But as we encounter other energy boundaries, sometimes our own are constricted or redefined or whatever and that's the interplay of energy. One of the reasons for today's conflict, I think — is that a lot of people are marshalling their energy at security points. They are trying to reinforce their security patterns, they're trying to strengthen patterns of life which are basically security patterns, so that energy is being misused actually. It's not being used to meet the real risks, it's being used to meet the risk of change. In other words, if you face the risk of living (and living

is full of risks), then you are using your energy in a productive and creative way because you exercise yourself. If you use your energy to protect patterns already established, you are not using yourself, in fact you're using your energy to avoid using yourself. In other words, you're letting the patterns work for you. You use structures instead of using your own direct resources.

R: Well, there are two things there. First of all the idea that the patterns that we've learned may be patterns that no longer fit the nature of our experience.

E: Yeah, right. Well, this is the nature of patterns. You see, I think of travel as a way of testing patterns. All patterns have to be tested periodically because patterns are simply models of reality. They're models we set up to cope with reality and reality is an ever changing flux, so naturally it's perfectly logical that we have to periodically test our patterns, throw out those that are becoming inefficient, modify ones that need to be changed, etc. But there's no means that people have systematically to test patterns — so I like the idea of travel as a systematic means of testing patterns, because when you go off to a foreign land or when you put yourself in what is basically a new situation, you again fend for yourself, you strip yourself of the patterns you have which normally protect you from your environment. And you see how that happens, you see what works.

R: But then there's another thing. Maybe we have been educated in the wrong pattern, the patterns that have stopped being tested and are unproductive and too rigid. Another thing behind that may very well be that all patterns should be thrown away. That is, we may be in a phase of culture that's so fluid and so changing so quickly that the very idea of pattern or of things that are formally worked out have to be left behind at every moment. I have an idea that form is simply your footprints in the sand. If you look back and concentrate on the footprints behind you — sort of encase them in concrete — then the cutting edge is lost and you become much too rigid, much too brittle. And I thought, well, maybe that's what that little biblical story of Lot's wife meant. She looked back over her shoulder and became a pillar of salt — she became too rigid to encounter the experiences ahead and she was looking back to the destroyed city.

E: That's a good metaphor for that, for people who look to the past for their security, who cannot face the future and who literally solidify.

CONCLUSION. In conclusion, I find I don't have much else to say—no smash ending, no final philosophical pronouncements. This book represents a large and personal part of me, and I offer it to you in friendship and with affection. Writing it, I realized that my role as a popularizer and spokesman for vagabonding has made me less a vagabond than ever. So I've determined not to write any more about vagabonding, just do it. Maybe we'll meet somewhere on the road. God bless you. God bless America. Happy Vagabonding.

The last days of traveling,
a need to mark them,
the end of a saga
that has no end.
and i could write forever
about beginnings and endings
within and without me
in this universe of wheels.
in denver and shasta
in idaho and tennessee
in taos and albuquerque
clear eyed and gentle people
wherever we go.

and i say to you
write your songs of the journey
sing them with friends
'round country campfires
all the world wide
and your search will be met
by other brave searchers
in this heavy metallic world.
while the sun keeps on shining
while the rivers keep on flowing
there will be songs to keep singing
and singers full of love.
So bow your head in thankfulness
for the blessings upon us
recieve Gods fragrant energy
and flourish in joy.

All relationships
are
KARMIC.
All relationships
are
EQUAL.
There is really only
ONE
relationship.

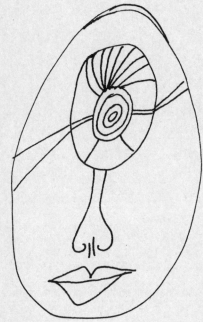

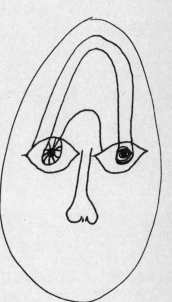

Appendixes

Information Sources

These appendixes represent, we hope, an exciting compilation of information about America. For all that's here — and it's a lot — it's still only a beginning, a taste of what America has to offer.

Contents

1 — AMERICAN TRIPS

2 — USA BOOKSHELF

3 — USA GUIDEBOOKS

4 — TOURIST INFORMATION OFFICES

5 — OIL COMPANY SERVICES

6 — TRAVEL CLUBS

7 — NATIONAL PARKS

8 — NATIONAL MONUMENTS

9 — NATIONAL FORESTS

10 — WILDERNESS AND PRIMITIVE AREAS

11 — OTHER NAT'L RECREATION FACILITIES

12 — OUTDOOR EQUIPMENT SUPPLIERS

13 — STATE LIQUOR LAWS

American Trips

Things to see and do: selected information sources. Let this list stimulate your imagination, getting you in touch with that wild fun "trip" you've always wanted to do. It's pretty sure that, whatever the trip, you'll be able to do it in America.

AMUSEMENT PARKS

Six Flags Over Texas
Arlington, TX
(between Dallas and Fort Worth)
450 years of Texas history make one big fantasyland.

Six Flags Over Georgia
I-20, just beyond the limits of
Atlanta, GA

Six Flags Over Mid-America
St. Louis, MO

Knott's Berry Farm
8039 Beach Bl
Buena Park, CA
See Chapter 10 for a history of one of the first big amusement parks in America.

Disneyland
26 miles S of Los Angeles
Anaheim, CA
Endless extravagence from the world of Mickey Mouse.

Disney World
15 miles SW of Orlando
Lake Buena Vista, FL
See Chapter 2 to find out how this enormous place is just a "small world."

Coney Island
Surf Ave from Ocean Parkway to 37th St
Brooklyn, NY
Beach, boardwalk, amusement park. Four roller coasters. This is America.

Enchanted Forest
Old Forge, NY

Fantasy Island
2400 Grand Island Blvd
Buffalo, NY

Ocean Beach Park
Long Island Sound
New London, CT
Good old-fashioned amusement park, complete with fireworks and free bath-house (great if you need to clean up from the road).

Belle Isle
Detroit, MI
An island park on the Detroit River, between the US and Canada.

Windmill Island
Holland, MI
This town was settled by Dutch refugees in 1847 and still retains the feel of a village in Holland. The amusement park is on the site of a 200 year-old working grainmill.

Cascade and Elwood Parks
Washington Ave
Elyria, OH
Water cycle rides on the Black River.

King's Island
Lebanon, OH
Has the world's largest roller coaster.

Pleasure Island
Eagle River, WI

Seaquarium
Rickenbacker Causeway
Miami, FL
Porpoise and sea lion shows, boat rides, and a monorail. More fish than you knew existed.

Fabulous Fairyland
US 441
Pigeon Force, TN

Calico Ghost Town
Barstow, CA
A restored mining town, dusty and dry in the summer heat, it gives you a sense of what the world was like then. Saloon, burro rides, tramway.

Santa Claus Land
Santa Claus, IN
There are lots of "Santa Claus Lands" across America—Santa Claus having become a kind of American god because he gives away expensive things. This one, like the others, is really a potpourri of gigantic toys to tantalize your children into wanting more—wax museum, hall of famous Americans, deer farm, miniature circus, and toys and dolls from all countries.

Magic Mountain
2610 N Tourney Rd
Saugus, CA

Land of the Magic Lamp
Moab, UT

Atlantic City, NJ has five amusement piers. It's convention city—an American trip if ever there was one. Vaudeville, bands, water sports, rides, games. You shouldn't miss it.

Land of Oz
Linville, NC

Dogpatch USA
Harrison, AR
L'il Abner, Daisy Mae and the folks—go ahead, play at being a hillbilly.

Lumbertown, USA
Brainerd, MN

This, of course, is only a selected list. Discover your own amusement parks in America, and tell us about the special ones.

ANTIQUES

Dover Books, 180 Varick St, NY 10014, publishes a series of books on antiques. Send for their catalog. Some titles are: *Shaker Furniture, Teach Yourself Antique Collecting, The Gentle Art of Furniture Faking, Decorative Antique Ironwork, Steigel Glass,* and more.

Golden Guide to Antiques, Western Publishing Co, 1220 Mound Ave, Racine, WI 53404, $1.25.

Antique and Auction News is a newspaper published by Joel Sater, Box B, Marietta, PA 17547. $4 per year. Articles about antique sales, places to buy and sell.

Something old to keep around

ART WORKSHOPS

The deYoung Museum, Golden Gate Park, San Francisco, CA 94117, has art workshops and organized field trips. This year they are offering craft tours of Pueblo, Papago and Zuni Indian reservations; photography workshops in Death Valley; raku firing workshops in Pt. Reyes. Write them for information.

The John C. Campbell Folk School, Brasstown, NC 28902, offers courses in folk crafts (woodcarving, instrument making, music, folk dancing, Appalachian folk songs). Two week workshops in woodcarving, weaving, and wrought-iron work are also available. Write for their catalog.

Summer Arts Study Center, Box 280, Grand Rapids, MN 55744: workshops in crafts, drama, music, dance, sponsored by the University of Minnesota.

For a directory of craft shops, studios and workshops, get the *American Crafts Guide*, Gousha Publications, Box 6227, San Jose, CA 95150, 1972, $3.95.

See "Festivals" in this appendix for a list of American craft fairs. Also see "Music Festivals" and "Theaters."

AUTO FACTORIES

For tours of major auto factories contact:

City of Detroit
Department Report and Information
    Committee
1008 City County Building
Detroit, MI 48226

BACKPACKING
(also see "Hiking" and "Walking")

Chapter 13 is about hiking and backpacking.

The Backpacker, Albert Saijo, 101 Productions, 79 Liberty St, San Francisco, CA 94110, 1972, $1.95. Highly recommended. Readable, terse, complete.

Pleasure Packing, Robert S. Wood, Condor Books, 1000 Mariposa, Berkeley, CA 94707, 1971, $3.95. Good nitty-gritty information on equipment, cooking, clothing, trip planning, packing.

Handbook of Wilderness Travel, George S. Wells, Colorado Outdoor Sports Corp, Denver, CO 80216, 1968, $3.25. Describes all of America's public outdoor areas; also contains basic backpacking information. An important reference.

Outdoor Survival Skills, Larry Dean Olsen, Brigham Young University Press, Provo, UT 84601, 1967, $2. How to build a shelter, find food and water, make a fire, fish . . . everything you need to know for living on and from the earth without modern tools.

Camping and Woodcraft, Horace Kephart, Macmillan Co, $6.95. First written in 1917, this book is quaint, to say the least. Full of old wisdoms and funky-isms, but not too useful anymore.

The Golden Book of Camping, William Hillcourt, Golden Press Inc, 850 Third Ave, NY 10022, $3.95. "Wonderfully clear information" says The Whole Earth Catalog.

At Home in the Wilderness, Sun Bear, Naturegraph Publishers, 8339 W Dry Creek Rd, Healdsburg, CA 95448, $3. Whole Earth Catalog says: "unusual outdoor book."

Backpacking, R. C. Rethmel, Burgess Publishing Co, 426 S Sixth St, Minneapolis, MN 55415, $3.95. Good, practical advice for the completely inexperienced. Lots of useful tables and lists. A thoro technical manual.

Advanced Camping Techniques, James Johnson, David McKay Co, $3.75. "A good book, maybe the only book in its field that really accomplishes very much. Maybe the only book in its field." (Whole Earth Catalog)

How to Stay Alive in the Woods, Bradford Angier, Macmillan Co, 1956, $.95. Interesting but not of much relevance to modern backpacking.

Going Light—With Backpack or Burro, David Brower, Sierra Club, 1962, $3.50. One of the first basic backpacking guides. Good stuff.

The Wilderness Route Finder, Calvin Rutstrum, Macmillan Co, $4.95. Basic navigation anywhere.

Food for Knapsackers and Other Trail Travelers, Hasse Bunnelle, Sierra Club, $1.95. Basics of buying, packing, and preparing food for backpacking trips. Information on how to do it for large groups, too. Some information on edible wild plants. List suppliers of lightweight foods.

Cooking for Camp and Trail, Hasse Bunnelle and Shirley Sarvis, Sierra Club, 1972, $3.95. Recipes for exotic trail dishes like Lamarou, Flemish Beef Stew, Argentine Roast Beef Ribs.

Some other interesting titles:

Backpacking One Step at a Time, Harvey Manning, Touchstone Press, Box 81, Beaverton, OR 97005, $7.95.

The Hikers and Backpackers Handbook, W. K. Merrill, Winchester Press, 460 Park Ave, NY 10022, 1971, $5.95.

Backpack Techniques, R. Mendenhall, La Siesta Press, Box 406, Glendale, CA 91206, 1968, $1.

Back Country Travel in the National Park System, a pamphlet from the US Government Printing Office, Washington DC 20402, $.35.

If you'd like to go on a group backpack trip, contact one of these organizations:

Sierra Club Wilderness Outings
1050 Mills Tower
San Francisco, CA 94104

The Wilderness Society
A Way to the Wilderness Outings
4260 East Evans Ave
Denver, CO 80222

Two new magazines about hiking, backpacking, and related wilderness activities:

Wilderness Camping
1255 Portland Place
Boulder, CO 80302
(One year: $4)

Backpacker
28 W 44 St
New York, NY 10036
(One year: $6)

The newsletters and magazines of the wilderness organizations are another source of information (see "Wilderness and Environmental Organizations").

For equipment, see Appendix 12, "Outdoor Equipment Suppliers."

I am a BALLOON a child HOLDS my STring on the earth.

BALLOONING

Ballooning, Peter L. Dixon, Ballantine, 1972, $1.50

Book of Balloons, Eric Norgaard, Crown, 1972, $7.50

ABC's of Avionics, Lex Parrish, Howard Sams & Co, 4300 W 62nd St, Indianapolis, IN 46268, 1970, $3.50.

Open The Sky, E. M. Quittenden, Pergamon Press, Elmsford, NY 10523, 1965, $1.50.

Balloons: The First Two Hundred Years, Antonio Sotomayor, Putnam, 1972 $4.69.

Basic Aeronautics, Merrill E. Tower, Aero Publishers Inc, 329 Aviation Rd, Fallbrook, CA 92028, 1952, $4.50.

Modern Airmanship, Neil D. VanSickle, Van Nos Reinhold, 1971, $15.95.

BASE CAMPING

See BACKPACKING; HIKING.

BATTLEFIELDS

Almost all significant battlefields in this country are state or national monuments; see Appendix 8 (National Monuments) and Appendix 11 (Other National Recreation Facilities). Also consult your gas station road map for location.

BEACH ACTIVITIES
(See also "Shell Collecting")

Golden Guides to *Seashores, Fishes, Rocks and Minerals,* Western Publishing Co, 1220 Mound Ave, Racine, WI 53404, $1.25 ea.

BICYCLING

Chapter 11 is about bicycling.

Bicycle Camping and Touring, Tobey Publishing Co, Box 428, New Canaan, CT, 06840, 1972, $3. A really fine book about touring and camping.

Anybody's Bike Book, Tom Cuthbertson, 10 Speed Press, 2510 Bancroft Way, Berkeley, CA 94704, 1971, $3. Thoro, easy and fun to read. Complete general information about your bike. And from the same author and publisher, *Bike Tripping,* 1972, $3. How to ride bikes and have fun.

The Complete Book of Bicycling, Eugene A. Sloan, Simon and Schuster, 1970, $9.95. Straight-forward and well-organized compendium of what you need to know to become a biker.

North American Bicycle Atlas, Warren Asa, American Youth Hostels Inc, 1970, $1.95. Maps, guided tours, food suggestions. Indicates locations of youth hostels.

Clear Creek Bike Book, Hal Aigner, New American Library, 1972, $2.95.

The Bicycle Book, Earth Action Council, Box 24390, Los Angeles, CA 90024, 1972, $.50. Buying, maintenance, theft prevention, repairs. For 10-speeds only.

Biking for Fun and Fitness, Award Books, 235 E 45th St, NY 10017, $.95.

Aerobics, Major Kenneth H. Cooper MD, Bantam Books, $1. A planned system of bicycle endurance exercises.

A Handbook on Bicycle Tracks and Cycle Racing, Huffman Manufacturing Co, Box 1036, Dayton, OH 45401. Free.

How to Fix Your Bicycle, Helen Garvey, Shire Press, 69½ Harriet St, San Francisco, CA, $.50. "Good preventative maintenance for 3 and 10 speeds" says the New Earth Catalog.

There are also some regional bike-tour books like these:

California Bike Tours, Gousha Publications, Box 6227, San Jose, CA 95150, 1972, $2.95. And, from the same publisher, *Bicentennial Bike Tours* — tours to celebrate America's bicentennial, $3.95.

Bicycling the Back Roads Around Puget Sound, Bill & Erin Woods, The Mountaineers, Box 122, Seattle, WA 98111, $4.95.

50 Northern California Bicycle Trips, The Touchstone Press, Box 81, Beaverton, OR 97005, $3.95.

And, if you still need more books, send for a free catalog from:

Books About Bicycling
Box 208
Nevada City, CA 95959
or
National Technical Information Service
Springfield, VA 22151
(They've listed all references to bicycles since 1900.)

You can get a lot of help and information from bicycle clubs, many of which have their own publications and sponsor group bicycle trips.

Bicycle Institute of America
122 East 42nd St
NY 10017.
They have a lot to offer, like free do-it-yourself plans for car bicycle racks, a free catalog of bicycle movies, safety purlications, and information about how to start a bicycle club. They publish the "Bicycle Clubs Directory" which lists national and regional clubs in all areas of bicycling: touring, racing, bike polo.

Amateur Bicycle League of America
4233-205th St
Bayside, Long Island, NY

American Youth Hostels, Inc
20 W 17th St
NY 10011
In addition to publishing the *North American Bicycle Atlas,* listed above, they also publish *The Family Hostelling Manual* and the *Hostel Guide and Handbook.*

League of American Wheelmen
5118 Foster Ave
Chicago, IL 60630
or
5540 S Westmont
Whittier, CA 90601

International Bicycle Touring Society
846 Prospect St
LaJolla, CA 92037
Scheduled tours, bulletins, newsletters.

British Cycling Federation
26 Park Crescent
London W1 England

There are also some clubs specializing in bicycling matters:

Antique Bicycle Club of America
260 W 260th St
NY

Bicycle Stamp Collectors
1457 Cleveland Rd
Wooster, OH

Veteran Wheelmen's Association
Franklin Institute
Philadelphia, PA

The Wheelmen (High Wheel Riders)
32 Dartmouth Circle
Swarthmore, PA 19081

Unicyclists Association of America
67 Lion Lane
Westbury, NY

I know of two bicycling magazines:

Bicycling!
256 Sutter St
San Francisco, CA 94108
($6 per year)
and
The Two Wheel Trip
440 Pacific
San Francisco, CA 94133
($10 per year)

MY NAME IS BIKE.

RIDE ME.

but the bicycle industry has some publications which might be useful:

The American Bicyclist
461 Eighth Ave
NY 10001
($4 per year, $12 if you are non-industry affiliated)

The Bicycle Journal
3339 West Freeway
Fort Worth, TX 76101
($3 per year)

See Appendix 12—"Outdoor Equipment Suppliers" — for sources of general equipment, but to supplement that here are some specialty suppliers:

Bicycle Parking Racks:

J. E. Burk Co
US No. 1, College Bridge
New Brunswick, NJ 08901

Everwear Park Equipment
36535 W Highway 16
Oconomowoc, WI 53066

Rainwear for Cyclists:

Shaker Velo-Sport
18734 Chagrin BL
Cleveland, OH 44122

Bike Racks for Cars:

Gerard Metal Craftsmen, Inc
151 West Rosecrans
Gardena, CA 90247

JC-1 Industries
904 Nogales St
Industry, CA

These are shops that specialize in bicycles and bicycling equipment:

Eurocycle Inc
960 N San Antonio Rd
Los Altos, CA 94022

Wheel Goods Corp
2737 Hennepin Ave
Minneapolis, MN 55408

Big Wheel Ltd.
310 Holly St
Denver, CO 80217

Cyclo-Pedia
311 North Mitchell
Cadillac, MI 49601
($1 for handbook and catalog)

Stuyresant Distributors
404 E 11th St
NY 10009
(Catalog: $.75)

Turin Bicycle Co-op
2112 N Clark St
Chicago, IL 60614

Thomas Arenia
131 E 119th St
NY 10035

If you want to travel the bike trails of America and need maps or further information, write to one of the following:

Lake Washington Bicycle Path
610 Municipal Bldg
Seattle, WA 98104

Fairmont Park Bikeway
West Park
Philadelphia, PA 17131

Illinois Prarie Path
Rt 3, Box 1517
St Charles, IL 60174

Foot Circle Parks Trail
U S Department of the Interior
Washington DC 20240

Highline Canal Trail
1806 W Littleton
Littleton, CO 80120

South Mountain Park Trail
251 W Washington
Phoenix, AZ 85003

If you would like to see a bike trail designated in your area, write the Bicycle Institute of America (see above) and they will tell you how.

See "Museums" in this appendix for a list of bicycle museums.

BIRDWATCHING

The Field Guide Series, Peterson, Houghton-Mifflin Co, each $5.95, has several volumes on birdwatching. For birdwatching clubs in a specific area, contact:

National Audubon Society
1130 Fifth Ave
NY 10028

Friends of Animals
11 West 60th St
NY 10023

or the local Chamber of Commerce.

BOATING

Golden Guide to Power Boats, Western Publishing Co, 1220 Mound Ave, Racine, WI 53404, $1.25.

Handbook of Wilderness Travel, George S. Wells, Colorado Outdoor Sports Corp, 1968, $3.25. See page 42, "Outboard Cruising."

The Outboard Boating Club of America (307 N Michigan Ave, Chicago IL) publishes *Your Outboard Vacation Guide.*

Boat Owners Guide, Yachting Publishing Corp, Davenport, CA 95017, $1.95.

Federal Requirements for Motorboats, A publication of the US Government Printing Office, Washington DC 20402.

Boating Regulations in the National Park System, also published by the US Government Printing Office, $.40.

For information about the Arkansas River International White Water Boat Race write:

Fibark Boat Races, Inc
Box 762
Salida, CO 81201

For equipment, see "Outdoor Equipment Suppliers," Appendix 12. For related activities see "Canoeing and Kayaking" and "Float Trips" in this appendix.

BOTTLE COLLECTING

Bottle Collecting in America, John P. Adams, New Hampshire Publishing Co, 1 Market St, Somersworth, NH 03878, 1971, $5.95. And, from the same author and publisher:

Bottle Collecting in New England, 1969, $4.95.

Bottles (guide to identifying and pricing), 1972, $7.95.

Bottle Book, Bob Ashton, Exposition Press Inc, 50 Jericho Turnpike, Jericho, NY 11753, 1972, $3.95.

Poor Man's Guide to Bottle Collecting, Ferol Austen, Doubleday, 1971, $7.95.

Cembura and Avery (139 Arlington Ave, Berkeley, CA 94707), publishes the following:

Bischoff Bottles, $4.75.
Garnier Bottles, $4.95.
Jim Beam Bottles, $5.
Luxardo Bottles, $4.75.
A Guide to Miniature Bottles, $3.95.

From Old Time Bottle Publishers, 611 Lancaster Dr. NE, Salem, OR 97301:

Bottle Rush USA, $4.25.
Old Time Bottles Found in Ghost Towns, $2.50.
Redigging The West for Old Time Bottles, $4.25.

Bottler's Year Book 1972-73, British Book Center, Elmsford, NY 10523, $9.50.

BREWERIES

Falstaff Museum of Brewing
1920 Shenandoah
St Louis, MO
Free tours and refreshments.

Miller Brewing Co
4000 W State St
Milwaukee, WI

Joseph Schlitz Brewing Co.
235 W. Galena St.
Milwaukee, WI
                    and
11111 N 30th St
Tampa, FL
Guided tour begins at the Brown Bottle Hospitality Center
                    and
4791 Schlitz Ave
Winston-Salem, NC
                    and
1400 W. Cotton St
Longview, TX

Pabst Brewing Co
901 W Juneau Ave
Milwaukee, WI

Anheuser-Busch Inc
111 Busch Dr
Jacksonville, FL
    and
on US1 in Newark, NJ
    and
610 Pestalozzi St
St Louis, MO
    and
775 Gellhorn Dr
Houston, TX
    and
3000 Busch Blvd
Tampa, FL
This brewery is in Busch Gardens, an amusement park and zoo.

Walter Brewing Co
Hickory and LaCrosse Sts
Pueblo, CO

Lone Star Brewing Co
600 Lone Star Blvd
San Antonio, TX

Olympia Brewing Co
Custer Way
Tumwater, WA

Rainier Brewing Co
3100 Airport Way
Seattle, WA

BUS TOURS

Contact:

Greyhound Bus Lines
(Ask about USA Bus Pass, Ameripass and Amazing America Vacations.)
60 Seventh St
San Francisco, CA 94103

Continental Trailways Tours, Inc
1669 Broadway
Denver, CO 80202
    or
315 Continental Ave
Dallas, TX 75207

or check in the "Yellow Pages" for a local office.

CANOEING AND KAYAKING

Canoeing Waters of Northern California, Ann Dwyer, 125 Upland Rd, Kentfield, CA 94904, 1972. Also sold by Sierra Designs, Berkeley. Guided canoe trips with maps. A funky hand-made book. $3.95.

Kayak and Canoe Trips in Washington, Werner Furrer, Signpost Publications, 16812-36th Ave West, Lynnwood, WA 98036, $2. Printed on waterproof paper. Table of river classifications.

Adventure Trip Guide, Adventure Guides Inc, 36 E 57th St, NY 10022, 1972, $2.95, page 115: "Canoe and Kayak Trips."

Bark Canoes and Skin Boats of North America, Superintendent of Documents, US Government Printing Office, Washington DC 20402, $3.75.

A Whitewater Handbook for Canoe and Kayak, Appalachian Mountain Club, 5 Joy St, Boston, MA 02108, 1969, $1.50. From the same publisher: *New England Canoeing Guide,* $6.

Canoeing Textbook, Joseph L. Hasenfres, American National Red Cross, 1625 Van Ness Ave, San Francisco, CA 94109, 1956, $1.75. A booklet condensed from this textbook is available for $.50.

Pole, Paddle, and Portage, Bill Riviere, Van Nostrand Reinhold, 1969, $6.95. "This is the authoritative book on canoes and canoe-tripping. I paddled Northern Wisconsin lakes and rivers for six summers without learning a fraction of the useful information here."—Whole Earth Catalog.

55 Ways to the Wilderness in Southcentral Alaska, Helen Nienhueser, The Mountaineers, Box 122, Seattle, WA 98111, 1972, $7.95 (includes kayaking and canoeing).

Handbook of Wilderness Travel, George S. Wells, Colorado Outdoor Sports Corp, 5440 North Valley Highway, Denver, CO 80216, $3.25, Chapter 4: "The Canoe Trip."

The following books are available from Chicagoland Canoe Base, 4019 North Narragansett Ave, Chicago, IL 60634:

Basic River Canoeing, Robert McNair, $1.50.
Basic Rowing, Charles Russell, $.50.
Canoe Camping and *Canoeing,* Carle Handle, $5 each.
Canoeing, John Malo (an instruction book for young people), $1.95.
Canoeing Complete, Brian Skilling, $4.50.
Makens Guide to US Canoe Trails, J Makens, $4.95.
Canoeing Skills and Canoe Expedition Techniques for Teachers and Leaders, P E Williams, $4.
Fundamentals of Kayaking, Robert Evans, $4.
A Guide to Canoe Camping, Luther Anderson, $.95.
Living Canoeing, Alan Byde, $6 (has a chapter on home-made molds).
North American Canoe Country, Calvin Rutstrum, $6.95.
Paddling Kayaks and Canoes, $7.

When you order books from Chicagoland Canoe Base, include 20 cents for postage and handling. Illinois residents include 5% tax.

There are two magazines for the canoe and kayak enthusiast:

Amateur Boat Building
3183 Merrill
Royal Oak, MI 48067
($6 per year/monthly)

The American Canoeist
(a publication of the American Canoe Association)
4260 East Evans St
Denver, CO 80222

SaiLing on the water is like Dancing On the Ocean of LiFe.

If you are interested in undertaking a group canoe/kayak expedition, one of the following organizations can help you:

Sierra Club Family Canoe Trips
1050 Mills Tower
San Francisco, CA 94104

Canoe California
Box 61
Kentfield, CA 94904

Wilderness Society
4260 East Evans Ave
Denver, CO 80222

American Whitewater Affiliation
2019 Addison St
Chicago, IL 60618

United States Canoe Association
1818 Kensington
Fort Wayne, IN 46805

American Youth Hostels
2710 North Clark St
Chicago, IL 60613

These organizations can also answer any questions you might have about canoeing and kayaking.

Check in Appendix 12, "Outdoor Equipment Suppliers" to find a supplier near you, and here are some more who can answer your specific needs for kayak and canoe supplies—they all will send you their free catalogs:

Old Town Canoe Co
Old Town, ME 04468

Grumman Boats
General Sales Office
Marathon, NY 13803
(Whole Earth Catalog says they make the best aluminum canoe on the market.)

Chicagoland Canoe Base (see address above), also recommended by the Whole Earth Catalog, publishes a list of National Canoe Trails and midwest canoeing organizations as well as producing a good line of canoes.

Quicksilver Canoe and Kayak Kits
115 McGavock Pike
Nashville, TN 37214

Klepper Co
35 Union Square West
NY 10003
("Klepper is the best line of folding boats and kayaks" says Whole Earth Catalog.)

Dedham Kayaks Inc
Box 281
Milles, MA 02504

CAR CAMPING

Camping Around California: The South and *Camping Around California: The North*, Jim Crain and Terry Milne, Fifth Street Press, 1409 Fifth St, Berkeley, CA 94710, 1972, $3.95 each. Index to campgrounds with maps, some information for the first-time camper, sources of gear, list of environmental organizations. We used it while camping in California and it's good. And a new book from these authors: *Camping Around New England*, $3.95.

Leisure Camping, Camping Enterprises, 923 Dodd Rd, St Paul, MN, $3.95. Tells you how to convert a school bus to a family camping van.

How To Keep Your Volkswagon Alive, John Muir, John Muir Publications, Box 613, Santa Fe, NM 87501, 1969, $5.50. The Bible for VW owners.

Golden Guide to Camping, Western Publishing Co, 1220 Mound Ave, Racine, WI 53404, 1971, $1.25. Good general information.

Sunset Camping Book, Lane Books, Menlo Park, CA 1972, $1.95. "It would probably be a big help to the person getting started, but kind of a bore for the experienced camper." New Earth Catalog. And from the same publisher, *Sunset Western Campsites*. New Earth Catalog says about this one: "Regional but more complete. Includes several useful hints about camping in general."

Woodall's Trailer Parks and Campgrounds. See USA GUIDEBOOKS.

Roll Your Own (The Complete Guide to Living in a Truck, Bus, Van, or Camper), Jodi Palladini and Beverly Dubin, Collier/McMillan Co, 1973, $3.95. The nitty-gritty of buying a used bus: procedures, legalities, red tape. The heart of the book is the emphasis on the unique creation of your traveling-living space: what to do with beds, stoves, lighting, etc. What to take and where to get it. Trucking with children. How to get involved with people as you travel. Lots of quotes and photographs and words from people who have done it/are doing it. Also trucking in Canada and Mexico.

Camping Today, S Blackwell Duncan, Rand McNally, 1972, $3.95. It all reads like an advertising campaign for rec vecs. "The out-of-doors is everybody's campground" they say. I'm trying hard but I can't find any value in this book except that it teaches you to pretend—pretend you're an outdoorsman as you drive your Winnebago; pretend you're a man as you whip thru the backwoods on your mini-bike.

The Trail-R Club of America (Box 1376, Beveraly Hills, CA 90213), publishes books on trailering which I haven't seen (I should probably be thankful). Some of the titles are:

How to Select, Buy and Enjoy a Motor Home, Van Camper, Tent Top or Tent, Clinton Hull, 1970, $4.95.
Trailer Owners Manual, Lambert Eliel, 1969, $3.75.
Trailer Owners Driving Manual, Duane Newcomb, $2.95.
Trailer Trails in the Mid Atlantic States, $1.50.
Trailering in New England, Richard L. Hayes, $1.
Trailerists Cookbook, Charlotte Dawson, $2.50.
Trailering to Alaska, David Nelson, $3.95.
How to Buy Recreational Vehicles, John Kneasse, 1969, $2.95.

Another book which I haven't seen but which sounds interesting:

America's Camping Book (the Encyclopedia of Camping), Scribners, 1968, $10.

Plans and patterns for trailers and campers can be gotten for 50 cents from:

Glen-L-Campers
9152 Rosecrans
Bellflower, CA 90706

Camping and Trailering Guide is a monthly magazine about car-camping. Rajo Publications, 319 Miller Ave, Mill Valley, CA, $5.50/12 issues per year.

Camping in the National Park System, $.35 to the US Government Printing Office, Washington DC 20402.

For equipment suppliers, see Appendix 12.

For more information about camping, see "Backpacking" and "Hiking" in this appendix.

Also see Chapter 7 in this book, "Camping and Car Camping," and the USA Guidebooks Appendix.

CATTLE DRIVES AND COVERED WAGONS

Farm and Vacation Guide, Farm and Ranch Vacations Inc, 36 E 57th St, NY 10022, $2.50. Tells who to contact if you want to join a cattle drive or take a trip in a covered wagon.

CAVES

Introduction to Caving, John Thraikill, Alpine Rec, Box 54, Mt Vernon, NY 10552, $1.

Place Magazine (Box 2708, Menlo Park, CA 94025) is gathering data on caves of the United States.

Also, see SPELUNKING.

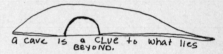

a cave is a clue to what lies BEYOND.

COMMUNES

Spiritual Community Guide (see "USA Guidebooks," Appendix 3).

How to Live in the New America, page 302-309, list of communes. (See "USA Bookshelf," Appendix 2)

Cooperative Communities, Kriyanda, Naturegraph Books, 1188 Chiquita Rd, Healdsburg, CA 95448, $1.50.

The Joyful Community, Benjamin Zablocki, Penguin Books, 1971, $1.45. Highly recommended by the Whole Earth Catalog.

Armed Love, Eliz Katz, Harper and Row, 1971, $5.95. " . . . through the profound maturity of his feelings and his gift for sharing them, Katz . . . communicates what is important in the hippies communal lifestyle and what is self-delusion."—LA Free Press.

The New Communes, Ron Roberts, Prentice-Hall, 1971, $1.95.

Communes USA, Richard Fairfield, Penguin Books, 1972, $3.50. Richard Fairfield is the founder and director of the Alternatives Foundation which publishes "Alternatives Journal" and "The Modern Utopian." His book is interviews and commentary from a tour of American communes.

"Alternatives Journal" is about alternate ways of living. It is an information source provided by Dick who investigates alternatives and tells you about them. Primary emphasis is on communal living and free schools, but there are articles about pollution, drugs, theater, sex, funding for projects, buying land. One year/5 issues/$5.50.

"The Modern Utopian" is a book series including:
Communes Japan, $2.95.
Communes Europe, $3.95.
In Search of Utopia, $3.95.
Utopia USA, $3.95.

Both "Alternatives Journal" and "The Modern Utopian" books are available from:

Alternatives Foundation
Box 36604
Los Angeles, CA 90036

For more about communes in general, see Chapter 14, "Staying Awhile."

For a list of spiritual organizations, some of which are communes, see this appendix under "Spiritual Centers."

CRUISES

Harman's Official Guide to Cruise Ships, Jeanne and Harry E. Harman III, Simon and Schuster, 1971, $3.95. A "how to cruise" guide with good information on what's available, how much to spend, how much you need, and how to get your money's worth. Lists and evaluates all cruise ships.

DUDE RANCHES

National Dude Ranchers Assoc
Box 1363 A
Billings , MT

Dude Rancher Magazine
2822 Third Ave N
Billings, MT 59101
(Publish a brochure listing dude ranches.)

Farm and Ranch Vacation Guide, Farm and Ranch Vacations Inc, 36 E 57th St, NY 10022, $2.50. Lists dude ranches with guest facilities.

ECOLOGY

Concepts of Ecology, Edward J. Kormandy, Prentice-Hall, 1969, $3.95. "This book is about the science, unhindered by rhetoric." Whole Earth Catalog.

The Population Bomb, Dr. Paul Ehrlich, Ballantine Books, 1968, $.95. "This book is the best first hard book that's around." Whole Earth Catalog.

Population, Resources, Environment, Dr. Paul Ehrlich, W H Freeman & Co., 630 Market St, San Francisco, CA 94104, 1970, $8.95. " . . . a 400 page textbook on the ecology crisis." Whole Earth Catalog.

The Environmental Handbook, Garrett DeBell, editor, Ballantine Books, 1970, $.95. The Bible of new conservation.

What To Do? What To Do?, Jo Robinson, 1535 S E Adler, Portland, OR 97214, 1970, $2.50. "If you know someone who doesn't know yet that there is an environmental problem, give them this book for Gound Hog Day." Whole Earth Catalog.

A Survey of Environmental Science Organizations in the USA, Ecology Center Press, 1360 Howard St, San Francisco, CA 94103, 1970, $5.50.

How to be a Survivor, Paul Ehrlich and Richard Harriman, Ballantine Books, 1971, $1.25.

Ecology At Home, 101 Productions, 79 Liberty St, San Francisco, CA 94114, 1972, $1.95.

The Breather's Guide to Invisible Air Pollution, Last Gasp Eco Press, 320-10th St, San Francisco, CA 94103, $1.25. "A handy little booklet about the various types of air pollutants." New Earth Catalog.

What To Do With Your Bad Car, Ralph Nader, Bantam Books, $1.50. "Nader and sidekicks go into great detail on course of action to take to get satisfaction and/or a new vehicle." New Earth Catalog.

Air and Water Pollution, Gerald Lienwand, editor, Simon and Schuster, $.75. A basic text if you want to know about this problem.

Two Sierra Club Books dealing with specific environmental crises: *Oil on Ice*, $1.95 and *Mercury*, $2.25. The latter contains a state-by-state survey of mercurial contamination.

Two classic books: *Silent Spring*, Rachel Carson, Fawcett Publications, $.75 and *Where Have All the Flowers, Fishes, Birds, Trees, Water and Air Gone*, David McKay Co, 750 Third Ave, NY 10017, $2.95.

Books about the wilderness concept:

The Sierra Club Wilderness Conference Books are:

Wilderness: The Edge of Knowledge, $6.50.
Wilderness and the Quality of Life, $6.50.
Wilderness in a Changing World, $6.50.
Wilderness: America's Living Heritage, $5.75.
The Meaning of Wilderness to Science, $5.75.

Wilderness and the American Mind, Roderick Nash, Canyonlands Press, Box 21021, Salt Lake City, UT 84212, $2.25. The wilderness concept traced from its beginnings.

Our Vanishing Wilderness, Mary Louise Grossman and John Hamlet, Grossett and Dunlap, $14.95.

A Sand County Almanac: With other essays on conservation from Round River, Ballantine Books, $.95.

Three publications of interest to those who care about our disintegrating planet:

The Environmental Monthly
420 Lexington Ave
NY 10017
($35 per year/12 issues)

Environmental Action
1346 Connecticut Ave NW
Washington DC 20036
($7.50 per year/bi-weekly)

For a list of wilderness and environmental organizations, and their publications, see this appendix under "Wilderness and Environmental Organizations."

Dream Farms come true.

FARMING

A lot of books and magazines have appeared lately about starting a farm, written for city people who are changing to a rural, often organic, life style. A few of them are:

First Time Farmer's Guide, William Kaysing, Straight Arrow Books, 625 Third St, San Francisco, CA 94107, 1971, $7.95; and, by the same author, *How to Live in the New America* (also listed in *USA GUIDEBOOKS*). The second expands on the first, giving you more ways to drop out and save money. The first concentrates on how to be a farmer and live cheaper, reaping a good life harvest.

Grow It!, Richard W Langer, Saturday Review Press, 230 Park Ave, NY 10017, 1972, $8.95. A beginner's guide to small farming: vegetables, grains, livestock.

Grow Your Own, Jeanie Darlington, Bookworks/Random House, Westminster, MD 21157, 1970, $1.75. One of the first of the do-it-yourself-farming books. Simple, helpful, and fun to read. Good list of sources at the back—where to buy fertilizer, kelp, ladybugs, like that.

Two magazines that provide up-to-date information on the back to the organic earth movement, mostly supplied by the readership:

"Mother Earth News"
Box 38
Madison, OH 44057
($5 per year)
For more about this magazine and some words about farming, see Chapter 14.
                and
"The Green Revolution"
Route 1, Box 129
Freeland, MD 21053
($4 per year/monthly)

Rodale Publications (Emmaus, PA 18049), publishers of "Organic Gardening and Farm Magazine" ($5.85 per year—essential for organic farmers), also publish books and pamphlets like the following. Write to them for a list of their publications.

These pamphlets are $1 each:

"Organic Fertilizing"
"Control Garden Pests Without Poison Sprays"

Country Gardener's Cookbook"
"Organic Foods Shopping Guide"
"Compost in 14 Days"
"All About Mulch"

Some books by J I Rodale, $10.19 each:

The Encyclopedia of Organic Gardening,
1968.
The Organic Way to Plant Protection,
1961.
How to Grow Vegetables & Fruits by the
Organic Method, 1961.

For free pamphlets about gardening
write:

University of California Agricultural
Extension Service
Agricultural Publications
University Hall
Berkeley, CA 94720

Each of the 50 states provides
agricultural advice and services thru
county or area offices of their
Agricultural Extension Service. A wide
range of publications are available thru
the AES or the US Department of
Agriculture. Most are free and written
for the lay person. Most states will have
a catalog of their publications. AES
offices are listed in the phonebook under
county listings. To get a list of
government publications send 40 cents
to: US Department of Agriculture,
Washington DC 02050.

Garden Way Publishing Co, Charlotte,
VT 05445 is a small press dealing
exclusively in books like how to raise
poultry, home storage of vegetables and
fruits, raising milk goats, etc. One
particularly helpful book they publish is
Buying Country Property, by Herb
Moral, $3.

How to Make It On the Land, Ray
Cohan, Prentice-Hall, Englewood Cliffs,
NJ 07632, $5.

How to Have a Green Thumb Without an
Aching Back, Ruth Stout, Cornerstone
Library Publications, 630 Fifth Ave, NY
10020, 1955, $.95. Highly recom-
mended by everyone I know.

Sunset Western Garden Book, Lane
Magazine and Book Co, Menlo Park, CA
94025, 1971, $5.95. We have it and use
it for our struggling city garden patches.

Farmers Almanac, Judson Hale, Dublin,
NH 03444, published every fall, $.50.

Farm and Ranch Vacation Guide, 36 East
57th St, NY 10022 at $2.50. Lists how
you can go spend your vacation down on
the farm!

A pamphlet listing correspondence
courses on farming available from
colleges and universities thruout the
country can be gotten by sending 50
cents to:

National University Extension
Association
1 Dupont Circle
Washington DC 20036

FESTIVALS

Festivals in California, Christine Austin,
101 Productions, 79 Liberty St, San
Francisco, CA 94110, 1972, $1.95. Lists
all kinds of events from the Tournament
of Roses to the International Sea
Festival. Dates, locations, descriptions.

American Crafts Guide, Gousha
Publications, Box 6227, San Jose, CA
95150, 1972, $3.95. Calendar of major
US craft fairs and festivals.

For Indian pow-wows and festivals get
the *American Indian Calendar* by
sending $.25 to the US Government
Printing Office, Washington DC 20402.
For a schedule of dances at the New
Mexico pueblos write the Chamber of
Commerce, Box 1928, Santa Fe, New
Mexico 87501. The Navajo Tribal Fair is
held at Window Rock, New Mexico,
September 2-4, and the Intertribal
Ceremonials are held at Gallup, New
Mexico, August 10-13. To get the most
out of these events, read some of the
books listed under "Indians" in this
appendix.

See also "Music Festivals" and
"Theaters".

What follows is a selected list of
American festivals. Find your own
festivals, and if you can't find one—live
one, make one, be one.

Georgia Mountain Fair
Hiawassee, GA
(the second full week in August)

Aspen Summer Festival
Aspen, CO
(June 27-September 14)

Festival of the Arts
on the Green in New Haven, CT
(10 days late May)

Maine Seafoods Festival
Old County Road
Rockland, ME
(1st weekend in August)

Skowhegan State Fair
Skowhegan, ME
(mid-August—this fair is 153 years old!)

Village Art Festival
Nappanee, IN
(German bands and folk dancing. 3rd
week in August)

Plymouth-Marshall County Blueberry
Festival
Centennial Park
Plymouth, IN
(Labor Day weekend)

Tulip Time Festival
Holland, MI
(In this Dutch village which has the only
wooden shoe factory in the US see
Dutch pagaents, eat Dutch food, help
wash the streets. May.)

Oktoberfest
German Village
Columbus, OH
(A restored German village. September-
October.)

Johnny Appleseed Festival
Lisbon, OH
(In the Village Square—3 days in
mid-September.)

Fyr-Bal Fest
Ephraim, WI
(A Scandinavian welcome to summer.
Third weekend in June.)

Lumberjack World Championships
Hayward, WI
(3 days late July or early August)

Old Milwaukee Days and Schlitz Circus
Parade
For information write:
Visitor Information Center
828 N Broadway
Milwaukee, WI
(June 30-July 3)

The town of New Glarus, WI was settled
by Swiss immigrants. Their ethnic
festivals are:

Heidi Festival
1420 - 2 — St
(end of June)

Swiss Volksfest
North end of 2 St
(August 6)

Wilhelm Tell Festival
Tell Amphitheater
(Labor Day weekend)

The July 4 celebration in Birmingham,
AL is supposed to be the biggest in the
country. For information write the
Birmingham Chamber of Commerce,
Birmingham, AL.

DeSoto Celebration
Bradenton, FL
(Everyone in town who can grows a
beard. Mid-March)

Turtle Crawl and Leif Eríkson Day
Pagaent
Jensen Beach, FL
(The first is May-July, the second—a
re-enacting of the landing of the Vikings—
is on the Saturday and Sunday nearest
October 10.)

Gasparilla Pirate Invasion
Tampa, FL
(Fully rigged pirate ships invade the
harbor and take the city. Festivities
continue for five days. 2nd week in
February.)

Savannah Arts Festival
Forsythe Park
Savannah, GA
(April)

International Banana Festival
Fulton, KY
(3 days late summer)

Shrimp Festival
Biloxi, MS
(at the Gulf of Mexico, early June)

Folk Festival of the Smokies
For information write:
Box 8
Crosby, TN 37722

Fiesta de Mayo
Nogales, AZ
(first week of May—celebrated by the two Nogales)

Helldorado
Tombstone, AZ
(third Friday in October)

Fiesta de los Vaqueros
6th Ave and Irvington Rd
Rodeo Grounds
Tucson, AZ
(last weekend in February)

Tucson Festival
For information write:
    2720 Broadway
    Tucson, AZ 85716

Gold Rush Days
Wickenburg, AZ
(You can pan for gold and keep whatever you find! 2nd weekend in February)

Lodi Grape Festival and National Wine Show
E Lockford and Calavares St
Lodi, CA
(3 days in mid-September)

Danish Days Festival
Solvang, CA
(Good just for the pastries! 3rd weekend in September)

Valley of the Moon Vintage Festival
Sonoma, CA
(last weekend in September)

Bon Odori
Buddhist Temple
Stockton. CA
(Buddhist street dance, late July)

National Basque Festival
Elko, NV
(1st weekend in July)
For information write:
    Chamber of Commerce
    Box 149
    Elko, NV 89801

Festival of American Folklife
The Mall
Washington DC
(5 or 6 days in July, including July 4. Sponsored by the Smithsonian Institute.)

Platdeutsches Volksfest
Schuetzen Park
32nd and Kennedy
North Bergen, NJ
(2nd and 3rd Sunday in August)

Craftsman's Fair of the Southern Highlands
City Auditorium
Asheville, NC
(5 days in July)

Pennsylvania Dutch Folk Fair
Hamburg, PA
(2 days in mid-July)

Original Pennsylvania Dutch Days
Hershey Park
Hershey, PA
(1st weekend in October)

Pennsylvania Dutch Folk Festival
Kulztown, PA
(8 days in early July)

National George Washington Birthday Celebration
For information write:
    Board of Trade
    400 S Washington St
    Alexandria, VA 22314

Appalachian Arts and Crafts Festival
Raleigh County Armory
Beckley, WV
(late August or early September)

International Pancake Race
Liberal, KS
(Americana. The women compete on shrove Tuesday by seeing who can run a quarter of a mile, flipping a pancake on a skillet twice. At the same time, women in Olney, England are having the same competition. See it!)

Mennonite Folk Festival
Newton, KS
(late March or early April)

Mid-America Fair
Fairgrounds
Topeka, KS
(2nd week in September)

Mardi Gras & Spring Fiesta
For information write:
    Tourist and Convention Commission
    400 Royal St
    New Orleans, LA 70130

National Festival of Craftsmen
Silver Dollar City
Branson, MO
(October)

Basque Festival
Boise, ID
(The largest Basque colony in North America lives here, yes—here in Boise. Mid-summer)

Nordic Fest
Decorah, IA
(3 days in late July)

All American Square Dance Festival
Oskaloosa, IA
(2 days in early July)

Winter Carnival
St Paul, MN
(late January thru early February. One of America's leading festivals.)

FISHING

How to Fish Good, Milford "Stanley" Paltroon, Wretched Mess News, 460 Park Ave, NY 10022, 1972, $2.95.

The Fisherman's Handbook, John Power and Jeremy Brown, Charles Scribner Sons, 1972, $7.95. List of how to find fishing holes.

For free catalogs of fishing equipment, write:

    Cabela's
    823 - 13th Ave
    Sidney, NB 69162

    The Orvis Co
    Manchester, VT 05254

Also see Appendix 12, "Outdoor Equipment Suppliers."

A magazine for fishermen which the Whole Earth Catalog says is "the saltiest publication I know":

    National Fisherman
    22 Main St
    Camden, ME 04843
    ($4 for 1 year)

Fish Catching Methods of the World, Fishing News Books Ltd, 110 Fleet St, London EC 4, England.

Guide to Fresh and Salt Water Fishing, George S. Fisher and Phil Francis, Western Publishing Co, 1220 Mound Ave, Racine, WI 53404, $1.25.

And, yes, Virginia, there is a fishing school:

    Orvis Vermont Fly Fishing School
    The Orvis Co
    Manchester, VT 05254

For information about the Virginia Salt Water Fishing Tournament write:

    Virginia Salt Water Fishing Tournament
    25th and Pacific Ave
    Virginia Beach, VA 23451

Fishing in the National Park System, a pamphlet from the US Government Printing Office, Washington DC 20402, $.30

GONE
FISHING

FLEA MARKETS

Flea Marketing is rapidly becoming a popular American sport. Best to rummage among the local populace for exact locations in any area. Try funky looking antique dealers and the local newspaper as well.

See also ANTIQUES.

FLOAT TRIPS

Adventure Trip Guide, Adventure Guides, Inc, 36 E 57 St, NY 10022, 1972, $2.95. See page 135 for a list of river guides.

Snake River Guides, Verne Huser and Buzz Belknap, Westwater Books, Box 365, Boulder City, NV 89005, 1972, $3.95. Maps, history, geology of the Snake River region. Names and addresses of Grand Teton National Park concessioner-river guides.

River Runners Guides to the Canyons of the Green and Colorado Rivers, Powell Society, 750 Vine St, Denver, CO 80206. Volume 1: *Flaming Gorge--Ouray,* $2; Volume 2: *Labyrinth, Stillwater, and Cataract Canyons,* $3; Volume 3: *Marble Gorge and Grand Canyon Gorge,* $4; Volume 4: *Canyons of the Green and Colorado Rivers,* $3 Supplement: *Yampa River,* $1. *The Exploration of the Colorado River and Its Canyons,* J.W. Powell, Dover, 1961, $3. Wonderful reading.

The Exploration of the Colorado River and its Canyons, J. W. Powell, Dover, 1961, Wonderful reading.

Standing Up Country, Dr. C. Gregory Crampton, Alfred Knopf, 1965, $15.50. Background on where the river runners operate. Recommended by Western River Guides Association.

Handbook of Wilderness Travel, George S. Wells, Colorado Outdoor Sports Corp, 5440 North Valley Highway, Denver, CO 80216, chapter 5: "The Float Trip."

River guidebooks available from Canyonlands Press (Box 21021, Salt Lake City, UT 84121) are:

> *Grand Canyon River Guide,* $3.95, waterproof, $5.95.
> *Colorado River Guidebook,* $4.45.
> *Guidebook to the Colorado River,* Part 1: $2.80, Part 2: $3.30.
> *Exploration of the Colorado River and its Canyons,* $3.30.

There are two organizations devoted to the preservation of the canyonlands country and to publishing books and pamphlets to further the appreciation and proper use of those river regions:

Powell Society Ltd
750 Vine St
Denver, CO 80206

Western River Guides Association
994 Denver St
Salt Lake City, UT 84111
(They publish a "List of Professional Outfitters" and a "Directory of Outfitters, Associates, Guides and Members." Both are free.)

If you would like to make a river expedition, contact one of the following:

Sierra Club Wilderness
    Outings
1050 Mills Tower
San Francisco, CA 94104

Hell's Canyon and
    Colorado River Runs
Mountain Travel
1398 Solano Ave
Albany, CA 94706

Grand Canyon Expeditions
Box 0
Kanab, UT

American River Touring Association
1016 Jackson St
Oakland, CA 94607

Hatch River Expeditions
411 East Second North
Vernal, UT

Adventure Bound
Whitewater Expeditions
Denver, CO

Quayle Expeditions
Box 8026
Salt Lake City, UT 84108

Grand Canyon Dories
Box 5585
Stanford, CA 94305

FOOD FACTORIES, INDUSTRIAL FACTORIES, ETC.

A good way to check out the karma of the food that becomes you and the goods you consume is to take a tour of a major factory or processing plant in action. Check the "yellow pages" for location and time of tours.

See also AUTO FACTORIES, BREWERIES, WINERIES.

FORTS

Many old forts are now state or national monuments. Check out Appendix 8. Many others are lost in the sands of time; check with the local populace for locations you suspect still exist.

A trip into Civil War history books can add a dimension to any trip into the South.

FOSSIL HUNTING

America's Ancient Treasures, Franklin Folsom, Rand McNally, 1971, $2.95.

Field Guide to Fossils, Houghton--Mifflin, 1971, $1.60.

Beginning Knowledge Book of Fossils, Anne O. Epple, Macmillan, 1969, $3.95.

Two books from Doubleday by Fenton Carroll;
    Tales Told By Fossils, 1966, $5.95
    Fossil Book, 1959, $17.95.

Handbook of Paleontological Techniques, Kummel and Raup, W H Freeman Co, 660 Market St, San Francisco, CA 94104.

Fossils in America, Jay Ransom, Harper & Row, 1964, $8.95.

Fossils, Frank H. Rhodes (a Golden Nature Guide), Western Publishing Co, 850 Third Ave, NY 10022, 1962, $4.95.

GIDDY YAP!

JEEP

FOUR-WHEEL DRIVE TRIPS

Jeep Trails to Colorado Ghost Towns, Robert L Brown, Caxton Printers, Caldwell, ID, $5.50.

Adventure Trip Guide, Adventure Guides Inc. 36 E 57th St, NY 10022, $2.95, page 26: lists organized jeep trips.

Expeditions in land rovers: Mountain Travel, 1398 Solano Ave, Albany, CA 94706.

FUCKING

Nevada Paymate: A Guide to Nevada Sporting Houses, Nevada Pocket Books, Box 290, Las Vegas, NV 89101, 1972, $5.

Total Orgasm, Jack Rosenberg, Random House/Bookworks, 1973, $3.95.

GAMBLING

Beat the Dealer, Edward O Thorpe, Random House, 1966, $6.95.

Complete Guide to Gambling, John Scarme, Simon and Schuster, 1961, $10.

The World's Greatest Gambling Systems, Holloway Publishing Co. , 8060 Melrose Ave, Los Angeles, CA 90046, $1.25.

GHOST TOWNS

California and Nevada Ghost Town Atlas, Robert N. Johnson, Naturegraph Books, 1188 Chiquita Rd, Healdsburg, CA 95448, $2. Also by the same author: *Southwestern Ghost Town Atlas* ($2) and *Northwest Gem Fields and Ghost Town Atlas,* ($2).

Guide to Colorado Ghost Towns, Perry Eberhart, Sage Books, 2679 S. York St, Denver, CO 80210, $6.50.

You can get a list of ghost towns by sending for "Room to Roam—A Recreational Guide to Public Lands" ($.75) from the US Government Printing Office, Washington DC 20402.

GOLD PANNING AND PROSPECTING

Diving and Digging for Gold, Naturegraph Books, 1188 Chiquita Rd, Healdsburg, CA 95448, $1.

Prospecting and Operating Small Gold Placers, William F Boericke, John Wiley & Sons, 605 Third Ave, NY 10016, 1933, $5.95.

Miners Catalog, Miners & Prospectors Supply, 177 Main St, Newcastle, CA 95658. Free.

Two pamphlets from the government might be worth sending for:

"Staking a Mining Claim on Federal Lands"
"Prospecting for Gold in the United States"

15 cents each to the US Government Printing Office, Washington DC 20402.

GRAVEYARDS AND GRAVESTONE RUBBING

Early New England Gravestone Rubbings, Edmund Vincent Gillon Jr, Dover Publications, 1966, $3.50.

The Early American Gravestone as Primitive Art, Richard Friswell, 88 Beach St, Belmont, Ma 02178, $1.25.

Stranger Stop and Cast an Eye, J. Walker Jacobs, Oldstone Enterprises, Box 462, Marblehead, MA 01945, $1.50 The "definitive handbook" of gravestone rubbing. Oldstone Enterprises will also sell you a Gravestone Rubbing Kit for $7.50 (paper, wax, tape, brush, and a copy of *Stranger Stop and Cast an Eye,* to tell you how to use all these things).

Gravestone of Early New England, Harriette Forbes, Houghton-Mifflin, $15.00.

Graven Images: New England Stone-carving and Its Symbols, Allan Ludwig, Wesleyan University Press, $40.

Antiques Journal (Box 1046, Dubuque, IA, $6/monthly) often has articles about gravestone rubbing.

HARBOR TOURS

See the "yellow pages" in any ocean, bay or river city under Harbor Tours; it's a vigorous tourist business, a mixture of information and corn.

HEALTH AND SURVIVAL

Diet For a Small Planet, Francis Moore Lappe, Ballantine Books, 1971, $1.25. A book on protein—what it is, why we need it, and how to get it.

The Adelle Davis books are a must for anyone interested in being healthy. They are all published by New American Library, $1.75 each:
Let's Have Healthy Children
Let's Get Well
Let's Eat Right to Keep Fit
Let's Cook it Right

Here are some general medical guides:

Emergency Medical Guide, John Henderson, McGraw-Hill, 1963, $3.95.

Better Homes & Gardens Family Medical Guide, Meredith Press, 1964 $9.95.

And a brand new one, *The Well Body Book,* Hal Bennet and Mike Samuels, Random House/Bookworks, 1973, $5.95.

Mountaineering Medicine, see this appendix under "Mountaineering."

Our Bodies Ourselves: A Course By and For Women, Boston Women's Health Collective, New England Free Press, 791 Tremont St, Boston, MA 02118, $.30. A book that tells women how to examine themselves, information about sex that you never got in school, the real story on birth control, and how to keep your body healthy.

You can find out where to get pregnancy tests, pre-natal care, prepared childbirth classes, and information about free clinics and VD tests in the Bay Area from the *People's Yellow Pages,* Box 31291, San Francisco, CA 94131, $1.50.

If you are pregnant and want to know what it will be like to have a baby, or if you are just curious about how you got here, read our book, *Two Births,* Jane Brown, Eugene Lesser, Stephanie Mines, photographs by Ed Buryn, Bookworks/Random House, 1972, $3.95.

Survival, Evasion and Escape is published by the Superintendent of Documents, US Government Printing Office, Washington DC 20402, $3.50.

"Desert Survival" is a free pamphlet available from the Maricopa County Department of Civil Defense and Emergency Services, 2035 North 52nd St., Phoenix, AZ 85008. Excellent.

How to be a Survivor, Paul Ehrlich and Richard Harriman, Ballantine Books, 1971, $1.25.

See also chapter 15 in this book, "Medical Matters" and "Herbs and Plants" in this appendix.

Some recommended cookbooks for making healthy food:

Ten Talents, Dr. Frank J. Hurd and Rosalie Hurd, Box 86A—Route 1, Chisholm, MN 55719, 1968, $7.95. The best cookbook I've ever seen.

The Soybean Cookbook, Dorothea Van Gundy Jones, ARC Books, 219 Park Avenue South, NY 10003, 1971, $1.45.

The Tassajara Bread Book, Edward Espe Brown, Shambala Publications, 1409 Fifth St, Berkeley, CA 94710, 1970, $2.95. Janet Brown, who makes the best bread in the world, gets glassy eyed when she talks about this book. She loves it and you will too.

Diet for a Small Planet, (see above) has good recipes for getting complete, high-quality protein.

HIKING

Many mountaineering clubs publish hiking guides. Check these:

The Mountaineers
Box 122
Seattle, WA 98111
They publish:
> *101 Hikes in the North Cascades*, $4.95.
> *102 Hikes in the Alpine Lakes, South Cascades, and Olympics*, $4.95.
> *50 Hikes in Mt. Rainier National Park*, $3.95.
> Trips and Trails: 2 volumes of *Hikes in the North Cascades and Olympics*, $4.95 each.
> *Footloose Around Puget Sound*, $4.95.

Appalachian Mountain Club
5 Joy St
Boston, MA 02108
They publish hiking maps for New Hampshire, Main, Massachusetts, and Rhode Island, and:

> *AMC White Mountain Guide*, $6.

A national hiking organization is:
> The National Campers and Hikers Association
> 7172 Transit Road
> Buffalo, NY 14221.

The Handbook of Wilderness Travel, George S. Wells (Colorado Outdoor Sports Corp, Denver, CO, $3.25) lists hiking clubs and other outdoor societies in each state. Chapter 8 is about hiking trails.

Hiking expeditions for groups are organized by:
Sierra Club
1050 Mills Tower
San Francisco, CA 94104

The Wilderness Society
729-15th St NW
Washington DC 20005

The Wilderness Press, 2440 Bancroft Way, Berkeley, CA 94704, publishes these hiking guides:
> *High Sierra Hiking Guides*, $1.95 each.
> *Sierra North and Sierra South*, $4.95 and $3.95.
> *The Tahoe-Yosemite Trail*, $2.95.
> *Trails of the Angeles*, $4.95
> *Mammoth Lakes Sierra*, $4.95
> *Deepest Valley*, $3.95.

The Touchstone Press, Box 81, Beaverton, OR 97005, publishes:
> *100 Oregon Hiking Trails*, $5.95.
> *100 Northern California Hiking Trails*, $5.95.
> *100 Southern California Hiking Trails*, $5.95.

Exploring Mt. Rainier, Ruth Kirk, University of Washington Press, Seattle, WA, 1968, $2.50. From many hikes on Mt. Rainier, Ruth Kirk gives information about wildflowers, geology, wildlife and the history of the region. Other books by her are:

> *Exploring Death Valley*, Stanford University Press, $1.95.
> *Exploring the Olympic Peninsula*, University of Washington Press, $2.50.
> *Exploring Yellowstone*, University of Washington Press, $2.95.
> *The Olympic Rain Forest*, University of Washington Press, $6.95.

Grand Canyon Treks, Harvey Buthchart, La Siesta Press, Box 406, Glendale, Ca, 91209. Hiking the inner Grand Canyon.

Starr's Guide to the John Muir Trail, Walter A. Starr, Sierra Club, 1959, $2. The Sierra Club publishes other books of interest to the hiker:
> *Hiker's Guide to the Smokies*, $7.95.
> *Food for Knapsackers*, $7.95.

The Hikers and Backpackers Handbook, Winchester Press, 460 Park Ave, NY 10022, $5.95.

See chapter 13 in this book, "Hiking and Backpacking."

For equipment, see appendix 12, "Outdoor Equipment Suppliers."

HISTORIC HOMES

See also Appendix 8, National Monuments, and Appendix 11, Other National Recreation Facilities.

American Heritage Press publishes *An American Heritage Guide: Historic Houses of America*, 1971, $6.95, and Bruce Catton's *Book of Great Historic Places*, $16.50. Also, *The American Heritage History of Notable American Houses*, $19.95.

Great Houses of American History, Andrew Hepburn, Crown Publishers, 1972, $25.00.

Many towns conduct guided tours thru their historic homes. These are scheduled at different times each year. Check with the local Chamber of Commerce or ask at the antique shops or cafe.

HOME EXCHANGE

Elliott's Worldwide Vacation Home Exchange
5624 Proctor Rd
Castro Valley, CA 94546

Home Exchange Bureau
Box 55
Grants, NM 87020

Home Exchange Club of California
Box 2445
San Leandro, CA 94577

HORSES

Horses: Their Selection, Care and Handling, Margaret Cabell Self, A S Barnes & Co, Box 421, Cranbury, NJ 08512, $5.95. Published in 1943, this remains the classic, encyclopedic source of information on all phases of horse management.

Breaking and Training the Stock Horse, Charles Williamson, Hamilton, MT, 59840, 1950, $8.

Horses, Hitches and Rocky Trails, Joe Back, Swallow Press, 1139 S Wabash Ave, Chicago, IL 60605, 1959, $4. Written by a packer.

The Wilderness Society (4260 East Evans Ave, Denver, CO 80222) organizes horse riding expeditions.

There are more than 300 horse farms open to the public in Lexington, KY. Tours can be arranged by writing:
Blue Grass Tours
239 N Broadway
Lexington, KY 40509

HOT SPRINGS

How to Live in the New America, William Kaysing (see USA Bookself) has a section, beginning on page 309, showing the location of more than 1000 hot springs situated west of Denver.

Place Magazine, Star Route 1, volume 1, number 2 of a unique magazine (Box 2708, Menlo Park, CA 94025, $2), has an article on page 105 called "Thermal Springs of the United States"—20 pages of listings of over 1500 hot springs in the continental United States with maps.

Hot Springs of the United States and Other Countries of the World, Gerald A Waring, US Government Printing Office, Washington DC 20402. The classic source—compiled in 1965. Place magazine says the data is incomplete.

HOUSEBOATING

Family Houseboating
($4 yr/bimonthly magazine)
Box 2081
Toluca Lake, CA 91602

You can buy, rent or lease houseboats now in many parts of the country. See the "yellow pages."

INDIANS

Seven Arrows, Hyemeyohsts Storm, Harper & Row, 1972, $9.95. Highly recommended. Will give spirit-insight into The People of our heritage, those who freely inhabited this continent until we stole it.

Ishi in Two Worlds, (A biography of the Last Wild Indian in North America), Theodora Kroeber, University of Chicago Press, 1961, $1.95. The story of the Yahi Indians of northern California (Mount Lassen) and of Ishi the Yahi who in 1911 walked out of the wilds into the white man's civilization for the first time. Classic and required reading. Also by Theodora Kroeber and about California Indians: *Almost Ancestors*, Sierra Club Books, 1050 Mills Tower, San Francisco, CA 94104, $15.00.

Book of the Hopi (The first revelation of the Hopi's historical and religious world-view of life), Ballantine Books, 1963, $1.25. Ritual and mythology of the Hopi. The Hopi story of creation, told here for the first time in print, is an epic poem like The Odyssey or The Bible.

The Patriot Chiefs (A Chronicle of American Indian Resistance), Alvin M. Josephy, Viking Press, 1958, $2.95. Nine biographies: Hiawatha, King Philip, Pope, Pontiac, Tecumseh, Osceola, Black Hawk, Crazy Horse and Chief Joseph.

Crazy Horse (The Strange Man of the Oglala Sioux), Mari Sandoz, University of Nebraska Press, 1961, $1.95. Mari Sandoz reconstitutes the world of the Oglala Sioux to tell us the story of Crazy Horse's life. Reads like a novel.

Black Elk Speaks (Being the Life Story of a Holy Man of the Oglala Sioux), John G. Neihardt (Flaming Rainbow), University of Nebraska Press, 1961, $1.50. Meridel LeSueur said, when I told her I was about to read this book, "Oh, you have a treat in store for you", And Eugene Lesser says it's one of the best books he's ever read. What more can *I* say: Read it!

In the Trail of the Wind (American Indian Poems and Ritual Orations), John Bierhorst, editor, Farrar, Strauss and Giroux, 1971, $4.95. A finely made book.

Naturegraph (1188 Chiquita Rd, Headlsburg, CA 95448) publishes a series of books about the Indians, most of which I haven't seen, but they sound interesting. Some examples are:

Warriors of the Rainbow—$2.25
Great Upon the Mountain—Crazy Horse of America—$1.95
A Bag of Bones: Tales of the Wintu Indians—$2.25

I have seen Naturegraph's *Good Medicine Books*—stories and art from the out-of-doors. How to make mocassins, herb cures, smoke meat. $1.50.

The Lost Universe, Gene Weltfish, Ballantine Books, 1965, $1.65. "Here is the whole life of the Pawnee, told in a way that you could go now and live it."—Whole Earth Catalog.

Tales of the North American Indians, Stith Thompson, editor, Indiana University Press, 10th and Morton Streets, Bloomington, IN 47401, 1966, $2.95. "It is a fine readable collection of far out stories." —Whole Earth Catalog.

Book of the Indians, American Heritage Series, Simon and Schuster, 1961, $16.50. See review in "USA Bookshelf."

Some well-touted books which I haven't read:

Bury My Heart at Wounded Knee, Dee Brown, NY, Bantam Books, 1972, $1.95.

Custer Died For Your Sins, Vine Deloria, Jr, NY, Avon Books, 1969, $1.25.

Snake Dance of the Hopi Indians, Earl R. Forrest, Tower Publications, 1961, $7.50.

Sun Chief: The Autobiography of a Hopi Indian, Leo Simmons, Yale University Press, 1970, $3.75.

Akwesane Notes (the official publication of the Mohawk Nation) via Rooseveltown, NY 13683. Fifty cents per issue, $5 per year. Information on contemporary Native American struggles, political and cultural.

For 35 cents you can have a fine map of *Indian Land Areas*. The map shows Federal reservations, interstate highways, National Forests, Parks and Monuments, National Wildlife Refuges, and tourist complexes in the areas of the reservations. The back of the map lists area and agency offices for the Bureau of Indian Affairs. Send your request to:

U.S. Department of the Interior
Bureau of Indian Affairs
U.S. Government Printing Office
Washington DC 20402

Some books by John Collier Sr., a former head of the Bureau of Indian Affairs. Highly recommended.

American Indian Ceremonial Dances, NY, Crown, 1972, $3.95.
Indians of the Americas, 1952, NY, Norton, $.95. A classic.
On the Gleaming Way: Navajos, Eastern Pueblos, Zunis, Hopis, Apaches and Their Land and Meaning to the World, The Swallow Press, 1139 S. Wabash Ave., Chicago, IL 60605, $2.25.

LIGHTHOUSES

Most lighthouses are to be found along the east coast, with the heaviest proliferation in New England. Some are open to the public; all are really great to see. For locations, ask the natives as you drive the coastline. See also Other National Recreation Facilities, Appendix 11.

LIGHTHOUSES. Guidance. Direction. Houses of Light. WISDOM. Clarity. Hope Knowledge. Light is Life. LIGHT. HEALS.

MAPS

Gousha Publications, Box 6227, San Jose, CA 95150, offers a menu of maps:

Rec Vec Traveler: combination of road maps and touring information. Indicates winding roads, windy areas, congested areas, curves, steep grades, alternate routes—all for the Rec Vec driver. Shows picnic and rest areas, scenic tours, toll roads. Tells where to camp near major cities. 6 maps in the series: Texas, Florida, New York, Vermont/New Hampshire, Northern California, Southern California. $1.95 each.

Family Fun Maps. Street and area maps showing tours in 3 cities: Chicago, Los Angeles, Washington DC. $1.25 each.

Tourmaps. Three maps, each emphasizing a tour based on a different aspect of America: "Landmarks of the Revolution," "Rodeos," "The First Americans." $1.50 each.

Travel Planners. Maps to plan your trip with. Locates major points of interest and gives detailed maps of national parks and major cities: Northeastern US, Southeastern US, Midwestern States. $1.25 each.

Bicentennial Tourguide. Maps of every state and 25 cities. $1.

Gulf Tourguide Map of the United States. Available from your Gulf dealer, free.

Rand McNally, Box 7600, Chicago, IL 60680 offers us these guides:

Rand McNally Road Atlas, $2.95. See USA Guidebooks for more about this one.

1972 Rand McNally Interstate Road Atlas, $1.
Interstate Highway Atlas, pocket edition, $.50.
Regional Travel Guides, $1.95 and $2.95.
America's Ancient Treasures. Listing of archeological sites and museums, plus all museums with archeological collections. Information on prehistoric Indians. Data on admission, fees, hours, location, and how to get there. $2.95.

For maps of the national forests, write the regional director of the region you are interested in. See Appendix 9, "National Forests," for addresses.

For a list of maps published by the US Geological Survey (Washington DC 20242) send for their free brochure: "Information Sources and Services."

The US Geological Survey has maps of our land masses; for maps of our coastal regions and waterways write the US Coast and Geodetic Survey, ESSA Washington Science Center, Rockville, MD 20852 and ask for their free catalog listing their maps. See also "Sailing" in this appendix for more information about water charts.

MARIHUANA MARIJUANA CANNABIS SATIVA WEED POT GRASS TEA DOPE

A short pot bibliography:

Pot Report, Ronald Bruce, 1971, Universal Publishers and Distributors, 235 E 45th St, NY 10017, $1.25.

Cultivator's Handbook of Marijuana, Bill Drake, Agrarian Reform, Box 1701, Eugene, OR 97401, 1970, $2.50. The Whole Earth Catalog says: "How to grow good pot. The best book on the subject."

Drug Beat: A Complete Survey of the History, Distribution, Uses and Abuses of Marijuana, LSD, and the Amphetamines, 1969, Cowles Book Corp, 114 W Illinois St, Chicago, IL 60610, $6.50.

Marijuana Smokers, Erich Goode, Basic Books Inc, 404 Park Ave S, NY 10016, 1970, $10.

Marijuana, Erich Goode, Aldine Atherton Inc, 529 S Wabash Ave, Chicago, IL 60605, 1969, $7.95.

Marijuana: Teenage Killer, Norman Hill, 1970, Popular Library, $.95.

Everything You Always Wanted to Know About Marijuana, Daniel Klien, 1972, Capital Distributing Co, Charlton

Capital Distributing Co, Charlton Blvd, Derby, CT 06418, 1972, $.95. And, by the same author, *The Marijuana Question and the Marijuana Answer.*

The Sexual Power of Marijuana, Barbara Lewis, NY, David McKay, 1970, $5.95.

A Child's Garden of Grass, Jack Margolis and R. Clorfene, NY, Simon and Schuster, 1972, $1.25. Cliff Houdek says, "The funniest book I ever read."

Man and Marijuana, Mark Merlin, Fairleigh Dickinson University Press, Box 421, Cranbury, NJ 08512, 1972, $8.00.

Marijuana, The Facts, The Truth, Will Oursler, Paul S Eriksson, 119 W 57th St, NY 10019, 1970, $2.95.

Pot, John Rosevar, Lancer Books, 1560 Broadway, NY 10036, 1971, $1.25.

Marijuana Papers, David Soloman, NY, New American Library, 1968, $1.50.

Uses of Marijuana, Solomon Snyder, NY, Oxford University Press, 1972, $1.95.

New Social Drug: Cultural, Medical, and Legal Perspectives on Marijuana, David E Smith, Prentice-Hall, Englewood Cliffs, NJ, 1970, $1.95.

On Being Stoned, Charles Tart, Science and Behavior Books, Box A-J, Cupertino, CA 95054, 1971, $7.95.

MOTORCYCLING

Two Wheel Travel: Motorcycle Camping and Touring, Tobey Publishing Co, Box 428, New Canaan, CT 06840, 1972, $3. See Chapter 10, "Motorcycle Touring," for high praise of this book.

Intelligent Motorcycling, William Kaysing, Paradise Publishers, Box 5372, Santa Barbara, CA 93102, $2. How to survive and enjoy your bike.

Modern Motorcycle Mechanics, J B Nicholson, 225 Third Ave No, Saskatoon, Saskatchewan, Canada, 1942, $8.

The magazine most dedicated to the concept of bike touring is Road Rider (Box 678, South Laguna, CA 92677, $5/12 issues). *Two Wheel Travel* says: "On the whole, this is a fine magazine. It's funny and relaxing and sometimes very helpful. It will certainly urge you to take your bike on the open road." Other bike mags are:

Bike and Rider
Box 8617
La Cresceta, CA 91214
($7.50/12 issues)

Cycle
Box 1092
Flushing, NY 11352
($6/12 issues)

Cycle World
Box 1757
Newport Beach, CA 92660
($7/12 issues)

Motor Cyclist
Box 638
Sierra Madre, CA 91024
($6/12 issues)

Easyriders
Box 2086
Seal Beach, CA 90740
($.75 per issue)

MOUNTAINEERING

The Mountaineers (Box 122, Seattle, WA 98111) publish:

Mountaineering: Thee Freedom of the Hills, 1960, $7.50 (classic instruction manual).
Medicine for Mountaineering, James A. Wilkerson MD, $7.50.
The Challenge of Rainier, Dee Molenaar, $12.95.
Challenge of the North Cascade, Fred Beckey, $7.95.
Mountain Rescue Techniques, Dr. Otto Trott & Kurt Beam, $3.50.
Trail Country (a guide to the Olympics), Robert L. Wood, $6.95.
Wilderness Trails of Olympic National Park, $3.95.

The American Alpine Club (113 East 90th St, NY 10028) publishes a yearly journal, The American Alpine Journal, ($5 per copy) and a newsletter, American Alpine Club News (5 issues/$2.50). They also publish these books:

320

Bibliography of American Mountain Ascents, Joe Fisher, $5.
Knots for Mountaineering, $1.
Frostbite, $1.

and many more. Send for their list of publications.

The Appalachian Mountain Club (5 Joy St, Boston, MA 02108) organizes group expeditions and publish:

  White Mountain Guide, $6.
  Maine Mountain Guide, $5.
  Maps of Mt. Washington, Franconia, Katahdin, Mt Desert, $1 each.

The Sierra Club (1050 Mills Tower, San Francisco, CA 94104) also sponsors group mountaineering adventures and publsihes:

  The Manual of Ski Mountaineering, 1962, $4.95.
  Mountaineer's Guide to the High Sierra, $7.95.

Some other books of interest:

Mountaineering, Alan Blackshaw, Penguin Books, 1968, $4.95.

Mountaineering Handbook, C. Casewit and R. Pownall, Lippincott, 1968, $5.95.

Mountaineering in the Sierra Nevada, Clarence King, University of Nebraska Press, 1970, $2.25.

Organizations sponsoring mountaineering workshops and expeditions:

Palisade School of Mountaineering
6201 Medau Place
Oakland, CA 94611

Mt Hood Meadows School of Mountaineering
9920 SW Terwilliger Rd
Portland, OR 97219

Mountain Travel
1398 Solano Ave
Albany, CA 94706

Jackson Hole Mountain Guides
Teton Village, WY 83025

Sierra Club
1050 Mills Tower
San Francisco, CA 94104

Potomac Appalachian Trail Club
1718 N Street NW
Washington DC 20336

Iowa Mountaineers
Box 163
Iowa City, IA 52240

Colorado Mountain Club
1723 E 165h Ave
Denver, CO 80218

Mazamas
909 NW 19th St
Portland, OR 97209

Some mountaineering magazines are:

Ascent (the mountaineering journal of the Sierra Club)
1050 Mills Tower
San Francisco, CA 94104
($3.50 per issue)

Mountain (publication of the Youth Hostels Association of England)
30 Collingwood Ave
London N10 England
($6 yr/bimonthly)

Climbing (publication of American Mountaineering & Rock Climbing)
310 E Main
Aspen, CO
($4.50 per year)

Off Belay
12416 — 169th Ave SE
Renton, MA 98055
($6/6 issues)

Summit, Box 1889, Big Bear Lake, CA 92315, $7/yr.

A good book to have is: *Mountaineering Medicine,* Fred Darvill Jr, MD, Skagit Mountain Rescue Unit, Box 2, Mt Vernon, WA 98273, 1966, $1.

MUSEUMS

This is a selected list of museums of special interest. Find some more and make your own list. Unless otherwise noted, admission is free.

Navajo Tribal Museum
Window Rock, AZ 86515

Heard Museum of Anthropology and Primitive Arts
22 E Monte Vista Bl
Phoenix, AZ
(50 cents, children: 25 cents)

Arizona Museum
University Park
Phoenix, AZ

Sonora Desert Museum
Tucson Mountain Park
Tucson, AZ
($1.50)

Roy Rogers Museum
Apple Valley, CA 92307
(Where Trigger waits, mounted and stuffed—$1, children: 50 cents)

San Francisco Museum of Art
McAllister & Van Ness Sts
San Francisco, CA 94102

M H deYoung Memorial Museum
Golden Gate Park
San Francisco, CA 94117
(Has the famous Brundage collection of Oriental art.)

Otis Art Institute
2401 Wilshire Blvd
Los Angeles, CA

Berkeley Art Museum
Bancroft Way
(on the campus of the University of California at Berkeley)
Berkeley, CA
(The building of this museum gives you an exciting sense of freedom and spaciousness. A wonderful place to be.)

Oakland Museum
10th and Fallon Sts
Oakland, CA

Henry E Huntington Library and Art Gallery
1151 Oxford Rd
San Marino, CA 91108
(Home of Gainsborough's "Blue Boy" and Lawrence's "Pinkie," the Gutenberg Bible, Shakespeare's First Folio, and the Ellesmere manuscript of Chaucer's *Cantebury Tales.*)

Art Institute of Chicago
Michigan at Monroe
Chicago, IL
(Collection of French impressionists is supposed to be better than the Louvre.)

Chicago Museum of Science and Industry
57th St and South Shore Dr
Chicago, IL

Museum of Contemporary Art
237 East Ontario
Chicago, IL
(50 cents)

DuSable Museum of African-American History
3806 South Michigan
Chicago, IL
(50 cents)

Field Museum of Natural History
Roosevelt Rd and Lake Shore Dr
Chicago, IL
(Free on Fridays, otherwise $2.50 for your whole family.)

Baltimore Museum of Art
Charles and 31st Sts
Baltimore, MD

The Walters Art Gallery
Charles at Centre
Baltimore, MD

Boston Museum of Fine Arts
465 Huntington Ave
Boston, MA
(50 cents)

Gardner Museum
280 The Fenway
Boston, MA

University Museum
11 Divinity Ave
Cambridge, MA
(5 museums including Peabody Museum of Archaeology and Ethnology which has fine Indian exhibits.)

You can get a complete catalog of Massachusetts Museums by writing the the Massachusetts Department of Commerce and Development, Box 1775, Boston, MA 02105.

Museum of Indian Heritage
6040 DeLong Rd
Indianapolis, IN
(90 cents)

Green Village
Dearborn, MI
(Restored Wright Bros Cycle Shop,
Luther Burbank's home, and other
settings of creative Americans. American
craft demonstrations.

American Museum of Atomic Energy
Jefferson Circle
Oak Ridge, TN

Museum of African Art
(Frederick Douglass Town House)
316 - 318 A St, NE
Washington DC
(50 cents, children: 25 cents)

North Carolina Museum of Art
109 E Jones St
Raleigh, NC
(Gallery for the Blind.)

American Indian Museum
705½ Joyce St
Golden, CO 80401

Koshare Indian Kiva Museum
18th St & Santa Fe Ave
La Junta, CO 81050

Museum of Indian Arts and Crafts
103 W 66th Ave
Gallup, NM 87301

Museum of Navajo Ceremonial Art
704 Camino Lejo
Santa Fe, NM
(a stoned place)

International Folk Art Building
Camino Lejo
Santa Fe, NM

Palace of the Governors
Santa Fe, NM
(In the main square and in the oldest
American public building still standing—
a combination of five outstanding
museums including Indian folk art
museum.)

New Orleans Jazz Museum
340 Bourbon St
New Orleans, LA

Polynesian Cultural Center
Laie, Oahu, HI

Mission Houses Museum
Honolulu, HI

Iolani Palace
Honolulu, HI

Wadsworth Atheneum
600 Main St
Hartford, CT

Mystic Seaport
Greenmanville Ave
Mystic, CT
(A restored seaport, showing life in old
shipping days. $3, children: $1.25)

Bath Marine Museum
963 Washington St
Bath, ME
($1.50, children: 40 cents)

William A. Farnsworth Library and Art
  Museum
Elm St (on US 1)
Rockland, ME

Old Sturbridge Village
Sturbridge, MA

Thomas Gilcrease Institute of American
  History and Art
2500 W Newton St
Tulsa, OK

Minneapolis Institute of Art
201 E 24th St
Minneapolis, MN

Museum of the Plains Indians
Browning, MT

Willa Cather Pioneer Memorial &
  Museum
Webster St
Red Cloud, NB

Sioux Indian Museum
1002 Joe St
Rapid City, SD

Temple Museum of Religious Art and
  Music
University Circle & Silver Park
Cleveland, OH

Ringling Museums
Sarasota, FL
(The estate of John Ringling and a
Circus Museum with the largest
collection of circus gear in the country.
$2.50)

Detroit Institute of the Arts
5401 Woodward Ave
Detroit, MI
(The history of man thru his art. Murals
by Diego Rivera.)

The Brooklyn Museum
Eastern Parkway and Washington Ave
Brooklyn, NY

The Cloisters
Fort Tyron Park
NY City

The Guggenheim Museum
1071 Fifth Ave (15 89th St)
NY City
(50 cents)

The Jewish Museum
1109 Fifth Ave (at 92nd St)
NY City
(Jewish ceremonial objects. $1)

The Museum of Primitive Art
15 West 53rd St
NY City
(25 cents)

Whitney Museum of American Art
945 Madison Ave
NY City
(50 cents)

Studio Museum in Harlem
2033-5th Ave (15 125th St)
NY City

Jacques Marchais Center of Tibetan Art
338 Lighthouse Ave
Staten Island, NY
(50 cents)

Black History Museum
106A Main St
Hempstead, Long Island, NY

Portland Art Museum
SW Park Ave and Madison St
Portland, OR

Franklin Institute Science Museum
20th St and the Parkway
Philadelphia, PA
($1.25, under 19: 75 cents)

Philadelphia Museum of Art
26th and the Parkway
Philadelphia, PA
(50 cents, children: 25 cents)

McNay Art Institute
Austin Highway
San Antonio, TX

The Bayue Bend Collection
(The former residence of Miss Ima Hogg)
For reservations write:
    Curator
    1 Westcott St
    Houston, TX 77007

Corcoran Gallery of Art
17th and E Sts, NW
Washington DC

National Gallery of Art
Constitution Ave and 6th St
Washington DC

The Phillips Gallery
1600 - 21st St NW
Washington DC

Smithsonian Institute
The Mall
Washington DC
This is it. America's Achievements. A
world of its own. Includes: Museum of
National History, Museum of History
and Technology, Arts and Industries
Building, National Portrait Gallery, Air
and Space Building, Freer Gallery of Art,
a great bookstore of Americana. Better
than DisneyWorld.

BICYCLE MUSEUMS:

Cars and Music of Yesterday
Sarasota, FL

Martin County Historical Society
Elliott Museum of Vehicular Evolution
Stuart, FL

Science and Industry Museum
Chicago, IL

Childrens Museum
Indianapolis, IN

Pioneer Village
Minden, NB

Ford Museum
Greenfield Village
Dearborn, MI

NY Historical Society
Central Park West at 76th St
NY City

Staten Island Historical Museum
Staten Island, NY

Carillon Park Museum
2001 South Patterson
Dayton, OH

Don Adams
The Wheelmen
Antique Bicycle Club
214 Maywinn Rd
Defiance, OH

Franklin Institute
Philadelphia, PA

Ponderosa Museum
Quarryville, PA

Witte Museum
San Antonio, TX

Smithsonian Institute
Washington DC

MUSIC FESTIVALS

Tennessee Valley Old Fashioned
    Fiddler's Contest
Athens College
Athens, AL 35611
(1st Saturday in October)

Stephen Foster Story
My Old Kentucky Home State Park
Bardstown, KY 40004
(June 17—September 3, nightly)

American Folk Song Festival
Crater Caves State Resort Park
Olive Hill, KY 41164
(2nd Saturday and Sunday in June)

Country Music Week
Elizabethtown, TN 37643
(June 19-24, nightly)

Brewery Gulch Days
Bisbee, AZ 85603
(Fiddler's contest, September 2-4)

Monterey Jazz Festival
Write:
    Box JAZZ
    Monterey, CA 93940
(September 15-17. Write well in
advance.)

August Moon Concerts
Charles Krug Vineyards
For information write:
    Box 535
    Napa, CA 94558
(3 Saturdays in August)

Mid Summer Music Festival
Sigmund Stern Memorial Grove
San Francisco, CA
(June—mid-August at 2 p.m.)

Burlington Steamboat Days and
    Dixieland Jazz Festival
Burlington, IA 52601
(1st week in June)

Music at the Vineyards
Old Paul Masson Winery
For information write:
    330 Jackson St
    San Francisco, CA 94111

Shady Grove Music Fair
Gaithersburg, MD 20760
(late February—early December)

Mountain Dance and Folk Festival
City Auditorium
Asheville, NC
(3 days in August. Renowned for
5-string banjo and gut-string fiddle
playing. Also folk songs and precision
dance contests.)

Bach Festival
Bethelem, PA
(2nd and 3rd weekends in May)

Hampton Jazz Festival
For information write:
    Box 126
    Hampton, VA 23369

Shenandoah Valley Music Festival
For information write:
    Box 12
    Woodstock, VA 22664

Ozark Folk Festival
Eureka Springs, AK 72632
(mid-October)

Rackensack Folk Musicals
Courthouse
Mountain View, AK 72560
(every Friday nite—free song fest.
Banjoes, fiddles, dancing)

National Oldtime Fiddler's Contest &
    Festival
High School Gym
Weiser, ID 83672
(3rd week in June. While you're in
Weiser, see the National Fiddler's Hall of
Fame. We know some great people from
Weiser—Dalpha and Delmar—and Delmar
sent us a record from the last fiddler's
contest and it really moves.)

International Music Camp
Bottineau, ND 58318
(8 weeks, June-July)

Original All Northwest Barbershop
    Ballad Contest
For information write:
    Box 13
    Forest Grove, OR 97116

Berkshire Music Festival
Tanglewood
Lenox, MA
(June 30—August 20)

The oldest music festival in the country
(113 years) is held in late October in
Worcester, MA at the Memorial
Auditorium.

Central Park Concerts
Free performances by the NY
Philharmonic, the Metropolitan Opera
Co, and the Goldman-Guggenheim Band
at the Central Park Mall in NY. Entrance
on 72nd St. Summer.

Marlboro Music Festival
Marlboro College
Marlboro, VT
(July—mid-August)

NATIONAL MONUMENTS
See Appendix 8.

Pamphlets on many of the national
monuments can be obtained by writing
the Superintendent of Documents, US
Government Printing Office, Washington
DC 20402. Prices range from 10 to 40
cents.

NATIONAL WILDLIFE
REFUGES

Directory of National Wildlife Refuges,
US Department of the Interior, Fish and
Wildlife Service, Bureau of Sport
Fisheries and Wildlife, US Government
Printing Office, Washington DC 20402.

NIGHTCLUBBING

In the souvenir shops of major cities you
can find pamphlets and books guiding
you toward the nightlife. Also see the
weekend editions of local newspapers.
These things will get you to the biggest
attractions, the ones with the most
money, but not necessarily the best.
Personal taste and familiarity with an
area are the best tools in the last
analysis. Ask friends or strangers.

NUDE BEACHES

California probably has most of the few
designated nude beaches in this country.
Best to check with local headshops,
underground newspapers, college information services or friends. Actually, any
beach is a nude beach. However, don't
offend others. Do your thing in private
by searching out a deserted spot.

The Bronx was a one-industry town. All it produced was INSANITY.

ONE-INDUSTRY TOWNS

East Liverpool, Ohio 43942: A pottery center and site of the Tri-State Pottery Festival in mid-June.

Holland, MI 49423: Has the only wooden shoe factory in the country, tours daily. Holland was settled by Dutch immigrants and holds onto its ancestral heritage.

Burlington, WI 53105: Home of Nestle's (637 S Pine St), free tours daily and samples of chocolate, cocoa, and other confectionary products.

Neenah-Menasha, WI 54956: Paper and paer products center. Factories can be toured, but arrangements must be made in advance. Contact:
Chamber of Commerce
315 - 1 St
Neenah, WI 54956

Tarpon Springs, FL 33589: One of the world's largest sponge markets. Tarpon Springs is a community of Greek fishermen. Sponge diving exhibitions are held daily on the Sponge Docks (810 Dodecanese Blvd). On January 6, at the Festival of the Ephiphany, the waters are blessed. Church dignitaries, a Byzantine choir, costumed children march thru the streets from St. Nicholas Church to Spring Bayou. The Bishop tosses a golden cross into the water and the young men plunge to recover it. Banquets and a ball follow.

Hershey, PA 17033: The chocolate capital of the world. Street lights are shaped like candy kisses. Tours of Hershey Foods Corporation are free.

Weirton, WV 26062: Steel is Weirton and Weirton is steel. If you want to see what working in the steel mills does to people, go to Weirton.

International Falls, MN 56649: Producing paper from America's trees is what they do here. Free tours of the Boise Cascade Corporation.

Oregon City, OR 97045 is also devoted to turning our trees into paper. Free tours of the Crown Zellerbach Corporation.

Tillamook, OR 97141: Cheese and butter. Free tours of the Tillamook County Creamery Association.

See also "Breweries" and "Wineries" in this appendix.

These towns, of course, are only a taste of the kinds of things American cities can specialize in.

PACK TRIPS

Going Light With Backpack or Burro, David Brower, Sierra Club, 1951, $3.50.

Names of packers, guides and services they offer in Idaho:

Idaho Outfitters and Guides Assoc
Box 95
Boise, ID 83701

List of packers and pack trips in California:

California State Chamber of Commerce
Travel and Recreation Dept
350 Bush St
San Francisco, CA 94104

Handbook of Wilderness Travel, George Wells, Colorado Outdoor Sports Corp, 5440 North Valley Highway, Denver, CO 80216, $3.25. Chapter 3: "The Pack Trip" lists outfitters.

Another source of information about packers is:

Eastern Sierra Packers Assoc
Box 147
Bishop, CA

For organized pack trips contact one of these organizations:

Sierra Club Wilderness Outings
1050 Mills Tower
San Francisco, CA 94104

The Wilderness Society
4260 East Evans Ave
Denver, CO 80222

OH, TO FLY FREE

PARACHUTING, SKY-DIVING

These activities are usually connected with small, private airports and are operated through local parachuting or sky-diving clubs. Since they require skill and training up front, plan to put in the necessary hours before you go up. Begin with a friend who knows how, check the "yellow pages" for clubs or airport locations, or watch the skies on Sundays.

PHOTOGRAPHY

Photography is a constant, easy trip within your trip—the best pictures come when you least expect them. If nothing else, photography will teach you to always expect the unexpected. There is a vast array of gear to choose from. Start simple and cheap and see where you go.

One word of caution: do not let your shutter substitute for your eyes. Enjoy the scenery as well as take a picture of it. Otherwise you'll have no trip until you get home.

PLANTS AND HERBS

Outdoor Survival Skills, Larry Dean Olsen, Brigham Young University Press, $2. Chapter 5: "Plants as Food and Medication."

Common Edible and Useful Plants of the West, Muriel Sweet, Naturegraph Books, 1188 Chiquita Rd, Healdsburg, CA 95448, 1962, $1.50. Also from Naturegraph:
Natural Remedies for Better Health, $2.25.
Wild Edible Plants of the Western US, Donald Kirk, $3.95.

Euell Gibbons is, of course, the dean of herb gurus. The budding master who we picked up outside of Las Vegas was the first one to turn us onto Euell Gibbons, and since then we've heard a lot about him. Check him out. See where he leads you. These are his books, all published by David McKay and Co:

Stalking the Healthful Herbs, $2.95, 1966.
Stalking the Wild Asparagus, $2.95, 1962.
Stalking the Blue Eyed Scallop, $2.95, 1964.
Stalking the Good Life, $5.95, 1971.

Edible Wild Plants of Eastern North America, Fernald, Kinsey & Reed, Harper and Row, 1943, $10.

Mushroom Hunter's Field Guide, Alexander Smith, University of Michigan Press, Ann Arbor, MI 48106, 1967, $8.95.

The Peterson Field Guide Series (Houghton-Mifflin) has titles like: *Field Guide to Ferns and Their Related Families, Field Guide to Rocky Mountain Wild Flowers,* $4.95 each.

Edible Wild Plants, Oliver Perry Medsger, Collier Books, 1966, $2.95. Lovingly written. Oliver Perry Medsger is a wise woodsman.

Edible and Poisonous Plants of the Western United States, Burt & Heyl, Touchstone Press, Box 81, Beaverton, OR 97005, $4.95. From the same publishers: *Wildflowers 1: The Cascades,* $6.95.

Back to Eden, Jethro Kloss, Beneficial Books, Box 404, NY 10016, 1971, $2.95. The definitive book on herbal cures. A great book to read. It's beneficial.

A Modern Herbal, Mrs. M. Grieve, Hafner Publishing Co, 31 East 10th St, NY 10003, 1931, $29.50. Highly recommended by the Whole Earth Catalog.

Herbs: Their Culture and Uses, Rosetta Clarkson, Macmillan Co, 1970, $5.95.

The Edible Wild, Berndt Berglund and Clare Bolsby, Charles Scribner Sons, 1971, $2.45. A complete cookbook and guide to edible wild plants in Canada and North America—that's the subtitle. Designed for beginners.

Place Magazine, Star Route 1 (volume 1, number 2), Box 2708, Menlo Park, CA 94025, $2. See page 74 for an article called "Chasing the Wild Chickweed" with recipes for sorrell soup and wilted green salad.

Nature's Medicines, Richard Lucas, Award Books, $.95, has a list of herb distributors.

REGIONAL FOODS AND SPECIALTIES

Sampling regional foods can be the high point of any trip—if you can find them. To do this trip well, you have to be local or lucky. Have patience; don't expect to buzz into town and eat dinner at the truely best restaurant in the area. It probably won't happen, because tourists and natives rarely eat at the same places; the natives know what the tourists don't, and vice versa.

See REGIONAL GUIDES and also Chapter 6, "Food and Lodging."

REGIONAL GUIDES

San Francisco At Your Feet, Margot Patterson Doss, NY, Grove Press, Inc, 1964, $1.95. Walks around San Francisco for visitors, tourists, and residents who want to experience their city more deeply. Each walk is a bit of history, culture, and experience as well as good exercise.

Up Against New York, John Bereny, NY, William Morrow and Co, 1971, $2.95. For visitors who want to crack the shell of the real NY and for residents who are slowly being done in by New York but who can't get up the courage or the money to go to California. Fun reading for someone with lots of time before a trip to New York.

Country Inns and Back Roads, The Berkshire Traveller Press, Stockbridge, MA, 01262, 1972, $3.50. Personalized descriptions, with bits of history thrown in, of inns from another time in America. Wonderfully written in a style reminscent of colonial New England. For those who can afford the somewhat luxurious American Plan Inns (meals included), this book is a delightful way to discover these homey escapes from the present.

Great Escapes (A Guide for Weekend Escapes from the Bay Area), Great Escapes Publications, 1671 Greenwich Street #4, San Francisco, CA 94123, 1972, $2.25. "Great Escapes is not a comprehensive travelogue but rather a selective guide for nine special week-end getaways from the Bay Area . . . essential information for travelers and campers looking for gorgeous locations with smogless skies and unlimited activity." If you are visiting Northern California and want to discover some new and wonderful places, read this book.

All About Arizona, Thomas B. Lesure, Harian Publications, Greenlawn, NY 11740, 1971, $2.95. Arizona is the state full of the history of the great Hopi people. This book doesn't tell you much about that. Aimed at the older traveler, the retired couple who wants a healthy vacation or a sunny place to spend their later years.

All About California, Thomas B. Lesure, Harian Publications, Greenlawn, NY 11740, 1970, $2.50. Good information for the middle class traveler.

Norman Ford's Florida, Norman Ford, Harian Publications, Greenlawn, NY 11740, 1972, $3.00. Another Harion book for "A good trip or Successful retirement." Lots of emphasis on healthy climate for older people.

California Bike Tours, Gousha Publications, San Jose, CA, 1972, $2.95. H.M. Gousha Co is a well-known and reputable map-maker. Gives tours around California with good maps. Tells about points of interest surrounding the region you are touring. Highly recommended. Also from Gousha: *Explorer's Guide to the West*, $1.95 each for a series of 6 guidebooks on different aspects of the West (California, Oregon, Washington, Nevada). The individual titles are: *Cities, Coast, Desert, Rivers and Lakes, Northern Mountains, Southern Mountains.* and *Weekend Guide to San Francisco*, $1.95. 10 tours.

Ritchie Press Publishes the following. guides by Russ Leadabrand:

> *Guidebook to the Mojave Desert (including Death Valley Joshua Tree National Monument and Antelope Valley)* 1964, $1.95.
> *Guidebook to the San Bernardino Mountains*, 1964, $1.95.
> *Guidebook to the San Gabriel Mountains*, 1967, $1.95.
> *Guidebook to the Southern Sierra Nevada*, 1968, $1.95.

These are available from Ward Ritchie Press, 3044 Riverside Drive, Los Angeles, CA 90039.

New York on $5 and $10 A Day, Joan Feldman and Norma Ketay, NY, Arthur Frommer Inc, distributed by Simon and Schuster, 1970, $2.50. Good only for hotel and restaurant recommendations.

Instant Chicago, Jory Graham, Rand McNally, 1972, $2.95.

Philadelphia Guide, Nancy Love, Philadelphia Magazine, 1968.

Collegiate Guide to Greater Philadelphia, Mixed Media, 1972, $3.

A Guide to San Francisco and the Bay Region, James Benet, Random House, 1963, $1.95.

From Golden Guides: *Everglades National Park* and *Acadia National Park*, $1.25 each.

Grand Canyon National Park, Robert Scharff, Canyonlands Press, Box 21021, Salt Lake City, UT 84121, $2.25.

RIVER STEAMERS

The Delta Queen: for brochures, rates and information write:
Greene Line Steamers
Public Landing
Cincinnati, OH 45202
The only remaing river boat still functioning. Week-long trips (Cincinnati to New Orleans) and week-end trips available. Baby-sitting on board.

THIS IS A ROCK. IT Sits in my Heart.

ROCK CLIMBING

The following books are available from The Ski Hut, 1615 University Ave, Berkeley, CA 94703:

> *High Over Boulder*, Ament and McCarty, $5.50.
> *Climber's Guide to Oregon*, Nicholas Dodge, $3.95.
> *Guide to the Sandia Mountains*, Lawrence Kline, $1.75.
> *Guide to the Colorado Mountains*, Robert Ormes, $6.
> *Climber's Guide to the Tetons*, Leigh Ortenburger, $6.
> *Climber's Guide to the Pinnacles National Monument*, Steve Roper, $2.75.
> *Climber's Guide to Yosemite Valley*, Steve Roper, $6.95.
> *Climber's Guide to the High Sierra*, Harvey Voge, $5.95.
> *Desert Peaks Guide*, Walt Wheelock, $1.
> *Climber's Guide to Tahquitz and Suicide Rocks*, Chuck Wilts, $4.

From The Mountaineers, Box 122, Seattle, WA 98111, the following books are available:

> *Guide to Leavenworth Rock Climbing Areas*, $2.75.
> *Routes and Rocks*, D.F. Crowder & R.W. Tabor, $5.
> *Routes and Rocks in Mt. Challenger Quadrangle*, R.W. Tabor, $2.95.

Rocky Mountain Trails, Pruett Publishing Co, Box 1560, Boulder, CO 80302, $3.95.

On Snow and Ice and Rock, Gaston Rebuffat, Oxford University Press, $12.50. Step-by-step photos of vanced and artificial technique. Beautiful book.

Fundamentals of Rock Climbing, Appalachian Mountain Club, 5 Joy St, Boston MA 02108, $1.

Royal Robbins, the noted climber, teaches his skill thru his school:
Rockcraft
906 Durant St
Modesto, CA 95350

For equipment, see Appendix 12, "Outdoor Equipment Suppliers." See also "Mountaineering" in this appendix for related material.

RODEOS

Rodeo Sports News
2929 W 19th Ave
Denver, CO 80204
(303) 244-8657
Published every two weeks with
approved listings of rodeos. List
coordinated by the Rodeo Cowboys
Assoc, Inc.

Also try the local Chamber of
Commerce, but you have to be in season.

The best way to see a rodeo is to be
driving into a little western town just as
they are having one. But don't expect to
find any on the interstates.

SAILING

Sailing Illustrated, Patrick M Royce,
Royce Publications, Box 1967, New port
Beach, CA 92663, $4.15. Whole Earth
Catalog says "It's a nice job of
information packaging with easy
retrieval designed in."

The Glenans Sailing Manual, Philippe
Harle, John de Graff Inc, 34 Oak Ave,
Tuckahoe, NY 10707, 1961, $10. Whole
Earth Catalog says "This is the closest
thing we've seen to a definitive text on
small boat sailing."

Golden Handbook of Sailing, Western
Publishing Co, 1220 Mound Ave, Racine,
WI 53404, $1.25.

For information on fine old-fashioned
wooden rowing and sailing dinghies send
for the free catalog from:

The Old Boathouse
2770 Westlake North
Seattle, WA 98109

Charts (maps of the waters) are essential
if you're going sailing unless, like Huck
Finn, you don't care where you're going.
Charts of the Atlantic, Pacific, and Gulf
coasts and the Intra-coastal waterway
come from the Coast and Geodetic
Survey (ESSA Washington Science
Center, Rockville, MD 20852). The
Mississippi River and its tributaries are
on Army Corps of Engineers charts (look
in your phone directory for a local
office), and the Great Lakes are handled
by Lake Survey (630 Federal Building
and US Court House, Detroit, MI
48226). Index maps are free. Charts of
the rivers come in books, and prices vary
but are usually somewhere around $2.
Catalogs of what maps are available are
also free from the proper agency.

The Last Whole Earth Catalog
(distributed by Random House) lists the
sources for some charts on page 285.

SCUBA DIVING
(See Skin Diving)

Golden Guide to Scuba Diving, Western
Publishing Co, Inc, 1220 Mound Ave,
Racine, WI 53404, $1.25.

SHELL COLLECTING

Exploring Pacific Coast Tidepools,
Earnest Braun & Vincent Brown,
Naturegraph Books, 1188 Chiquita Rd,
Healdsburg, CA 95448, $2. Also from
Naturegraph: *Gems of the World's
Oceans,* Dr. A G Melvin, $2.95.

Golden Guide to Sea Shells of the World,
Western Publishing Co, 1220 Mound
Ave., Racine, WI 53404, $1.25.

Houghton-Mifflin's Peterson Field Guide
Series has:

*A Field Guide to Shells of the Pacific
Coast and Hawaii,* $5.95.
*Field Guide to Shells of Our Atlantic
and Gulf Coasts,* $5.95.

SKI TOURING,
CROSS COUNTRY SKIING,
SNOWSHOEING

Complete Cross Country Ski Touring,
William J. Lederer, W W Norton & Co,
1970, $3.50. Easy to read, friendly
lessons on how to ski x-c (cross
country).

From the Mountaineers, Box 122, Seattle, WA 98111:
*Snowshoe Hikes in the Cascades and
Olympics* Gene Prater, $3.95.
*55 Ways to the Wilderness in South-
central Alaska,* Helen Nienhueser,
$7.95.
Northwest Ski Trails, Ted Mueller,
$4.95.

*Nordic Touring and Cross Country Ski-
ing,* Arthur Vanous Co, 20 Bonita Pl,
Hackensack, NJ 07601, $3.

Ski Tours in California, David Beck,
Wilderness Press, 2440 Bancroft Way,
Berkeley, CA 94704, $4.95.

The New Cross Country Ski Book,
Johnny Caldwell, Stephen Greene Press,
Brattleboro, VT, 1972, $3.95. Family
x-c. How to have fun doing something
new and inexpensive.

Sierra Spring Ski Touring, Hans Joachim
Burhenne, Mountain Press, 3445 Wash-
ington, San Francisco, CA, $7.95.
Descriptions of 28 tours in the Sierras.

The Wilderness Society (4260 East Evans
Ave, Denver, CO 80222) has planned x-c
outings.

Complete information on ski touring
clinics and clubs can be obtained by
sending $2 to:
Ski Touring Council Inc.
West Hill Rd
Troy, VT 05868

SKIING, DOWNHILL

Golden Guide to Skiing, Western Publishing Co, 1220 Mound Ave, Racine, WI
53404, $1.25.

Northwest Ski Trails, Ted Mueller, The
Mountaineers, Box 122, Seattle, WA
98111, $4.95.

Skiing Western America, Charles Miller,
101 Productions, 79 Liberty St, San
Francisco, CA 94110, 1972 $3.95. A
skier's appraisal and evaluation of ski
resorts. A handsome book with breakdowns on each resort giving motel rates,
lifts available, ski schools and ski rental
information. Thoro but concerned with
slick resorts, expensive accommodations.

A Guide to Western Skiing, Curtis Case-
wit, Chronicle Books, 54 Mint St, San
Francisco, CA 94103, 1972, $2.95.
Guide to ski resorts, restaurants, etc.
Information on ski conditions, type of
snow, climate.

United States Ski Association, Rocky
Mt. Division, 1463 Larimer Square, Denver, CO 80202. They publish a newspaper, "The Rocky Mountain Skier"
which comes with membership in the
organization.

Winter Activities in National Parks, $.15.
A publication of the US Government
Printing Office, Washington DC 20402.

SKIN DIVING

*The New Science of Skin and Scuba
Diving,* Association Press, 291 Broadway, NY 10007, 1968, $2.95. "Now in
its newest edition, it is more complete
than any other book ever written on this
subject by anyone." Whole Earth
Catalog.

US Navy Diving Manual, Superintendent
of Documents, US Government Printing
Office, Washington DC 20204, $7.95.

Free Catalogs of equipment available
from:
New England Divers
42 Water St
Beverly, MA 01915

M & E Marine Supply
Box 601
Camden, NY

and for $1 you can get a catalog from:
US Divers
3323 West Warner Ave
Santa Ana, CA 92702

SOARING, GLIDING

See PARACHUTING and SKY-DIVING.

SPELUNKING

National Spelunking Society
Cave Avenue
Huntsville, AL 35810
Write them for a list of their
publications.

Spelunking library:
  21 William St
  Closter, NY 07624

SPIRITUAL CENTERS
(A Selected List)

Ali Akbar Kahn School of Music
234 Hawthorne St
Larkspur, CA 94399

Ananda Marga Yoga Society
3453 E 12th St
Wichita, KS 67200

Ananada Meditation Retreat
Allegheny Star Route
Nevada City, CA 95959

Association of Research and
  Enlightenment
Box 959
Virginia Beach, VA 23451

Bahai House of Worship
12 Lindon
Wilmette, IL 60091

Blue Mountain Center of Meditation
Box 381
Berkeley, CA 94701

Christian Spiritual Alliance
Lakemont, GA 30552

JOHREI (The Art of Channeling Light)
3068 San Marino St
Los Angeles, CA 90006

Cultural Integration Fellowship &
  Ashram
2650 Fulton St
San Francisco, CA 90006

Dasashram Satsang Centers
Lokoya Tapoyan
Napa, CA 94558

Divine Light Mission
695 South Harvard Blvd
Los Angeles, CA

Eckankar
Box 5325
Las Vegas, NV 89102

The Foundation
(See Chapter 14 for some information
about "The Farm" — the commune
where members of The Foundation live.)
Route 1 Box 197A
Summertown, TN 38483

Fransisters
2168 S Lafayette St
Denver, CO 80210

3HO—Healthy, Happy, Holy
  Organization
8802 Melrose Ave
Los Angeles, CA 90069

House of Love and Prayer
1456 - 9th Ave
San Francisco, CA 94100

Inner Light Foundation
Box 761
Novato, CA 94967

Integral Yoga Institute
500 West End Ave
NY 10000

International I Ching Studies Institute
10985 Bluffside Dr
Studio City, CA 91604

International Society for Krishna
  Consciousness
3764 Watseka Ave
Los Angeles, CA 90034

International Swananda Yoga and
  Vedanta Society
115 N Larchmont Blvd
Los Angeles, CA 90004

Krishnamurti
Box 216
Ojai, CA 93023

Lama Foundation
Box 444
San Cristobal, NM 87564

Macrobiotics (Ohsawa Foundation)
1434 N Curson Ave
Los Angeles, CA 90000

Meher Baba
Box 487
Myrtle Beach, SC 29577

One World Family of the Messiah's
  World Crusade
2340 Piedmont Ave
Berkeley, CA 94704

Radha Soami
2922 Las Flores
Arlington, CA 92503

Rosicrucian Fellowship
Box 713
Oceanside, CA 92054

Ruhani Satsang
11404 Laken Pl
Oakton, VA 22124

Self Realization Fellowship
3880 San Rafael Ave
Los Angeles, CA 90065

Society of Brothers
Rifton, NY 12471

Sri Chinmoy Centers
85-45 - 149th St
Jamaica Hills, Queens, NY 11435

Sufi Order
410 Precita Ave
San Francisco, CA 94100

T'ai Chi Ch'Uan
211 Canal St
NY10001

Universal Life Church
601 Third St
Modesto, CA 95351

Vedanta Society
2963 Webster St
San Francisco, CA 94123

Wailua University of Contemplative Arts
Kapaa, Kauai, HI 96746

Zen Center
300 Page St
San Francisco, CA 94100

Tassajara Hot Springs
Carmel Valley, CA 95705

For more about these organizations, see
the *Spiritual Community Guide*, listed in
USA Bookshelf (Appendix 2). Other
books in that section (under "Soul
Books for Americans") may prove
helpful.

STATE FAIRS

See Appendix 4, which lists state Tourist
Information Offices. Write them — the
dates change in each state every year.

STATE PARKS

All the standard camping and trailer
guide books list state parks. See
"Camping Guides" in Appendix 3, USA
GUIDEBOOKS.

STEAM TRAINS AND RAILROADS

The Silverton Train
Rio Grande Depot
Durango, CO 81301

American Rail Tours
210 Post St
San Francisco, CA 94108

The National Railroad Passenger Corp
955 L'Enfant Pl SW
Washington DC 20024

Ohio Railway Museum
990 Proprietors Road
Worthington, OH 43085

California Western Railroad
Box 907-B
Fort Bragg, CA 95437

The Durango Gray Line
Rio Grande Depot
Durango, CO 81301

Green Mountain Railroad Corp
Box 57
Chester Depot, VT 05144

The Valley Railroad Co
Essex Station
Exit 3, CT

White Mountain Scenic Railroad
Box 496
McNary, AZ 85930

Reader Railroad
Box 6049
Shreveport, LA 71106

Colorado Central Narrow Gauge Railway
409 Lookout View Dr
Golden, CO 80401

Cripple Creek &
    Victor Narrow Gauge Railroad
Box 459
Cripple Creek, CO 80813

Colorado Railroad Museum
Box 641
Golden, CO 80401

Cumbres & Toltec Scenic Railroad
Railroad Depot
Chama, NM 87520

National Museum of Transport
3015 Barretts Station Rd
St. Louis, MO 63122

Black Hills Central Railroad
Hill City SD 57745

I THINK I CAN
I THINK I CAN
aum shanti
I THINK I CAN

SURFING

Surfer, a magazine which Whole Earth Catalog says is "well ahead of its imitators and miles ahead of most other sports/hobby magazines" is $5 per yr. Write to: Surfer, Box 1028, Dana Point, CA 92629.

Organizations with information about surfing:
    Hawaii Surfing Assoc
    Box 8125
    Honolulu, HI 96815

    Hawaii Visitors Bureau
    2270 Kalakaua
    Honolulu, HI 96815

Surfboard Builders Yearbook, Michael Morgan, Transmedia, 9811 Edgelake Rd, LaMesa, CA 96815, 1971, $4.

SWIMMING

Drownproofing, Fred Lanoue, Prentice Hall, Englewood Cliffs, NJ 07632, $4.95.

For guidance to local "swimming holes," best to contact the local Chamber of Commerce or local park and recreation office. Do not swim anywhere unless you're sure it's safe.

Also see Place Magazine, Spring 1972, Vol 1, No 1, "Swimming Holes and Hot Springs."

THEATERS

West Coast Theatrical Directory, Gousha Publications, Box 6227, San Jose, CA 95150, 1972, $6.95.

What follows is a selected list of American theaters. I know you can discover some unique ones of your own. And forming a traveling theater company would be fun.

Eugene O'Neill Memorial Theater Center
Waterford, CT
(This includes: The National Theater of the Deaf, Playwright's Conference, Critics Institute, Barn Theater, Instant Theater, Amphitheater. For schedules and reservations write: Box 206, Waterford, CT 06385.)

American Shakespeare Festival Theater
1850 Elm St
Stratford, CT

Westport Country Playhouse
Boston Post Road
Westport, CT

Lakewood Theater
Skowhegan, ME

Karamu House & Theater
2355 East 89th St at Quincy Ave
Cleveland, OH
(For more information write: Convention and Visitors Bureau, 511 Terminal Tower, Cleveland, OH 44113.)

Asolo Theater
Box 1393
Sarasota, FL
(The state theater of Florida, on the grounds of the John Ringling estate.)

Padua Hills Theater
Padua Ave
Claremont, CA
(Traditional Mexican plays performed for gringos.)

Old Globe Theater
(For information write: Box 2171, San Diego, CA 92112)

American Conservatory Theater
450 Geary St
San Francisco, CA

Marin Shakespeare Festival
Forest Meadows Theater
San Rafael, CA
(For schedules write: Box 2306, San Rafael, CA 94902)

Ford's Theater
511 - 10th St NW
Washington DC

Kennedy Theater
New Hampshire Ave & F St NW
Washington DC
(For schedules write: 726 Jackson Rd NW, Washington DC 20566)

Shakespeare Summer Festival
Sylvan Theater, Washington Monument
Washington DC
(For Schedules write: 1000 - 6th St SW, Washington DC 20024)

Annapolis Summer Garden Theater
Annapolis, MD

The Music Circus
Lambertsville, NJ

The Paper Mill Playhouse
Brookside Dr
Millburn, NJ

Flat Rock Playhouse
Hendersonville, NC
(State theater of North Carolina, performances by the Vagabond Players.)

Town Theater
1012 Sumter St
columbia, SC
(One of America's first little theaters — established 1919.)

Ice House Theater
1 Hill St
Hannibal, MO
(In the town where Huck Finn and Tom Sawyer came from — early American vagabonds.)

Guthrie Theater
725 Vineland Pl
Minneapolis, MN

Oregon Shakespeare Festival
Luthia Park
Ashland, OR
(For information write well in advance to Oregon Shakespeare Festival, Ashland, OR 97250 — June 17 - September 10 are the dates for this famous festival.)

TREE, FLOWER AND OTHER PLANT IDENTIFICATION

Flowers, Trees, Non-Flowering Plants, Trees of North America are all publications of the Western Publishing Co (Golden Books), 1220 Mound Ave, Racine, WI 53404, $1.25 each.

Common Wildflowers of the Grand Canyon, Canyonlands Press, Box 21021, Salt Lake City, UT 84121, $1.45. Also from Canyonlands Press:
> *Field Guide to Rocky Mountain Wildflowers*, J Craighead, $4.25.
> *Grand Canyon Wildflowers*, W B McDougall, $2.80.

The Peterson Field Guide Series (Houghton Mifflin Co, 2 Park St, Boston, MA 02107) publishes a lot of interesting guides, $5.95 each. Here are two of them — send for their list of publications:
> *A Field Guide to Trees and Shrubs*
> *A Field Guide to Ferns*

From Naturegraph Books (1188 Chiquita Rd, Healdsburg, CA 95448):
> *Lake Tahoe Wildflowers*, Kenneth Legg, $2.25.
> *Redwood Empire Wildflower Jewels*, Dorothy Young, $2.95.

See also "Plants and Herbs" in this appendix.

WALKING

The classic is *The Complete Walker* by Colin Fletcher (Alfred Knopf, $7.95). Here's some of the Whole Earth Catalog review: "Besides just the stuff, what to take and waht to leave behind, it also takes you on a trip thru Colin Fletcher, which is an outing all by itself."

The Magic of Walking, Aaron Sussman and Ruth Goode, Simon and Schuster, $2.95. A lot about the philosophy and poetry of walking, as well as a walking guide. Good reading.

Handbook of Wilderness Travel, George Wells (cited elsewhere in this appendix), has information on the organized trails: Appalachian Trail, Pacific Crest Trailway, California State Trail, and The Long Trail.

The Long Trail Guidebook, The Green Mountain Club (an organization for walkers), 63 Center St, Rutland, VT, $1.

Guide to the Pacific Crest Trailway, Pacific Crest Trail System Conference, Hotel Green, Pasadena, CA, $2.25.

The Appalachian Trail, Appalachian Trail Conference, 1916 Sunderland Place NW, Washington DC, $.15.

New York Walk Book, American Geographic Society, $9.95.

San Francisco At Your Feet, Margot Patterson Doss, Grove Press, $1.95. Guided walking tours in a walker's town.

See Appendix 12 — "Outdoor Equipment Suppliers" and "Hiking" in this appendix for related information. Read Chapter 13.

WILDERNESS AND ENVIRONMENTAL ORGANIZATIONS

California Tomorrow
681 Market St
San Francisco, CA 94105
Publishes "Cry California"

California Coastal Alliance
Box 4161
Woodside, CA

California Native Plant Society
2490 Channing Way
Berkeley, CA 94062

California Trout
Box 2046
San Francisco, CA 94126

Desert Protective Council
Box 33
Banning, CA 92220

Environmental Defense Fund
1910 N St NW
Washington DC 20036
Publishes a "Newsletter"

Friends of Animals
11 W 60th St
NY 10023

Friends of the Earth
451 Pacific Ave
San Francisco, CA 94133
Publishes "Not Man Apart"

The Izaak Walton League of America
1326 Waukegan Rd
Glenview, IL 60025

National Audubon Society
1130 Fifth Ave
NY 10028

National Parks Assoc
1701 Eighteenth St NW
Washington DC 20009

National Wildlife Federation
1412 - 16th St
Washington DC 20009

Nature Conservancy
215 Market St
San Francisco, CA 94105

Palnned Parenthood
810 - 7th Ave
NY 10019

Planning and Conservation League
909 - 12th St
Sacramento, CA 95814

Outward Bound
Andover, MA 01810

Rocky Mountain Center on Environment
580 E Jewell
Denver, CO 80222

Sierra Club
1050 Mills Tower
San Francisco, CA 94104
Publishes "Sierra Club Bulletin"

Wilderness Society
729 Fifteenth St NW
Washington DC 20005
Publishes "Wilderness Society Bulletin"

World Wildlife Fund
901 - 17th St NW
Washington DC 20005

Zero Population Growth
Los Altos, CA 94022

See also "Ecology" in this appendix.

WINDJAMMING

Windjammer Cruises
Box 120
Miami Beach, FL 33139

WINERIES
(A Selected List)

All the wineries listed below conduct daily free tours.

Weibel Champagne Vineyards
1250 Stanford Ave
Fremont, CA

Wente Bros Winery
5565 Tesla Rd
Livermore, CA 94550

Guild Wine Co
1 Winemasters Way
Lodi, CA 95240

Christian Bros Mont LaSalle Vineyards
4411 Redwood Rd
Napa, CA 94558

Christian Bros Wine and Champagne Cellars
2555 Main St
St. Helena, CA 94574

Louis Martini Winery
St. Helena, CA 94574

Hanns Kornell Champagne Cellars
Larkmead Lane
St. Helena, CA 94574

Charles Krug Winery
St. Helena, CA 94574

Beringer-Los Hermanos Vineyards
2000 Main St
St. Helena, CA 94574

Beaulieu Vineyard
Rutherford, CA

Inglenook Vineyard
Rutherford, CA

Paul Masson Champagne Cellars
13150 Saratoga Ave
Saratoga, CA 94070

Sebastiani Vineyards
389 - 4th St E
Sonoma, CA 95476

Buena Vista Winery
18000 Old Winery Rd
Sonoma, CA 95476

Kluxen Winery
28 Fairview Ave
Madison, NJ 07940

Wiederkehr Wine Cellars
Altus, AR 72821

Stone Hill Winery
Stone Hill Highway
Hermann, MO 65041
(This is a German town; German is
taught in the schools and they have a
Maifest. Some of the original sturdy
German buildings are still standing. Ja
wohl!)

Honeywood Winery
501 - 14th St SE
Salem, OR

Italian Swiss Colony
Asti, CA

WORKING

If you want to find work, check the
following sources:
Summer Employment Directory of
the United States
National Directory Service
266 Ludlow Ave
Cincinnati, OH 45220 ($5.95)

Norman Ford, How to Travel and
Get Paid For It, Harian Publications, Greenlawn, NY 11740,
$2.50. Tells you how to get a job
that takes you traveling. This
book is mostly about working and
traveling abroad, but there are
some hints for us in the US.

The Student Guide to Employment:
How to Earn a Lot of Money in
College, Harvard Student
Agencies, 993 Massachusetts Ave,
Cambridge, MA 02138, 1968,
$1.95.

Summer Jobs in Federal Agencies,
Announcement #414 (free) from:
United States Civil Service
Commission
Washington DC 20415

Who's Hiring Who, Richard Lathrop.
A directory of employers avail-
able from:
Who's Hiring Who
Box 3651
Washington DC 20007.

If you want to drop out of the daily
rigors so that you can travel and work on
your own terms, check these sources:

Working Loose, New Vocations Project, American Friends Service
Committee, 1972, $1.95. A book
about people looking for good
work. People who have found or
created meaningful and energizing
work tell how they did it. Lots of
straight talking by real folks.
Order from:
American Friends Service Committee
2160 Lake Street
San Francisco, CA 94121.

What Color is Your Parachute? (A
Practical Manual for Job Hunters
and Career Changers), Richard
Nelson Bolles, Ten Speed Press,
Box 4310, Berkeley, CA 94704,
1972, $3.95. A whimsical and
valuable book about how to get a
job when you want one. Aimed at
that growing class of 35-45 year
old youngsters who have dropped
out. A technical book that is
funny and Very Serious about
explaining the structure and
operation of job hunting. Contains list of job counsellors and
others who can help you find a
job.

How to Live in the New America,
William Kaysing, Prentice-Hall,
Englewood Cliffs, NJ, $8.95.
Chapter 2: "How Do I Make a
Living?"

An organization that has been working
for some time on the problem of new
vocations for new people—they'll help
you with information if you help them
with a donation (at least to cover
mailing):
Vocations for Social Change
Canyon, CA 94516.

A fine magazine that always has lots
of articles about how to support
yourself in the style you choose is
(some examples: "I Drive for
Money," "How to Find Work as a
Picker," "Your Own Home Typ-
ing Business"):
Mother Earth News
Box 38
Madison, WI 44057

Work When You Want to Work, John
Fanning, NY, Collier Books,
1969, $1.25.

The Back to Work Handbook for
Housewives, Barbara Prentice,
NY, Collier Books, 1971, $1.50.

If you're about to drop out and find a
new way to live but need the support of
others and a few suggestions, contact
Black Bart who publishes the Outlaw
Newsletter:
Outlaw Institute
c/o Shirley Nice
1349 Greenwich
San Francisco, CA 94109

New York temporary agencies that pay
in full at the end of each day:

Johnny on the Spot
110 W Houston St
982-7224

Office Substitutes
565 Fifth Ave
OX7-5311

Kelly Industries
393 Canal St
966-0040

Perlowitz Temporary Agency
135 Norfolk St

Labor Pool Inc
130 W Houston St
OR4-8650

Aames Temporary Staff
41 E 42nd St
867-1177

Hourly Helpers
219 Thompson St
533-7600

Everyday Helpers
88 W Third St
673-6190

Dependable Temporary Help
171 W 23rd St
691-9040

Midtown Help Agency
307 W 39th St
868-3310

Laboraids
207 - 7th Ave
6:30 am shapeup

ZOOS: A SELECTED LIST

"Wild things in captivity
while they keep their own wild purity
won't breed, they mope, they die.

All men are in captivity
active with captive activity
and the best won't breed,
    though they don't know why."
                        —D H Lawrence

Jimmy Morgan Zoo
Lane Park
Birmingham, AL

Papago Park
Tempe, AZ
(The first zoo to attempt to save
antelopes from extinction.)

Greater Los Angeles Zoo
Griffith Park
Hollywood, CA
(Displays of endangered species.)

San Diego Zoological Gardens
Balboa Park
San Diego CA
(The Louvre of zoos.)

Fleishacker Zoo
Zoo Avenue
San Francisco, CA

Cheyenne Mountain Zoo
South of Colorado Springs in
Broadmoor, CO

Crandon Park Zoological Gardens
Key Biscayne, FL
(Where the first ardvark in America was
born.)

Honolulu Zoo
Kapabula and Kalakaua
Honolulu, HI

Chicago Zoological Park
8500 West, 3100 South
Brookfield, IL
(The largest elephant in captivity.)

Lincoln Park Zoo
Chicago, IL
(America's gorilla headquarters.)

Detroit Zoological Park
Ten Mile Road
Royal Oak, MI
(The first zoo to do away with bars and
cages.)

Como Park Zoo
1200 Lexington Parkway
St. Paul, MN
(The National Student Association says:
"Wide variety of animals and hippies.")

St. Louis Zoo
Forest Park
ST. Louis, MO

New York Zoological Gardens
(The Bronx Zoo)
Bronx Park
Bronx, NY
(Scheduled bat demonstrations.)

Buffalo Zoological Gardens
Delaware Park
Buffalo, NY
(Established 1870.)

Central Park Zoo
64th St and Fifth Ave
NY (Birds, monkeys, lions, seals, camels
and a fascinating collection of homo
sapiens.)

Cinciannati Zoological Gardens
Forest Park
Cincinnati, OH
(The world's finest cat compendium.)

Cleveland Zoological Park
Brookside Park
Cleveland, OH
(Has the only Bongo antelope in captiv-
ity as well as the Nubian ibex.)

Toledo Zoological Park
2700 Broadway
Toledo, OH
(Birds of Paradise, llamas, vicunas, tapirs,
rheas, yaks.)

Oklahoma City Zoo
Lincoln Park
Oklahoma City, OK

Portland Zoological Gardens
Washington Park
Portland, OR

Philadelphia Zoological Gardens
Fremont Park
Philadelphia PA
(Established 1874.)

The Pittsburgh Zoo
Highland Park
Pittsburgh, PA

Overton Park Zoo
Memphis, TN

Forth Worth Zoological Park
Forest Park
Fort Worth, TX

Houston Zoological Gardens
Herman Park
Bellaire, TX

Woodland Park Zoological Gardens
Seattle, WA

The National Zoo
Rock Creek Park
Washington DC
(Animals that were diplomatic gifts: a
dragon lizard, pygmy hippos, kiwis.
Smokey the Bear and his wife live here,
along with Ham, the chimp that went
into outer space.)

Milwaukee County Zoo
Bluemound Road
Milwaukee, WI

Catskill Game Farm
Catskill, NY
(The world's largest collection of horned
and hooved animals.)

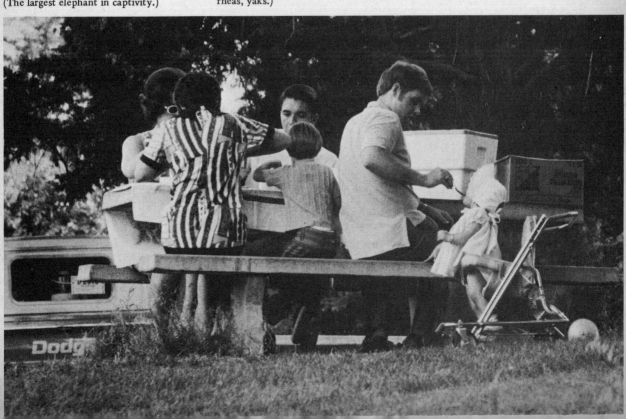

APPENDIX 2

USA Bookshelf

Listening to America, Bill Moyers, Dell Publishing Co, 1971, $1.25. Interviews conducted on a journey to America by an ex-assistant to President Johnson who goes out to meet the people. And he does. He even met us once in San Francisco. Highly sophisticated reporting and good reading — makes you feel like you're lying down, ear to the ground, listening to America Speak.

The Greening of America, Charles Reich, Bantam Books, 1970, $1.95. The origins of the revolution in consciousness. Where is it taking us? What does it really mean?

How to Live in the New America, William Kaysing, Prentice-Hall Inc, 1972, $8.95. A manual for dropping out of straight society and falling into the country. A treasure house of hints, guidelines, how-to-do-it. From how to make bread to all about the motorcycle. Lists, with maps, all the thermal springs of the US. Lots of goodies.

Living Poor With Style, Ernest Callenbach, Bantam Books, 1972, $1.95. Like *How to Live in the New America*, this is a manual for dropping out. But its emphasis is on city rather than country life, and on how to stop being a consumer rather than "how-to-do-it" hints. How to construct a free household. Readable.

Travels With Charley: In Search of America, John Steinbeck, Viking Press, 1962, $1.65. "A journey is a person in itself; no two are alike. And all plans, safeguards, policing, and coercion are fruitless. We find after years of struggle that we do not take a trip; a trip takes us." Steinbeck's sentimental journey to America is enlightening now, ten years later. Full of travel wisdoms and literate tho stodgy whimsey.

On The Loose, Terry and Renny Russell, Ballantine Books, 1967, $7.95. The record of two vagabonds' experiences in the American wilderness. Photographs and poetry that put you in touch with the intense beauty of America and the energy that is generated from seeing it naked and raw.

Total Loss Farm, Raymond Mungo, E.P. Dutton Co, 1970, $1.65. One trend in America that now seems irreversible is the movement by young people out of the city and into the country . . . to farm, to roam, or to just be there. Learn why this movement is happening and who the people in it are.

The Time Life Library of America and *The American Wilderness* series, Time-Life Books, Chicago, IL 60611. These two sets of books try to tell the story of America. The first includes: *USA: A Visitor's Handbook* (1969, $4.95) and *Pictorial History of the American Negro* (1970, $9.95). The Wilderness series has, for $5.95 each: *The High Sierra, The Grand Canyon, The Northeast Coast,* and *Wild Alaska*. *The High Sierra,* by Ezra Bowen has beautiful photographs by David Cavagnaro and Harald Sund, among others. The rambling text is primarily concerned with history, geologic as well as socio-political. *The Grand Canyon,* by Robert Wallace, has a similar thrust, and like *The High Sierra,* takes you thru the valleys and canyons slowly, making you long to leave your armchair and start roaming the high country.

American Heritage Books on America, McGraw Hill Book Co. Here are a few selections from the dean publisher of Americana:
American Album, American Heritage and Ballantine Books, 1970, $3.95. "The purpose of this book is to revisit an utterly vanished earlier America by means of old photographs . . ." Many trips.

Book of Natural Wonders, Simon and Schuster, 1963, $16.50. Maps, photographs, drawings of the wondrous places of America like Acadia National Park, the Okefenoke Swamp, the Great Lakes, the Indiana Dunes, Isle Royale National Park, the Gulf of Alaska.

Book of the Indians, Simon and Schuster, 1961, $16.50. Introduction by John F. Kennedy: "Before we can set out on the road to success, we have to know where we are going, and before we can know that we must determine where we have been in the past. It seems a basic requirement to study the history of our Indian people." Very scholarly, somewhat paternalistic, but thoro and informative. (For more books about Indians, see that heading in *Appendix 1.*

Some more, but not all, books in the American Heritage collection (all are $16.50):
Book of the Revolution, Simon and Schuster, 1958.
Book of the Pioneer Spirit, Simon and Schuster, 1959.
Book of Great Historic Places, Bruce Catton, Simon and Schuster, 1957.
Pictorial Atlas of US History, American Heritage, 1966.

SOUL BOOKS FOR AMERICANS
(see also "Indians" in *Appendix 1*)

Caravan, Stephen, Random House/Bookworks, 1972, $3.95. Transcripts of services/lectures/discussions conducted by Stephen Gaskin when he was touring American with a caravan of followers. The book embodies Stephen's religion and is an attempt to spread certain life precepts like total honesty and compassion. This is a spiritual guidebook as well as a record of the caravan's experiences in the heartland of America. It will help you on your trip. (See chapter 14, "Staying Awhile," to find out what happened to the caravan when it found a home.)

Centering, M.C. Richards, Wesleyan University Press, 1962, $2.45. How to find your center and act with it in tune. The image of centering comes from pottery: to feel the whole in every part. This knowledge could make a trip to America, or anywhere, a high experience. Like *Caravan*, this is personalized spiritual guidance, but less demanding in its approach. You can learn to "center" no matter what you do and without altering your general life stye. A guidebook to a richer life.

How to Find God: The Yoga Aphorisms of Patanjali, translated and with commentary by Swami Prabhavanda and Christopher Isherwood, New American Library, 1969, $.75. This book will help you see the reality that is America compassionately, ("to love Atman in ourselves is to love it everywhere. And to love the Atman everywhere is to go beyond any manifestation of Nature to the Reality within Nature."). This book also has exercises to keep you from boredom and depression. In the privacy of your car, for instance, chant the name of God (Aum, or whatever name you pick) and see if it doesn't change the climate of your mind. ("It cannot do otherwise.") The object of the Aphorisms of Patanjali is to give you some control over the stream of reverie that substitutes for thought in most of our minds. The tendency to let this reverie overcome us is especially prevalant in car travel and leads to boredom and frustration, not to mention accidents. Patanjali will help show you the way out of this trap. And he also has a general attitude that will help you look at America: "Undisturbed calmness of mind is attained by cultivating friendliness toward the happy, compassion for the unhappy, delight in the virtuous, and indifference toward the wicked.''

How to Win Games and Influence Destiny (A Manual for Apprentice Gods), translated and adapted from diverse sources by Rick Strauss. A series of four books. Gryphon House, Box 1483, Studio City, CA 91604, 1969, $2.25 each.
Book I: How to Win Games and Influence Distiny. ". . . any behavior which prevents us from living up to our full potential is stupid and inefficient." An exercise for boredom and unhappiness: "Do a good deed . . . one from which you yourself DO NOT derive any benefit."
Book II: How to Win Games and Influence Destiny. A manual on gaining conscious control over what happens to you. Lots of help for travelers and others in search of truth. For example: "The universe fills all space with splendor, using precisely the minimum effort necessary to achieve each effect. Man is a creature of the universe. Should he be different?"
Book III: The Book of Changes. About the energy of the universe and how to use it. How to improve the quality of your life — instantly.
Book IV: The Masters of Destiny. How to find the highest level of existence and stay there. Another exercise:

"Become fully conscious of what you are doing.
When you talk to a person, talk to them.

When you eat, eat.
When you sit, sit.

Nothing else.
Just that."

Remember that "pain and misery are extinguished when we adopt intelligent, enlightened attitudes and behavior, and drop the old, confused, pain-generating ones."

Integral Yoga Hatha, Swami Satchidananda, Holt, Rinehart and Winston, 1970, $4.95. This book will give you physical exercises to get in touch with your body, calm yourself, and be centered. A methodology for changing the way you are. Clear descriptions of the exercises and lovely photographs of Swamaji doing them.

Be Here Now, Baba Ram Dass, Crown Books, 1971, $3.33. In this compilation of spiritual aphorisms in contemporary language, Baba Ram Dass reveals the ancient truth: Be here now.

Tao Te Ching, Lao Tse, Vintage Books, 1972, $2.95. The slow unraveling of the way of the Tao. Photographs, poetry, beauty, growth, insight.

The Sufis, Idries Shah, Doubleday, 1971, $2.45.

The three "Don Juan" books by Carlos Castaneda are vital contemporary reading. They tell the story of an American sociologist-anthropologist who becomes an apprentice to a Yaqui wise man ostensibly to learn about Indian peyote rituals. He learns much more. Entering the world of Don Juan is sure to give you a powerful energy shot. The books are, in order of their publication:

The Teachings of Don Juan: A Yaqui Way of Knowledge, Ballantine Books, 1971, $.95.
A Separate Reality, Simon and Schuster, 1972, $1.25.
Journey to Ixtlan, Simon and Schuster, $6.95. (Due to be out soon in paper.)

Some essential books for the soul:

Bhagavad-gita As It Is, Swami Prabhupada, Collier Books, 1972, $4.95.

The I Ching or Book of Changes, Cary F. Baynes, Bollingen Series, Princeton University Press, 1950, $6.

The Holy Bible, World Publishing Co, $2.45.

And finally, we feel our book, *Two Births*, belongs on this list. Photographs and poetry revealing the glorious birth process. By Janet Brown, Eugene Lesser, and Stephanie Mines. Photographs by Ed Buryn. Bookworks/Random House, 1972, $3.95.

APPENDIX 3

USA Guidebooks

Student Travel in America, US National Student Assoc, Pyramid Publications, 2115 "S" St, NW, Washington DC 20008, $2.25. Written for foreign students in America, this book includes a list of travel organizations that serve them. A standard travel guide with useful addresses and phone numbers (museums, theaters, libraries). Tho it claims to be uniquely for young people, anyone can use it.

Students Guide: North America, Travel Aid Services 231 Tottenham Court Rd, London WIE England $2.50. For English-speaking foreign students traveling in America. Good, concise, clear advice for Americans too. This book is superior to the one above — perhaps because it was not written by Americans and thus its appraisal of America is more realistic and insightful.

Where the Fun Is: USA, two volumes: *East of the Mississippi* and *West of the Mississippi*, Simon and Schuster, $2.95 each. This book tries hard to be hip. Selected parts of the country described by students. Very subjective and middle-class evaluations. Addresses, rates, hotels, blue laws, night spots, shops.

USA: Student Accommodations Guide, Council on International Education Exchange (CIEE), USA Desk, 777 United Nations Plaza, NY 10017 or CIEE Student Travel Service, 607 S Park View, Los Angeles, CA 90057, $1. 100-page booklet listing 1000 facilities in 50 states where students can spend the night for as little as $1.

Let's Go: United States and Canada, Harvard Student Agencies, EP Dutton Co, $2.95. Brief descriptions of cities followed by listings of attractions, accommodations, entertainment, restaurants, city maps. All standard, and written by slumming students from Harvard and Radcliffe. Incomplete information for the vagabond, but the listings are usable.

New Horizons USA, Pan-Am's guide to travel in the USA, Simon and Schuster, $4.95. Classic guidebook style — miles, temperature charts, etc. Boring and organized.

Tour America Guide, Rand McNally, $3.95. Eight regional sections, each introduced with an article by a different writer — a kind of public relations guy. Then a series of pre-planned tours with maps. Total packages. Some good suggestions and some nice tid-bits like regional recipes, but the tours themselves are inherently restricting.

What to See in All America, Norman D. Ford, $2.95; also by Norman Ford: *Off the Beaten Path*, $2.50 and *America By Car*, $3.50. All from Harian Publications, Greenlawn, NY 11740. These are unusual and good. *What to See in All America* is primarily about family car travel, with some information about bus and train trips. *Off the Beaten Path* tells about unique and quaint places in America that are especially interesting if you're looking for a place to retire. Many of the places, tho, are no longer so off the beaten path. *America By Car* has tour descriptions. Similar to *What to See in All America*, so don't get both.

National Park Guide, Michael Frome, Rand McNally, $3.95. Introduction by ecologist Paul Ehrlich. Well written. Good descriptions of each of the parks. Also describes other National Recreation Areas, Monuments, Seashores, Historical Areas, etc.

1972 Campground and Trailer Park Guide, Rand McNally, $4.95. A state-by-state directory of camping facilities, listing State Parks, National Forests, Corps of Engineers campgrounds, and private campgrounds. Computerized tables list each campground and information like how to find it, physical environment, tent spaces, fees, hook-ups, and additional facilities. There are maps with numbered locations of the campgrounds and selected tables, maps, and data of related interest. We used this book on our trip and it gave us a good idea of what was available. We never used the coupons for private campgrounds.

Camping and Trailering 1971-72 (Western and Eastern) and *Regional Tourbooks*, AAA, 1712 G St NW, Washington DC. These guides are free to AAA members. Encourages use of AAA approved private campgrounds. Listings of campsites and campgrounds, public and private. Regional tourbooks list towns, describe them and recommend hotels, motels, restaurants. Layout and design of these books is particularly unattractive.

Mobil Travel Guides, Mobil Oil Corp, Simon and Schuster, Box A, Bloomfield, NJ 07003. 7 volumes, $2.95 each: *California and the West, Northeastern States, Northwest and Great Plains States, Southwest and South Central Area, Middle Atlantic States, Great Lakes Area, Southeastern States*. These are primarily collections of rated accommodations and restaurants, but also include road maps, town descriptions and facts, things to see and do, animal events, radio station listings, selected regional tours, and other miscellaneous information. This collection is bulky if you are going across country, but they are the best of all the standard-type guidebooks.

Woodall's 1972 Trailering Parks and Campgrounds, Woodall Publishing Co, 500 Hyacinth Pl, Highland Park, IL, $5.95. Lists public and private campgrounds. 64 pages of maps. Articles on camping integrated into the book. Lots of ads for the most magnificent rec vec's. Great emphasis on RV travel — articles about servicing your RV, repairing the toilet, the air conditioner, etc. For other books about car camping see Appendix 1 under that heading.

Guide to Spiritual Centers, The Spiritual Community, Box 1080, San Rafael, CA 94902, $2.95. This is a wonderfully usable guidebook, full of information that will make your trip interesting and even healthy. It lists, by state, health food stores and restaurants, meditation centers, Yoga centers, spiritual, metaphysical and occult bookstores, organic bakeries, and other "businesses of interest to the Spiritual Community." The front part of the book describes existing spiritual organizations. For those who have never heard of the Happy, Healthy, Holy Organization or Meher Baba, this is a way to find out about them. Thruout the book are statements by spiritual leaders which can be read and pondered as you travel. Other goodies: chart of the chakras, glossary of spiritual terminology, and a list of "new age" magazines and periodicals. See also "Spiritual Centers" in Appendix 1 and Soul Books for Americans in Appendix 2, "USA Bookshelf."

Exploring Our National Parks and Monuments, Devereux Butcher, Houghton-Mifflin, $4.95. One of the best of the National Park guides. For each park and monument, a geological and ecological history is given. An extensive bibliography at the end provides information for those who want to know more about the parks and their wildlife, flora, fauna, archaeology, and geology.

Hitchhiker's Handbook, Tom Grimm, New American Library, $2.95. An outlandishly conservative book which is short on practical information — a grim combination.

Side of the Road: A Hitch Hiker's Guide to the United States, Ben Lobo and Sara Links, Simon and Schuster, $1.95. Written by people who know about the road. There's philosophy too, and it's worth considering. Unlike *Vagabonding*, tho, the emphasis is on political rather than spiritual consciousness ("We are the mutant stepchildren of the Men Who Broke a Continent. Only now they drive Ford Customs and they're out to break us."). The section on city crashing lists underground community services. Hitchhiking tales are fascinating and real — often scary, sometimes ecstatic. There's a chapter for women, by a woman, and a lot about protecting yourself from cops and other threats.

Vacationlands USA, National Geographic Society, Washington DC, $9.95. A glossy, starry-eyed, wide 'n wonnerful look at America. And expensive too. Other books in the National Geographic series on America are:

> *America's Wonderlands*, $9.95
> *America's Historylands*, $9.95
> *Indians of the Americas*, $7.50
> *Wild Animals of North America*, $7.75.

The Black American Travel Guide, Bob Hayes, Straight Arrow Books, 625 Third St, San Francisco, CA 94107, $6.95. Covers selected US cities for the black traveler. The book is based on that old white technique of letting someone do the evaluating for you . . . funny trip, and something of a rip-off, whether you're white or black. Good tips: soul food restaurants, black clubs, brief history of black population in each city, soul radio stations, soul TV shows, and monuments to black history.

Steal This Book, Abbie Hoffman, Grove Press, $1.95. A guide to America on zero dollara a day, or how to put out lots of bad energy and get back even more bad karma. Special emphasis on four cities: Fuck NY, Fuck Chicago, Fuck LA, Fuck SF. Tells you how to steal food from restaurants, sneak into movies, ride the subway free. Sprinklings of hard-core information like how to organize a food conspiracy, how to find land in the country, how to be an anarchist. Crash pads are listed for the four fucked cities. Some listings of museums, underground papers and services (these tend to be undependable), theaters, libraries. The best parts of this book are about how to use what's already here. The worst parts are about how to destroy everything else.

Road Atlas, Rand McNally, $2.95. See chapter 3 for a general discussion of road maps. This is what we recommend but with the reservations discussed in that chapter. See also "Maps" in Appendix 1.

Some other books which I haven't seen but which you might want to check out:

American Wilderness, Gousha Publications, Box 6227, San Jose, CA 95150, $4.95. Maps and guides to 900 wilderness and primitive areas. Shows campsites and trails.

The NY Times Guide to Outdoors USA, Ben Cameron, Quadrangle Books, $4.95.

See America Free, Sallie Robbins, Hearthside Press Inc, 445 Northern Blvd, Great Neck, Long Island, NW 11021, $4.95.

Travel America Almanac and Yearbook, David McKay Co, 750 Third Ave, NY 10017, $1.25.

APPENDIX 4

Tourist Information Offices

Bureau of Publicity and Information
State Highway Building
Montgomery, AL 36104

Alaska Travel Division
Pouch E
Juneau, AK 99801

Department of Economic Planning
and Development
3003 N Central Ave
Phoenix, AZ 85012
and
Department of Travel and Information
Phoenix, AZ 85005

Department of Parks and Tourism
101 State Capitol
Little Rock, AR 72201

Office of Tourism and Visitors Service
1400 Tenth St
Sacramento, CA 95814

Additional tourist information
sources for California:

Northern Calif.:

San Francisco Convention & Visitors
Bureau
Fox Plaza
San Francisco, CA 94102

Redwood Empire Assn
476 Post St
San Francisco, CA 94102

Shasta-Cascade Wonderland Assn
Box 155
Redding, CA 96002

Southern Calif.:

Southern Calif. Visitors Council
705 W 7th St
Los Angeles, CA 90017

San Diego Convention & Visitors Bureau
225 Broadway
San Diego, CA 92101

California Mission Country Visitors Assn
25 W Anapamu St
Santa Barbara, CA 93104

Colorado Visitors Bureau
225 Colfax Ave
Denver, CO 80202

Colorado State Division of Commerce
and Development
602 State Capitol Annex
Denver, CO 80203

Denver Visitors Bureau
Denver, CO 80202

Connecticut Development Commission
Box 865
Hartford, CT 06115

Travel Development Bureau
45 The Green
Dover, DE 19901

Bureau of Marketing & Tourism
107 West Gaines St
Tallahassee, FL 32304

Miami Metro Dept of
Publicity and Tourism
499 Biscayne Blvd
Miami, FL

Georgia Dept of Industry and Trade
Box 38097
Atlanta, GA 30334

Hawaii Visitors Bureau
2270 Kalakaua Ave
Honolulu, HI 96815

Idaho Dept of Commerce and
Development
State Capitol Bldg, Room 108
Boise, ID 83707

Illinois Dept of Business & Economic
Development
222 South College Ave
Springfield, IL 62706

Chicago Convention and
Tourism Bureau
332 South Michigan Ave
Chicago, IL 60604

Indiana Dept of Commerce
323 State House
Indianapolis, IN 46204

Iowa Development Commission
250 Jewett Bldg
Des Moines, IA 50309

Department of Economic Development
Room 1225
Topeka, KS 66612

Kentucky Dept of Public Information
Capitol Annex
Frankfort, KY 40601

Tourist Development Commission
Box 44291
Baton Rouge, LA 70804

Greater New Orleans Tourist and
Convention Commission
334 Royal St
New Orleans, LA 70130

Dept of Economic Development
State House
Augusta, ME 04330

Division of Tourism
State Office Building
Annapolis, MD 21401

Dept of Commerce & Development
100 Cambridge St
Boston, MA 02202

Boston Convention and
Visitors Bureau
125 High St
Boston, MA 02202

Michigan Tourist Council
Stevens T. Mason Building
Lansing, MI 48926

Minnesota Dept of Economic
Development
51 East 8th St
St. Paul, MN 55101

Agricultural and Industrial Board
Box 849
Jackson, MS 39205

Missouri Tourism Commission
Box 1055
Jefferson City, MO 65101

Montana Highway Commission
Helena, MT 59601

Nebraska Dept of Economic
Development
State Capitol
Lincoln, NB 68509

Dept of Economic Development
State Capitol
Carson City, NV 89701

Division of Economic Development
Box 856
Concord, NH 03301

Division of Economic Development
Box 5400
Trenton, NJ 08625

Department of Development
113 Washington Ave
Santa Fe, NM 87501

State Dept of Commerce
112 State St
Albany, NY 12207

New York Convention and
    Visitors Bureau
90 E 42nd St
NY 10017

For recorded phone message on
city wide activities call:

Parks, Recreation, & Cultural Affairs
    Administration:
Manhattan, Bronx: 755-4100
Brooklyn, Queens, Staten Island:
    691-5858
Park Events: 472-1003

For a book on attractions in NYC, write:

"PRCA Where Book"
830-5th Ave
NY 10021 (10¢)

Dept of Conservation and Development
Box 27687
Raleigh, NC 27611

North Dakota Highway Dept Bldg
Travel Division
Bismark, ND 58501

Ohio Dept of Development
Box 1001
Columbus, OH 43216

Oklahoma Tourist & Information Div
500 Will Rogers Memorial Bldg
Oklahoma City, OK 73105

Oregon State Highway Division
101 State Highway Building
Salem, OR 97310

Oregon Coast Association
Drawer 1266
Newport, OR 97365

Bureau of Travel Development
Pennsylvania Dept of Commerce
Harrisburg, PA 17120

Philadelphia Convention and
    Tourist Bureau
1525 John F Kennedy Blvd
Philadelphia, PA 19102

Rhode Island Development Council
207 Roger Williams Bldg
Providence, RI 02908

Dept of Parks, Recreation & Tourism
Box 1358
Columbia, SC 29202

Department of Highways
Travel Section Communications
Pierre, SD 57501

Black Hills, Badlands, & Lakes Assoc
Sturgis, SD 57785

Department of Conservation
2611 W End Ave
Nashville, TN 37203

Texas Tourist Development Agency
Box 12008, Capitol Station
Austin, TX 78711

Travel Council
Council Hall, State Capitol
Salt Lake City, UT 84114

Travel Development
61 Elm St
Montpelier, VT 05602

Virginia State Travel Service
911 East Broad St
Richmond, VA 05602

Washington Dept of Commerce &
    Economic Development
General Administration Bldg
Olympia, WA 98501

Seattle Visitors Bureau
215 Columbia St
Seattle, WA 98104

Washington DC Convention &
    Visitors Bureau
1129 - 20th St NW
Washington DC 20036

West Virginia Dept of Commerce
1900 Washington St E
Charleston, WV 25305

Dept of Natural Resources
Box 450
Madison, WI 53701

Wyoming Travel Commission
2320 Capitol Ave
Cheyenne, WY 82001

APPENDIX 5

Oil Company Services

Atlantic Richfield Touring Service
111-8th Ave
NY 11001
Map making and touring information.

Chevron Travel Service
555 Market St
San Francisco, CA 94120
Map making, hiway log, travel guide. Use tour request card available at Chevron and Standard stations.

Cities Service Touring Bureau
70 Pine St
NY 10005
Map making service.

Gulf Tourguide Bureau

1375 Peachtree St NE
Atlanta, GA 30309

710 Main St
Houston, TX 77002

7th and Grant Sts
Pittsburgh, PA 15219

Map making service and touring information.

Humble Touring Service

15 West 51st St
NY 10019

800 Bell St
Houston, TX 77001

Map making service and touring information.

Mobil Travel Routing Service
Box 265
NY 10011
Road maps and touring information.

Shell Touring Service
Ask dealer for tour request card.

Standard Oil Touring Service
3rd and Guthrie Sts
Louisville, KY 40402
Map making service.

Texaco Travel Service Office

312 S Michigan Ave
Chicago, IL 60624

1111 Rusk Ave
Houston, TX 77052

3350 Wilshire Blvd
Los Angeles, CA 90005

1501 Canal St
New Orleans, LA 70160

135 E 42nd St
NY 10017

Write or visit for touring information.

There are no doubt others; ask at your local gasoline dealer.

APPENDIX 6

Travel Clubs

American Automobile Association (AAA)
Washington, DC 20006
(or one of 840 local branches)
The big daddy of them all, offering most travel services known to man and/or beasts: maps, guides, "Motorland" magazine, insurance, emergency service, legal aid, travel agency, etc. $5 initiation plus $23/yr plus $6 for spouse.

American Oil Motor Club
111 W Jackson Blvd
Chicago, IL 60604
Write or visit for information.

Allstate Motor Club
2882 Sandhill Road
Menlo Park, CA 94025
Trip planning, travel information, "Discovery" magazine, insurance, etc. $15/yr.

Gulf Travel Club
Box 4852
Chicago, IL 60680
Travel planning services, trip atlas, "Odyssey" magazine, tours, charter flights, discount books. $12 / yr.

National Automobile Club (NAC)
65 Battery St
San Francisco, CA 94111
Similar to AAA but on a more modest scale: maps, guides, travel information, emergency service. $22/yr.

National Travel Club
Travel Bldg
Floral Park, NY 11001
Travel information, motor touring service, "Travel" magazine, insurance. $8.50/yr.

The Globetrotters Club
BCM Roving
London W.C. 1
England
See Chapter 8 for information on this organization of vagabonds.

Traveler's Directory
51-02 — 39th Ave
NY 11377
See Chapter 8 for details

Travelers Information Exchange
Box 368, Kenmore Station
Boston, MA 02215

"Free"
1623 East 6th St
Eugene, OR 97401
Not a club but a magazine which is a source of information about vagabonding. When last we heard from Bill, the young editor, he was planning to pub together a Traveler's Exchange like Travelers Directory.

There are, no doubt, other major travel organizations. Let me hear about them if you think they're any good.

APPENDIX 7

National Parks

Acadia National Park
Box 388
Hulls Cove, ME 04644

Big Bend National Park
TX 79834

Bryce Canyon National Park
Bryce Canyon, UT 84717

Canyonlands National Park
Post Office Building
Moab, UT 84532

Carlsbad Caverns National Park
Box 1598
Carlsbad, NM 99220

Catoctin National Park
Thurmont, MD 21788

Crater Lake National Park
Box 7
Crater Lake, OR 97604
(October-May)
Box 672
Medford, OR 97501

Everglades National Park
Box 279
Homestead, FL 33030

Glacier National Park
West Glacier, MT 59936

Grand Canyon National Park
Box 129
Grand Canyon, AZ 86023

Grand Teton National Park
Moore, WY 83012

Great Smokey Mountains National Park
Gatlinburg, TN 37738

Guadalupe Mountains National Park
Box 1598
Carlsbad, NM 88220

Haleakala National Park
Box 456
Kahulaui, Maui, HI 96732

Hawaii Volcanoes National Park HI 96718
HI 96718

Hot Springs National Park
Box 1219
Hot Springs, AR 71902

Isle Royale National Park
87 North Ripley Street
Houghton, MI 49931

Kings Canyon and Sequoia National Park
Three Rivers, CA 93271

Lassen Volcanic National Park
Mineral, CA 96063

Mammoth Cave National Park
Box 68
Mammoth Cave, KY 42259

Mesa Verde National Park
CO 81330

Mount McKinley National Park
McKinley Park, AK 99755

Mount Rainier National Park
Longmire, WA 98397

North Cascades National Park
311 State Street
Sedro Wooley, WA 98284

Olympic National Park
600 East Park Avenue
Port Angeles, WA 98362

Petrified Forest National Park
Holbrook, AZ 86025

Platt National Park
Box 201
Sulphur, OK 73086

Redwood National Park
501 H Street
Crescent City, CA 95531

Rocky Mountain National Park
Box 1080
Estes Park, CO 80517

Sequoia and Kings Canyon National Park
Three Rivers, CA 93271

Shenandoah National Park
Luray, VA 22835

Virgin Islands National Park
Box 803
Charlotte Amalie, VI 00801

Voyageurs National Park
1709 Jackson Street
Omaha, NB 68102

Wind Cave National Park
Hot Springs, SD 57745

Yellowstone National Park
WY 83020
Yosemite National Park
Box 577, Yosemite Village
Yosemite National Park, CA 95389

Zion National Park
Springdale, UT 84767

APPENDIX 8

National Monuments

Agate Fossil Beds National Monument
Box 427
Gering, NB 69341

Arches National Monument
Moab, UT 84532

Aztec Ruins National Monument
Route 1, Box 101
Aztec, NM 87410

Badlands National Monument
Interior, SD 57750

Bandelier National Monument
Los Alamos, NM 87544

Black Canyon of the Gunnison
    National Monument
334 South 10th Street
Montrose, CO 81401

Booker T Washington National
    Monument
Route 1, Box 195
Hardy, VA 24101

Cabrillo National Monument
Box 6175
San Diego, CA 92106

Canyon de Chelly National Monument
Box 588
Chinle, AZ 86503

Capitol Reef National Monument
Torrey, UT 84775

Capulin Mountain National
    Monument
Torrey, UT 84775

Casa Grande Ruins National
    Monument
Box 518
Coolidge, AZ 85228

Castillo de San Marcos National
    Monument
1 Castillo Drive
St Augustine, FL 32084

Cedar Breaks National Monument
Springdale, UT 84767

Chaco Canyon National Monument
Star Route
Bloomfield, NM 87414

Channel Islands National Monument
Box 1388
Oxnard, CA 93030

Chesapeake & Ohio Canal National
    Monument
Box 158
Sharpsburg, MD 21782

Chiricahua National Monument
Dos Cabexas Star Route
Wilcox, AZ 85643

Colorado National Monument
Montrose, CO 81401

Craters of the Moon National Monument
Box 29
Arco, ID 83213

Custer Battlefield National Monument
Box 416
Crow Agency, MT 59022

Death Valley National Monument,
CA 92328

Devils Postpile National Monument
Box 577, Yosemite Village
Yosemite National Park, CA 95389

Devils Tower National Monument,
WY 82714

Dinosaur National Monument
Box 101
Dinosaur, CO 81610

Effigy Mounds National Monument
Box K
McGregor, IA 52157

El Morro National Monument
Ramah, NM 87321

Florissant Fossil Beds National
    Monument
Estes Park, CO 80517

Fort Frederica National Monument
Box 816
St Simons Island, GA 31522

Fort Jefferson National Monument
Box 279
Homestead, FL 33030

Fort McHenry National Monument
    and Historic Shrine
Baltimore, MD 21230

Fort Matanzas National Monument
1 Castillo Drive
St Augustine, FL 32084

Fort Pulaski National Monument
Box 98
Savannah Beach, GA 31328

Fort Sumter National Monument
Box 428
Sullivans Island, SC 29482

Fort Union National Monument
Watrous, NM 87753

George Washington Carver National
    Monument
Box 38
Diamond, MO 64840

Gila Cliff Dwellings National
    Monument
Gila Hot Springs, NM 88061

Glacier Bay National Monument
Box 1089
Juneau, AK 99801

Gran Quivira National Monument
Route 1
Mountainair, NM 87036

Grand Canyon National Monument
Box 129
Grand Canyon, AZ 86023

Grand Portage National Monument
Box 666
Grand Marais, MN 55604

Great Sand Dunes National Monument
Box 60
Alamosa, CO 81101

Homestead National Monument
Beatrice, NB 68310

Hovenweep National Monument
Mesa Verde National Park, CO 81330

Jewel Cave National Monument
Hot Springs, SD 57747

Joshua Tree National Monument
Box 875
Twentynine Palms, CA 92277

Katmai National Monument
McKinley Park, AK 99755

Lava Beds National Monument
Box 867
Tulelake, CA 96134

Lehman Caves National Monument
Baker, NV 89311

Montezuma Castle National
    Monument
Box 218
Camp Verde, AZ 86322

Mound City Group National Monument
Box 327
Chillicothe, OH 45601

Muir Woods National Monument
Mill Valley, CA 94941

Natural Bridges National Monument
Moab, UT 84532

Navaho National Monument
Tonalea, AZ 86044

Ocmulgee National Monument
Box 4186
Macon, GA 31208

Oregon Caves National Monument
Box 7
Crater Lake, OR 97604

Organ Pipe Cactus National Monument
Box 38
Ajo, AZ 85312

Pecos National Monument
PO Drawer 11
Pecos, NM 87552

Perry's Victory and International Peace
    Memorial National Monument
Box 78
Put-in-Bay, OH 43456

Pinnacles National Monument
Paicines, CA 95043

Pipe Spring National Monument
Springdale, UT 84767

Pipestone National Monument
Box 727
Pipestone, MN 56164

Rainbow Bridge National Monument
Box 1507
Page, AZ 86040

Russell Cave National Monument
Route 1, Box 175
Bridgeport, AL 35740

Saguaro National Monument
Box 17210
Tuscon, AZ 85710

Scotts Bluff National Monument
Box 427
Gering, NB 69341

Sitka National Monument
Box 1089
Juneau, AK 99801

State of Liberty National
    Monument
26 Wall Street
NY 10033

Sunset Crater National Monument
Tuba Star Route
Flagstaff, AZ 86001

Timpanogos Cave National Monument
RR 1, Box 200
American Fork, UT 84003

Tumacacaro National Monument
Box 67
Tumacacori, AZ 85640

Tonto National Monument
Box 707
Roosevelt, AZ 85545

Tuzigoot National Monument
Box 68
Clarkdale, AZ 86324

Walnut Canyon National Monument
Rout 1, Box 790
Flagstaff, AZ 86001

White Sands National Monument
Box 458
Almogordo, NM 88310

Wupatki National Monument
Tuba Star Route
Flagstaff, AZ 86001

Yucca House National Monument
Mesa Verde National Park, CO 81330

APPENDIX 9

National Forests

For information on visiting a national forest, write to the office of the region in which the state is located. Some states are administered by more than one region, so it may be necessary to check listings in several regions to find the forest in which you are interested.

EASTERN REGION: 633 W. Wisconsin Avenue, Milwaukee, Wisconsin, 53203.

State	*National Forest*
Illinois	Shawnee National Forest
Indiana	Hoosier National Forest
Kentucky	Daniel Boone National Forest
Michigan	Hiawatha National Forest
	Huron National Forest
	Manistee National Forest
	Ottawa National Forest
Minnesota	Chippewa National Forest
	Superior National Forest
Missouri	Clark National Forest
	Mark Twain National Forest
New Hampshire	White Mountain National Forest
Ohio	Wayne National Forest
Pennsylvania	Allegheny National Forest
Vermont	Green Mountain National Forest
Virginia	George Washington National Forest
	Jefferson National Forest
West Virginia	Mononqaheia National Forest
Wisconsin	Chequamegon National Forest
	Nicolet National Forest

SOUTHERN REGION: 50 Seventh Street NE, Atlanta, Georgia 30323.

Alabama	William B. Bankhead National Forest
	Conecuh National Forest
	Talladega National Forest
	Tuskegee National Forest
Arkansas	Ouachita National Forest
	Ozark National Forest
	St. Francis National Forest
Florida	Apalachicola National Forest
	Ocala National Forest
	Osceola National Forest
Georgia	Chattahoochee National Forest
	Oconee National Forest
Louisiana	Kisatchie National Forest
Mississippi	Bienville National Forest
	Delta National Forest
	DeSota National Forest
	Holly Springs National Forest
	Homochitto National Forest
	Tombigbee National Forest
North Carolina	Croatan National Forest
	Nantahala National Forest
	Pisgah National Forest
	Uwharrie National Forest
South Carolina	Francis Marion National Forest
	Sumter National Forest
Tennessee	Cherokee National Forest
Texas	Angelina National Forest
	Davy Crockett National Forest
	Sabine National Forest
	Sam Houston National Forest

NORTHERN REGION: Federal Building, Missoula, Montana 59801.

Idaho	Clearwater National Forest
	Coeur d'Alene National Forest
	Kaniksu National Forest
	Nez Perce National Forest
	St. Joe National Forest
Montana	Beaverhead National Forest
	Bitterroot National Forest
	Custer National Forest
	Deerlodge National Forest
	Flathead National Forest
	Gallatin National Forest
	Helena National Forest
	Kottenai National Forest
	Lewis and Clark National Forest
	Lolo National Forest
Washington (see also Pacific Northwest region)	Colville National Forest

INTERMOUNTAIN REGION: Federal Office Building, Ogden, Utah 84401.

Idaho	Boise National Forest
	Caribou National Forest
	Challis National Forest
	Payette National Forest
	Salmon National Forest
	Sawtooth National Forest
	Targhee National Forest
Nevada	Humboldt National Forest
	Toiyabe National Forest
Utah	Ashley National Forest
	Cache National Forest
	Dixie National Forest
	Fishlake National Forest
	Matni-LaSal National Forest
	Uinta National Forest
	Wasatch National Forest
Wyoming	Bridger National Forest
	Teton National Forest

SOUTHWESTERN REGION: Federal Building, Albuquerque, New Mexico 87101.

Arizona	Apache National Forest
	Coconino National Forest
	Kaibab National Forest
	Prescott National Forest
	Sitgreaves National Forest
	Tonto National Forest
New Mexico	Carson National Forest
	Cibola National Forest
	Lincoln National Forest
	Santa Fe National Forest

CALIFORNIA REGION: 630 Sansome Street, San Francisco, California 94111.

California
Los Angeles National Forest
Cleveland National Forest
Eldorado National Forest
Inyo National Forest
Klamath National Forest
Lassen National Forest
Los Padres National Forest
Mendocino National Forest
Modoc National Forest
Plumas National Forest
San Bernardino National Forest
Sequoia National Forest
Shasta-Trinity National Forest
Sierra National Forest
Six Rivers National Forest
Stanislaus National Forest
Tahoe National Forest

ALASKA REGION: Federal Office Building, Juneau, Alaska 99801.

Alaska
Chugach National Forest
North Tongass National Forest
South Tongass National Forest

PACIFIC NORTHWEST REGION: Box 3623, Portland, Oregon 97212.

Oregon
Deschutes National Forest
Fremont National Forest
Malheur National Forest
Mount Hood National Forest
Ochoco National Forest
Rogue River National Forest
Siskiyou National Forest
Siuslaw National Forest
Umatilla National Forest
Umpqua National Forest
Wallowa-Whitman National Forest
Willamette National Forest
Winema National Forest

Washington
Gifford Pinchot National Forest
Mount Baker National Forest
Okanogan National Forest
Olympic National Forest
Snoqualmie National Forest
Wenatchee National Forest

PUERTO RICO: Box AQ, University Agricultural Exp. Sta., Rio Piedras, Puerto Rico 00928.

Puerto Rico   Caribbean National Forest

APPENDIX 10

Wilderness and Primitive Areas

State	National Forest	Headquarters	Approx. Acreage
ARIZONA			
Blue Range (also in N M)	Apache	Springville	180,000
Chiricahua	Coronado	Tucson	18,000
Galiuro	Coronado	Tucson	53,000
Mazatzal	Tonto	Phoenix	205,000
Mount Baldy	Apache	Springerville	7,000
Pine Mountain	Prescott	Prescott	16,000
	Tonto	Phoenix	
Sierra Ancha	Tonto	Phoenix	21,000
Superstition	Tonto	Phoenix	124,000
Sycamore Canyon	Coconimo	Flagstaff	50,000
	Kaibab	Williams	
	Prescott	Prescott	
CALIFORNIA			
Agua Tibia	Cleveland	San Diego	226,000
Caribou	Lassen	Susanville	19,000
Cucamonga	San Bernardino	San Bernardino	9,000
Desolation	Eldorado	Placerville	41,000
Dome Land	Sequoia	Porterville	62,000
Emigrant	Stanislaus	Sonora	97,000
High Sierra	Sierra	Fresno	10,000
	Sequoia	Porterville	
Hoover	Toiyabe	Reno, Nev.	43,000
	Inyo	Bishop, Calif.	503,000
John Muir	Sierra	Fresno	503,000
	Inyo	Bishop	
Marble Mountain	Klamath	Yreka	213,000
Minarets	Inyo	Bishop	109,000
	Sierra	Fresno	
Mokelumne	Eldorado	Placerville	50,000
	Stanislaus	Sonora	
Salmon Trinity Alps	Klamath	Yreka	223,000
	Shasta-Trinity	Redding	
San Gabriel	Angeles	Pasadena	36,000
San Gorgonio	San Bernardino	San Bernardino	35,000
San Jacinto	San Bernardino	San Bernardino	21,000
San Rafael	Los Padres	Santa Barbara	143,000
South Warner	Modoc	Alturas	69,000
Thousand Lakes	Lassen	Susanville	16,000
Ventana	Los Padres	Santa Barbara	53,000
Yolla Bolly-Middle Eel	Mendocino	Willows	108,000
	Shasta-Trinity	Redding	
COLORADO			
Flat Tops	White River	Glenwood Springs	102,000
Gore Range-Eagle Nest	Arapaho	Golden	61,000
	White River	Glenwood Springs	
La Garita	Gunnison	Gunnison	48,000
	Rio Grande	Monte Vista	
Maroon Bells-Snowmass	White River	Glenwood Springs	71,000
Mt. Zirkle	Routt	Steamboat Springs	72,000
Rawah	Roosevelt	Durango	238,000
San Juan	San Juan	Durango	238,000
Uncompahgre	Uncompahgre	Delta	53,000
Upper Rio Grande	Rio Grande	Delta	53,000
West Elk	Gunnison	Gunnison	61,000
Wilson Mountains	San Juan	Durango	27,000
	Uncompahgre	Delta	

State	National Forest	Headquarters	Approx. Acreage
IDAHO			
Idaho	Boise	Boise	1,225.000
	Challis	Challis	
	Salmon	Salmon	
	Payette	McCall	
Sawtooth	Boise	Boise	201,000
	Challis	Challis	
	Sawtooth	Twin Falls	
Salmon River Breaks	Nezperce	Grangeville	217,000
	Bitterroot	Hamilton, Mont.	
Selway-Bitterroot (see Montana) . .	Claerwater	Orofino	989,000
	Nezperce	Grangeville	
	Bitterroot	Hamilton, Mont.	
MINNESOTA			
Boundary Waters Canoe Area . . .	Superior	Duluth	747,000
MONTANA			
Absaroka	Gallatin	Boseman	64,000
Anaconda-Pintlar	Beaverhead	Dillon	158,000
	Bitterroot	Hamilton	
	Deerlodge	Butte	
Beartooth	Gallatin	Boseman	230,000
	Custer	Billings	
Bob Marshall	Flarhead	Kalispell	950,000
	Lewis & Clark	Great Falls	
Cabinet Mountains	Kootenai	Libby	94,000
	Kaniksu	Sandpoint, Idaho	
Gates of the Mountains	Helena	Helena	29,000
Mission Mountains	Flathead	Kalispell	73,000
Selway-Bitterroot (see Idaho) . .	Bitterroot	Hamilton	252,000
	Lolo	Missoula, Mont.	
Spanish Peaks	Gallatin	Bozeman	50,000
NEVADA			
Jarbidge	Humbolt	Elko	65,000
NEW HAMPSHIRE			
Great Gulf	White Mountain	Laconia	6,000
NEW MEXICO			
Black Range	Gila	Silver City	169,000
Blue Range (see Arizona)	Apache	Springerville, Ariz.	37,000
Gila Wilderness	Gila	Silver City	434,000
Gila Primitive Area	Gila	Silver City	131,000
Pecos	Santa Fe	Santa Fe	167,000
	Carson	Taos	
San Pedro Parks	Santa Fe	Santa Fe	41,000
Wheeler Peak	Carson	Taos	6,000
White Mountain	Lincoln	Alamogordo	31,000

State	National Forest	Headquarters	Approx. Acreage
NORTH CAROLINA			
Linville Gorge	Pisgah	Asheville	8,000
Shinning Rock	Pisgah	Asheville	13,000
OREGON			
Diamond Peak	Deschutes	Bend	35,000
	Willamette	Eugene	
Eagle Cap	Wallowa-Whitman	Baker	220,000
Gearhart Mountian	Fremont	Lakeview	19,000
Kalmiopsis	Siskiyou	Grants Pass	77,000
Mt Hood	Mt. Hood	Portland	14,000
Mt. Jefferson	Deschites	Bend	100,000
	Mt. Hood	Portland	
	Willamette	Eugene	
Mount Washington	Deschutes	Bend	47,000
	Willamette	Eugene	23,000
Mountain Lakes	Winema	Klamath Falls	33,000
Strawberry Mountain	Malheur	John Day	197,000
Three Sisters	Deschutes	Bend	
	Willamette	Eugene	
UTAH			
High Uintas	Ashley	Vernal	237,000
	Easatch	Salt Lake City	
WASHINGTON			
Glacier Peak	Mt. Baker	Bellingham	464,000
	Wenatchee	Wenatchee	
Goat Rocks	Gifford Pinchot	Vancouver	83,000
	Snoqualmie	Seattle	
Mount Adams	Gifford Pinchot	Vancouver	42,000
Pasayten	Okanogan	Okanogan	518,000
	Mt. Baker	Bellingham	
WYOMING			
Bridger	Bridger	Kemmerer	383,000
Cloud Peak	Bighorn	Sheridan	137,000
Glacier	Shoshone	Cody	177,000
North Absaroka	Shoshone	Cody	351,000
Popo Agie	Shoshone	Cody	70,000
South Absaroka	Shoshone	Cody	483,000
Stratified	Shoshone	Cody	204,000
Teton	Teton	Jackson	564,000

APPENDIX 11

Other National Recreation Facilities

Abraham Lincoln Birthplace National
   Historic Site
RFD 1
Hodgenville, KY 42748

Adams National Historic Site
135 Adams Street
Quincy, MA 02169

Allegheny Portage Railroad National
   Historic Site & Johnston Flood
   National Memorial
Box 216
Johnstown, PA 15907

Andersonville National Historic Site
Citizens Trust Co Building

Atlanta, GA 30303
Andrew Johnson National Historic
   Site
Greeneville, TN 37743

Ansley Wilcox House National Historic
   Site
143 South Third Street
Philadelphia, PA 10106

Antietam National Battlefield Site &
   Cemetary
Box 158
Sharpsburg, MD 21782

Apostle Islands National Lakeshore
143 South Third Street
Philadelphia, PA 19106

Appomattox Court House National
   Historic Park
Box 218
Appomattox, VA 24522

Arbuckle Recreation Area
Box 201
Sulphur, OK 73086

Arkansas Post National Memorial
Gilett, AR 72055

Armistad National Recreation Area
Box 1463
Del Rio, TX 78840

Assateague Island National Seashore
Route 2, Box 11
Berlin, MD 21811

Battleground National Cemetary
1100 Ohio Drive SW
Washington DC 20242

Bent's Old Fort National Historic Site
Box 581
La Junta, CO 81050

Big Hole National Recreation Area
c/o Yellowstone National Park, WY 38020

Bighorn Canyon National Recreation Area
Box 458
Hardin, MT 59035

Blue Ridge Parkway
Box 1710
Roanoke, VA 24008

Brices Cross Roads National
   Battlefield Site
Box 948
Tupelo, MO 38802

Cape Cod National Seashore
Box 428
Eastham, MA 02642

Cape Hatteras National Seashore
Box 457
Manteo, NC 27954

Cape Lookout National Seashore
Box 177
Beaufort, NC 28516

Carl Sandburg Farm National Historic
   Site
400 North Eighth Street
Richmond, VA 23240

Chalmette National Historical Park
Box 125
Arabi, LA 70032

Chamizal National Memorial
300 East Main Drive
El Paso, TX 79901

Chicago Portage National Historic Site
Cummings Square
River Forest, IL 60305

Chickamauga and Chattanooga National
   Military Park
Fort Ogelthorpe, GA 30741

Christiansted National Historic Site
Box 160
Christiansted, VI 00820

City of Refuge National Historical Park
Honaunau, Kona, HI 96726

Colonial National Historical Park
Box 210
Yorktown, VA 23490

Coronado National Memorial
Star Route
Hereford, AZ 85615

Coulee Dam National Recreation Area
Box 37
Coulee Dam, WA 99116

Cowpens National Battlefield Site
Box 31
Kings Mountain, NC 28086

Cumberland Gap National Historical Park
Box 840
Middlesboro, KY 40965

Curecanti National Recreational Area
334 South Tenth Street
Montrose, CO 81401

Custis-Lee Mansion
1100 Ohio Drive SW
Washington DC 20242

Delaware Water Gap National Recreation
   Area
Highway I-80
Columbia, NJ 07832

De Soto National Memorial
Box 1377
Bradenton, FL 33505

Dorchester Heights National Historic Site
33 Beacon Street
Boston, MA 02108

Edison National Historic Site
Box 126
Orange, NJ 07051

Eisenhower National Historic Site
143 South Third Street
Philadelphia, PA 19106

Federal Hall National Memorial
26 Wall Street
NY 10003

Fire Island National Seashore
Box 229
Patchogue, Long Island, NY 11772

Foothills Parkway
Great Smokey Mountains National
   Park
Gatlinburg, TN 37738

Ford's Theatre (Lincoln Museum)
1100 Ohio Drive
Washington DC 20242

Fort Bowie National Historic Site
Dos Cabezas Star Route
Wilcox, AZ 85643

Fort Caroline National Memorial
1 Castillo Drive
St Augustine, FL 32084

Fort Clatsop National Memorial
Route 3, Box 604FC
Astoria, OR 97103

Fort Davis National Historic Site
Box 785
Fort Davis, TX 79734

Fort Donelson National Military Park &
Cemetary
Box F
Dover, TN 37058

Fort Laramie National Historic Site
Fort Laramie, WY 82212

Fort Larned National Historic Site
Box 135
Larned, KS 67550

Fort Necessity National Battlefield
Route 1, Box 360
Farmington, PA 15437

Fort Point National Historic Site
450 Golden Gate Avenue
San Francisco, CA 94102

Fort Raleigh National Historic Site
Box 457
Manteo, NC 27954

Fort Scott Historic Area
Box 49
Larned, KS 67550

Fort Smith National Historic Site
Box 1406
Fort Smith, AR 72902

Fort Union Trading Post National Historic
Site
c/o Theodore Roosevelt National
Memorial Park
Medora, ND 58645

Fort Vancouver National Historic Site
Vancouver, WA 98661

Frederick Douglass Home
National Capital Region, National Park
Service
Washington DC 20242

Fredricksburg & Spotsylvania County
Battlefields Memorial
Box 679
Fredricksburg, VA 22401

General Grant National Memorial
26 Wall Street
NY 10003

George Rogers Clark National Memorial
115 Dubois Street
Vincennes, IN 47591

George Washington Birthplace National
Monument
Box 679
Fredricksburg, VA 22401

George Washington Memorial Parkway
National Park Service
Washington DC 20242

Gettysburg National Military Park &
Cemetary
Box 70
Gettysburg, PA 17325

Glen Canyon National Recreation Area
Box 1507
Page, AZ 86040

Golden Spike National Historic Site
Box 639
Brigham City, UT 84302

Greenbelt Park
6501 Greenbelt Road
Greenbelt, MD 20770

Guilford Courthouse National Military
Park
Box 9145, Plaza Station
Greensboro, NC 27408

Gulf Islands National Seashore
Box 10008
Richmond, VA 23240

Hampton National Historic Site
c/o Fort McHenry National Monument
Baltimore, Md 21230

Harper's Ferry National Historical Park
Box 117
Harper's Ferry, WV 25425

Herbert Hoover National Historic Site
Box B
West Branch, IA 52358

Home of Franklin D. Roosevelt National
Historic Site
Hyde Park
Dutchess County, NY 12538

Hopewell Village National Historic Site
RD 1
Elverson, PA 19520

Horseshoe Bend National Military Park
Box 608
Dadeville, AL 36853

House Where Lincoln Died
1100 Ohio Drive SW
Washington DC 20242

Hubbell Trading Post National Historical
Site
Box 38
Ganado, AZ 86505

Independence National Historical Park
313 Walnut Street
Philadelphia, PA 19106

Indiana Dunes National Lakeshore
Box 12
Chesterton, IN 46304

Jefferson National Expansion Memorial
Historical Site
11 North Fourth Street
St Louis, MO 63102

John Fitzgerald Kennedy National Historic
Site
Box 160
Concord, MA 01742

Kennesaw Mountain National
Battlefield Park
Box 1167
Marietta, BA 30060

Kings Mountain National Military Park
Box 31
Kings Mountain, NC 28086

Lake Mead National Recreation Area
601 Nevada Highway
Boulder City, NV 89005

Lincoln Boyhood National Memoarial
Lincoln City, IN 47552

Lincoln Memorial
1100 Ohio Drive SW
Washington DC 20242

Lyndon Baines Johnson National Historic
Site
Box 329
Johnson City, TX 78636

Manassas National Battlefield Park
Manassas, VA 22110

Minute Man National Historical Park
Box 160
Concord, MA 01742

Moores Creek National Military Park
Currie
Pender County, NC 28435

Morristown National Historical Park
Box 759
Morristown, NJ 07960

Mount Rushmore National Memorial
Keystone, SD 57751

John Muir National Historic Site
4202 Alhambra Avenue
Martinez, CA 94553

Natchez Trace Parkway
Box 948
Tupelo, MS 38802

National Capital Parks
1100 Ohio Drive SW
Washington DC 20242

Nez Perce National Historic Park
Spalding, ID 83551

Ozark National Scenic Riverways
Box 448
Van Buren, MO 63965

Padre Island National Seashore
Box 8560
Corpus Christi, TX 78412

Pea Ridge National Military Park
Pea Ridge, AR 72751

Pennsylvania Avenue National Historic
Site
1100 Ohio Drive SW
Washington DC 20242

Petersburg National Battlefield
Box 549
Petersburg, VA 23804

Pictured Rocks National Lakeshore
Box 32
Munising, MI 49862

Piscataway Park
National Park Service
Washington DC 20242

Point Reyes National Seashore
Point Reyes, CA 94956

Poplar Grove National Cemetary
Box 549
Petersburg, VA 23804

Prince William Forest Park
Triangle, VA 22172

Richmond National Battlefield Park
3215 East Broad Street
Richmond, VA 23223

Roger Williams National Battlefield
Park
143 South Third Street
Philadelphia, PA 19106

Sagamore Hill National Historic Site
26 Wall Street
NY 10003

Saint-Gaudens National Historic Site
Windsor, VT 05089

St. Croix Island National Monument
Box 388
Bar Harbor, ME 04609

St. Croix National Scenic Riverway
143 South Third Street
Philadelphia, PA 19106

St. Paul's Church National Historic Site
Box 1707
Charlotte Amalie, St Thomas, VI 00801

St. Thomas National Historic Site
Box 1707
Charlotte Amalie, St. Thomas, VI 00801

Salem Maritime National Historic Site
Custom House Derby Street
Salem, MA 01970

Sanford Redreation Area
Box 325
Sanford, TX 79078

San Jose Mission National Historic Site
6539 San Jose Drive
San Antonio, TX 78214

San Juan National Historic Site
Box 712
San Juan, PR 00902

San Juan Island National Historic Park
Box 549
Friday Harbor, WA 98250

Saugus Iron Works National Historic Site
244 Central Street
Saugus, MA 01906

Saratoga National Historic Park
RFD 1, Box 113C
Stillwater, NY 12170

Shadow Mountain National Recreation
Area
Box 1080
Estes Park, CO 80517

Shiloh National Military Park & Cemetary
Shiloh, TN 38376

Sleeping Bear Dunes National Lakeshore
143 South Third Street
Philadelphia, PA 19106

Stones River Ntiaonal Battlefield &
Cemetary
Box 1039
Murfreesboro, TN 37130

Theodore Roosevelt Birthplace National
Site
26 Wall Street
New York, NY 10003

Theodore Roosevelt Island
1400 Wilson Blvd.
Arlington, VA 22209

Theodore Roosevelt National Memorial
Park
Medora, ND 58645

Thomas Jefferson Memorial
1100 Ohio Drive SW
Washington DC 20242

Tupelo National Battlefield
RR5
Tupelo, MS 38801

Touro Synagogue National Historic Site
85 Touro Street
Newport, RI 02840

Vanderbilt Mansion National Historic Site
Hyde Park
Dutchess County, NY 12538

Vicksburg National Military Park &
Cemetery
Box 349
Vicksburg, MS 39180

Washington Monument
900 Ohio Drive SW
Washington DC 20242

Whiskeytown-Shasta-Trinity National
Recreation Area
Box 188
Whiskeytown, CA 96095

White House
1100 Ohio Drive SW
Washington DC 20242

Whitman Mansion National Historic Site
Route 2
Walla Walla, WA 99362

Wilson's Creek National Battlefield Park
Box 38
Diamond, MO 64840

Wright Brothers National Memorial
Box 457
Manteo, NC 27954

Yorktown National Cemetary
Box 210
Yorktown, VA 23940

APPENDIX 12

Outdoor Equipment Suppliers

Catalogs are available from all the companies listed below and are free unless otherwise indicated.

Two books about equipment:

Lightweight Camping Equipment and How to Make It, Colorado Outdoor Sports Corp, 5440 North Valley Highway, Denver, CO 80216, $2.50.

The Potomac Appalachian Trail Club Lightweight Equipment Guide, PATC, 1718 North Street Northwest, Washington DC 20036.

Alpine Designs
6185 East Araphoe
Boulder, CO 80302
No mail order facilities. Tents, sleeping bags, climbing packs which are suitable for motorcyclists.

Alpine Recreation
Mail orders:
 4b Henshaw St
 Woburn, MA 02139
In Maine and New York, this company has branches selling camping, climbing and mountaineering equipment. They will send you funky mimeographed leaflets with information on xc skiing, winter hiking, and the story of their tents, sleeping bags, down clothing, boots, skis, snow shoes and much more.

Antelope Backpacking Equipment
10268 Imperial Ave
Cupertino, CA 95014
Packframes and bags, hip-packs, tent poles.

Eddie Bauer, Expedition Outfitters
417 East Pine
Seattle, WA 98122
High quality down bags and clothing for hikers, climbers, backpackers and mountaineers. Tents, boots, pack frames.

L L Bean Inc
Freeport, ME 04032
This company started in 1912 with the development of the Maine hunting shoe. Hunting, fishing, camping supplies.

Big Wheel Ltd
310 Holly St
Denver, CO 80217
Bicycle supplies.

Bellweather Get-A-Way Gear
1161 Mission St
San Francisco, CA 94103
Bicycle packs, bicycle shirts, jackets, parkas, down sleeping bags.

Bishop's Ultimate
Outdoor Equipment
6804 Millwood Rd
Bethesda, MD 20034
(Tents, mountaineering supplies.)

Thomas Black and Sons
930 Ford St
Ogdensburg, NY 13669
Tent manufacturers from England with mail order and retail facilities in the US.

Boy Scouts of America
655 E 14th St
Oakland, CA 94606
(or a regional branch)

Bugaboo Mountaineering
170 Central Ave
Pacific Grove, CA 93950
Sleeping bags with shifting down, down jackets (custom made), waterproof gear for sailing, custom work (tarps, belay seats).

Cabela's Inc
812-13th Ave
Sidney, NB 69162
Boots, clothes, fishing equipment.

Camp 7 Inc
3235 Prarie Ave
Boulder, CO 80301
Sleeping bags.

Camp Trails
3920 W Clarendon Ave
Phoenix, AZ 85019
Packs, tents, hip belts.

Chicagoland Canoe Base
4019 N Narragansett Ave
Chicago, IL 60634
Canoes, kayaks, car-top carriers, paddles, life perservers, cushions and other canoe accessories. See appendix 1--"Canoeing and Kayaking"--for a list of their books.

Cloud Cap Chalet
1127 SW Morrison St
Portland, OR 97205
Mountaineering and backpacking equipment.

Cyclo-Pedia
311 North Mitchell
Cadillac, MI 49601
Touring, sports and racing bikes. Bicycle packs and parts, child carriers, bicycle tools.

Dedham Kayaks, Inc
Box 218
Millis, MA 02504
Kayak building kits.

Denali Co
2402 Ventura
Fresno, CA 93721
Rock climbing equipment.

Eastern Mountain Sports
1041 Commonwealth Ave
Boston, MA 02215
"The EMS catalog is incredible" says Two Wheel Travel. Lightweight gear. Manufacturers of kits for making parkas, ponchos and ruckscaks. Stores also in Wellesley, Springfield, and New Platz, NY.

Examino Establishment
Segundo, CO 81070
Mining supplies.

Frostline Outdoor Equipment
Box 1378
Boulder, CO 80302
Do-it-yourself lightweight kits for tents, sleeping bags, down clothing.

Gerry Outdoor Sports
Industries
5450 North Valley Highway
Denver, CO 80216
and
228 Grant Ave
San Francisco, CA 94108
Fine lightweight gear. Sleeping bags, hiking boots, ski equipment, packs.

Gloy's
11 Addison St
Larchmont, NY 10034
Boating equipment, accessories, heavy camping supplies.

Gokey Co
21 W Fifth St
St Paul, MN
Boots, sports clothes, parkas, Gerry
equipment.

Harley Davidson
Box 653
Milwaukee, WI
Motorcycles and accessories.

Herter's Inc
Rural Route 1
Waseca, MN 56093
Their catalog costs $1, but it's worth it.
Herter's has everything—fishing tackle,
archery equipment, down sleeping bags,
backpacks, gems, fabrics, and much
more.

High Performance Products
Hingham Industrial Center
Hingham, MA 02043
Canoes and kayaks.

Himalayan Industries
Box 950
Monterey, CA 93940
Packs, sleeping bags, tents.

Holubar Mountaineering
Box 7
Boulder, CO
"Holubar makes the best sleeping bag in
the world," says Two Wheel Travel.
Sew-it-yourself kits.

Jan Sport
17010 Aurora Ave N
Seattle, WA
Makers of lightweight packs that are
suitable for bicycling. Also motorcycle
rucksacks.

Kelty Pack Co
Box 3453
Glendale, CA 91201
The most famous of the pack makers.

Klepper Co
35 Union Square W
NY 10003
Whole Earth Catalog says: "Klepper is
the best of the folding boats and
kayaks."

Peter Limmer and Sons
Intervale, NH 03845
Backpacking gear. Famous for
hand-crafted, custom-made boots, ski
boots and mountaineering equipment.

M & E Marine Supply
Box 601
Camden, NJ
Skin diving equipment.

Moor and Mountain
14 Main St
Concord, MA 01742
Backpacking and Nordic ski equipment.
Kayaks and canoes. Clothing, tents,
frame packs, rucksacks and packs made
in Norway. Northmark sleeping bags.
Canoeing guides and maps.

New England Divers
42 Water St
Beverly, MA 01905
Skin diving equipment.

The North Face
308 Columbus Ave
San Francisco, CA 94133
Mountaineering equipment. Also has
excellent equipment for the biker.
Rucksacks suitable for hikers and bikers.
Stores also in Palo Alto, Orinda,
Berkeley.

The Old Boathouse
2770 Westlake N
Seattle, WA 98109
Sailing equipment.

Old Town Canoe Co
Old Town, ME 04468

The Orvis Co
Manchester, VT 05254
Tents, snowshoes, sleeping bags.

Quicksilver Canoe
and Kayak Kits
115 McGavock Pike
Nashville, TN 37214

Rainier Equipment
900 N 137th St
Seattle, WA 98133
Tents.

Recreational Equipment Co
1525-11th Ave
Seattle, WA 98122
A cooperative: membership is $1. Wide
range of rucksacks from European
makers. Skis and Ski accessories, down
clothing. Also at 523 Pike St, Seattle,
WA.

Sierra Designs
4th and Addison Sts
Berkeley, CA 94710
Their catalog gives a thoro and direct
explanation of their materials and
methods of construction. Bags, clothing,
ponchos. Mountaineering equipment.
Touring and racing boats. Materials for
constructing packs, tarps, ponchos,
down-filled items. A mellow store with
mellow folks.

Sierra Mountain Equipment
Box 15251
San Francisco, CA 94115

Ski Hut ("Trailwise" label)
1615 University Ave
Berkeley, CA 94703
Sleeping bags of high quality. Tents, air
mattresses, ski touring gear, climbing
gear. Down filled jackets.

The Smilie Company
575 Howard St
San Francisco, CA
Sleeping bags made by Sierra Designs,
Pacific Tents, snowshoes, parkas,
climbing and hiking equipment.

Stephenson's
23206 Hatteras Street
Woodland Hills, CA 91364
Warmlite tents and sleeping bags.

Stow-A-Way Products
103 Ripley Road
Cohasset, MA 02025
Packs, frames, bicycle panniers, horse
packs, sleeping bags, Gerry products,
hiking boots.

Swiss Ski Sports
559 Clay St
San Francisco, CA 94111
Packframes, rucksacks, sleeping bags,
hiking boots, down clothing, tents.

Todd's
5 South Wabash Ave
Chicago, IL 60603
Boots and shoes only.

Universal Field Equipment
Mira Loma Space Center
Mira Loma, CA 91752
Everything in backpacks for the hiker
and mountaineer.

U S Divers
5323 West Warner Ave
Santa Ana, CA 90064
Skin diving equipment. Send $1 for their
catalog.

West Ridge Mountaineering
12010 W Pico Blvd
Los Angeles, CA 90064

Wheel Goods Corp
2737 Hennepin Ave
Minneapolis, MN 55408
Bikes, accessories, tools, parts, touring
bags, technical information.

Yakima Tent and Awning Co
1316 S First St
Yakima, WA 98901

Zodiac Inflatable Boats
111 Lee St
Annapolis, MD 21401

APPENDIX 13

State Liquor Laws

(Age limit is 21 unless otherwise noted.)

ALABAMA: It is illegal to bring liquor into a dry county. Liquor is sold by state stores only, and by the drink. Alcoholic beverages cannot be sold to anyone on Sunday.

ALASKA: You can purchase liquor anywhere if you're 21.

ARIZONA: Beer, wine and liquor are available by the drink. Bottles are available at package, drug, and grocery stores. Age limit is 21. Nonresident driver's license, ID card, or draft cards are *unacceptable* as proof of age.

ARKANSAS: Beer can be purchased in grocery stores or by the drink. Liquor is available in package and drug stores and by the drink in licensed hotels, motels, and restaurants.

CALIFORNIA: Beer, wine, and liquor are sold by the drink and bottle.

COLORADO: Liquor is available at package stores or by the drink, except in some hotels and restaurants.

CONNECTICUT: Available by the bottle at package stores and some drugstores. Liquor stores are closed on Sunday.

DELAWARE: Available by the bottle or drink at restaurants, clubs, taprooms, hotels, and liquor stores.

FLORIDA: Liquor is sold at package stores only, and by the drink.

GEORGIA: Bottled liquor is sold at package stores and by the drink. In Atlanta, in order to drink hard liquor in a bar after 8 PM, you must be wearing a coat and tie. Have ID.

HAWAII: You can purchase liquor anywhere if you're 21. The lady at the travel agency I called said, "Take a flight bag and fill it with all you need" because booze is very expensive in Hawaii.

IDAHO: Liquor is available by the drink or at state liquor stores.

ILLINOIS: Available by the drink under local option, and at package stores. Have ID.

INDIANA: Sold by the drink or bottle. No children allowed where liquor is sold except in cafes with separate bar where children must be accompanied by parents.

IOWA: Available by the bottle at state liquor stores and by the drink.

KANSAS: Liquor can be bought at package stores only, under local option.

KENTUCKY: By the package and by the drink. Local option reigns. Great variation in counties.

LOUISIANA: Beer, wine, and liquor sold by the drink. Bottles are sold in various places.

MAINE: Liquor is sold by the bottle at state liquor stores and by the drink in restaurants and hotels.

MARYLAND: Sold by the package or drink; regulations may vary locally.

MASSACHUSETTS: Beer, wine, and liquor are sold by the drink or at package stores and at some grocery stores, under local option. Night spots are strict about ID.

MICHIGAN: Under local option, liquor is available in Michigan by the drink or by the bottle.

MINNESOTA: Liquor is sold by the drink in restaurants from noon to midnight. Also available by the bottle.

MISSISSIPPI: Of Mississippi's 82 counties, 42 are partially or totally wet. In these places, beverages of more than 4% alcoholic content may be purchased by the bottle. Liquor by the drink is available in resort areas daily, 24 hours; in other areas it is available Monday - Saturday, 10 a.m. - midnight. Drinking age is 21 for liquor; 18 for beer.

MISSOURI: Sold by the drink and by the bottle.

MONTANA: Available at state stores by the bottle and by either drink or bottle at licensed dealers.

NEBRASKA: Liquor is sold by the drink or by the bottle. No package sales.

NEVADA: By the bottle and by the drink.

NEW HAMPSHIRE: Available by the bottle at state stores only. Beer, wine, and liquor are sold by the drink.

NEW JERSEY: Available by the drink and by the bottle at package stores and taverns. Drinking age for men is 21, for women 18. Local option.

NEW MEXICO: Beer, wine, and liquor are sold by the drink and in package stores.

NEW YORK: By the bottle and by the drink. 18 is the drinking age. ID required.

NORTH CAROLINA: By the package at state stores. Wine and beer are sold by the drink at local option. If you're 18, beer and wine may be bought at grocery stores and consumed in restaurants. At 21, you can buy liquor at the grocery store.

NORTH DAKOTA: Sold by the bottle and the drink.

OHIO: Alcohol is sold by the package at state-owned stores. 3.2% alcohol, regular beer, wine, and mixed beverages are sold by licensed retailers by the bottle. Liquor is available for "on-premise" drinking. Only 3.2 beer is sold on Sunday. 18 years old for beer; 21 for hard liquor.

OKLAHOMA: Sold only at package stores.

OREGON: Sold by the drink and by the bottle at state stores.

PENNSYLVANIA: Available at state stores by the bottle, and also by the drink under local option. No alcohol served to those under 21. Strictly enforced. Adult ID available from Liquor Control Board.

RHODE ISLAND: Beer, wine, and liquor sold by the package, and by the drink under local option. The town of Barrington is dry.

SOUTH CAROLINA: Available by the package from state-licensed stores from sunrise to sunset. Beer and wine are sold at taverns, some groceries, drugstores, and restaurants.

SOUTH DAKOTA: Sold by the bottle at stores and by the drink, under local option.

TENNESSEE: Sold by the package only. Davidson and Shelby counties have legalized the sale of liquor by the drink. You must be 21 and have ID.

TEXAS: In most large cities, liquor is available by the drink; in some places only beer is permitted; in others no more than 14% alcoholic content is permitted. In some counties hard liquor is sold only at package stores. For the most part, north Texas is dry; south Texas is wet. There are private clubs in both wet and dry cities.

UTAH: Available by the bottle from state-run stores. Tenth size bottles of wine can be purchased with meals in restaurants so licensed, under local option. 3.2 beer is sold at bars and restaurants.

VERMONT: State liquor stores sell bottles. Local option forbids sale of liquor in some Vermont towns, but it is legal to bring your own and buy set-ups.

VIRGINIA: Alcohol is sold by the package at state stores. Beer, wine, and whiskey and mixed beverages are sold by the drink in licensed establishments, under local option. Drinking ages — 18 for 3.2% beer; 21 for high beer (6.4%) and wine.

WASHINGTON: By the bottle at state-owned liquor stores. Beer and wine are sold by the bottle in grocery stores and taverns.

WASHINGTON D.C.: By the drink and by the bottle. You must be 18 for beer and wine; 21 for hard liquor.

WEST VIRGINIA: By the bottle at state stores only. By the drink in private clubs only; under local option. Age for liquor is 21; beer is 18.

WISCONSIN: By the bottle and by the drink. Under local option. Hard liquor age is 21; beer is 18.

WYOMING: By the bottle and by the drink.